THE ECHO OF THE NAZI HOLOCAUST
IN RABBINIC LITERATURE

The Echo of the Nazi Holocaust in Rabbinic Literature

by

Rabbi Dr H. J. Zimmels

KTAV PUBLISHING HOUSE, INC.
1977

Library of Congress Cataloging in Publication Data

Zimmels, Hirsch Jakob.
  The echo of the Nazi holocaust in rabbinic literature.

  Includes bibliographical references and index.
  1. Holocaust and Jewish law. 2. Holocaust, Jewish
(1939-1945) 3. Responsa—1800-   I. Title.
D810.J4Z55   1977   296.1'8   76-56778
ISBN 0-87068-427-2

Printed in the Republic of Ireland

IN MEMORY OF MY DEAR MOTHER
—ONE OF THE SIX MILLION MARTYRS
OF OUR PEOPLE

Contents

PART I

THE FOUR PHASES

Boycott of Jewish shops—prohibition of *shehitah*—
Jewish anti-German boycott—business on the
Sabbath—segregation and limitation in cultural
respects—disposal of synagogues and cemeteries—
emigration—*herem* against return to Spain—
Austria—Evian Conference.

Expulsion of Polish Jews from Germany—*Kristallnacht*—refugees—premonition of war—conditional
bill of divorce.

Attacks on Jewish life—beard plucking—creation
and administration of ghettos—deportations—the
final solution—*Kiddush Ha-Shem*—change of identity — suicide — concentration and extermination
camps—'Why did the Jews not rise against their
tormentors?'

Cultural revival — monuments — museums —
memorial days — memorial prayers — return to
Judaism—rescue of children—exhumation and
reburial—treatment of *kapos*—restitution.

PART II

PART III

ANTHOLOGY OF RESPONSA

Preface

As its title suggests this book intends to convey to the reader the relationship between the Nazis and their victims and the problems which faced the Rabbis in the days of the holocaust and immediately after the liberation. The work is based on Rabbinical *teshuboth* (*Responsa*), i.e. replies by the Rabbis to questions on various problems sent to them for their guidance and decisions. The role of this branch of Rabbinic literature is well known; the *Responsa* are unique, most reliable and objective. Any personal colouring and deviation from fact would often require a different decision. While I have quoted the facts and the queries in full (as far as relevant to purpose) the decisions of the Rabbis are mentioned only briefly. The reader must not take the decisions as quoted in this book as a guide for practical cases without studying the sources and examining carefully the *halachic* reasoning in the Rabbis' replies.

The first writer to draw the attention of historians of the Nazi holocaust to the material contained in the *Responsa* of contemporary Rabbis was Joseph Wulf in his essay 'Rabbinic Books Aiding Research into the Holocaust' (Yiddish), in *Probleme*, Paris 1950, pp. 566f. A list of authors of *Responsa* on the Nazi holocaust was given by Philip Friedman, *Bibliography of Books in Hebrew on the Jewish Catastrophe and Heroism in Europe*, Yad Vashem-YIVO, Jerusalem 1960, pp. 139ff.; Rabbi Dr Joseph Schafran wrote on 'Sheeloth Halachah Bi-Yeme Shoah Ve-Hurban Be-Europa' in *Sinai*, Kislev-Tebeth, Jerusalem, 5729, pp. 190ff. (further references by R. H. Schmelzer ibid. Ab-Ellul, p. 335) and also published a paper under the same title in *Torah She-Beal-Peh*, Jerusalem, 5732, pp. 134ff, he had read at the '14th Kinnus for Torah She-Beal-Peh'. I too read a paper entitled 'The Echo of the Nazi Holocaust in the Rabbinic Literature' at the Fifth World Congress of Jewish Studies held by the University in Jerusalem, 1969 (subsequently published there in vol. II, 1972, pp. 186ff.). I pointed out that it was only a synopsis of a major work which I intended to publish.

Unfortunately for reasons beyond my control I was unable to publish my work until now. I have tried to do justice to the numerous religious problems which arose in the Nazi era as well as during the reconstruction until today. I have made use of almost all available printed *Responsa* to date.

After a general introduction, an historical review of the life of the Jews under the Nazis and after the liberation is given in Part I. In Part II the relation between the Nazi legislation and *halachah* is discussed. Part III forms an anthology of *Responsa*—a collection of historical Rabbinic records.

I wish to express my gratitude to all those who assisted me to produce this book.

H.J.Z.

'No monuments need be put up for the righteous,
their words are their monument (*Shekalim* 7a)'

This quotation can justly be applied to my father, the author of this work, who was tragically taken from our midst on Sabbath 24th Heshvan 5735 (9th November 1974).

Alas he did not have the good fortune to see the conclusion of this work which was only partly in proof form at the time of his sudden death. The manuscript was almost completed two years ago but for reasons beyond his control its publication was delayed.

I am most grateful to Rabbi C. D. Kaplin for his keen interest in this work and am indebted to Dr L. V. Snowman for having read the proofs and for making valuable suggestions and to Mr A. Schischa for his constant advice and guidance.

Sincere thanks are due to the Emeritus Chief Rabbi, Sir Israel Brodie, Mr A. Hubert, O.B.E., and other well-wishers who were instrumental in making this publication possible.

My father instilled in me the love for Torah, the appreciation of true scholarship and scholastic discipline. During recent years I was privileged to assist him in his literary work. Thus I felt I had to accept the responsibility of undertaking completion of this work, but were it not for the encouragement of my dear mother I doubt I would have been able to bring this matter to a satisfactory conclusion.

The Talmud states: 'It is a legal presumption that a scholar would not allow anything unprepared to pass out of his hand (*Erub.* 32a).' My father was always aware of the importance of meticulous presentation and all his writings were checked many times over before being allowed to go to press. This work, however, has been bereft of his final touches and it is therefore almost inevitable that errors have occurred. For those I take full responsibility.

My father bore his great erudition with true humility and matched his piety with his kindness. He will always remain a shining example to all those who came into contact with him.

May his memory be for a blessing.

London, 1975   M.Z.

Prologue

OF THE GREATEST TRAGEDY OF ALL TIMES

'Come and see,' says the Midrash,[1] 'how much blood of the righteous and pious people Esau has shed and no burial been given to them, as it is written "They have shed their blood like water around Jerusalem, with none to bury them" (Ps. LXXIX 3). What does the Holy One, blessed be He, do? He takes from the life-blood of each of the martyrs and dips His cloak in it until the colour resembles blood. When the day of judgement comes He will put on His cloak and show Esau the body of every righteous man marked on it.'

When reading this one must ask oneself: How red is the purple mantle of the Holy One, blessed be He, now, after He has dipped it six million times in the blood of the martyrs of the last great tragedy to befall mankind? How many martyrs are marked on it joining those who sanctified the name of the Lord during the past two thousand years alone! They will be shown not only to the Esau of our time who perpetrated the crimes but also to those who witnessed them and stood by transgressing the prohibition 'Neither shalt thou stand idly by the blood of thy neighbour' (Lev. XIX 16), the blood, which cries from the earth (Gen. IV 10) and rises and seethes like that of Zechariah, the son of Jehoiada,[2] and cannot cease to effervesce. It cries: 'Remember what the German Amalek did unto thee. . . . Thou shalt not forget.' (See Deut. XXV 17.)

'Remember . . . thou shalt not forget.' When Sir Hartley Shawcross, British Attorney-General and Chief Prosecutor at the Nuremberg Trial, saw on his visit to Poland the ghastly exhibits in the Polish National Museum of Nazi torture of the Jews he is reported to have said that 'it is the most horrible and convincing testimony of German degradation and should be shown in every country as a reminder of what the Germans did and would do again if ever they were allowed to re-arm.'[3]

'Remember . . . thou shalt not forget' is also the wish of honourable gentiles today, twenty-nine years after the liberation from tyranny. 'While the trial was in progress,' writes Lord Denning, M.R., in his Foreword to *Auschwitz in England, A Record of a Libel Action*, 'many thought: "All this is too horrible. Let us turn over this page of history

---

1. *Yalkut* Num. No. 785; Ps. 869.
2. See *Gittin* 57b.
3. *Jewish Chronicle*, 28 June 1946, p. 1. That there are still criminal elements among the Germans who ignore the past can be seen from two short notices which appeared together in the press twenty-five years later. They run as follows:
   'Fourteen gravestones were overturned and damaged in the ancient Jewish cemetery at Hochberg in the Ludwigsburg district, recently.
   Swastikas were scratched on all twelve glass doors of the historic Paulus Church in Frankfurt, where an exhibition on the theme of "Anti-Fascist Resistance, 1933–1945" was being held.' *Jewish Chronicle*, 2 April 1971, p. 6.

and forget it." Yet the truth should be made known, if only to show at one time a civilized country reverted to barbarism, and thus remind us of the perils that are not far away.'[4]

The national press and the Jewish newspapers in London reported some time ago under the heading 'Cardinal's Belsen Warning' a lecture given by Cardinal Heenan, archbishop of Westminster, to students at the London School of Economics on 'Ethics 1970 Style' in which he said: 'The greatest shock in modern times was not the bomb at Hiroshima, but the persecution of the Jews in Nazi Germany. . . .

'The realisation that national leaders in the twentieth century could plan the systematic destruction of the whole race put an end to the belief in the myth of human progress.

'It would be educationally good to show the films of Belsen to young people every year. They should be allowed to see what was done in the name of national purity and eugenics by twentieth-century men and women.

'Although the trials of criminals responsible for the torture and murder continue to this day the full horror is scarcely known to citizens under forty years of age.'[5]

'Remember . . . thou shalt not forget.'

4. Mavis M. Hill and L. Norman Williams, *Auschwitz in England, A Record of a Libel Action,* London, 1965.
5. See *Daily Telegraph,* 18 November 1970, p. 3; *Jewish Chronicle,* 27 November 1970, p. 1; *Jewish Tribune,* 27 November 1970, p. 9. How right these words are that the crimes committed by the Germans must be remembered can be judged from 'a lengthy article full of admiration for Adolf Hitler and denigration of the Jews' published by a new Afrikaans magazine *Brandwag,* twenty-five years after the war. The author of this article, J. A. Rio-Neuhof, claims that the liberal Jewish and American powers had invented the crimes ascribed to Hitler. He regards it as impossible that six million Jews had died during World War II. When the vice-chairman of the South African Publications Control Board was asked about the article he claimed he had not received any complaints. (See *Jewish Chronicle,* 4 June 1971, p. 36.) If contemporaries of the sadistic crimes have the audacity to deny them what can one expect from future generations?

Introduction

The greatest of all persecutions to which our people has been subject since the destruction of the Second Temple[1] was no doubt the Nazi holocaust. There were several factors which made the persecution of the Jews by the Nazis unique in the history of mankind in general and in that of the Jews in particular. These factors were:

1. the nature of the persecution;
2. the plan of the extermination of the whole Jewish race;
3. the number of countries affected and the number of their victims;
4. the use of modern methods of science and technology in the extermination of Jews;
5. the misuse of the victims and their bodies for forced labour, for medical, commercial and private purposes, and
6. the difficulties of finding places of refuge.

All these factors are reflected to a greater or lesser extent in the *Responsa* and have been dealt with by the Rabbis for religious, legal and matrimonial purposes.

THE NATURE OF THE PERSECUTION

The attitude of National Socialism towards the Jews had been expressed several years before Hitler came to power. One of the articles of the National Socialist party, adopted on 25 February 1920, declared that 'a Jew by virtue of his blood, could not become a member of the nation'.[2] Other articles stated that non-citizens (Jews) are only 'guests' in Germany, that they are to fill no public office, that (Jewish) aliens should be expelled in periods of unemployment, and that all East European Jews who entered Germany after 2 August 1914 should be expelled too, etc.[3]

This degradation of the Jews did not, as is well known, assume practical importance until 1933 when Hitler came to power and the Nazi legislative machinery began working: the programme planned in 1920 was completed in the following years. Until then (1933), on the basis of Article 109 of the Weimar Constitution all citizens of the Reich enjoyed parity in the eyes of the law.[4] In spite of that, encroachment

---

1. According to one Rabbi it even surpassed in its severity the destruction of both Temples and all other persecutions, cf. R. Hayyim Yizhak Jeruchem, *Birkath Hayyim*, New York, 1956, Introduction 'Alim Bochim, p. 20. Cf. also R. Z. H. Meisels, *Kuntras Takkanoth Agunoth*, no. 49, p. 16. R. Eliezer Yehudah Waldenberg, *Ziz Eliezer*, V, no. 17.
2-3. Cf. Jacob Marcus, *The Rise and Destiny of the German Jew*, Cincinnati, 1934, p. 47.
4. See Bruno Blau, *Das Ausnahmerecht für die Juden in Deutschland 1933–1945*, Düsseldorf, 1954, p. 7.

upon the rights and life of the Jews in Germany occurred even before
Hitler's rise to power. Two facts feature among the acts of the Nazis
against the Jews. First, the bills prohibiting *shehitah,* i.e. ritual slaughtering of animals without prior stunning by electric shock (such bills were
presented at various *Landtags*);[5] secondly, the desecration of Jewish
cemeteries which had become a common evil suffered by the Jews in
Germany. While attempts to prohibit *shehitah* do not expressly bear an
anti-Jewish character since they were ostensibly 'to avoid cruelty to
animals', the desecration of cemeteries were acts directed specifically
against the Jewish people. In the *Jüdisches Lexikon*[6] which appeared in
Berlin in 1928 there is a special entry on *Friedhofsschändungen.*
Among other facts we are told that desecrations were mainly for
political, National-Socialist motives (unlike those in previous centuries
which bore only a religious character). During the years 1923–28 fifty-
eight Jewish cemeteries were desecrated, forty-two of them in two and
a half years. Such desecrations continued in the years prior to Hitler's
rule and affected synagogues too. By September 1932 fifty synagogues
and one hundred and twenty-eight Jewish cemeteries had been defiled
and desecrated.[7] Physical attacks on Jews also occurred. In September
1931, as the Berlin Jews left the synagogue on *Rosh Ha-Shanah* they
were assaulted by Nazis in an organized attack with the result that
one hundred and thirteen Jews were injured.

The Nazi Programme of 1920, the various acts against the Jews,
Hitler's book *Mein Kampf* and the wild anti-Jewish tirades which
accompanied the elections in the 1930s showed the German Jews
clearly what the Nazis had in mind should they come to power.

Indeed with Hitler's rise on 30 January 1933, the systematic and
'legal' destruction of German Jewry began. After brushing aside the
Weimar Constitution (which guaranteed parity in the eyes of the law
to all citizens) Hitler and his cabinet had the power to enact laws
without parliament which might deviate from the constitution on the
basis of the 'Enabling Act' (*Ermächtigungsgesetz*) of 24 March 1933.[8]

A series of anti-Jewish laws was issued culminating in the humiliation,
segregation and degradation of German Jews.

Of great significance and with far-reaching consequences were the
laws issued at the party rally at Nuremberg on 15 September 1935,
which became known as 'The Nuremberg Laws'. There were two funda-
mental issues involved: 'The Reich Citizenship Act' (*Reichsbürgergesetz*)
and 'The Act for the Protection of German Blood and German Honour'
(*Gesetz zum Schutze des deutschen Blutes und der deutschen Ehre*), known

5. *Vide infra* 'Shehitah'.
6. Vol. II, p. 820.
7. Marcus, *The Rise and Destiny of the German Jew,* p. 49.
8. See Blau, *Das Ausnahmerecht;* Johan M. Snoek, *The Grey Book,* Assen, 1969, p. 33.

as 'The Blood Protection Act' *(Blutschutzgesetz)*.[9] Under the former, Jews were deprived of their German citizenship. They were only *Staatsangehörige* (subjects of the State) unlike the Aryan Germans who were *Reichsbürger*.[10] Only the latter enjoyed all political rights.[11]

According to the second law, marriage and extramarital relations between Jews and Aryans were prohibited under penalty of imprisonment. In order to humiliate the Jews even more, the Jews were not to employ female domestics under forty-five years of age.[12]

The second law played an important role in Jewish religious life as we shall see later. Indeed when comparing the anti-Jewish laws of Nazi legislation with those of the various European countries in the Middle Ages one would find little difference between them. However, and this is the main characteristic of the Nazi legislation, unlike the Middle Ages when the Jew could save himself from outlawry and death by performing mere lip-service, in the Nazi era nothing whatsoever could help him whereby he could in a 'legal' way escape his fate as decreed by the Nazis. All their actions were aimed at humiliating and degrading the Jew forcing him to cease his occupation and compelling him to emi-

Reichsbürgergesetz vom 15. September 1935

§ 1

i Staatsangehöriger ist, wer dem Schutzverband des Deutschen Reiches angehört und ihm dafür besonders verpflichtet ist.

ii Die Staatsangehörigkeit wird nach den Vorschriften des Reichs—und Staatsangehörigkeitgesetzes erworben.

§ 2

i Reichsbürger ist nur der Staatsangehörige deutschen oder artverwandten Blutes. . . .

ii Das Reichsbürgerrecht wird durch Verleihung des Reichsbürgerbriefes erworben.

iii Der Reichsbürger ist der alleinige Träger der vollen politischen Rechte nach Massgabe der Gesetze.

Gesetz zum Schutze des deutschen Blutes und der deutschen Ehre (15. September 1935)

§ 1

Eheschliessungen zwischen Juden und Staatsangehörigen deutschen oder artverwandten Blutes sind verboten. . . .

§ 2

Ausserehelicher Verkehr zwischen Juden und Staatsangehörigen deutschen oder artverwandten Blutes ist verboten.

§ 3

Juden dürfen weibliche Staatsangehörige deutschen oder artverwandten Blutes unter 45 Jahren in ihrem Haushalt nicht beschäftigen.

Reichsgesetzblatt, Jahrgang 1935, Teil I, pp. 1146f. (copy from the Wiener Library). For the text and interpretation, see Blau, *Das Ausnahmerecht*, pp. 29ff.; Helmut Krausnick; 'The Persecution of the Jews', in *Anatomy of the SS State*, London, 1968, pp. 32ff., Arthur D. Morse, *While Six Million Died*, London, 1968, p. 180; Raul Hilberg, *The Destruction of the European Jews*, London, 1961, pp. 46ff.; Gerald Reitlinger, *The Final Solution*, pp. 7f.

10. On this distinction, see Blau, *Das Ausnahmerecht*, pp. 7, 29f.

11. *Vide supra* note 9, para 2, no. iii.

12. On the use of the term 'Jude' instead of 'non-Aryan' in the Nazi legislation for the first time and its significance, see Blau, *Das Ausnahmerecht*, pp. 7, 33.

B

grate and (during the war when emigration was not possible) at massacring him in cold blood. At first the cold pogrom was used and later the bloody pogrom was set in operation.[13]

THE PLAN OF THE EXTERMINATION OF THE WHOLE JEWISH RACE

As the persecution under the Nazis differed from all previous persecutions of the Jewish people so were the plans for exterminating them different from those of other enemies. Complete extermination dictated by the head of state is almost unprecedented in history. Hitler's goal was the total destruction of the Jewish race as he firmly expressed in his speech on 30 January 1939.[14]

It is rather significant that a new expression was coined to denote the mass murder committed by the Nazis which has been included in standard dictionaries: it is 'genocide'.[15]

The policy of genocide was of the utmost importance for the Rabbis as it served as an auxiliary factor in deciding leniently cases of *agunoth* (women whose husbands had disappeared).[16]

THE NUMBER OF COUNTRIES AFFECTED AND THE NUMBER OF THEIR VICTIMS

Never in the history of the Jews had it happened that such a large number of countries was involved as during the Nazi extermination campaign and similarly never in Jewish history was the number of the localities 'purged' of their Jewish inhabitants as great as in the holocaust.

In the 'First Count of the Indictment of Adolf Eichmann' the following item is mentioned:

'The accused, together with others, caused the killing of still more hundreds of thousands of Jews during the years 1939–1945 . . . in the following countries: Germany; Austria; Italy; Bulgaria; Belgium; U.S.S.R. and the Baltic States; Lithuania, Latvia and Estonia which were annexed to U.S.S.R. and that part of Poland which was annexed to U.S.S.R. after September, 1939; Denmark; Holland; Hungary; Yugoslavia; Greece; Luxembourg; Monaco; Norway; Poland; Czechoslovakia; France; Rumania.'[17] The total number of localities 'purged'

13. For particulars *vide infra*.
14. *Vide infra*, p. 32.
15. See *Brewer's Dictionary of Phrase and Fable*, London, 1970, *s.v.* 'Genocide' where the following explanation is given: 'A word invented by Professor Raphael Lemkin, of Duke University, U.S.A., and used in the drafting of the official indictment of war criminals in 1945. It is a combination of Gr. *genos*, race and Lat. *caedere*, to kill. It is defined as acts intended to destroy, in whole or in part, national, ethnical, racial, or religious groups, and in 1948 was declared by the United Nations General Assembly to be a crime in international law.'
16. *Vide infra*.
17. See 'The Indictment', The Attorney General *v* Adolf Eichmann (copy at the Wiener Library, p. 4); cf. also Peter Papadatos, *The Eichmann Trial*, p. 114; Bar-Zohar, *The Avengers*, p. 13; Manvell and Fraenkel, *The Incomparable Crime*, London, 1967, pp. 4f.

of their Jewish population is given as 33,914.[18] Poland tops the list with 16,782 localities.

When dealing with an *agunah* case where the members of the family had been deported with other Jews from Larissa (Greece) and Corfu to the extermination camp of Birkenau a Sephardi Rabbi remarks: 'The whole of Germany had become a place of stoning (*beth ha-sekilah*) for the Jews.'[19] With bitter irony an inmate of the Warsaw Ghetto when speaking of a particular camp calls it: 'An Ingathering of the Exiles on foreign soil'.[20]

Action and Achievement: Mass murder. Never in human history is such a large number of innocent victims known to have perished during a persecution, the number is estimated at around six million.[21]

In fact the Nazis intended to exterminate eleven million Jews including those of England, Portugal, Turkey, Sweden, Spain, the whole of U.S.S.R. and of all German satellites.[22]

THE USE OF MODERN METHODS OF SCIENCE AND TECHNOLOGY IN THE EXTERMINATION OF THE JEWS

For the first time in history the method used for mass killings was not only shooting but the quicker, more 'effective' and modern method of gassing followed by burning in crematoria. Once the fate of the victim had been decided as many as two thousand people of one transport could disappear within a short period without leaving any witness to testify to the death of any particular person as he who had witnessed another's death was himself killed. When the thousands of *agunah* problems came before the Rabbis, direct evidence could hardly ever be

---

18. Bar-Zohar, *The Avengers*. During the persecution under Chmielnicki in 1648–49. which was one of the greatest persecutions before the Nazi holocaust, 744 communities were destroyed. See I. Halperin, *Pinkas Vaad Arba Arazoth*, p. 79, no. 210, and S. Bernfeld, *Sepher Ha-Demaoth*, III, p. 32. The number of victims was about 650,000. According to R. Samuel Pheivish, *Tit Ha-Yaven*, quoted by Bernfeld, *Sepher Ha-Demaoth*, p. 157, the number of communities known to the author to have been destroyed was 740, and the known number of family-heads (women and children excluded) was 600,070.

19. R. Uzziel, *Mishpete Uzziel, E.H.* no. 40.

20. Chaim A. Kaplan, *Scroll of Agony*, p. 289.

21. The exact figure varies. According to some reports 5,700,000 or 5,721,000 Jews were exterminated, according to another estimate the number of victims was 5,978,000. On these and other figures, see Reitlinger, *The Final Solution*, London, 1968, pp. 553f.; Manvel and Fraenkel, *op. cit.*, pp. 4f.; Hilberg, *The Destruction of European Jews*, p. 631. Eichmann's figure was: six million. Mr Joseph Fraenkel, London, drew my attention to an article by Nahman Blumenthal in *Folk un Zion*, Jerusalem, 21st year, no. 12, August 1972, p. 45, according to which '7,000,000 Jews and no less' were exterminated.

22. See Gideon Hausner, *Justice in Jerusalem*, London, 1967, p. 94.

given about the death of the husbands. There are a few exceptions.[23] This was unlike *agunah* cases of the other persecutions where evidence could be taken from people who had witnessed the actual death of a particular person.

This method of mass extermination was the most severe crime committed in Nazi Germany; the wonderful gift of the human intellect, the gift of invention and discovery brought curse instead of blessing. In fact Hitler and his henchmen put all branches of technology into service for the destruction of the Jewish people.

Scientists were busy inventing the deadly gases to exterminate the Jews, technicians and engineers competed in constructing 'foolproof' ovens to burn the victims[24] and one firm produced 'a continually-operating High-Volume Corpse Incinerator' being 'an ingenious machine which made full use of the body fat of the corpses to assist in providing the fuel of destruction'.[25] Had anything like this happened during former persecutions of the Jews?

THE MISUSE OF THE VICTIMS AND THEIR BODIES FOR FORCED LABOUR, MEDICAL, COMMERCIAL AND PRIVATE PURPOSES

The crime committed on the living

The victims in the concentration camps classified as fit were not only exploited for forced labour particularly in the various factories established in some camps but they were used as human guinea-pigs for the advancement of science and medicine. Is there any greater crime committed against humanity and science? Yet all this was done by doctors notwithstanding the 'Hippocratic oath'!

There exists a long list of tests carried out on the inmates of the camps to see the effect of numerous vaccines, new drugs, etc.[26] Most cruel were the experiments made on men and women by various methods of sterilization. They were to serve a double purpose: as a medical experiment as far as drugs were concerned, and as a means of extermination,[27] or at least of limiting the birth-rate of the Jews and other races after the final victory of the Germans making them the masters of Europe.

23. See e.g. R. M. J. Breisch, *Helkath Yaakob*, I, no. 15 (*vide infra*, p. 89); *Hazon Ish* on *Eben Ha-Ezer, Hilchoth Ishshuth*, no. 28, p. 90, quoted in *Peer Ha-Dor*, Bene Berak, 1970, III, p. 176; 'A woman gave evidence that she had seen her husband who had been among the Jews taken by the Germans to be massacred, shot in the head and fall to the ground.' The *Hazon Ish* was inclined to permit the woman to remarry.

24. *Vide infra* 'Camps'.

25. See Manvel and Fraenkel, *The Incomparable Crime*, London, 1967, p. 294, n. 11.

26. On these experiments, see Jacques Delarue, *The History of the Gestapo*, London, 1964, pp. 307ff.

27. *Vide infra*, pp. 102ff.

The crime committed on the dead

The desecration of the corpses of the victims. As long as the inmates of the concentration camps were still fit for work, they were used for forced labour. If they were no longer fit or were found unfit on their arrival at the camp, they were doomed to death. But even then they were exploited and parts of their bodies were used for various purposes for the benefit of the German people.[28]

THE DIFFICULTIES OF FINDING PLACES OF REFUGE

Another great tragedy which makes the Nazi holocaust distinguishable from all the other persecutions and expulsions was the fact that the Jews in the countries under the Nazi heel, had great difficulties in finding places to which they could emigrate. Only a small proportion of Jews were successful. When the Jews were expelled from Spain, Turkey opened her gates to the exiles and Sultan Bayazid declared: 'You call Ferdinand a wise king who had impoverished his country and enriched ours!'[29] In the Nazi era no country opened its gates freely to anyone. For that reason emigration became deportation, leading to extermination. Had the gates of Palestine been opened, six million Jews might not have perished.[30]

There is still another point to be mentioned. In the same way as the persecution was unique, so its literary consequences differ from all other persecutions. Unlike those in Germany during the Crusades in 1096 and 1146 and during the Black Death in the fourteenth century and the persecution of the Jews in Spain beginning with the Holy War in 1391 and ending with the expulsion of the Jews from the Iberian Peninsula in 1492 or the massacre under Chmielnicki in 1648, when chronicles and *kinoth* were composed, the Nazi holocaust found its expression in many diverse ways. Monuments in memory of the martyrs were erected, museums and institutes were established and a special chair for studies of the Nazi persecution was created.[31] Special research centres and archives were opened.[32] However, most outstanding is the literary activity covering all branches of literature in various languages. It includes history, poetry, biography, diaries, memorial volumes, folk songs, *kinoth*, etc., many of them written in the shadow of death. We also possess rich Rabbinic literature, sermons delivered in the ghettos, Talmudical discourses written down as well as one of the most important

---

28. See previous note.
29. See H. Graetz, *Geschichte der Juden*, VIII, Leipzig, 4th ed., p. 354.
30. On emigration, *vide infra*. See also R. Hayyim Ozer Grodzinski, *Ahiezer, Kobez Iggeroth*, vol. I, nos. 139ff., for the plea by R. H. O. Grodzinski to Chief Rabbi Herzog.
31. At the Yeshivah University in New York. See *Jewish Chronicle*, 28 August 1970, p. 14.
32. See Hausner, *Justice in Jerusalem*, p. 286.

branches of Rabbinic literature, the *Responsa* which play a special role. From the time the Nazis came to power until today, there is hardly a collection of *Responsa* which does not deal with the problems connected with the Nazi persecution. Some works are devoted exclusively to such problems, as their names suggest: *Mi-Maamakkim*,[33] *Kuntras Me-Emek Ha-Bacha*,[34] *Ezrath Nashim*,[35] *Me-Emek Ha-Bacha*,[36] *Mi-Ge Ha-Haregah*,[37] *Seride Esh* (vol. I, and some *Responsa* in vols. II and III).[38] Some collections include in their introductions or at the end biographical notes giving valuable material in connection with the Nazi holocaust.

There are also *Responsa* written by the Rabbis who had themselves been inmates of the ghettos. Their replies concern the life of the Jews under the Nazis. Their decisions were in many cases very lenient and could be regarded as *horaoth shaah* i.e. decisions in emergency which cannot be taken to serve as a precedent. And yet the Rabbis who wrote them down collected them and published them after the Nazi regime had collapsed although most such *Responsa* serve little practical purpose today. The reason for their being published is that they are of great historical value. 'Now fifteen years after I wrote down these *Responsa*,' writes one Rabbi,[39] 'I went through the scraps of paper which had begun to be eaten away in the course of time. I noticed that they contain extraordinary historical material of great value which gives us a picture depicting the spiritual life of the inmates of the Ghetto and of the background of the daily war for existence, then I said to myself "this was the Lord's doing" (Ps. cxviii 23) to cause me to note these *Responsa* to set up a memorial for the righteous of Lithuania who sanctified the Name of God in their life and death. . . .'

We also possess some decisions made by Rabbis on the basis of their own observations in the extermination camps. The decisions were written down later after the liberation.[40]

The historical value of the *Responsa* of the holocaust is also stressed by some other authors.[41] Indeed the *Responsa* reflect the life, particularly the spiritual life, of the inmates of the ghettos and camps. For the first

33. By R. Ephraim Oshry, vols. I–III, New York, 1959–69.
34. In *Dibre Ephraim* by R. E. Oshry, New York, 1949.
35 Vols. I–III, by R. Meir Meiri (Feuerwerger), Brussels-London, 1950–55.
36. By R. S. Efrati, Jerusalem, 1948.
37. By R. S. Efrati, Jerusalem, 1961.
38. By R. J. J. Weinberg, vols. I–III, Jerusalem, 1961–66.
39. R. E. Oshry, Introduction to *Mi-Maamakkim* I.
40. R. Z. H. Meisels, *Kuntras Takkanoth Agunoth*, Bergen-Belsen, 1946; *Mekaddshe Ha-Shem*, vol. I, Chicago, 1955, vol. II, New York, 1967; *Binyan Zebi*, vol. II, New York, 1956, nos. 33ff. R. Jacob Avigdor, 'Iggunah De-Iththa', in *Helek Yaakob*, II, Mexico, 1956.
41. Cf. R. J. J. Weinberg *infra* p. 186; *Ozar Ha-Poskim* on *E.H.*, cap. XVII, no. 36, vol. VII, p. 124.

time in the history of the *Responsa* their publication serves more for historical than practical purposes and they are an important source for the historian writing on this period.

Rabbi Weinberg[42] who was expelled from Berlin before the war and spent some time in the Warsaw Ghetto and in German concentration camps stresses on several occasions the historical importance attached to the *Responsa* (on the prohibition of *shehitah* and lecturing in synagogues).

We possess *Responsa* dealing with the life of the Jews in Germany, in the ghettos of Poland, Hungary, Lithuania, etc., in the bunkers, in the hiding places, on the 'death marches', on the trains to the extermination camps and inside the camps, as well as those which tackle the numerous problems arising after the liberation.

---

42. He hailed from Lithuania and settled in Berlin where he was appointed head of the Hildesheimer Seminary, Berlin.

Part 1

The Four Phases

There are four important phases in the history of the Jews under the Nazi regime. (1) The period from the beginning of Nazi rule in Germany in 1933 until the deportation of the Polish Jews to Zbonszyn in October 1938. (2) The period from the deportation of the Polish Jews to Zbonszyn until the outbreak of World War II. (3) World War II, and (4) the aftermath and reconstruction.

The story told of the persecution of the Jews in Spain can, to some extent, be regarded as characteristic of the Jews under the Nazis. 'In the great city of Seville', writes R. Solomon ibn Verga,[1] 'there lived R. Judah ibn Verga. . . . Before the inquisition was established there he knew what was about to happen. He put into his window three pairs of turtle-doves. One pair was plucked and slaughtered upon whose necks he wrote "These will be those Marranos who go out last". The other pair was plucked but not slaughtered. "These," he said, "will be the middle ones." The third pair alive with their plumage untouched bore the writing "These will be the first ones".' This can be applied, to some extent, to the Jews in Germany under the Nazis during the first three periods mentioned above. Those who remained in Germany during World War II (and also the Jews in countries overrun by the Nazis during the war) were 'plucked and slaughtered'. The Jews who left Germany between the *Kristallnacht*[2] and the beginning of World War II could only leave alive but 'plucked' (this also applies to those who survived the war). Those, however, who left Germany or who left the occupied countries, Austria and Czechoslovakia, before or immediately after the Nazis had come to power could emigrate alive 'with their plumage' taking with them some or all of their property.

1. *Shebet Yehudah*, ed. by Wiener, Hanover, 1855, p. 94.
2. Or 'The Night of the Broken Glass'. On it *vide infra*, pp. 25ff.

1

The period from the beginning of Nazi rule in Germany in 1933 until the expulsion of the Polish Jews in October 1938

This period is marked by humiliation, segregation and emigration. It is characterized by the attempts of the Nazi government to deprive the Jews of all basic rights, to drive them out of economic life and to make their existence in Germany and Austria (after the annexation in March 1938) as difficult as possible. For that reason the Nazis assumed emigration of the Jews would follow, thus making the Reich first free of Jews.

Also sporadic acts of physical violence by the SS occurred. The following event should be mentioned which took place immediately after the Nazis had come to power. A Rabbi who hailed from Poland and acted as Rabbi in Duisburg reports his miraculous escape from the Nazis. On the conclusion of the Sabbath, 21st of Adar 693 (the night 18–19 March 1933) five armed SS men came and beat him mercilessly. On the 25th of Adar (23 March 1933) a band of SS men came into his house and led him outside through the streets accompanied by hundreds and thousands of people. Not one who saw the beatings and humiliation intervened on his behalf. After one hour he was led into a wide open place near the theatre and was surrounded by thousands of people who beat him, pulled his hair and plucked his beard. A huge fire burned nearby and the Rabbi thought he would be led to the bonfire. 'However, due to the mercy of the Almighty, a high-ranking officer was present who implored the wicked people to set me free.' This was done. The Rabbi returned home and soon afterwards left Germany for Switzerland. He was appointed Rabbi in Zurich.[3]

The degradation and segregation of the Jews were achieved by 'legal' means by the Enabling Act (*Ermächtigungsgesetz*) authorizing Hitler to issue decrees which were in contradiction with the constitution and which did not require parliamentary approval.[4]

The boycott of Jewish shops observed and enforced by the Nazis on 1 April 1933, is mentioned in two *Responsa*. Both were written by R. Spira of Mukacevo (Munkatsch). The Rabbi deals with the boycott from the religious-moral point of view. In one *Responsum* written to R. Weinberg in connection with the prohibition of *shehitah* he remarks: 'It is a finger of God' (Exodus VIII 15), that the beginning of the *gezerah*

3. R. M. J. Breisch, Introduction to *Helkath Yaakob* I.
4. *Vide supra*, p. xvi and note 8.

3

(evil decree) was the boycott on the Sabbath prohibiting non-Jews from buying in Jewish-owned shops and in spite of that it did not cross the Jews' minds that they ought to keep their shops closed every Sabbath.[5] The same view was expressed by him in a *Responsum* to the Rabbi of Ungvar.[6]

From April 1933 a series of decrees was issued, all of them aimed at the expulsion of the Jews from various professions. A special system can be observed in the legislation against the Jews. It did not begin with drastic measures applying to the majority of Jews but was directed first against selected professions and went on to embrace all positions held by them[7] thus segregating them and finally making them outcasts and pariahs.

The prohibition of *shehitah*, i.e. ritual slaughtering of animals without prior stunning by electric shock issued on 21–22 April 1933, was harsh.[8] Although this law was an encroachment on the religious way of life of the Jews, it was by no means intended, as we shall see later, as an act of religious persecution. Its purpose was merely to annoy the Jews.[9]

The harsh treatment of the Jews in Germany was also felt by the Jews abroad who sought to combat it. A suitable weapon with which to fight German tyranny was thought to be a boycott of German goods. Indeed a great boycott movement began in March 1933. In the Jewish press[10] headings like 'Boycott Movement in Full Swing', 'Jewry's Reply: Boycott German Goods! World Wide Campaign has its Effect', etc., were widely acclaimed.[11] A still greater anti-German boycott movement began after the pogrom of 1938. The Nazis naturally were enraged at this act of international Jewry as they were at the other reports of the ill-treatment meted out to the German Jews. There occurred a most interesting event unprecedented in the history of the Jews. While the Nazis were afraid of damage to their 'good name' abroad and the Jews in Germany feared reprisals a book appeared (Berlin 1933) which was to serve as a first-class documentation that the Jews were living in peace, undisturbed by their Nazi environment. This was maintained by the Nazi leaders themselves and confirmed by influential Jews who implored their coreligionists abroad not to believe in the atrocity propaganda and to refrain from action against the

5. Cf. R. J. J. Weinberg, *Seride Esh*, I, p. 223.
6. Cf. *Sepher Darche Hayyim Ve-Shalom, Ozar Kol Ha-Minhagim* of R.H.E. Spira, ed. by J. M. Gold, Munkatsch, 1940, new edition: Brooklyn, 1948, p. 221, no. 655.
7. For details see Blau, *Das Ausnahmerecht für die Juden in Deutschland 1933–1945*, pp. 7ff.
8. *Vide infra*, pp. 181ff.
9. *Vide infra*, Part II, pp. 192, 244.
10. See *Jewish Chronicle*, 24 March 1933, p. 26; 31 March 1933, pp. 18, 23.
11. On the anti-German boycott movement and its effect also in 1938 cf. particularly Hilberg, *The Destruction of the European Jews*, London, 1961, pp. 20, 25.

German state. The book entitled *Atrocity Propaganda Is Based On Lies, Say The Jews Of Germany Themselves*, was written in German, English and French consisting of four sections with reports of interviews, speeches and letters from: (1) the members of the Nazi government (Hitler, Göring, Goebbels, etc.); (2) various Jewish organizations in Germany; (3) leading Jewish personalities (lay and religious leaders, financiers, industrialists, etc.); and (4) press reports.

The most striking feature of the book is that the editor—a Jew named Jakov Trachtenberg—tells us in his preface (dated: 15 May 1933) that he was a foreigner and because of the hospitality given to him by Germany for the previous fourteen years had to take this stand for the honour of this country. 'I must state expressly that I am doing this of my own accord . . . the book should prove that the German Jews themselves regard the atrocity propaganda as lies and are eager to oppose it with every means in their power. . . .'

However, the writer who was living in Germany at the time knew of the little truth that lay in the assurance of the Nazis and of Trachtenberg and in the statements of the Jews who under great duress composed those letters. Trachtenberg's motive in publishing the book is not quite clear. According to one view he was in the service of Goebbels. 'Der Hausjude des Goebbels' is the heading of an article which appeared in the press. According to another view he was coerced by the Nazis to do so. The publication was financed by the Nazis.[12]

What was indeed the attitude in Rabbinic circles towards the attempt to boycott German goods? We possess a few very interesting documents on this point.

R. Judah Leb Zirelsohn, Rabbi of Kischinev (he was killed by a bomb dropped by German planes in 1941), wrote two addresses in which he expressed the view that only total boycott of German goods could halt German aggression and persecution of the Jewish people. He demanded the use of therapeutic prescription: 'Similia similibus curantur'. We had to make use of the press, radio, etc., and to boycott all German productions. It was not directed against the German people as such but against Hitlerism. He then enumerated four types of Jews who tried to avert the boycott and refuted their views.

The second letter appears to have been written later as the Rabbi speaks of Dante's *Inferno* which had been created in Germany for the Jews and their great misfortune which was not less than that caused by the Inquisition. In it the Rabbi sees the only possibility of quenching

---

12. The book appeared in 'Jakow Trachtenberg Verlag, Berlin-Charlottenburg'. For the views on Trachtenberg, see *Europaeische Hefte*, Prague, no. 2, 26 April 1934; *Aufbau*, New York , 18 January 1952. My thanks to the Wiener Library for these two references.

the fire of the *Gehennah* by the announcing of a general boycott of German goods and tries to show how wrong was the attitude of those who were indifferent for one reason or another to such a boycott.[13]

More moderate and careful was the opinion expressed by R. Hayyim Ozer Grodzinski in a letter addressed to R. Silver, Rabbi of the 'Agudath Ha-Kehilloth' in Cincinnati, of Friday, 3rd Kislev, 5694.[14] R. Hayyim Ozer Grodzinski refers to the question he had been asked about the boycott. He replied that at first he was of the opinion that the Rabbis should refrain from intervening and remain passive as the boycott had already had evil consequences. 'However, the Rabbis have to consider the matter in accordance with the Torah (*be-daath Torah*) . . . as our brethren there complain bitterly and are afraid of blood being shed . . . .'
    From R. Hayyim's letter we learn that the 'Agudath Ha-Rabbanim' had decided to boycott (without *herem* or religious prohibition).[15]

There exists another source which shows us how nervous the Germans were about a boycott by the leading religious organizations 'of international Jewry'. They tried to exert pressure upon the Jews in Germany to intervene on their behalf among the Jews in Poland that no boycott be announced. The following account illustrates the anxiety of the Nazi authorities.
    It was one Thursday before the beginning of the *Selihoth*-days 5694, when the Nazi officer responsible for the interests of orthodox Jews called on R. Jacobson, chairman of the representatives of the orthodox Jews in Germany and of the World Agudath Yisrael and informed him that on the following Sunday (the first day of *Selihoth*) a *herem* (boycott) of German goods would be announced in Warsaw. He warned him that this would have repercussions on the Jews in Germany. When R. Jacobson replied he had no influence on Polish Jewry the Nazi leader of the department retorted there existed an Agudath Yisrael Movement and the majority of the congregation of Warsaw knew all particulars of it. Thereupon Dr Hildesheimer, vice chairman, went to Warsaw and succeeded in having the boycott abandoned. He immediately returned to Germany—he was there the following Sunday (the first day of *Selihoth*). The matter would not have become known had not a Jewish newspaper in Warsaw, ignorant of the background to Dr Hildesheimer's visit and the threat of the Gestapo, attacked him calling him 'Hitler's agent'.[16]

13. See R. J. L. Zirelsohn, *Leb Yehudah*, Jerusalem, 1961, pp. 70ff.
14. This corresponds to 21 November 1933, however, that day was a Tuesday!
15. R. H. O. Grodzinski, *Ahiezer, Kobez Iggeroth*, I, Bene Berak, 1970, p. 296, no. 182.
16. R. B. Z. Jacobson, *Essa Dei Le-Merahok*, Bene Berak, 1967, p. 123.

Reference to that episode is made by R. J. J. Weinberg, head of the Rabbinical Seminary in Berlin. This Rabbi was occupied with a problem which affected the whole of German Jewry: the prohibition of *shehitah* without prior stunning by electric shock. R. Weinberg went to Poland in September to consult the leading Rabbis on this problem.[17] He went to Wilno between *Rosh Ha-Shanah* and *Yom Kippur* and discussed the matter with R. Hayyim Ozer Grodzinski. 'Despite all the care I had taken', writes R. Weinberg, 'my journey to Lublin and my stay in Poland in general did not escape the eyes of the press. They suspected I had come to Poland to help R. Hildesheimer against the boycott of Germany. In view of this, incitement was stirred up against me. Naturally, this limited the freedom of my movements and I was forced to refrain from visiting more Rabbis . . . .'[18]

The following years brought only new misery and humiliation through the Nazi legislation. The professional and cultural life of the Jew in Germany was being constantly restricted.[19]

As early as in summer 1933 (Tuesday 27 June 1933) R. Weinberg remarked:

'In general one has nowadays to look for reasons to permit dealing in things which are prohibited by arranging a *shetar mechirah*, etc., to save the life of Jewish families.'[20]

On Wednesday, 7th of Nisan (10 April 1935)[21] he was approached by the Rabbi of Barken on the question of *shetar mechirah* for a man to keep his shop open on the Sabbath. R. Weinberg had some misgivings about granting such permission from the religious point of view, however, 'since it is a time of emergency and distress, and there is economic calamity, one must have mercy on our Jewish brethren who still keep the Law and Commandments and make life as easy as possible for them to prevent them from disregarding the laws completely. . . .' He then gives some directives how to deal with the matter.[22]

In a *Responsum* written to R. Klein in Nuremberg in the 'years of indignation' (*shenoth ha-zaam*) R. Weinberg who tries to adopt a lenient view with regard to business with a non-Jew on the Sabbath

---

17. See the entire correspondence, etc., in *Seride Esh*, I, pp. 371ff.

18. R. Weinberg's *Responsum* is dated: beginning of winter, 694 (1933). In it he mentions his journey from Cracow to Warsaw on his way to Wilno to see R. H. O. Grodzinski. This journey took place on Sunday, 17 September, and must have been made in 1933, for only in that year did 17 September fall on a Sunday (and not in 1934). This shows us that the boycott episode occurred in 1933.

19. For particulars see Blau, *Das Ausnahmerecht*, p. 46.

20. Weinberg, *Seride Esh*, II, no. 51.

21. No year is mentioned. However, as 7th of Nisan occurred on a Wednesday only once between 1932–39, i.e. in 1935, our *Responsum* was written in that year.

22. Weinberg, *Seride Esh*, no. 155.

under certain conditions justifies his action by saying: 'Whenever it affects the livelihood of a Jew I try giving permission.'[23]

Similarly, he writes to R. David Ochs in Leipzig that one must endeavour to find reasons for permitting various forms of business in order to save the life of Jewish families, *verb. sap.*[24]

When the position of the Jews under the Nazis became intolerable and they were deprived of their livelihood and their entire economic situation grew desperate, R. Weinberg was asked by the Rabbi of Kissingen about a butcher who had a partnership with a non-Jewish butcher and would be unable to earn his living were he not to allow the non-Jewish butcher to sell meat on the Sabbath. The questioner added that several Rabbis did not permit this. However, R. Weinberg adopted a more lenient view and laid down the conditions under which the partnership could be maintained, since, as he remarked, 'it is a matter which concerns *pikkuah nephesh* (saving life) of a Jewish family particularly at this time when the livelihood of the Jews is more difficult than the division of the Red Sea' (*Pes.* 116a). The conditions, he mentioned, applied only as far as the principle of Sabbath was concerned. With regard to the question of dealing with forbidden food (non-*kosher* meat) some other arrangements had to be made, and he wished also to know whether the customers were only gentiles or included also Jews. He would then express his view.[25]

It is interesting to know that R. Weinberg himself tells us of a decision he gave while still Rabbi in the Lithuanian town Pilviski. He was asked by several Jews to permit work to be done for them by non-Jews on the Sabbath by means of a *shetar shuthphuth* (partnership). They threatened that should they not get permission, they would be forced to work on the Sabbath. R. Weinberg remarked that his predecessor did not want to permit this, unlike another Rabbi who lived in the neighbouring town. Being in a great dilemma, he went to Radin to ask the famous 'Hafez Hayyim' for advice. The saintly Rabbi replied that a decision could be given either way.[26] He, therefore, did not want to take the responsibility upon himself. 'In the end', says R. Weinberg, 'I refused to comply with the request of the congregants.'[27] One can see how great the plight of the Jews in Germany under the Nazis must have been that R. Weinberg adopted a lenient view later.

The segregation can also be seen in the refusal of the non-Jewish neighbours to co-operate and help Jews. Jewish farmers had to ask the Rabbi of Würzburg (who then presented the case to R. Weinberg)

23. Ibid., no. 73.
24. Ibid., no. 74.
25. Ibid., no. 21.
26. Cf. however, R. J. J. Weinberg, *Eth Ahai Anochi Mebakkesh*, Bene Berak, 1966, p. 22.
27. Weinberg, *Seride Esh*, II, no. 21.

whether they might milk their cows on the Sabbath as non-Jews refused to do it for them.[28] The Rabbi was inclined to permit this. There were two reasons for this: cruelty to animals and danger to the Jewish community as non-Jews would say that the Jews did not care for animals or that they wasted food, etc.

R. Weinberg tried to refute the reasons, as the non-Jews could be asked to milk the cows and keep the milk for themselves. 'This they would surely do (as it would benefit them greatly). Only the reason of monetary loss remains . . . .' R. Weinberg then quoted the suggestion made by the Sephardi Chief Rabbi in Tel Aviv how cows could be milked on the Sabbath. However, this suggestion was not accepted by the Rabbis in Israel. R. Weinberg pointed out that in Israel one could be lenient because of *yishub Erez Yisrael* (to maintain the cultivation of Israel). This did not apply in Germany. On the other hand, in Germany it would mean a loss of livelihood to Jewish families who had no other source of income.

R. Weinberg refused to give a decision and advised the Rabbi of Würzburg to do the same, but he should have explained that the views are divided 'For whenever the question of *parnasah* (maintenance) is involved, one cannot insist that people follow the view of those who are stringent'.

The same problem arose in Fulda. The Jews of that town and its neighbourhood were generally cattle dealers. In view of the prohibition of the Nazi government against employing non-Jews,[29] the Dayan of Fulda, R. Baruch Kunstadt, had to deal with the question of milking cows on the Sabbath. (The *Responsum* was written before 1936.)[30]

R. Hayyim Ozer Grodzinski of Wilno who when dealing with the question of milking cows on the Sabbath in Palestine adopted a very stringent view, tells us that he had been asked by a great Rabbi in Germany what Jews should do concerning milking cows on the Sabbath where non-Jews were not available. He then thought in view of 'the great emergency' (*shaath ha-dehak gadol*) of adopting a lenient view and gave directives how Jews should act.[31]

An attempt made by the Nazis to segregate the Jews and limit their activity in cultural respects was the prohibition imposed on the Jews against holding lectures and concerts, etc., except in the synagogue. They were forbidden also to assemble other than in a synagogue. In

28. Weinberg, *op. cit.*, no. 24.
29. I could not find this prohibition quoted in Blau. According to the Nuremberg Laws of 15 September 1935, Jews were permitted to employ in their homes Aryan women over forty-five years of age, *vide supra*, p. xvii n.9.
30. See his *Responsum* printed in *Sepher Ha-Zikkaron li-Kebod R. J.J. Weinberg*, Jerusalem, 1970, pp. 41ff.
31. *Ahiezer*, III, Wilno, 1939 (Jerusalem, 1960), no. 34. The *Responsum* is dated Tebeth 12, 696 (7 January 1936).

C

a *Responsum*[32] which R. Weinberg says in a footnote had been written
when the Jews of Germany and the neighbouring countries (Czechoslovakia and Austria?) were under Nazi domination when, apart from
other decrees the Jews were not permitted to gather in public places
except in synagogues,[33] he discusses the following question.

Is one permitted to lecture on secular subjects in a synagogue and to
hold a concert there? The questioner whose name is not mentioned
remarked that since it was a time of great emergency, people suffered
greatly from insults and it was a great *mizvah* to give them moral support
and encourage them in their cultural pursuits. Furthermore (if such
permission were refused), 'they might go to the liberals who hold such
meetings and concerts in their "synagogues", and consequently they
might become influenced in their religious outlook'.

R. Weinberg deals with this case in a lengthy *Responsum*. He tries to
shed light on it from many aspects. His exposition contains a few
interesting facts about differences between German and East European
Jewries.[34] Summing up his discussion he gives the following ruling:

> From the halachic point of view there is no prohibition against deliver-
> ing a lecture in the synagogue, though, preferably, one should recite
> a few verses of Psalms or words of Torah before the lecture is given.
> It must be understood that the lecturers should be people who are
> known to be God-fearing men and not those who are 'free' in their
> religious outlook since otherwise they may speak about heretical
> matters. For that reason, permission should not be given to anyone
> without the consent of the local Rabbi.
>
> Under no circumstances should a discussion take place after the lecture.
> Apart from the fear that among the participants in the discussion
> there might be freethinkers, R. Weinberg fears that frivolity (*kalluth
> rosh*) may occur which is prohibited in a synagogue under any
> circumstances. Discussions are often spiced with criticism and with
> sarcasm or ridicule (*lezanuth*). They may cause laughter and mockery
> which are prohibited in a synagogue.
>
> Concerts of a secular nature cannot be allowed under any circum-
> stances. It is the Rabbi's duty to refuse to permit them even if he loses
> his position as a result.
>
> Concerts of a religious nature are a different matter, though the Rabbis

---

32. Weinberg, *Seride Esh*, II, no. 12. He adds in a footnote that apart from its historical
    value it had also practical importance for Jews living in far places where no possibility
    existed of their coming together except in synagogues and houses of study.
33. From the very fact that there were still synagogues standing it is obvious that this
    Responsum was written before 9 November 1938.
34. On this difference see also his remarks in *Yad Shaul, Sepher Zikkaron Li-Kebod R. S.
    Weingorth*, Tel Aviv, 1953.

do not entirely favour them either. However, if a quarrel might arise, perhaps one should permit them.

God forbid that men and women should sit together. This is an absolute prohibition as we can see from the Talmud. Women should be in the women's gallery. 'I declare it explicitly', concludes R. Weinberg, 'that my permission is confined solely to these days which are "a time of emergency" as is well known. When, please God, conditions change, we shall then be careful again with the sanctity of our Synagogue.'

Ostracized by their neighbours, boycotted by their non-Jewish friends, forced out of their professions, expelled from their businesses[35] which were Aryanized, and often in danger of their lives the Jews in Germany began to move. At first their movements were inside Germany from villages and small towns to larger places. Later there followed emigration from Germany.

As far as movement inside Germany is concerned, this tendency can be found in the years prior to Hitler's rise even among non-Jews and was due to the industrialization of the country. However, in the Nazi era, many Jewish families were compelled to leave their homes. How could a Jew remain in a place when in the district of Hanover (in all towns and villages) the following slogan appeared: 'Jews live in this village at their own risk' and posters were erected with the words 'Jews not welcome'? As a result the Jews moved to larger places where they thought they were safer. Jewish shopkeepers and businessmen were even forced to give up their businesses and leave their homes.[36]

No wonder, the Jews tried to emigrate. The result was that many communities disappeared. In summer 1938 one Rabbi wrote in a *Responsum*: 'Through our great sins, the affliction, i.e. the oppression[37] in our country is becoming more and more severe. May God have mercy.' Small communities became still smaller, some disappeared completely so that no Jewish inhabitant was left. 'One goes to this place, the other goes to that place.'[38]

The dwindling communities and the difficulty in obtaining a quorum for prayer caused the 'Freie Vereinigung für die Interessen des ortho-doxen Judentums' (Frankfurt am Main) and the 'Verein zur Wahrung des gesetzestreuen Judentums in Baden' (Mannheim) to publish jointly a pamphlet[39] entitled *KEIN MINJAN!* (No Minyan) *Eine Gottesdienst-*

---

35. See Blau, *Das Ausnahmerecht*, p. 8; *The Yellow Spot*, London, 1936, p. 112.
36. *The Yellow Spot*, pp. 122, 178, 180.
37. Phrase taken from the Passover Haggadah: *Ha-lahaz zeh ha-dehak*.
38. R. S. Bamberger, *Sheerith Simhah*, Jerusalem, 1969, no. 3.
39. Printed in Frankfurt a.M., 1937. I am indebted to the Central Archives for the History of the Jewish People, Jerusalem, for sending me a photostat of the pamphlet.

ordnung für Gemeinden ohne Minjan (Order of the divine service for communities without quorum).

The following regulations are given:

1. No *Kaddish* and *Barachu* should be recited.
2. The *Amidah* should be recited only by the congregants quietly. The reader should not repeat it.
3. The *Sepher Torah* may be taken out with the recital of the traditional prayers and songs but no one should be called up to the Torah. The weekly portion should be read without interruption, without the benedictions usually recited before and after the reading. The *Haphtarah* should be read without benedictions.
4. Special prayers[40] to be recited instead of *Kaddish*, *Barachu* and *Kedushah* on weekdays after *Tahanun*, on Sabbath after the *Amidah* and on festivals after *Hallel*.
5. Special prayers to be recited during the *Minhah* service.
6. The same applies to the *Maarib* service.
7. On Friday night the prayer *Magen Aboth* (*Ahath Me-Eyn Sheba*) should not be recited. Neither should *Kiddush* be said in the synagogue.
8. On festivals all *Piyyutim* (poetical insertions) should be recited after the *Amidah*. The *kohanim* do not recite the priestly blessing.
9. On fastdays the prayer *Anenu* is omitted in the morning service. *Selihoth* are to be recited after the *Amidah* with the omission of the 'Thirteen Attributes' (*El Melech* . . .). They are followed by the reading of the Torah. In the *Minhah* prayer those who fast recite *Anenu* in the benediction *Shema Kolenu*.
10. In the days when *Selihoth* are said: the prayers *El Erech Appayyim*, *Kaddish*, the Thirteen Attributes, *Maran De-Bishmayya*, *Mahe U-Masse* are omitted.
11. On *Purim* the *Megillah* should be read after *Maarib* with the recital of the three benedictions before the reading, but the benediction after the reading (*Ha-Rab eth Ribenu*) should not be said. The same applies to the morning service.

These rules are followed by an admonition to those who take part in the service without a quorum of ten to be well acquainted with these rulings and to ensure the service is held with due respect. In that way, even the smallest congregation would form a valuable part of the company in the service of God. 'Let us endeavour to maintain the dwindling congregation until the end. No day, Sabbath or festival, should pass without prayer even where there is no public service. This

---

40. (4) and (5) are contained in Baer's *Siddur, Abodath Yisrael*, pp. 120f., and printed in the pamphlet.

is only a temporary measure. It is a holy duty to keep up the *minyan* (quorum of ten) whenever possible even with great sacrifice.'

In view of the economic hardship of the German Jews, the dissolution of smaller communities and the emigration of many people a training centre for Rabbis became superfluous. The number of students decreased also due to the fact that students from abroad did not come to Germany to study. The authorities of the Hildesheimer Seminary in Berlin intended to transfer the seminary to Israel. However, this plan did not materialize owing to strong opposition, particularly from R. Hayyim Ozer Grodzinski.[41] Although he admired R. Meir Hildesheimer and R. J. J. Weinberg and also the seminary in particular, calling it 'an honourable institution' which he regarded as essential for German Jewry,[42] he strongly opposed such a transfer. In a letter addressed to R. Hildesheimer (dated 3rd *Hanukkah* 5694=15 December 1933) he writes that he heard of the latter's intention of going to the Holy Land for the purpose of transferring the Berlin seminary to Tel Aviv as he did not obtain permission to transfer to Jerusalem. R. Hildesheimer said that his reason for the transfer of the seminary was to serve the Sephardim of Eastern countries. R. Hayyim regarded it his duty to write to R. Hildesheimer to urge him to give up his plan. He writes that his father the *Zaddik* (R. Esriel Hildesheimer) when establishing the seminary had a holy aim in mind.

It was the time of the spread of the Reform movement and its adherents filled communities and appointed 'Ra-banim'[43] freethinkers who were highly cultured. Hence R. Hildesheimer when founding the 'Adath Yisroel' congregation was forced to contend with them and see that the traditional communities also had Rabbis who had attended universities and acquired culture. He, therefore, founded a seminary to serve that purpose. Such action was appropriate in Germany which was regarded as cultured in those days.[44] But how could it cross one's mind to establish a 'factory' for Rabbis in the Holy Land, to appoint Rabbis of a new type for whom culture was their main object and Torah of secondary importance as Israel was

---

41. On the opposition of R. H. O. Grodzinski to the planned transfer to Palestine see his letters in *Ahiezer, Kobez Iggeroth*, Bene Berak, 1970, II, no. 289 (letter to *Hazzon Ish*) containing a copy of the letter written to R. Meir Hildesheimer (no. 290), no. 291 (letter to R. Joseph Zebi Duschinsky), nos. 229, 293 (to R. J. J. Weinberg, in which R. Hayyim thanks R. Weinberg for easing his mind concerning the transfer of the seminary to Palestine). See also *Peer Ha-Dor, Hayye Ha-Hazon Ish*, R. Abraham Yeshayahu Karelitz, I, pp. 315ff.

42. See his letter to R. Weinberg, *Seride Esh*, I, p. 380.

43. Lit. 'Evil sons'—a pun on the word *Rabbanim* (Rabbis).

44. This letter was written after Hitler had come to power and had unleashed his anti-Jewish legislation.

a country where great *yeshiboth* existed and famous God-fearing
Rabbis lived? The Sephardim of the East did not require such
Rabbis either . . . .[45]

Indeed the seminary stood until *Kristallnacht*. The seminaries in
Breslau, Berlin and Vienna survived until summer 1938, when on
10 November they were closed.

The disappearance of communities raised some questions concerning
the sale of synagogues as well as the handing over of ritual articles to
people going to Palestine. In 1934, we hear for the first time the question
of selling synagogues in places deserted by their Jewish inhabitants.
On 25 June 1934, the *Fränkischer Kourier* reported that the Synagogue
of Salzbach (Upper Palatinate) had been converted into a museum as
it could no longer fulfil its purpose because of the emigration of all
Jews of Salzbach.[46] The Synagogue of Mühlheim had to be sold. Most
tragicomic is a further report about this synagogue. During the
Kristallnacht it was burnt down on the order of a Nazi official. When he
was tried by the court in Duisburg his defence was that the synagogue
had been sold beforehand and had no longer been a 'house of worship'.[47]

In a *Responsum* of R. Hayyim Ozer Grodzinski to R. J. J. Weinberg
in Berlin, he agrees with him that it was forbidden and a shameful act
to sell the synagogue of a community which had become deserted by
Jewish inhabitants to the Congregation of Baptists. If the sale was
forced on the community, the latter was not responsible for that.[48]

We have the following report which deals with the disposal of
synagogue articles. In a *Responsum* written in the year 1938 R. Simhah
Bamberger (Stuttgart, left in 1939 for Israel, d. 1958) tells us of the
plight of the small communities in Germany which dwindled because
of the great oppression. Some of them had already disappeared
completely, due to the emigration of their members so that no single
person had been left. The members of a small community approached
the Rabbi asking him whether they were permitted to give a scroll of
the Law as a gift to a Jew who was going with members of other
communities to settle in Israel with the intention of setting up a new
community there. The question was asked as the community from
where the scroll was to be given still existed. The answer was in the
affirmative.[48a]

45. *Ahiezer, Kobez Iggeroth*, II, no. 290. See also *Kobez Iggeroth Hazon Ish*, Bene Berak,
    1957, p. 172.
46. *The Yellow Spot*, p. 89.
47. Lord Russell of Liverpool, *Return of the Swastika*, London, 1968, p. 109.
48. Weinberg, *Seride Esh*, p. 378 (dated: Wednesday, 5th of Nisan 694 — 21 March 1934);
    Ahiezer, Kobez Iggeroth, II, no. 231 (dated: Wednesday, 5th of Nisan 696 — 28 March
    1936). The former date is correct since the 5th of Nisan 696 was on a Saturday.
48a. *Sheerith Simhah*, no. 3.

Another problem which arose in those days concerns cemeteries, exhumations and the transfer of the bones to other places. The fear of desecration on one hand, the leaving them unattended because of emigration on the other, as well as the fact that the government might require the ground and force exhumation, raised various questions which were sent to R. Weinberg for his advice.

The greater part of the Old Cemetery of Cologne had been expropriated by the government. Only the smaller part remained in the possession of the community. The corpses removed from the greater part were then reburied. Afterwards, the government requested the community to hand over part of the small portion which hitherto had remained in the community's possession. The authorities wished to erect a *Markthalle* there. The government offered in exchange another plot of land near the other side of the cemetery. In the part which the government then wished to acquire there were no graves and no bones were found. It was suggested that it was permitted to exchange the land for two good reasons: (1) If the community refused to comply with the request the government might take it by force. (2) It was well known that hooligans had lately desecrated cemeteries. By handing over part of the grounds for the building of a *Markthalle* the cemetery might be protected. R. J. J. Weinberg thought that the part required by the government might be sold; however, he feared that within the course of time people would forget that there had ever been a cemetery on that site and *kohanim* would defile themselves when entering the *Markthalle*, as the cemetery might not have been properly cleared when the greater part was handed over to the government. The matter therefore still required consideration.[49]

R. Weinberg was asked by the Rabbi of Schweinfurt whether the corpses might be removed from the graves and sent to Israel where the relatives had emigrated. The Rabbi permitted this for three reasons. One of these reasons was the ruling laid down in the *Shulhan Aruch*, *Yoreh Deah*, cap. CCCLXIII, 1, that whenever there may be fear that the corpse might not be kept in its grave but taken out by non-Jews, it is a great *mizvah* to remove it and rebury it elsewhere. 'And in this country the fear is very great, *verb. sap.*'[50]

In 1936 (Shebat 696) R. Weinberg was asked by R. J. Carlebach of Altona-Hamburg about the question sent to the latter by the Rabbi of Ems whether it was permitted to exhume bodies buried at the Old Cemetery which was not guarded and rebury them in the new cemetery.

49. *Op. cit.*, II, no. 128.
50. *Op. cit.*, no. 129.

The answer was that it was permitted and some rulings were given how this was to be done. However, the Rabbi adds, that though that permission was given in accordance with the law, the matter had to be carefully considered, since the non-Jews might force the Jews to clear out all cemeteries.[51]

As mentioned already, the only salvation for the Jews of that period was emigration to free countries. They could still leave although not completely in accordance with the tale of the pair of turtle-doves which hung in the window alive with their plumage. The German Jews could emigrate with much of their 'plumage' (i.e. possessions) after paying the various taxes.

The desire to emigrate began immediately after Hitler had come to power. In those days it was not as difficult to find a place of refuge as it was a few years later. Indeed the number of emigrants from Germany was the highest in the first year.[52] In spite of that Jews inquired of the Rabbis in 1933 whether emigration to Spain was permitted as there was a wide-spread assumption that the exiles from Spain in 1492 had imposed a ban (*herem*) on themselves and their descendants never to return to that country. However, as this is never mentioned by contemporary Rabbis or in any authoritative book of later times the very existence of such a *herem* was doubted. Was it perhaps an unfounded rumour? The first Rabbi to mention this *herem* was, as far as I could find, Chief Rabbi Kook who, in a letter (dated 17th Tebeth 5674, i.e. 15 January 1914), wrote: 'With regard to living in Spain I have not found a clear mention of whether there existed a *herem* or an oath. Probably they (the exiles) did not regard this as more stringent than the prohibition of living in Egypt which applied only to one wishing to live there permanently but not to a person who intends to visit the country for business purposes with the intention of returning to his home country.'[53] Most probably Chief Rabbi Kook's letter was a reply to someone who wished to go to Spain for a short visit.

From 1933 onwards when the question of emigration to Spain for permanent residence became topical the existence of a *herem* was constantly discussed, even as recently as 1971.[54] We shall see, there are two diametrically opposed views on this matter.[55]

---

51. *Op. cit.*, no. 127.
52. See Werner Rosenstock, 'Exodus 1933–1939' in *Deutsches Judentum, Aufstieg und Krise*, Stuttgart, 1963, pp. 386f.
53. *Iggeroth Ha-Reayah*, II, no. 632, Jerusalem, 722, p. 252.
54. There appeared a *Responsum* by R. Yehudah Gershoni, on the question whether the alleged *herem* not to settle in Spain applies also to those who wish to visit the country or only to those who wish to take up permanent residence. *Hadorom*, no. 32, New York, 731, pp. 48ff.
55. On what follows, see the sources in Part III, cap. 1.

Those who reject the alleged *herem* mainly bring the following proofs to substantiate this view: (1) No author mentions such a *herem*; (2) the expulsions of the Jews from various countries in the Middle Ages (e.g. France, England and various towns in Germany) have never caused the Jews who suffered to proclaim a *herem* against returning to those countries.

According to one scholar,[56] the report about the *herem* concerning the resettlement in Spain is based on a misunderstanding. After mentioning the fact that we have never heard of Jews who were banished from a country (England, France) or various towns in Germany proclaiming a *herem*, and that 'there was in the 17th[57] and 18th centuries a constant trickle of visitors—most of them from North Africa, or later on merchants from the British stronghold of Gibraltar' he writes that some members of the Spanish community, after escaping from Spain and Portugal, went to Spain for business and pretended to be Christians. After returning to their new homeland they expected to be treated in the same manner as before they had left for Spain. As the Jewish authorities sought to discourage such conduct they imposed various sanctions on a person who had gone to Spain. He had to confess his 'sin' and submit himself to the penitence which the Haham imposed. This gave rise to the legend of the *herem* announced by the exiles from Spain when leaving the country.

On the other hand, one Rabbi[58] is of the opinion that there exists sufficient support for the assertion that there was a general *haskamah* not to return to Spain. After referring to the work of R. Yaakob Mosheh Toledano, *Ner Ha-Maarab* (p. 75, no. 9) who quotes the view that the origin of his name was meant to indicate 'never to return to Toledo' (Toledo—no), he then cites a *Responsum* of R. Moses Trani (b. Salonica, 1500, Rabbi of Safed, d. 1580) which, curiously enough, is claimed by another Rabbi[59] to show that there was *no* such *herem*, as a clear indication testifying amply to the existence of such a *haskamah* with or without a *herem*.

What puzzles the writer is the fact that none of the authors ever considers from the historical and practical points of view how such a *herem* could have been issued. When reading of the expulsion of the Jews from Spain we are told by the historians[60] that the deadline for leaving the

---

56. Cecil Roth, 'Was there a Herem Against The Return of the Jews to Spain?', in *Le Judaisme Sephardi*, London, no. XV, October 1957, pp. 675ff.
57. Mention is made of R. Jacob Sasportas, later Haham in London, who was the diplomatic representative of the Sultan of Morocco at the Spanish court.
58. R. Eliezer Waldenberg, *Ziz Eliezer*, V, no. 17 (*vide infra* pp. 255ff.).
59. R. Meshullam Rath, *Kol Mebasser*, I, no. 13 (*vide infra* pp. 254f.).
60. See e.g. S. Dubnow, *Weltgeschichte des jüdischen Volkes*, V, pp. 405f.; H. Graetz, *Geschichte der Juden*, VIII, p. 349.

country (31 July) was extended for two days (2 August). Some Jews left Spain on the former date. The bulk of exiles, however, numbering about 200,000[61] left on the latter date. Half went to Portugal, among them R. Isaac Aboab, R. Jacob Berab, the historian Abraham Zacuto, R. Isaac Caro (author of *Toledoth Yizhak*, and uncle of R. Joseph Caro), the parents of R. Joseph Caro with their son, R. Jacob ibn Habib with his son R. Levi,[62] and other exiles who later played an important role in Jewish life. Others left for Navarre, Italy, North Africa and Turkey. While all the exiles had to endure various privations and experienced great hardship on their journeys, the fate of those who immigrated to Navarre and particularly to Portugal was much worse. After spending six years in those countries they were expelled under much harsher conditions. In Portugal many were forced to embrace Christianity and were deprived of their children who were forcibly baptized.[63]

Seeing the fate of the Jews of Spain and that of the 100,000 Jews who went to Portugal, one must ask, if one shares the view of those who oppose the belief of a *herem*, how was it possible to announce a *herem* affecting 200,000 Jews without leaving a record of it? Surely such an important matter would have to be decided at a synod of Rabbis or representatives of the communities. There was no reason to fear should the decision become public.[64] The Spanish authorities would have been too glad to hear of that, and as far as the countries of refuge are concerned, we know that the rulers did not admit the newcomers on the condition that they return later to their country of origin. On the contrary, the sultans were pleased with the immigrants, as can be seen from the statement made by Sultan Bayazid quoted above.[65] Hence the lack of any information is no doubt a strong support for the view that a general *herem* did not exist. Furthermore, since the fate of the Jews in Portugal was similar to, if not worse than, that of their Spanish brethren, why do we not hear of any *herem* later against a return to Portugal?

On the other hand, it should be pointed out that the objection raised against the existence of a *herem* prohibiting a return to Spain on the grounds that we have never heard that the Jews expelled from England, France and German towns proclaimed a similar *herem*, is not quite true, for we indeed find such bans. This can be seen from statements in

---

61. There exists a difference of opinion about the number of exiles, see Dubnow, *Weltgeschichte*. According to another report (quoted by H. Graetz, *Geschichte*) 300,000 Jews left the country.
62. See also Rosanes, *Dibre Yeme Yisrael Be-Togarmah*, II, pp. 28, 201f.
63. Graetz, *Geschichte*, pp. 381ff.; Dubnow, *Weltgeschichte*, pp. 410ff.
64. See, however, Waldenberg, *Ziz Eliezer, ad fin.*
65. *Vide supra* p. xxi.

Sepher Hasidim[66] where the author objects to the practice of announcing a *herem*:

> If the communities or the scholars of the generation impose a *herem* on a settlement (*yishub*) that no Jew should live there, one should not proclaim that Jews should *never* live there, but only during the lifetime of the Nasi (president) or head of the *yeshibah* or as long as three of the leaders are alive. For there are many towns against which such a ban has been pronounced (and that everyone who would live there would be excommunicated) and yet Jews are living there. One should not pronounce a ban in a matter which many cannot endure. For who knows perhaps a future generation would be unable to live elsewhere but in that place . . . .

> In one town there was a wicked ruler (*sar*) who wished to force the Jews to renounce their religion whereupon they fled. The communities wished to proclaim a *herem* that no Jews should ever live in that town. The Rabbi (*Haham*) told them not to place any obstacle in the way of future generations but any *herem* should have effect only as long as the ruler is alive.

No doubt, the author of *Sepher Hasidim* when writing these rulings had in mind practical cases which had happened and he wished them to be avoided in future.

Finally, it should be pointed out that after the persecution by Chmielnicki in 1648–49 a *herem* was alleged to have been imposed on those who lived in the Ukraine. According to one version, the *herem* was revoked in 1705, when the ruler (*sar*) asked the Jews to settle in that country and granted them freedom.[67]

The fact that Jews visited Spain occasionally in an official capacity (Haham Sasportas on his mission for the Moroccan ruler, other Jews on business) is no proof or disproof as it was not a return of a permanent character. Such a visit was not forbidden even as regards Egypt.

In view of the above the writer was at first inclined to assume that there had been no *herem* or *haskamah* not to return to Spain but such rumour arose after the report of a *herem* against living in the Ukraine. However, it seems more correct to suggest that there was no *general herem* against a return to Spain. Most probably some Jews whose hearts were grieved at having been treated so ignominiously after having contributed to the development of the country accepted within their

---

66. *Sepher Hasidim,* ed. Wistinetzki, nos. 1302, 1402.
67. See Israel Halperin, *Pinkas Vaad Arba Arazoth,* pp. 79ff. It should, however, be pointed out that this *herem* is not mentioned by Nathan Hannover (d. 1663) who described the persecutions under Chmielnicki in his work *Yeven Mezulah,* nor is it found in *Pinkas Ha-Medinah* (*Pinkas Vaad Ha-Kehilloth Ha-Rashioth Be-Medinath Lita 383–521*) edited by S. Dubnow, Berlin, 1925. See also Halperin, *Pinkas, note.*

own families a personal undertaking never to return to that country.

After the Night of Broken Glass (*Kristallnacht*), the problem of a *herem* solved itself—Jews were very happy if they could find a place of refuge anywhere![68]

THE *Anschluss* OF AUSTRIA

It is in our period that the annexation of Austria occurred on 13 March 1938 when Hitler's army marched into Vienna. Austria became part of Germany and was called *Ostmark*, a name that country had in the early Middle Ages before it was separated from Bavaria (976). Through this annexation 191,000 Jews according to the 1934 census of whom nine-tenths lived in Vienna were now affected by the harsh decrees of the Nazis.[69]

There are two points which characterize the persecution of the Austrian Jews. First, the great majority of the population hailed the coming of Hitler and had been hostile to the Jews, unlike the inhabitants of other countries invaded by the Nazis who regarded the conquerors as enemies. Secondly, the humiliations and deprivations to which Jews in Germany were subject for more than five years, the Austrian Jews had to experience in a more severe manner within the course of a few weeks. While with the advent of Hitler the first attacks of the Nazis in Germany were directed against the Communists, Socialists and the Jews, in Austria the Jews were the first scapegoats. Anti-Semitism flourished in Austria long before the era of Hitler's Nazism. It was Austria where one of the first political apostles of the idea of the 'Super Race' proclaimed his doctrines. He was Georg Schönerer, a member of the Austrian parliament, who in a speech delivered on 28 April 1887 quoted the following remark by the 'much honoured German poet who died recently, Viktor von Scheffel': 'The antipathy of the Germanic nations to the Semites is not based upon the difference of religion and dogma, but upon the difference of the blood, the race, the origin (birth), the national customs and *Volksgemeinschaft*.' Schönerer then continues:

It is sheer nonsense to attack the Jews only because of their creed and he who maintains that we are standing up against the Jews because

68. On 14 August 1970, the *Jewish Chronicle*, p. 13, reported that a Rabbi, Rabbi Dr Chaim U. Lipschitz, who was writing a book on 'Franco and the Jews' was officially received by General Franco. The report adds that Rabbi Lipschitz who maintains in his book that Franco had saved sixty thousand Jews from extermination by the Nazis presented the general with a wine cup bearing the inscription 'In recognition for saving Jewish lives . . '. It should, however, be pointed out that Spain granted asylum also to Nazis and Fascists 'when the tide turned against them'. (See Michael Bar-Zohar, *The Avengers*, pp. 159ff.).
69. See Norman Bentwich, 'The Destruction of the Jewish Community in Austria 1938–1942', in *The Jews of Austria*, ed. by Josef Fraenkel, London, 1967, pp. 467ff.

of their religion belongs to those despicable people who are accustomed to defend every other religion and nationality—who, however, forget always their own nation.

Our anti-Semitism is not directed against the religion of the Jews but against the characteristics of the Jews which did not change with the pressure of the previous times or with the present freedom.[70]

As one can see, we have here a complete programme of the Nazi ideology. Who can say that it was not this address that influenced Hitler years later?[71] No practical importance was attached to this policy at that time. Jew-baiting was confined to those who professed to be of 'Mosaic' religion. Once the latter was changed, one 'obtained a ticket' for entrance into the highest aristocracy and professorship. However, the idea of the superiority of the 'Aryan' race remained dormant and its advocates were the 'Deutschnationalen' (Pan Germans) belonging to the *Grossdeutsche Partei*, who formed the vanguard of National Socialists in Austria.

For the first time the interpretation of the word 'race' as a distinction between Aryans and Jews gained practical significance in Austria in one instance after World War I. According to the peace treaty of St Germain (1919) those living in Austria but who hailed from countries which had been separated from the Austrian Empire could, if they wished, apply ('opt') for Austrian citizenship provided they belonged to the majority of the nation in respect of race and language. Indeed many Jews who had fled from Galicia and Bukovina (then Austria) to Vienna during World War I lived there and applied for Austrian citizenship. In the first months their applications were accepted. However, a change in the ministry then took place and a member of the Pan German party became minister of the interior. He gave the order to reject all applications as the Jews did not belong to the German race—a precursor of the first of the Nuremberg laws issued in Germany in 1935.[72]

Much has already been written on the wave of persecutions which followed the marching of Hitler's troops into Austria. The writer who

70. *Georg Schonerer*, ed. by Eduard Pichl, vol. III, 1873–89, 'Forty Speeches', Berlin, 1913 (2nd ed. 1938), p. 337. Cf. also his remarks ibid. pp. 290, 330, 351.
71. In his preface to the 1st vol. (12 February 1938) Walter Frank wrote: 'Schönerers Kampf is für das politische Werden Adolf Hitlers bedeutungsvoll gewesen.' How greatly Schönerer was admired by the Austrian Nazis can be gauged from the fact that immediately after the annexation of Austria by Hitler a street in the Jewish section of Vienna was named after him and a memorial exhibition was held in 1942; see *Encyclopaedia Judaica*, vol. 14, p. 989. According to Wilfred Daim, *Der Mann, der Hitler die Ideen gab*, Munich, 1958, p. 17, it was Jörg Lanz von Liebenfels, editor of the *Ostara*, who exerted a greater influence on Hitler than Schönerer.
72. The writer of these lines experienced this himself. See also Hugo Gold, *Geschichte der Juden in Wien*, p. 49. For another reference, concerning the census of 1923 when on the order of the minister of the interior who was a member of the Pan German party, a special question on 'Rassenzugehörigkeit' had to be answered, see ibid. p. 50.

was at that time in Vienna in the service of the 'Kultusgemeinde' can only confirm that the reports were not exaggerated. He witnessed the jubilation of the people in the streets on Saturday morning following the downfall of Chancellor Schuschnigg. He saw the looting of Jewish shops which followed in the next few days, the attacks on the Jews in the streets forcing them to scrub the pavements and to remove the slogans for Schuschnigg's intended plebiscite. He was present in the 'Kultusgemeinde' building when on one Friday morning trucks of SS men appeared, took out typewriters and calculating machines, arrested the leaders and closed the building. Although the latter was re-opened when a high fine had been paid for having supported Schuschnigg, the president and vice-president were taken to Dachau. What, however, puzzled the writer was the attitude of the general population to the Jews. It was not only a quarrel with a neighbour, an argument with a caretaker (let alone some affair in business) which sufficed to denounce a Jew and have him arrested and sent to a concentration camp (Dachau, Buchenwald or Mauthausen) but the hostility could be seen from the malicious pleasure and jeering of the crowd when the helpless Jews were attacked by the mob. He could not comprehend how it was possible that the same proverbial 'goldene Wiener Herz' (the golden Viennese heart) which could not let even a dog suffer (so that a policeman had to accompany the knacker when he went out to round up stray dogs in order to protect him should he be attacked) could turn to rock when a Jew was tortured. Of course, there were exceptions, but in general the population remained hostile.

Anxiously, some Jews watched the attitude of the Catholic Church towards the *Führer* and the new regime. Although it was a matter completely outside Jewish competence, they thought in their despair that the Church would raise its voice in their favour. In fact, an event occurred which caused great disappointment and consternation. When Hitler visited Vienna soon after the *Anschluss* Cardinal Innitzer paid him an official visit. On being greeted by the masses standing outside the cardinal responded with his arm raised as Hitler-greeting. Afterwards a pastoral letter was read and notices appeared in the press in which the cardinal admonished the Catholics to be faithful to Hitler and signed his name after the words: 'Heil Hitler'.[73]

The visit to Hitler by the head of the Church in Austria in 1938 was the reverse of the 'Bussgang nach Canossa' where the *summum imperium* bowed to the *summum sacerdotium* in 1077! Politically, the Jews who still had some ray of hope saw themselves completely isolated. As one

73. See Hugo Gold, *Geschichte*, pp. 79f.; Herbert Rosenkranz, in *The Jews of Austria*, ed. by Josef Fraenkel, p. 483; J. S. Conway, *The Nazi Persecution of the Churches 1933–1945*, London, 1968, p. 220.

can imagine, the position of the Jews became more precarious from day to day. The Aryanization of concerns and factories, the taking over of shops, appointing 'commissars' in business—in addition to compelling Jews to quit the civil service and other offices as well as the arrests, made their life intolerable.

The main task of the 'Kultusgemeinde' was the care for emigration, training for new occupations abroad and welfare.[74] Together with the Palestine Office, plans for emigration and assistance were made. Their leaders acted upon Eichmann's orders.[75] From those days (September 1938) dates a *Responsum* by the writer's saintly teacher R. Hayyim Yizhak Jeruchem, who was still in Vienna at that time, to his son R. Aharon in which the following passage occurs:

> The confiscations of businesses and houses, the setting up of 'commissars' and the expulsions from homes are an every day occurrence. The newspapers of the 'coachman'[76] write that in six months' time no trace of a Jew would remain in the whole of Austria. Our brethren hasten to arrange marriages. I myself have permitted many people to marry during the nine days of Ab as the authorities are about to issue a law[77] according to which it would be difficult for Jews to marry.
>
> People come to take leave and weep 'to whom shall we go now?', 'he turns aside and weeps and they turn aside and weep'. . . .[78]
>
> Israel needs mercy, The Holy One is full of mercy, He needs the mercy not for Himself but for His people, the House of Israel. May He let His great and abundant mercy shine on us speedily in our days, 'for the children are come to the birth, and there is not strength to bring forth' (cf. II Kings XIX 3; Isa XXXVII 3).[79]

CONFERENCE AT EVIAN

The main question was how to find countries which were willing to admit Jews from Germany and Austria. Great hopes were raised when the attempt made by President Franklin D. Roosevelt to convene an international conference to deal with the settlement of refugees from those countries was reported. This conference took place at Evian-les-Bains (on the French shore of Lake Geneva), on 6–15 July 1938, and was attended by representatives of thirty-two countries. All delegates

---

74. Cf. Bentwich, 'Destruction of the Jewish Community', p. 468.
75. See Herbert Rosenkranz in *The Jews of Austria*, pp. 486ff.
76. Hebrew 'Baal agalah'—a skit on the word 'Führer'. This was, as the editor R. A. Jeruchem (*vide infra* note 79) remarks, one of the nicknames the Jews gave Hitler.
77. Allusion to the decree which deprived the Jews from performing valid marriages.
78. Phrase taken from Mishnah *Yoma* I, 5.
79. R. H. Y. Jeruchem, *Birkath Hayyim*, ed. by his son R. Aharon Jeruchem, New York, 1956, no. 37.

were aware of the seriousness of the problem and how urgent it was to
help to avert a catastrophe for the Jewish people. But when concrete
proposals were to be made each delegate tried to let the other take the
responsibility. The result was that the conference did not have the
desired effect.[80] This naturally caused great disappointment among the
helpless people and malicious pleasure and satisfaction to Hitler. How
great such disappointment was in Jewish circles under the Nazi rule
can be seen from a letter of Rabbi Jeruchem in Vienna to his son. (The
Rabbi then emigrated with great difficulty to Poland but subsequently
was caught in the net of the Nazis after their invasion of Poland and
lost his elder son and other members of his family.) In his letter the
Rabbi expresses his consternation in the following words:[81]

> I do not fear for my own life but I wish to see speedily the salvation
> of all my children and that of all our brethren.
> People say that Switzerland[82] has been closed to the exiles. To
> where can the children of Israel go? The two destructions (of the
> Temple) and all expulsions are nought compared with this expulsion.
> The 'Ebionim'[83] deliver talks and that is all! 'Nobody enquires (of
> the plight of the Jews) and nobody prays (on their behalf). Upon
> whom can we rely? Upon our Father in heaven.'[84] And this is enough,
> only He can save us . . . .

There exist several decisions given by the same Rabbi, some of which
show great consideration for the position of the Jews in Vienna at
that time.[85]

80. On the conference and its outcome, cf. Gideon Hausner, *Justice in Jerusalem*, pp. 227f.;
     Arthur D. Morse, *While Six Million Died*, pp. 202ff.; Norman Bentwich, in *The Jews
     of Austria*, ed. by Josef Fraenkel, pp. 472f.; Herbert Rosenkranz, 'The Anschluss and
     the Tragedy of Austrian Jewry 1938–1945', ibid., p. 490.
81. R. Jeruchem, quoted in 'Alim Bochim', Introduction to *Birkath Hayyim*, pp. 20f.
82. This rumour was true, see Snoek, *The Grey Book*, p. 212. As is well known many tried
     to enter Switzerland illegally. Mention should be made here of a report which appeared
     some time ago in the Jewish press (*Jewish Chronicle*, 5 February 1971, p. 4) under the
     heading 'Policeman who helped Jews is vindicated'. He is the former captain of the
     St Gall police, Mr Paul Grueninger who had helped save about two to three thousand
     Jews, assisting them to enter Switzerland illegally and to obtain identity papers. He was
     dismissed from his office, lost his pension and since then lived in great poverty. In 1971
     he was morally exonerated by the cantonal government of St Gall. 'Mr. Grueninger's
     name occupies a place of honour in Israel, and it is engraved on the Jewish memorial
     in Washington.'
83. 'Referring to the members of the Evian Conference' (R. Aharon Jeruchem, *Alim
     Bochim*, p. 21)—a pun with the Hebrew word for 'poor men'.
84. Cf. *Sotah* IX, 15.
85. *Vide infra.*

2

The Period from the Deportation of the Polish Jews until the Outbreak of World War II

This period is characterized by complete lawlessness against the Jews in Germany and Austria, by acts of violence, murder and open robbery. They reached their peak in the so-called *Kristallnacht* (Crystal Night, The Night of the Broken Glass), a night which 'will go down in history with St Bartholomew's Eve as a lasting memory of human shame'.[1]

A prelude to the tragedy of *Kristallnacht* and its consequences was the expulsion of the Polish Jews from Germany on 29 October 1938 to Poland. The reason for this action is well known[2] and can be summed up briefly as follows. There were many thousand Jews of Polish nationality living in Germany and over three thousand Polish Jews in Vienna. Being afraid that in their plight the Jews might return to Poland the Polish government issued a decree that those Jews of Polish nationality who had lived permanently outside Poland or had been abroad for more than five years would lose their nationality from 30 October 1938 (and consequently they would have to remain in Germany). In order to prevent this and dispose of those Jews, about fifteen thousand with valid Polish passports were arrested one day before. (In Austria the arrests had taken place on Thursday night, 27 October 1938, but as almost all of them had no passports they were kept in the police stations until Friday morning when most were freed. Many of those who returned home on Friday morning found to their deep sorrow that their homes had been pillaged by their neighbours during the night.) The Jews rounded up in Germany were put on trains which left for the Polish border. *En route* they were deprived of their belongings and were left with only ten marks. Under the crack of whips they were driven into no-man's land. There were some fatal incidents on the way.[3] On their arrival at the Polish frontier the Polish sentries, after some trouble, let the refugees in and took them to a closed camp at the small town of Zbonszyn. Many old and infirm persons died of exposure during the first few days.

1. Words spoken by Mr Philip Noel-Baker, member of the Labour party, who later won the Nobel Peace Prize, in the House of Commons, quoted by A. D. Morse, *While Six Million Died*, p. 227.
2. On what follows see G. Reitlinger, *The Final Solution*, p. 10; L. Poliakov, *Harvest of Hate*, pp. 15f.; G. Hausner, *Justice in Jerusalem*, p. 41.
3. *Vide infra.*

25

D

In a letter written by R. H. Y. Jeruchem who had escaped on the eve of *Sukkoth* 699 (9 October 1938) from Vienna to Poland he made the following remarks about the deportation of the Polish Jews from Germany to Zbonszyn:

People say that on their way to Poland to where the Jews were forced to march through forests seven elderly persons died. Who knows whether they had the merit to be buried. People also say that one woman had a miscarriage during the escape and died and was thrown together with the foetus into the river. Another woman held her child in her arms. The child was thrown into the river, the mother then became insane. The frightening reports are innumerable. The faces of the refugees who come here (Poland) are full of fear. They had been taken from their beds and were not allowed to dress properly. They were deprived of all their money. There are about ten thousand Jews at the frontier who are not permitted to enter Poland or return to Germany. Their position is desperate—one cannot imagine. May God have mercy on them and all Israel . . . .[4]

Among those arrested and deported to Zbonszyn was Zindel Shmuel Grynszpan who reported his plight to his seventeen-year-old son Herszel who was in Paris at that time. The latter decided to seek revenge and shot the German diplomat Ernst von Rath who died two days later from his wounds. The diplomat's death served now as a pretext for launching an attack on the Jews in Germany and Austria, unprecedented in history. The 'spontaneous' reprisal against the Jews in Germany and Austria on the night of 9/10 November gave it the name of *Kristallnacht*. On that night and on the following day[5] 191 synagogues were burned down, a further 76 synagogues were totally demolished. Eleven community centres and cemetery chapels and 815 Jewish-owned businesses were demolished, 29 big stores destroyed,

---

4. In 'Alim Bochim', Introduction to *Birkath Hayyim*, p. 21. On a deportation from Breslau to Poland see R. I. J. Weiss, *Minchath Yizhak*, I, no. 43, (*infra* pp. 267f.).
5. On what follows see Reitlinger, *Final Solution*, pp. 16f.; Hausner, *Justice in Jerusalem*, p. 43; 'The Third Count, Indictment', The Attorney General *v* Adolf Eichmann, (Copy in the Wiener Library) pp. 6f. On the conditions in Austria see H. Gold, *Geschichte der Juden in Wien*, p. 89; Herbert Rosenkranz, 'Reichskristallnacht', Vienna, 1968. Little mention is made of the Torah scrolls which were burned by the Nazis on *Kristallnacht*. However, one can get an idea if one reads the short report which recently appeared in the Jewish press that charred remains of twelve Torah scrolls burnt in Schweinfurt (Bavaria) were brought to London by the Rabbi who on his visit to his former community found them stored in a museum. After negotiations with the mayor and the director of the museum he was able to bring them to London where the remains were buried in a proper manner at the cemetery of the Adath Yisroel Congregation, in Cheshunt, Herts. (See the *Jewish Tribune*, 22 January 1970, pp. 6, 7; 5 February 1971, p. 1.) The writer was present at the moving ceremony. If such a small community lost twelve scrolls how many scrolls must have fallen victim to the Nazis in 267 synagogues, among them synagogues of large communities!

7,500 shops looted, and 36 Jews were killed. More than 20,000 Jews had been taken into protective custody, half of whom were sent to Buchenwald and Dachau.

A few days later various families received boxes containing the ashes of their dear ones who had perished in the concentration camps. The question arose what laws of mourning should relatives observe and what should be done with the ashes. R. M. M. Kirschbaum (who later died a martyr in Belgium) compiled regulations which were printed under the title *Takkanoth Eych Lehithnaheg Ka-Eth Be-Epher Ha-Nisraphim—Ba-Avanothenu Ha-Rabbim* and contained the following twelve points:

1. No *shemirah* (watch, guard) is required.
2. The sitting of *shibah* should begin immediately news of death is received from the authorities.
3. The urn containing the ashes should be carried on a bier in honour of the deceased.
4. The ashes should be buried in a coffin. If this is not possible a small coffin may be used. If this too is impossible, the ashes should be buried in the urn sent from the concentration camp.
5. The urn containing the ashes should be wrapped with a *tallith*. Shrouds should be placed therein (to strengthen the belief that the deceased will rise at the Resurrection and to demonstrate that he was not one of those who did not believe in it).
6. If it is only possible to bury the ashes in the urn which was sent from the concentration camp one should see that shrouds be placed inside the urn and a small board or stone in between to prevent the shroud from becoming soiled.
7. On the day of burial which in most cases is after the *shibah* (sometimes even after thirty days, *shloshim*) the relatives should observe all laws of mourning for the entire day.
8. If *keriah* (tearing the garment) had been performed on the day the news of death was received it need not be repeated on the day of burial.
9. *Zidduk Ha-Din* (funeral prayers) should be recited and the customary standing-in-line (to give consolation) should take place.
10. It is not necessary to have a *seudath habraah* (first meal given to the mourner after the funeral) on that day.
11. *Tephillin* (phylacteries) should be put on on the day of burial unless it is 'the day of receiving the news of death' (*yom ha-shemuah*).
12. The day of death, if known, should be observed as the day of *yahrzeit* (anniversary of death).

These regulations were drawn up on Wednesday, 4 January 1939. As it was not possible to print them in Germany, R. Kirschbaum sent his manuscript to his brother in Cracow who had it printed there.[6] These regulations with an explanation were expounded by the Rabbi in a public sermon to the members of the *Hebrah Kaddisha* on Thursday night 21st of Shebat 699 (10 February 1939), so that they would know how to deal with such cases.

It appears that the following *Responsum* too dates from this period.

A Jew learned after thirty days that his father had been killed and cremated in *erez ha-damim* (Germany). The urn with the ashes had not yet been sent. As is well known, at the beginning of the persecutions the Nazis used to send the urn with the ashes to the family for burial. When does the time of mourning begin as the ashes had not yet been buried and the family had not given up hope of being able to bury them? The Rabbi answered that the day of death should be taken into consideration as the first of the days of mourning, regardless of whether the ashes had been buried or not. (The Rabbi gives the reasons for his decision.)[7]

Apart from the loss of life and material losses a curtailment of Jewish religious life and cultural activity ensued. The holding of services though not expressly forbidden was made impossible in many places because of the lack of synagogues and for the same reason lectures to the Jewish public could no longer take place.

It seems that Jewish-owned printing presses of Hebrew books had closed at that time as the printing of the above-mentioned regulations took place in Cracow and the printing of the second part of the *Responsa* 'Menahem Meshib' by R. M. M. Kirschbaum, Rabbi in Frankfurt am Main, which had begun in 1938 was not completed. The book appeared without title-page and without the last page.[8]

Apparently no Hebrew book was published in Germany after 10 November 1938. *Die Monatsschrift* ceased to be published as some cultural institutions and seats of research were closed. The Rabbinical seminary in Breslau was closed soon afterwards and its library confiscated.[9] The seminary in Vienna had been deprived of its library a few months before and no lectures were resumed in 1938. A short while later the Hildesheimer Seminary in Berlin closed.

The legal measures taken against the Jews amounted to strangulation of German Jewry.[10] On 12 November 1938, German Jews were ordered to pay a collective fine of 1,000 million Reichsmark and to repair all the damage done to their property at their own cost. All claims from

6. These regulations with explanatory notes were reprinted in *Ziyyun Le-Menahem*, ed. by R. J. Rubinstein, New York, 1965, pp. 363ff. On the burial of ashes of the victims of the extermination camps, *vide infra* (pp. 105, 152).
7. R. M. Breisch, *Helkath Yaakob*, I, no. 32.
8. See *Ziyyun Le-Menahem*, ed. by R. J. Rubinstein, New York, p. IX.
9. See Lothar Rotschild, 'Die Geschichte des Seminars von 1904 bis 1938' in *Das Breslauer Seminar*, Tübingen, 1963, p. 165.
10. See B. Blau, *Das Ausnahmerecht für die Juden in Deutschland 1933–1945*, pp. 53f.

insurances were taken over by the government for their own benefit. On the same day a decree was issued concerning the 'elimination of the Jews from German economic life' (*Ausschaltung der Juden aus dem deutschen Wirtschaftsleben*).

The only salvation from the hell in Germany which previously lay in emigration turned into flight. How staying in Germany (and Austria) already before the war was regarded by the Rabbis as a danger to life can be seen from the following report.[11]

One Rabbi, the son of a famous Rabbi, living in Vienna, obtained after great difficulty a visa to Luxembourg and on the basis of it a visa to emigrate to Switzerland. By chance the day he had to take his passport to the consulate was a Sabbath. As he did not want to carry the passport on the Sabbath he asked his nephew who was aged under thirteen to carry it for him. The boy was hesitant as he too did not wish to carry on the Sabbath. The Rabbi reports that on seeing this his father took his coat and went to the door to carry his son's passport, for 'there was in that case no prohibition of carrying in a public domain neither was there a prohibition of handling *mukzeh* (a thing not to be moved on the Sabbath). On the contrary, it is meritorious to help saving human lives . . .'. (Naturally on seeing that, the lad carried the passport.)

Unfortunately, the chances of leaving Germany and Austria and of finding a place of refuge were very slender. Happy were those who had the possibility of emigrating by getting permission on application made by relatives living abroad whose government granted it on account of a blood-relationship between the applicant and the prospective immigrant. Immigration to Palestine was limited, the German and Austrian quotas of immigrants to the U.S.A. were exhausted. Some countries which had hitherto admitted refugees (e.g. South Africa) closed their gates.[12]

Meanwhile many of the Jews kept in the concentration camps were released on the condition they would leave the country within a few weeks. They were to be re-arrested should they fail to fulfil the condition. They were caught between the devil and the deep sea! In their great despair they tried to cross the frontiers into neighbouring countries illegally, or to join illegal transports to Palestine. Indeed, even those

---

11. R. A. Jeruchem, 'Alim Bochim', Introduction to *Birkath Hayyim* of his father R. H. Y. Jeruchem, p. 19.
12. See W. Rosenstock, 'Exodus', in *Deutsches Judentum,* ed. by Weltsch, Stuttgart, 1963, p. 399. Much relief work was done by Britain who admitted many thousands of refugees to England under various categories, e.g. trainees, domestic helps, children, and those who had to wait until they would be eligible for admission to the U.S.A. or Palestine. However, the help though much appreciated was insufficient.

who had not yet been arrested endeavoured to leave.[13] Naturally such illegal emigration was most hazardous. Apart from the possibility of being discovered by the frontier police the escape often proved dangerous and sometimes fatal. Even after their arrival in a free country people felt unsafe as they had to register with the authorities. One Rabbi dealt with the question of having to recite the benediction *Ha-Gomel* (benediction recited after escaping danger) when one had succeeded in escaping illegally to a free country.[14]

Some Jewish families sought refuge in far-off places, e.g. China, Japan, Costa Rica and in Africa where no Jewish community existed. This later caused some problems. The following *Responsa* are illustrations.

A husband and wife escaped from Germany to one of the countries of Africa where no Jews could be found. The husband died before his wife had given birth to a son. The authorities did not give the woman and child permission to leave. A circumciser could not get there. The widow was at a great loss not knowing what to do. In her fear lest the child remain uncircumcised she asked a non-Jewish doctor to perform the circumcision, during which she was present and recited the benedictions from a prayerbook. After the war she succeeded in settling in Johannesburg. Her son grew up and was about twenty years old. It turned out, that in addition to what has already been mentioned his virile membrum was not normal (a description of it is given). After several years the young man who was an observant Jew was willing to undergo anything required by the Law. Several questions were then asked by R. Jacob Selzer of Johannesburg to which R. Weiss replied.[15]

In another *Responsum* we are told of an old man who reached a small town in Costa Rica, after having been driven from his home. In that town there was no special cemetery for Jews. Only one row was reserved for them and sometimes the authorities were not particular and a Jew was buried next to a non-Jew. As in that country there was a law that no corpse may be transferred from one place to another the old man approached a Rabbi and asked whether he could request his sons to cremate his body after death or whether it was better to be buried among non-Jews rather than to be cremated. The Rabbi was inclined to prohibit cremation and asked R. Breisch for his opinion.

13. See W. Rosenstock, 'Exodus', p. 388; Wolfgang von Weisl, 'Illegale Transporte' in *The Jews of Austria*, ed. by Josef Fraenkel, pp. 171ff.; Herbert Rosenkranz, ibid., pp. 503f.; also *vide supra* p. 24.

14. R. H.Y. Jeruchem, *Birkath Hayyim*, no. 16. *Vide infra* p. 262.

15. R. I.J. Weiss (formerly Dayan of Grosswardein later Ab Beth Din, Manchester; today Rosh Beth Din, Jerusalem), *Minhath Yizhak*, III, no. 101.

The latter replied that it was easy to reach a decision—in no circumstances might cremation be performed.[16]

Before leaving Germany and Austria all demands for taxes and other payments had to be met. The money received from the sale of their businesses had to be deposited in blocked accounts as early as after June 1938.[17] All shares, bonds and securities had to be deposited in a special account.[18] When emigrating, Jews could take only a small amount of cash with them. Indeed this state of the Jews during that phase reminds us of the second pair of turtle-doves which hung in the window: they were still alive but had been plucked. The Jews could emigrate thereby saving their lives but were deprived of most—if not all—of their possessions.

Most characteristic of the conditions at that time are the words written by R. J. Weinberg. About six months before the outbreak of the war he was ordered by the Gestapo to leave Berlin. 'They did not give me permission,' he writes, 'to take with me one book or garment or any other article. It was only with the clothes on my back that I left the city . . . .'[19] On another occasion he writes that he was unable to save even one book from his library. 'I mourn the loss of my books, for I left "the valley of overthrow" naked and lacking everything . . . .'[20]

Little wonder the refugees sought to outwit their robbers by taking out illegally whatever valuables they could. Josephus tells us[21] that during the siege of Jerusalem by the Romans the refugees crossed over to the enemy because of famine and smuggled out gold coins by swallowing them to use in captivity. Unfortunately the Romans soon learned of that practice and cut open the bowels of the captives. This led the Talmud to issue a special decree that 'one may not swallow gold denarii during the war because of danger'.[22] Different tricks were used by refugees from Nazi Germany and the countries occupied by the Germans. Being forbidden to take any jewellery or money above a small amount fixed by the Germans, people tried to overcome this. Apart from the case below where banknotes were sewn in the lining of a coat,[23] the following instance is reported in one *Responsum* where a precious stone was to be used in the time of danger. 'During the Nazi persecution a woman hid a diamond in a hole in her tooth which had later been

16. Breisch, *Helkath Yaakob*, II, no. 4. For China and Japan, cf. *Hamaor*, ed. by R. M. Amsel, New York, 5727, p. 682.
17. See H. Rosenkranz, in *The Jews of Austria*, ed. by Josef Fraenkel, p. 490.
18. Rosenkranz in *The Jews of Austria*, p. 501, quoting Blau, *Das Ausnahmerecht*, p. 79, no. 247.
19. *Seride Esh*, I. p. 1; *Ha-Doar*, New York, Kislev, 13th, 5728, p. 112.
20. *Seride Esh*, III, no. 71.
21. *Bellum Judaicum*, V, 13, 4–5. See also Graetz, *Geschichte der Juden*, III, 2, p. 536; Dubnow, *Weltgeschichte*, II, p. 459.
22. *Tosephta Gittin*, III, 12. See also *Mizpeh Shemuel, ad loc.* who refers to Josephus.
23. Breisch, *Helkath Yaakob*, I, no. 146, *vide infra* p. 65.

stopped up by a dentist in order she should be able to make use of it in time of danger to save herself and her family from the Nazis. Does this form an interposition during *tebilah* (immersion)? It could be removed only by an expert and would constitute a great danger if it became known.' After taking various factors into consideration the Rabbi decided that it formed no interposition.[24]

It was on 30 January 1939 that Hitler made a speech in which he pointed out:

> In my life I have often been a prophet . . . . Today I wish to be a prophet once more: If international-finance Jewry inside and outside Europe should succeed once more in plunging nations into another world war, the result will not be the Bolshevization of the earth and thus the victory of Jewry, but the extermination of the Jewish race in Europe.[25]

Was this merely a threat or was it a serious warning? The fact is that in some circles little attention was paid to those words. However, Rabbi Herzog, Chief Rabbi in Palestine, soon foresaw the great upheaval which would be caused were war to break out. In his letter dated 22nd Iyyar 699 (11 May 1939), addressed to R. H. O. Grodzinski of Vilno, Rabbi Herzog informs the latter of an audience he intends to arrange with the pope.[26] He then continues his letter using the phrase of Ehud (Judg. III 20),

> I have a message from God, to his honourable excellency, the renowned Rabbi, which concerns the entire community of Israel. The fermentation of war goes on and becomes stronger in the world. Although I hope that God will deliver us from this destruction which is liable to destroy the world particularly Israel which is oppressed, crushed and broken, however, one must feel cause for anxiety. Although 'one should not hasten the approach of trouble (*Gittin* 18a, *Megillah* 5a)', nevertheless we must anticipate the evil as far as we

24. Weiss, *Minhath Yizhak*, I, no. 23.
25. *Der Führer vor dem ersten Reichstag Grossdeutschlands, Reichstagsrede vom 30. Januar 1939*, Zentralverlag der NSDAP, München, 1939. On this speech, see Hilberg, *The Destruction of the European Jews*, p. 257. (See also ibid., p. 266, where another speech of Hitler is quoted which he made on 30 September 1942, referring to a similar 'prophecy' of September 1939). Hausner, *Justice in Jerusalem*, p. 48; Poliakov, *Harvest of Hate*, p. 30; Roger Manvell and Heinrich Fraenkel, *The Incomparable Crime*, p. 31; Heinz Höhne, *The Order of the Death's Head*, London, 1969, p. 353. Nine days earlier Hitler is reported to have said to the Czechoslovak foreign minister, 'Our Jews will be destroyed' (ibid.).
26. Cf. Chief Rabbi Herzog, *Hechal Yizhak*, II, nos. 35-41. On the conditional bill of divorce, cf. R. S.J. Zevin, *Le-Or Ha-Halachah*, pp. 48ff.; R. E.J. Waldenberg, *Hilchoth Medinah*, II, pp. 211ff.; I. Z. Kahana, *Sepher Ha-Agunoth*, pp. 51ff.; R. M. Meiri, *Ezrath Nashim*, III, pp. 1ff.

can concerning the *iggun* (uncertainty of death of husband, thus leaving the wife 'tied') of the daughters of Israel, God forbid,—a matter which concerns myriads of daughters of Israel . . . .

The Chief Rabbi then mentions a practice which had been carried out by R. Malkiel Ha-Levi of Lomza during the Japanese-Russian war (1904). The husband before leaving for battle should have an authorization written at his request, by which he appoints each man living in his town (or in another town where he knows there are scribes and Rabbis acquainted with the law of divorce) to write a bill of divorce for his (the soldier's) wife. Any two people could attest the *get* and any one could be the husband's agent to hand over that *get* to his wife. Furthermore, the husband authorizes the agent to act conditionally. Immediately the husband leaves for battle, a *get* should be written and signed (by witnesses). The agent should hand it over to the wife with a stipulation that if when two years have elapsed she fulfilled a certain condition thereafter she would be divorced from her husband, the *get* taking effect retrospectively:

> However, although this method could be employed at the time of the Japanese-Russian war when the husband who had left for battle (if he survived) did not return home until the end of the war, the position in a coming war would be somewhat different. We know from experience that particularly in England and France during this great war (World War I) from which we have not yet recovered, that the government would grant all soldiers short periods of leave when they would return home. Great difficulties with regard to the bill of divorce or authorization might then arise.

There was no reply until 3rd Kislev, 700 (15 November 1939). Rabbi H. O. Grodzinski first refers to the exchange of telegrams concerning the *yeshiboth*. He mentions also the plight of the *yeshiboth* which could not maintain themselves both for spiritual and material reasons. It was indeed very difficult to get support from the inhabitants of Wilno to where all the *yeshiboth* (which he mentions) had been transferred, owing to political and other changes particularly since the currency was greatly devalued and became almost worthless. R. Grodzinski sought assistance from the Chief Rabbi for help in the transfer of the *yeshiboth* of Mir and Kamienec to Palestine, by obtaining certificates for *yeshibah* students and some Rabbis.

At the end of the letter R. Grodzinski refers to Rabbi Herzog's letter who 'at the very beginning predicted war at the end of summer'. As far as the bills of divorce are concerned R. Hayyim Ozer had adopted a method practised before. If the soldier came home another arrangement was made before he left again. 'But here no permission is given to make the matter public. Nevertheless, we have found means of informing the public . . . .'

On 16th Ellul, 699 (31 August 1939), Chief Rabbi Herzog submitted his suggestions for the procedure of authorizing a bill of divorce to the members of the Council of the Chief Rabbinate of Palestine. 'We hope and pray', he writes, 'that the danger of a World War will soon pass[27] but it is the holy duty of the Rabbis of Israel to prevent evil as far as possible in regard to the *iggun* of the daughters of Israel.' He then gives directives with regard to the authorization, etc. (He made an addition on 19th Ellul, 699=3 September 1939).

At the end of a subsequent *Responsum*[28] Rabbi Herzog remarks: 'As far as our brethren in Poland are concerned the time has already passed. But we have to make arrangements also for *Erez Yisrael* since we know that Jews have already registered for the British army and will shortly leave for the battle-field. No doubt there are married men among them.' He then makes suggestions how to deal with this delicate matter.

It is most remarkable that there exists a record from R. H. O. Grodzinski of an earlier date in which the Rabbi speaks in a prophetic way of the conditions of the Jews as they were after the outbreak of World War II and how Jews of various countries particularly those of Poland, Lithuania and Russia were affected. It is found in a preface to the *Responsa Ahiezer*, Vol. III, dated Sunday 3rd of Sivan 699 (21 May 1939) and was printed in Wilno 1939. In it the following words of R. Grodzinski occur:

How great is the duty of the hour—great responsibility is imposed on anyone who is able to act. How awful is the position of our people. There was none like that even in the Middle Ages when 'the whole exile is like a sea of fire' (*Rosh Ha-Shanah* II 4), Houses of Study and Scrolls of the Law being burned at the head of every street and harsh decrees are renewed by those who hate us and cast us out (see Isa. LXVI 5) to cause us to forego our holy Law. Great and important Jewish communities are uprooted and the gates of other countries are closed to them. Jews are fugitives and toss among the waves of the sea and myriads of families wander on dry land between waves of hatred which overflow and rage with all their strength. We have become a scorn, derision, a taunt and are being trampled on. Also the light which had shone to us from the East, from the land of our desire, from the Holy Land, has become dimmed by a heavy cloud, so that we do not know what the next day will bring forth (Prov.

27. War broke out between Germany and Poland on 1 September 1939, and on 3 September England and France declared war on Germany.
28. Herzog, *Hechal Yizhak*. no. 39.

XXVII 1). Many troubles have surrounded us, massacres and murders, expulsion, exile. The entire nation of Israel is sinking in rivers of blood and in a sea of tears, oppressed and crushed. Woe, what has befallen us . . . .[29]

29. While in former times (R. Hayyim says) whenever Jews were persecuted new centres of learning were established, in our time, unfortunately, religious laxity could be observed. He holds the Jews of Germany responsible for this decline seeing that the Reform had spread causing assimilation and non-observance of the Law. He exhorts the Jews to intensify the study of the Law, particularly to strengthen the *yeshiboth* in Poland and Lithuania which still were centres and beacons of Jewish learning. (All this shows us that these lines were written before the outbreak of World War II but after the *Kristallnacht* in November 1938.)

3

World War II (1939–45)

This period forms the saddest chapter in the history of the Jewish people. According to one Rabbi it is beyond our comprehension to grasp what the Germans did to the Jews while as we have seen another Rabbi regards the Nazi holocaust as greater than the destruction of both Temples and all expulsions.[1]

One lay writer remarks that 'the terror of Torquemada pales before the Nazi Inquisition' and that 'Dante's Inferno was established in the modern world'.[2] It is rather significant that even a SS doctor who visited Auschwitz for the first time wrote in his diary (entry: 2 September 1942): 'At 3.0 a.m. attended a *Sonderaktion* for the first time. Compared with this, Dante's Inferno seems almost a comedy. Auschwitz is not called the extermination camp for nothing.'[3]

The heading of this tragedy can be marked by the verse from Joel III 3: 'Blood, and Fire and Pillars of Smoke', and can be divided into five acts: evacuation, ghettoization, deportation, concentration and extermination or 'Final Solution'. The latter was the goal of the Nazis and was not confined to the Jews of Germany (*Altreich*) and Austria, but affected six million Jews of more than twenty countries all over Europe, stretching from the Baltic Sea to Italy, from France to Greece, and was intended to be applied to another five million Jews as we have already seen (*supra*, p. xix). It was the example of Ibn Verga who hung in his window one pair of turtle-doves which was slaughtered and plucked, for the Jews in this period were both 'plucked', i.e. deprived of all their belongings, and slaughtered.

The emigration of the Jews from Germany since 1933 and from Austria since March 1938 to make the countries *judenrein* was, particularly in Austria, partially successful. There the emigration (or better 'expulsion') was urged by Eichmann who created The Central Office for Jewish Emigration (Zentralstelle für jüdische Auswanderung), with whose administration Jews were entrusted.[4]

Even Jewish leaders from Berlin were sent to Vienna to study the system to be introduced there as well. However great the desire of both

---

1. R. E.J. Waldenberg, *Ziz Eliezer*, V, no. 17; R. H.Y. Jeruchem, *Birkath Hayyim*, Introduction, p. 20.
2. G. Schoenberner, *The Yellow Star*, pp. 5, 211.
3. Hauptsturmführer Professor Kremer, M.D., quoted by Schoenberner, *Yellow Star*, p. 137.
4. See Herbert Rosenkranz, 'The Anschluss and the Tragedy of Austrian Jewry 1938–1945', in *The Jews of Austria*, ed. by Josef Fraenkel p. 491; Gideon Hausner, *Justice in Jerusalem*, pp. 39ff.

the Nazis and the Jews that the latter should completely leave the country various factors existed (among them chiefly the limited number of places of immigration) which prevented Germany and Austria ridding themselves entirely of their Jewish inhabitants. When World War II broke out there were 375,000 Jews in the territory of the *Altreich* (Third Reich), Austria and Czechoslovakia.[5] Although at the beginning Jews could still leave Germany and occupied countries through a 'backdoor', i.e. through Italian ports or via unoccupied France to Portugal and Casablanca,[6] this could not, however, lead to a complete solution of the problem the Nazis had in mind: to make the countries entirely free of Jews.[7]

Following the defeat of Poland and the occupation of part of that country with a dense Jewish population of 2,500,000, or according to another version 2,700,000,[8] Jews the matter became aggravated and the first chapter in the suffering of Polish Jewry commenced.

Most Polish Jews were taken unaware. They did not believe at first that the Germans were capable of committing such sadistic atrocities against them. They knew that every war entails danger to a conquered nation. They thought they would be treated like the non-Jewish population. The older Jews still remembered that in 1915 during World War I the German general, Erich Ludendorf issued a manifesto in Yiddish addressed to the Jewish population of Poland when occupied by the enemies of Russia. He declared: 'We come to you as friends; the barbarian foreign regime has ended. The equal rights of the Jews will be built upon a firm foundation. It is now your sacred duty to increase your strength to help in the liberation.'[9]

The following episode too is highly characteristic. One day after the Germans had entered the town of Zgierz on 8 September 1939 a young German officer came to the local Rabbi and introduced himself adding that he was a native of Nuremberg. He wished to see the Rabbi and his house. Before leaving he expressed his satisfaction at having met the old Rabbi. 'But,' he added, 'it will be very bad for the Jews here.' The Rabbi expressed his doubts by saying: 'The Germans, as bearers

5. See Michael Bar-Zohar, *The Avengers*, p. 11.

6. See G. Reitlinger, *The Final Solution*, p. 31.

7. In a circular dated 25 January 1939, Ribbentrop, the Foreign Minister, declared that the Jewish 'problem would not be solved until the last Jew had left German soil', quoted by Peter Papadatos, *The Eichmann Trial*, p. 6, note 10.

8. Hausner, *Justice in Jerusalem*, p. 54; Bar-Zohar, *The Avengers*, p. 11.

9. Quoted in *The Economic Destruction of German Jewry by the Nazi Regime 1933–1937*, American Jewish Congress, New York, November 1937, p. 5. A proclamation with a different text in Hebrew signed by the Supreme General Staff of the United German and Austrian-Hungarian armies has been published in *Beth Jacob*, no. 88, September 1966, p. 12.

of culture, will not cause evil to Jews who are free of all sin.' The
officer made no reply.[10]

More still can be said about the Jews in Russia and in Russian-
occupied Poland. Until the outbreak of war between Germany and
Russia they were quite ignorant of the Nazi atrocities against the Jews
in Germany and Poland, because the Russian newspapers would
always praise Hitler as a friend without mentioning his policy towards
the Jews. It was therefore possible to find even among the Jews in the
Ukraine some who admired Hitler as a great statesman. Those who
were older even recalled their good treatment by the Germans because
their language was similar.[11]

Soon the Jews of the newly occupied territories of Russia and Poland
experienced the attitude of the Nazis. Beatings and shootings were the
first encounters between the Jews and the conqueror. Some Germans
when entering a town had lists of the Rabbis and other leaders of the
local Jews. They would first go to find the Rabbi and when the Rabbi
was not at home beat the Jews to tell them where the Rabbi was.[12]
Roaming about the streets, equipped with iron bars and knocking down
men and women was an enjoyable entertainment. Shooting innocent
people was a pleasant sport. But the most malicious and sadistic
attitude of the Germans in almost all the places they occupied in East
European countries was the plucking of the beards of Jews. Even
officers and high military officials, we are told by one author,[13] were not
ashamed to run after an old Jew with scissors in their hands to cut off
his beard. This 'sport' could be carried out everywhere in the newly
occupied countries. It is well known that unlike the Jews in Germany
most of those of the eastern countries had beards.[14] In fact Hitler's
occupation forces were not the first to issue a decree concerning the
beard. Long before Hitler's era the Jew's beard was subject to government control. Both the prohibition of shaving as well as the order to
shave feature in the legislation of various countries. Thus for instance,
in Spain where the Jews appear to have shaved their beards, the Jews
of Castille had been forbidden to do so according to the ordinance of
Donna Catalina in 1412.[15] Frederick the Great (1712–86) insisted on
applying the decree of 1737 that married Jews should not shave off

10. R. S. Huberband, *Kiddush Ha-Shem*, Tel Aviv, 1969, p. 273.
11. A. Anatoli (Kuznetsov), *Babi Yar*, London, 1970, p. 103. See also Heinz Höhne,
    The Order of the Death's Head. p. 359.
12. See the case mentioned by R. Moses Steinberg in his Introduction to the *Responsa
    Mahazeh Abraham* II, New York, 1964.
13. Chaim A. Kaplan, *Scroll of Agony*, p. 36 (entry: 20 October 1939).
14. On the importance attached by Jews to the beard, cf. *Peer Ha-Dør*, biography of
    R. Abraham Isaiah Karelitz, author of *Hazon Ish*, II, Tel Aviv, 1939, pp. 335ff.
15. See Simon Dubnow, *Weltgeschichte des jüdischen Volkes*, V, p. 349.

their beards.[16] A similar decree was issued by Maria Theresa (1753, 1764).[17] On the other hand Czar Nicolas I ordered (1827) that Jews cut off their sidelocks (*peoth*) and beards.[18] The writer could find no reference that prior to the nineteenth century non-Jews had attacked Jews by cutting off their beards forcibly. It was for the first time in 1863 when the Poles rebelled against the Russians that the Cossacks fell on the Jews in Warsaw and cut off their side-locks and beards.[19] Fifty-six years later, during the war between the Poles and Bolsheviks (1919), it was the Poles who attacked Jews and cut off their beards. On 3 October 1919 the *Jewish Chronicle* reported the suffering of the Jews during the war. After the battle the Polish soldiers repeated the beard-cutting exploits in the townlet of Smolevitch and Rabbi Abramski (later appointed Rav of the 'Mahzike Ha-Dath' congregation, Spitalfields, in 1932, a member of the London Beth Din in 1935, and after his retirement emigrated to Israel) for fear of losing his fine long beard, obtained a written permit from the Polish commandant to keep it. The most characteristic feature of the permit is the statement that it was only a temporary licence which had to be renewed from time to time.[20] The writer can still recall the reports which appeared in the newspapers in the following years about the *Hallerczycy(s)* (Polish soldiers serving under General Józef Haller) who would attack Jews in the trains and in the streets and cut off their beards.

This form of attack was taken over by the Germans in occupied Poland and Lithuania. Reproductions of photographs are included in R. Simon Huberband's *Kiddush Ha-Shem*. They were taken by the Germans and show their soldiers looking with malicious pleasure at the sadistic scenes when Jews had their beards cut off by the Germans who sometimes tore off skin as well as the hair. In Huberband's work there is a special chapter on the attitude of the Germans towards the Jews and their beards and the sadistic acts committed by them. After entering a town, one of the first assaults of the Germans upon religious Jews, we are told, was to shear, burn, cut off and pluck their beards. Sometimes the Jews were ordered on pain of death to assemble at a public place where, to the rejoicing of the militia and the local Polish population, the cutting of beards with various instruments, bayonets included, took place. Then the hair was collected at a certain place and a modern *auto-da-fé* was arranged. Several towns are enumerated

16. Ibid., VIII, p. 22.
17. Ibid., VII, p. 291.
18. *Jüdisches Lexikon*, I, p. 739; Huberband, *Kiddush Ha-Shem*, p. 96.
19. See *Beth Jacob*, nos. 55–56, Kislev-Tebeth, 724 (Nov-Dec 1963), p. 23, where a photograph of such a scene is reproduced.
20. See also *Jewish Chronicle*, 3 October 1969, p. 43.

where the Jews were subject to various humiliations and beatings before
they were deprived of their beards.

In view of the maltreatment of the Jews who had their beards plucked
the religious leader (*Moreh Horaah*) of Cracow gave a decision that
Jews should cut off their beards themselves. The religious Jews of
Cracow followed his decision.[21]

The question of shaving off the beard is reflected in the following
Responsum. During their stay in the ghetto the Jews were subject to
various kinds of insults and humiliations. Their tormentors issued daily
new decrees causing them to suffer physically and spiritually. One of
the accusations against the Jews was that they were dirty and spread
infectious diseases, particularly those who grew beards, as was customary among religious Jews. When they saw a Jew with a beard he was
immediately in danger of his life. Therefore many inmates of the
ghetto, Rabbis and great men of Israel included, removed their beards.
Furthermore, the intention of the Germans was to destroy Judaism
therefore they particularly attacked the spiritual leaders. The *Gedole
Yisrael* (the great men of Israel) tried to conceal the fact that they were
the leaders and were forced to shave off their beards to resemble
ordinary men and not to stand out as Rabbis and leaders.

There were, however (we are told by R. Oshry), two men in the
Ghetto of Kovno[22] who did not remove their beards. One of them was
the Rabbi of Kovno, R. Abraham Dob Schapira, who did not want to
shave off his beard as he was known to the Gestapo as the Chief Rabbi
of Kovno. Shaving off his beard would have concealed nothing. Apart
from that he wished to maintain the honour of Israel.

The second man was an important member of the town whose name
was R. Feivel (Phöbus) Zussmann belonging to the Hasidim of HBD.
Eventually he was caught during the *Kinderaktion* when the Germans
searched for children and killed them (3rd and 4th of Nisan 5704 = 27–
28 March 1944). In those troublesome days Rabbi Oshry was asked by
a Jew whether he could shave off his beard with a razor as there was
no other implement available. The Rabbi's reply was that because of
danger to life he was permitted to shave with a razor as no other
instrument could be found and no non-Jew was available to shave him.
The Germans forbade all non-Jews to do anything for the Jews.[23]

21. Huberband, *Kiddush Ha-Shem*, p. 85.
22. Another case was in Galicia where my saintly teacher, R. Hayyim Yizhak Jeruchem,
    who died in the Sambor Ghetto on 19th Tishri, 703 (30 September 1942), 'was almost
    the only person in the country (*medinah*) who kept his beard', reported by his son in
    'Alim Bochim', Introduction to *Responsa* of his father *Birkath Hayyim*, New York,
    1956, p. 26.
23. R. E. Oshry, *Mi-Maamakkim*, I, no. 19. On the *Kinderaktion*, cf. *infra* pp. 289, 353.

Also executions by hanging occurred now and then.[24] Such form of murder was used in cases of sabotage, disobeying Nazi orders, refusal to supply lists of Jews to be deported or killed. The German tormentors showed great cruelty and sadism to their victims.

In one *Responsum* we are told of immigrants to Israel who brought with them from Poland a thick rope which they had removed from one of the gallows after the Nazis had used it to hang their Jewish victims. The leaders of *Vaadath Har Zion* introduced the custom that on every 10th of Tebeth, when the congregation assembled in the synagogue *Har Zion* for prayer and to remember the victims of the Nazi persecution the reader would gird himself with that rope. The Rabbi was asked whether that was permitted. In his reply he shows us that the rope may not be used but must be buried.[25]

While the degree of participation by the army commanders and their troops in acts of maltreatment of Jews is controversial there are several reports of the army being involved in acts of violence immediately they entered a conquered town.[26]

When describing the occupation of Warsaw by the German troops one author tells us that 'legal and illegal robbery[27] of Jewish possessions was instituted immediately. German soldiers and officers, regardless of their status in the army, air force, in the police as well as SS and German civilians, participated in this robbery . . . . Jews were also captured just for the sake of a beating. This became a favourite sport[28] and source of enjoyment'.[29]

With regard to the massacres in the Ukraine and the participation of the army there exists a report dated 2 December 1941 stating *inter alia* that the shooting of Jews 'was done entirely in public with the use of the Ukranian militia and unfortunately in many instances also with members of the armed forces taking part voluntarily . . . . So far about 150,000 to 200,000 Jews may have been executed in the part of the Ukraine belonging to the Reich Commissariat; no consideration was given to the interests of the economy'.[30]

While all these atrocities against the Jews were going on the Nazi masterminds were busy solving the Jewish problem. Until the outbreak

---

24. Cf. e.g. Simon Wiesenthal, *The Murderers Among Us*, p. 232, on the execution of twelve members of the Jewish council of Lwow.
25. R. Meshullam Rath, *Kol Mebasser*, I, no. 58. On 10th Tebeth, *vide infra* p. 157.
26. See Roger Manvell and Heinrich Fraenkel, *The Incomparable Crime*, p. 292, note 20; Richard Grünberger, *A Social History of the Third Reich*, pp. 148ff.
27. *Vide infra* the case where a Nazi officer offered two Scrolls for sale, p. 138.
28. David Wdowinski, *And We Are Not Saved*, London, 1964, pp. 24ff.; see a so R. J.J. Weinberg, *infra* p. 124 about maltreatment of Jews by 'German soldiers and officers'.
29. Other 'sports' and 'enjoyments' were smashing babies' heads against the wall and forcing Jews to tear up scrolls of the Law, *vide infra*, pp. 213, 247, 320.
30. Manvell and Fraenkel, *The Incomparable Crime*, pp. 112ff.

E

of the war this problem was confined to the Reich, the *Ostmark* (Austria) and Czechoslovakia and attempts were made to solve it at first by voluntary and later by forced emigration. After the outbreak of the war two factors brought a change in the solution. First, mass emigration was quite impossible.[31] Secondly, through the conquest of the new territories in Poland the number of Jews increased enormously. This gave rise to two new ideas in the Nazi mastermind (21 September 1939)—deportations and ghettoization. The former was to be carried out by deporting the Jews from the Reich, Austria and other areas to the region south-west of Lublin near the little town of Nisko on the San, where they were to be settled under SS supervision. Extermination of the Jews was not yet explicitly discussed. In fact transports of Jews from Vienna, Stettin and Prague arrived in Poland and it was planned to transfer another 400,000 Jews from other so-called re-incorporated territories. However, owing to discontent among the Nazi leaders, the chaotic deportations and fear of an economic crisis the plan had to be given up.[32]

More successful was the other plan engineered by the Germans: the evacuation of the Jews from the country to towns and establishing ghettos there for the local Jews and those of neighbouring places.[33] All Jews from communities with less than 500 members were to be transferred to the nearest Jewish centre. Several reasons were given for the concentration of the Jews in ghettos: to guard the non-Jewish population from the spread of diseases prevalent among the Jews; to prevent black-market activities; for 'political and moral reasons'; to protect the Jews from attacks by the native Polish and Lithuanian population; to obtain better and more concentrated chances of employment, and in some places the reason was given as a punishment for an alleged attack on German soldiers. In fact, the ghettoization was done merely for the purpose of concentrating the Jews and to make it easier for the Germans to carry out their demands and sadistic plans leading to the 'Final Solution'.

The establishment of the ghettos began in winter 1939–40. The first major ghetto was established at Lodz (Litzmannstadt) on 30 April 1940, to be followed by others. The largest ghetto was that of Warsaw,

31. On emigration on a small scale see L. Poliakov, *Harvest of Hate*, p. 37.
32. On this plan as well as the proposed transfer to Madagascar, see Raul Hilberg, *The Destruction of the European Jews*, pp. 128ff., 138, 260; Höhne, *Order of the Death's Head*, pp. 350ff.; Hausner, *Justice in Jerusalem*, pp. 58ff., Leon Poliakov, *Harvest of Hate*, pp. 33ff., where all the relevant facts are given and dealt with at length.
33. On the formation of the ghetto, its structure and administration, cf. especially Hilberg, *The Destruction of European Jews*, pp. 128ff., 144ff., 151; Reitlinger, *The Final Solution*, pp. 37, 54ff.; Poliakov, *Harvest of Hate*, pp. 84ff.; L. Garfunkel, *The Destruction of Kovno's Jewry*, pp. 39f. 47, (concerning Kovno); Isaiah Trunk, *Judenrat*, New York, 1972, pp. 3ff.

erected in October 1940. Ghettoization was almost an accomplished fact in Poland in 1941. The last ghettos were set up in 1942.

The ghetto was a town in itself. The way in which the inmates were separated from their environment was not always the same. In some places the ghetto was surrounded by a wall (Warsaw) or barbed wire (Lodz) and generally one could leave the ghetto only when going out to forced labour. The Jews had to walk in columns in the middle of the road and wear the *Judenstern* (six-pointed yellow star). The death penalty was imposed on any Jew found outside the ghetto without permission.[34]

Ghetto inmates were not allowed without permission to come in contact with the non-Jewish population whilst working outside the ghetto. Nevertheless they did on some occasions succeed in transacting 'business' with non-Jews. How dangerous it was to attempt such a transaction can be seen from the following *Responsum*.

Owing to the unbearable and indescribable famine in the Ghetto of Kovno (we are told) which became worse every day, the inmates tried to sell their last possessions to buy food. Unfortunately, there were many sellers but no buyers. The Germans had prohibited non-Jews from entering the ghetto as strongly as the Jews had been forbidden to leave it. Any contravention of that ruling was punishable by death. There was, however, some opportunity for those who wished to sell their belongings. The Germans used every day to take out a certain number of Jews for forced labour and they returned in the evening. Being outside the ghetto those Jews sometimes succeeded in contacting non-Jews and doing some business without being noticed by the Germans. With the help of the forced labourers it was possible for a few to sell their remaining jewellery to the non-Jews (e.g. gold rings, bracelets, diamonds and pearls) as articles of greater size would have been noticed by the Germans who used to search them when they went to work and when they returned.

Naturally the forced labourers who did the transactions on behalf of the owners received commission from the owners of the articles sold. Such transactions enabled both to buy food. One Jew had given a precious stone to a forced labourer for the latter to sell to a non-Jew outside the ghetto. In order to be able to leave the place of work and come in contact with non-Jews to sell them the stone the labourer removed the yellow star (of David) from his sleeve for otherwise he would have been unable to get into touch with non-Jews outside the ghetto without the escort of a German guard. Furthermore, as the Jews were not permitted to walk outside the ghetto on the sidewalk like free

34. See Poliakov, *Harvest of Hate*, pp. 38, 40, 87; and *infra*.

men but had to walk in the middle of the road under escort of their German guards like prisoners, the forced labourer had to walk on the sidewalk in order not to be suspected as a Jew. Whilst walking on the sidewalk he was recognized by the Germans and shot. They took his body into the ghetto and handed it over to the Jews as a warning to the others. The murdered man was buried with the garments which were on him in accordance with Jewish law. It was only afterwards that they learned of the precious stone which the owner claimed was still sewn in his garment. Upon that stone he had set his desire and that of his family who were dying of hunger.

The Rabbi[35] was asked whether it was permitted to open the grave and remove the stone and return it to the owner so that he could keep his little ones alive who were crying to their father for bread. The answer was in the affirmative. On the other hand, another Rabbi[36] writes:

> It is well known that escape from the ghetto was often very easy as in many cases it depended completely on the civil administration of the town. In many places the inmates were permitted to leave the ghetto for several hours daily to buy necessary requirements in the town. In others they were permitted to go out for work and could seize the opportunity to escape. Some inmates even obtained special permission in writing to leave the ghetto whenever they wished. All this was unlike a concentration camp . . . .

The administration of the ghetto was in the hands of the Jewish Council or Council of Elders (*Judenrat, Ältestenrat*) headed by its president.[37] Their task was primarily to inform the ghetto population of the Germans' orders, to see that these orders were carried out, to represent the inmates of the ghetto, to care for the welfare of the ghetto population, to deliver labourers for work—and at the end they were ordered by the Germans to provide them with lists of people for 'resettlement', i.e. deportation to the gas chambers.

Of the various institutions subordinated to the Jewish Council mention should be made of the following: the Jewish police, the Rabbinate, the hospital, the orphanage and the soup kitchen.

---

35. Oshry, *Mi-Maamakkim*, II, no. 12. One of the reasons for the Rabbi's decision was that it was in the interest of the murdered man that the property be restored to its real owner, and to avoid people saying he had taken something belonging to others into his grave. Retrieving the stone would also benefit those who were alive, since the *mizvah* of *pikkuah nephesh* would be fulfilled.

36. R. Z.H. Meisels, *Binyan Zebi*, II, no. 59.

37. On the Jewish Council, cf. the study by Trunk, *Judenrat*.

The Jewish police

The ghetto had its own police force to discharge various duties.[38] At first they were used for regulating street traffic, taking care that the streets should be kept clean, fighting crime, guarding the institutions of the *Judenrat*, the walls and fences of the ghetto and carrying out the orders of their superiors, particularly concerning the collection of taxes and arranging forced labour. At the close of the ghetto they had unfortunately to assist the Germans in their 'resettlement' programme, i.e. rounding up people for transports to the death camps.

Most of the policemen were corrupt, cruel and severely criticized by the inmates of the ghetto.[39] The role they played is described by various writers. As far as the ghetto police of Warsaw is concerned, seldom has one a good word to say about them. There were, however, some Jewish policemen who endangered their lives to help the unfortunate inmates, e.g. in the Ghetto of Kovno.[40]

From a *Responsum* it appears that the Jewish police in the Ghetto of Kovno were entitled to perform civil marriages recognized to some extent by the German authorities.[41]

The Rabbinate

As far as the duties of the *Judenrat* towards the inmates of the ghetto are concerned spiritual and religious needs were not within its main charge. Nevertheless, the Councils or *Judenräte* in many ghettos kept close contact with the Rabbis.[42] In the two large ghettos of Lodz and Warsaw the Rabbis were organized into *Vaad Ha-Rabbanim* or *Agudath Ha-Rabbanim* (Rabbinical Committee, Rabbinical Association).

In the Ghetto of Warsaw R. J. J. Weinberg of Berlin, who after his expulsion from Germany happened to be in Warsaw at the outbreak of World War II, was elected by the leading Rabbis president of the General Association of Rabbis (*Agudath Ha-Rabbanim*) and president of the Association of the Rabbis of Warsaw (*Agudath Rabbane Warsaw*).[43] Whilst in Warsaw he witnessed the cruel and sadistic acts

---

38. On the Jewish ghetto police, cf. Trunk, *Judenrat*, chapter 18, 'The Ghetto Police', pp. 475ff.; Hausner, *Justice in Jerusalem*, pp. 200f.

39. Cf. Wdowinski, *And We Are Not Saved*, pp. 31ff., 41, 62, 64f.; Kaplan, *Scroll of Agony*, pp. 258, 293, 305, 308.

40. Oshry, *Mi-Maamakkim*, II no. 8 (*infra*, p. 140); Garfunkel, *Destruction of Kovno's Jewry*, pp. 77, 95, 141, 153n. 14; cf. also Trunk, *Judenrat*, pp. 515ff.

41. *Vide infra* p. 310. On fictitious marriages in the Ghetto of Kovno, see Garfunkel, *Destruction of Kovno's Jewry*, p. 255. For further references to marriages performed in the ghetto, see Trunk, *Judenrat*, pp. 177, 192f.

42. *Vide infra* p. 50.

43. See following note.

which the Germans perpetrated against the Jewish inhabitants, and gives us an account of them.[44]

On the attitude and fate of the last three Rabbis of Warsaw *vide infra.*[45]

Hospitals

The Germans themselves showed interest in establishing hospitals in places where no hospitals were available in the ghetto. One such hospital in the Ghetto of Kovno was equipped with modern appliances and was set aside for dealing with infectious diseases. During the destruction of the 'Small Ghetto', in October 1941, the hospital with its patients, doctors and sisters (about sixty people) was burned down by the Germans.[46]

In December 1941 a new hospital was opened. It deserves mention because public religious services being prohibited by the Nazis it was one of the places used in secret for such services on *Rosh Ha-Shanah* and *Yom Kippurim.* The services were arranged by the doctors who, although they belonged to the assimilated class, were prepared to sacrifice their lives for the sake of prayer.[47]

Orphanages

During the ghetto period the orphanages housed also children whose parents were alive but were about to be sent to concentration camps. Before the liquidation of the Ghetto of Cracow the orphanage with its inmates was burnt down by the Germans.[48]

Soup kitchens

In order to alleviate the sufferings of the starving ghetto population the *Judenrat* opened kitchens where 'the black soup' was cooked, made of kidney-beans (*sheuith*) which the Germans supplied together with the daily ration of bread (100 grams per person). The kitchen was open also on the Sabbath and food was prepared.[49]

RELIGIOUS LIFE IN THE GHETTO

There was full co-operation between the *Judenrat* and Rabbinate in almost every ghetto. The president and members of the former showed great respect to the latter and *vice versa.* The decisions of the Rabbinical

---

44. See R. J.J.Weinberg, *Eth Ahai Anochi Mebakkesh,* Bene Berak, 1966, pp. 34ff.; from *Yad Shaul in Memory of Rabbi Shaul Weingorth,* ed. by R. Weinberg and R. Pinhas Biberfeld, Tel Aviv, 1953).
45. p. 60.
46. *Vide infra* p. 319.
47. Garfunkel, *Destruction of Kovno's Jewry,* pp. 109, 153; Oshry, *Mi-Maamakkim,* II, no. 11 (*infra* Part II, p. 250).
48. *Vide infra* p. 54.
49. Oshry, *Mi-Maamakkim,* I, no. 5. The kitchen was opened in Kovno in April 1942. See Trunk, *Judenrat,* p. 125.

Councils were transmitted to the president of the *Judenrat* who announced them to the inmates of the ghetto. Thus, e.g. the *Vaad Ha-Rabbanim* of Lodz informed the president that in a plenary session held on 26th of Shebat, 701 (23 February 1941) the following decision had been made:

1. If in the opinion of doctors women before or after childbirth require meat, they may eat it without any qualms.

2. People who feel their strength fail them should be examined by a doctor and then consult the Rabbinate or a special Rabbi.

The Rabbinate requested the president further to draw the attention of the doctors to the weight of their decisions, namely that permission (to eat meat) should be given only in cases of danger to life, and with full professional integrity.[50]

On the 28th of Adar, 701 (27 March 1941) Rabbi Joseph Finer, a member of the Rabbinate of Lodz, approached its president in the name of the *Vaad Ha-Rabbanim* with the request that an analysis be made of *Zitronensäure* (citric acid) and *Krimatatra* (cream of tartar) to ascertain whether they were permitted for use on Passover. If possible an analysis was to be made of saccharin and margarine.[51]

Mazzoth (or flour for *mazzoth*) for Passover were available in various ghettos (e.g. Warsaw, Lublin, Lodz, Boryslaw, Drohobycz and Theresienstadt in 1940, 1941 and 1942.[52]

When in the Ghetto of Kovno the famine became daily more acute people inquired before *Pesah* how they should act on *Pesah* with regard to food in order not to transgress the law of *hamez* as not even an olive's bulk of *mazzah* for *mazzath mizvah* was available. They asked:

1. Are they permitted to eat the black peas given to them by the Germans?

2. There are some men who succeeded in obtaining dirty potato peels in the forced-labour camp. They intended to mix them with flour to make *mazzoth* from this mixture, as the moisture of the peel could be regarded as 'fruit juice' which does not cause the dough to leaven. However, as the peels had to be washed owing to the dirt one could not prevent some water coming into the dough. The water mixed with the juice would have the effect of accelerating the leavening of the dough. There are, however, various views on this. Is there any possibility of permitting this?

As far as the first question is concerned, Rabbi Oshry of Kovno

50–51. See Isaiah Trunk, *Ghetto Lodz*, New York, 1962, pp. 410f., 455; *Beth Jacob*, Jerusalem, Nisan, 702, no. 11, p. 11.

52. *Vide infra* p. 126; Richard Feder, *Terezin*, p. 56; Trunk, *Judenrat*, pp. 191f.

decided that the black peas could be used as it was a time of great emergency. The peas should, if possible, first be scalded in boiling water. If this was not possible, the peas could still be eaten.

With regard to the second question the famous Rabbi Abraham Dob Beer Schapira (d. 21st Adar 703) decided that in no circumstances should the potato peel be washed but only cleaned dry. After doing so, flour could be added and this dough could be even baked on *Pesah* (when more stringent rules concerning *hamez* apply). Before baking, one should perforate the 'cakes' with a fork that no bubbles should arise. This decision was to be publicized so that people would not act otherwise.[53]

The holding of public religious services and the observance of the Sabbath and festivals depended much on the mood and attitude of German authorities. In general with some occasional exceptions neither was possible. In the Ghetto of Kovno where people had to go to work ordered by the Germans, Sabbath observance was almost impossible. Similarly the *Judenrat* had to keep its offices open every day (Sabbath and festivals included). To annoy the Jews the Nazis especially chose Sabbaths and festivals as days when harder work was imposed.[54]

When in the first year of the establishment of the Ghetto in Kovno only a small number of Jews employed in forced labour, particularly at the aerodrome, reported for work on *Yom Kippurim* the Germans threatened the *Judenrat* with stringent measures should the required number of inmates not appear within one hour. In view of the great danger the Rabbi of Kovno, R. Abraham Dob Beer Schapira, let an announcement be made in the synagogue and places of worship that those ordered to work interrupt their prayers immediately and go to work.[55]

Religious observance was made difficult in other matters too. Thus on the pretext of avoiding the spread of disease the holding of public services and the use of *mikvaoth* (ritual baths) were often prohibited. A curfew imposed as a sign of humiliation affected religious observance as is illustrated by the following two *Responsa* written in Slovakia.

R. Yizhak Weiss of Werbau was asked the following question in Tammuz 701 (June-July 1941). *Tishah Be-Ab* of that year would fall on a Sunday. The non-Jews had imposed a curfew upon the Jews that the

53. See Oshry, *Mi-Maamakkim*, I, no. 17. Most probably this question was asked before *Pesah* 702 (March 1942) as R. Abraham Schapira died on 21st of Adar 703 (26 February 1943). Permission to eat peas on *Pesah* was also given by a Rabbi in the Ghetto of Warsaw after consultation with other Rabbis. See Menasheh Ungar, *ADMORIM Shenispu*, p. 234.
54. Oshry, *Mi-Maamakkim*, II, no. 11, p. 65; Garfunkel, *Destruction of Kovno's Jewry*, p. 256. On worship and keeping the Sabbath, see also Trunk, *Judenrat*, pp. 187ff.; Feder, *Terezin*, pp. 53f., 56.
55. Garfunkel, *Destruction of Kovno's Jewry*. p. 256.

latter were not to go out after 8 p.m. How should they act with regard to prayer and reading the book of 'Echah' in a public service on Saturday night? Could they recite the evening prayer after the beginning of *pelag ha-minhah* (i.e. one and a quarter of the twelfth portion of the day before nightfall)?

The decision was that the evening prayer was not to be recited before the termination of the Sabbath. With regard to the recital of 'Echah' the Rabbi advised that everyone should read it at home and it was to be repeated, this time in public, on the following morning.

Another *Responsum* sent to the Rabbi of Tyrnau (Trnava), in connection with the curfew was the following. A curfew had been imposed that the Jews were not to appear on the street after 6 p.m. The question arose how were women to act concerning immersion due to take place on Friday evening, which could not be performed on that evening nor on Saturday night owing to the decree. The immersion could also not take place on Sunday before noon as the *mikveh* was closed as it was 'their' day of rest. The Rabbi in his reply gave some rulings.[56]

In spite of all the difficulties there were still many people who tried to observe the law as far as possible and defy the Nazi orders.[57]

'RESETTLEMENTS'

The most difficult problem which the *Judenrat* and also the Rabbis had to face in the ghettos was the question of compliance with the order given by the Germans to hand over lists of people for 'resettlement', which was identical with being sent to extermination camps. It was a trial unprecedented in history, a fight between religion and conscience on the one hand and threat of death on the other.

Indeed these matters concerned one of the most important principles of the Jewish religion.

According to the Talmud and Codes[58] if idolaters say to Jews: 'Hand over one of your number to us, that we may put him to death, otherwise we will put all of you to death', they should all suffer death rather than hand over a single Jew to them. But if they specified an individual, saying: 'Hand over that particular person to us, or else we will put all

---

56. Both decisions are to be found in R. Z.H. Meisels, *Mekaddshe Ha-Shem*, I, nos. 70, 71.

57. *Vide infra* p. 247; cf. also Garfunkel, *Destruction of Kovno's Jewry*, p. 256; R. Simon Huberband, *Kiddush Ha-Shem*, pp. 88f.

58. Talmud Yerushalmi, *Terumoth*, VIII, 10, p. 46b; Maimonides, *Mishneh Torah, Hilchoth Yesode Ha-Torah*, V, 5; *Beth Yoseph* and *Bayyith Hadash* on *Tur Yoreh Deah*, cap. CLVII and Isserles on *Shulhan Aruch Yoreh Deah*, ibid. For Maimonides's reason for the decision, see the Commentaries on *Mishneh Torah* and on *Tur Shulhan Aruch, Yoreh Deah*, cap. CLVII. See also the suggestions put forward in *Torah She-Beal Peh*, ed. by Yizhak Raphael, Jerusalem, 1972, pp. 74ff., 82ff., 101ff., 109ff.

of you to death', there is a difference of opinion in the Talmud whether
or not the person asked for should be handed over. According to one
view he may be handed over. According to another view he may be
handed over only when he is guilty of a crime punishable by death like
Sheba, son of Bichri (who rebelled against David, see II Sam. xx 1ff.,
21ff.).

Maimonides decided according to the second view saying: 'If the
individual specified has not incurred capital punishment, they should
all suffer death rather than hand over a single Jew to them.'

Some presidents of the *Judenrat* committed suicide or refused to
co-operate with the Germans in the deportation of Jews and were
themselves executed.[59]

It also happened that the *Judenrat* in their struggle between the
pressure from the Nazis and their deep conscience went to ask the Rabbi
for advice. The following report given in various sources is very
moving.[60]

On 26 October 1941, an officer of the Gestapo called Rauke came to
the office of the *Judenrat* of Kovno informing them that he had been
appointed commandant of the ghetto by the Gestapo and would like
to get to know the inmates of the ghetto 'face to face'. The *Judenrat*
should therefore publish an announcement to the effect that on
28 October all the ghetto inmates young and old, men, women and
children should congregate at six in the morning at the Democratic
Square in the centre of the ghetto. All should bring their working papers
with them. Anyone hiding in the houses would be shot. They should be
assembled in a special order and in groups: members of the *Judenrat*;
at their sides the Jewish police force and workers of the *Judenrat*
according to their functions and institutes; behind them the labourers
at the aerodrome, and behind them the labourers at other places. The
last place should be occupied by those who had not yet any fixed work.
He, Rauke, would pass through all the groups and inspect the working
certificates of all men and women. Those who were regarded as unfit
for hard work would be removed from the ghetto to another place. He
did not mention the place; however, one could understand he meant
deportation into the Small Ghetto from where a few weeks before the
inmates had been evacuated and murdered. The members of the
Judenrat were very disturbed by this order. A discussion ensued among
them whether to comply with the Nazi order and make an announcement as demanded or to sabotage it. In the former case there was still

59. For references see Hausner, *Justice in Jerusalem*, pp. 197, 205; Huberband, *Kiddush Ha-Shem*, pp. 28, 30f.; Adam Czerniakow, *Warsaw Ghetto Diary*, 'Introduction', p. 27.
60. See Oshry, 'Kuntras Me-Emek Ha-Bacha', in *Dibre Ephraim*, no. 1; Garfunkel, *Destruction of Kovno's Jewry*, pp. 71f.; *Jewish Review*, London, 28 April 1971, p. 5; Trunk, *Judenrat*, 424ff.

hope, though only for the time being, of saving a part of the ghetto population, perhaps even the greater part of it. In the latter case the consequences might be terrible, sabotage might lead to the liquidation of the whole ghetto. After a lengthy discussion they decided to go and consult the venerable R. Abraham Dob Beer Schapira. The Rabbi who was ill (he died later in the ghetto on the 21st of Adar 703, 26 February 1943) fainted on hearing the report. When he recovered consciousness he told the delegation to come next morning as he wished to consult the Rabbinic sources how to act in such terrible conditions in accordance with Jewish law. On the following morning the Rabbi gave his decision as follows: if—God forbid—a decree is issued to destroy a Jewish community and means exist by which a part of the congregation could be saved the heads of the community must have the courage and take the responsibility upon themselves to comply with the order and save what is possible.

Consequently, posters in both languages, Yiddish and German, appeared requesting the inmates of the ghetto to assemble in the Democratic Square on 28 October 1941, not later than six o'clock in the morning. 'Those found after that time would be shot on the spot.'

The outcome of that 'resettlement' was that of the ghetto population numbering 26,400 who had assembled 17,400 people returned home towards evening. Those deported were later killed.

One scholar[61] appears to regard R. Schapira's decision as contrary to Maimonides's ruling. It appears, however, that the Rabbi considered the circumstances of the Nazi demand in the Ghetto of Kovno as different from those forming the background to Maimonides's ruling. In the Nazi order no direct mention was made of the fate of those to be deported (although it was clear that they would be killed). Furthermore, the *Judenrat* did not deliver the victims to the wicked ones. No list of candidates for deportation was made out or given to the Nazis, as was the case in other ghettos.

Great deliberations took place also in other ghettos where the Germans asked the *Judenräte* to make arrangements for 'resettlements'.[62] Sometimes the *Judenrat* invited Rabbis and members of the councils of other ghettos, and debates ensued whether or not to comply with the Nazi order as, by handing over elderly and sick people who had no chance of survival, part of the ghetto population could be saved. The views were often divided.

WORKING PERMITS

It is well known that the Germans very often used various strategies

---

61. J. Robinson in his Introduction to Trunk's *Judenrat*, p. xxxi.
62. For particulars, see Trunk, *Judenrat*, pp. 420f., where the ghettos, their presidents and the various views expressed are mentioned.

to mislead the Jews and to make them believe that their intentions were genuine and that no harm would befall them. The so-called 'Aussied-lungen' (evacuations) were said to be intended to place the Jews in areas with better sanitary conditions. The erection of the ghettos was said to be for the benefit of the inmates. The survival of some ghetto inmates, particularly of those fit to work or of skilled workers was 'guaranteed' by the distribution of special cards. They were working permits and granted 'immunity' to the holders. They were handed to the *Judenrat* for distribution among the inmates. One can imagine how everybody wished to obtain such a card and there was great confusion as the number of inmates far exceeded the number of cards. The Nazi sadists sometimes used to reduce the number of ghetto inmates step by step in an inconspicuous manner. They changed the colour of the cards and declared the previous set null and void, reducing the number of cards on each occasion. In the *Responsa* we find questions which arose in connection with these cards. One such *Responsum* is as follows.[63]

On Ellul 23, 701 (15 September 1941) the commandant of the Ghetto of Kovno, named Jordan, handed over 5,000 white cards, so-called *Jordan-Scheine*, to the *Ältestenrat* for distribution among the workmen and their families. Only they were to remain in Kovno. There were about 30,000 Jews in the ghetto at that time, among them about 10,000 trained men (*baale melachah*) and their families. Great confusion ensued. Whoever was strong was able to snatch a card from the *Ältestenrat*. Two questions, says R. Oshry, arose: was the *Ältestenrat* permitted to distribute the cards among the workmen to comply with Jordan's order? Was a workman permitted to snatch a card thereby depriving his fellow-workmen from being amongst the 5,000? While the first question was decided in the negative no clear decision was given concerning the second question in view of contradictory considerations. However, at the end of his *Responsum* R. Oshry quotes the decision of R. Abraham Dob Beer Schapira mentioned above. 'Similarly in our case', concludes Rabbi Oshry, 'the acceptance and distribution of the cards is a way of saving life. The *Ältestenrat* was bound to accept and distribute the cards.'

Another case concerning work-permits took place in the Wilno Ghetto. Rabbi Shalom Alter Perlow of Kojdanow and Rabbi Reuben Kohen were in that ghetto. The latter had formerly been editor of the Rabbinic weekly *Das Wort*. R. Shalom Alter was employed in the ghetto office of labour as assistant to R. Kohen. On the strength of this employment R. Shalom Alter obtained a card which gave him and his wife protection and some form of immunity. In October 1941 the whole

63. R. Oshry, 'Kuntras Me-Emek Ha-Bacha'. See also Garfunkel, *Destruction of Kovno's Jewry*, pp. 64ff.

section of the ghetto was given yellow cards which replaced the white cards in use hitherto. R. Alter and R. Kohen received only one card between them. The problem as to who should keep it was to be solved by casting lots. However, R. Alter objected to the casting of lots and wished to forego his right in favour of R. Kohen, saying that were he to draw the correct lot he would not save his life at the expense of another man. But R. Kohen also refused to cast lots. It seemed that both men would lose a chance of survival. A member of the *Judenrat* intervened and cast the lots and R. Alter was the winner. Unfortunately it did not help him for in spite of holding a yellow card he was seized by the Germans on 24 October 1941 during an action against yellow card holders and both he and his wife were killed.[64]

Cultural activity in the ghetto was rather strong in spite of the fact that it was sometimes carried on amid great difficulties and danger to life.[65] The study of Torah continued notwithstanding a strict order prohibiting it. Sermons and Talmudical discourses were delivered and sometimes written down. Special schools continued to operate underground. They taught Bible and Talmud. Elementary classes for young children were held in the ghettos of Warsaw, Lodz, Kovno and Wilno.

It is well known that the death-rate in the ghetto was very high. In Lodz, we are told, 14,000 Jews died within eighteen months.[66] It is also unbelievable how high the marriage-rate in the ghetto was. In one *Responsum* it is mentioned that the president of the Lodz *Judenrat* Hayyim Rumkowski performed marriages at the rate of twenty to thirty every Sunday.[67] Was this due to the fact that people felt lonely and tried through marriage and companionship to alleviate their grief and sorrow? Or was it because they thought that married couples had better chances of escaping deportation to the death camps? In the Ghetto of Kovno as has been mentioned above it was the Jewish ghetto police force who were entitled to perform (civil) marriages.[68]

The following ghettos are mentioned in the Rabbinic literature: BORYSLAW (BORISLAV), Galicia. A full account on the conditions in this ghetto and the deportations of its inmates is given in a later chapter.[69] CRACOW[70] (KRAKOW), Poland, erected in March 1941.[71] The Rabbi of

---

64. Ungar, *ADMORIM Shenispu Ba-Shoah*, Jerusalem, 1969, pp. 262f.
65. Cf. e.g. *Sepher Esh Kodesh* which contains sermons delivered on Sabbaths and festivals in the Warsaw Ghetto during 1940–42 by R. Kalonymus (Kalmish), who later died a martyr; Oshry, *Mi-Maamakkim*, II, no. 11 and ibid., pp. 177ff. See also Garfunkel, *Destruction of Kovno's Jewry*, p. 133; Moshe Dworzecki 'Jewish Education During the Holocaust' in *Bar Ilan*, IV–V, Jerusalem 1967, pp. 289ff.
66. Reitlinger, *Final Solution*, p. 93. On the Ghetto of Boryslaw, *vide infra* p. 126.
67. *Vide infra* p. 146.
68. *Vide supra* p. 45 and *infra* p. 310.
69. *Vide infra* p. 126.
70. Cf. Rath, *Kol Mebasser*, I, no. 84.
71. Hilberg, *Destruction of European Jews*, p. 148.

Beitsch (Galicia, Poland), whose four children were murdered by the Nazis, escaped with his other children to the Ghetto of Cracow. He tried to save one son by putting him into the care of the orphanage of Cracow where there were about five hundred children. On the 16th Heshvan 703 (27 October 1942) the Nazis fell upon the orphanage killing and burning the children. On *Taanith Esther* 703 (18 February 1942) the ghetto was liquidated and thousands of Jews among them the members of the Beth Din were massacred, the other inmates being sent to the labour camp of Plaszow.[72]

CZERNOWITZ (CERNAUTI, Bukovina, Rumania).[73]

DROHOBYCZ (Galicia, Poland),[74] see Boryslaw. There were two massacres there: one on Sabbath, 25th Ab 702 (8 August 1942) and the other on Wednesday, 10th Heshvan 703 (21 October 1942).

GROSSWARDEIN (Rumania). The ghetto there was erected on 3 May 1944 and the first transport of Jews to Auschwitz took place on 24 May 1944.[75]

KOVNO (Kaunas, Lithuania). The ghetto was in the area of Slobodka and consisted of two parts: 'the Small Ghetto' and 'the Big Ghetto' connected with each other by a wooden bridge. There were about 30,000 inmates among whom there were about ten thousand manual workers.[76] The ghetto was changed by the Nazis into a concentration camp in September 1943.

LENCZYC (Leczyca, Poland).[77] The Rabbi's mother was beaten by a SS Officer and because of that she fell ill and died on 9th Tebet 700 (21 December 1939). As no tombstone could be put up at the grave the Rabbi placed a note inside a bottle with the name and date and buried it in the grave.

LODZ (Litzmannstadt, Poland)[78] was the first ghetto to be set up in April 1940 with more than 200,000 (or, according to another report, 160,000) Jews. It lasted the longest, and was liquidated in September 1944. Deportations (*Aussiedlungen*) from there had taken place

---

72. R. I.B. Halpern, *Mishneh La-Melech,* Introduction, p. 12; see also Helmut Krausnick, 'The Persecution of the Jews', in *Anatomy of the SS State,* London, 1968, p. 118.
73. Cf. R. Shemuel Meir Ha-Kohen Holländer, *Shem Ha-Kohen,* I, Jerusalem, 1952, Introduction. From Czernowitz the Jews were deported to Transnistria (*vide infra* 'Camps').
74. R. J. Avigdor *infra* p. 126; R. Jeruchem in 'Alim Bochim', p. 27, n. 26, Introduction to *Birkath Hayyim.*
75. R. J.J. Weiss, *Minhath Yizhak,* I, pp. 265, 267; II, no. 62.
76. R. Oshry, 'Kuntras Me-Emek Ha-Bacha', R. M.J. Breisch, *Helkath Yaakob,* II, no. 31. (The *Responsa* 'Kuntras Me-Emek Ha-Bacha' and *Mi-Maamakkim* (3 volumes) written by R. E. Oshry, Rabbi in Kovno, deal with cases and problems connected mainly with the Kovno Ghetto.) Garfunkel., *Destruction of Kovno's Jewry.*
77. R. J.M. Aronzon, *Yeshuath Mosheh,* p. 307, n. 52.
78. Breisch, *Helkath Yaakob,* I, no. 18; Meisels, *Binyan Zebi,* II, no. 33; *Mekaddshe Ha-Shem (Shaar Mahmadim),* p. 14; Chief Rabbi I. Herzog, *Hechal Yizhak,* II, no. 84.

already before the erection of the ghetto (4th Tebet 700 = 16 December 1939). Further deportations were arranged by the Germans on 25 August 1944 and 29 September 1944. The president of the *Ältestenrat* was a certain Hayyim Rumkowski, a controversial figure.[79]

MATTERSDORF (Burgenland, Austria).[80]

SAMBOR (Galicia, Poland).[81]

SANOK (Poland).[82]

SLOBODKA, see Kovno.

TARNOW (Galicia).[83]

THERESIENSTADT (Czechoslovakia), an old fortress built in 1780 by the Austrian Emperor Joseph II and named after his mother, the Empress Maria Theresa, was set up as a ghetto for old people and invalid war veterans on 20 January 1942. It was meant to pacify the Jews to show that deportation did not mean death and it also served as a shop window, to Red Cross authorities and newspaper reporters to show that the treatment of the Jews was not bad. In fact Theresienstadt was a transit camp from where people were deported to extermination camps, but many of the inmates died beforehand.[84]

WARSAW (Poland). The ghetto there was the largest; it housed 500,000 Jews. It was established in October 1940. A description of the sadistic attitude of the Germans is given by R. J. J. Weinberg of Berlin who spent some time there, where he was president of the General Rabbinical Association and the Association of the Warsaw Rabbinate.[85] Jews were deported from the ghetto to Maidanek and other extermination camps.[86] The uprising in Warsaw left its imprint in a *Responsum*.[87]

79. Hilberg, *Destruction of European Jews*, p. 148; Krausnick, 'Persecution of the Jews', p. 58; L. Poliakov, *Harvest of Hate*, London, 1956, p. 104; Trunk, *Judenrat*, pp. 8f., 187, 191f., 282, 423, 430ff.; see also *infra* pp. 145f.
80. Rath, *Kol Mebasser*, no. 6.
81. Jeruchem, 'Alim Bochim', p. 25.
82. Aronzon, *Yeshuath Mosheh*, p. 5.
83. Breisch, *Helkath Yaakob*, I, no. 17.
84. See Aronzon, *Yeshuath Mosheh* ('the Jewish town Theresienstadt'); Breisch, *Helkath Yaakob*, I, no. 5. On Theresienstadt, cf. Zdenek Lederer, *Ghetto Theresienstadt*, London, 1953; H. G. Adler, *Theresienstadt 1941–1945*, Tübingen, 1955; Feder, *Terezin*, Prague, 1965. See also *infra* p. 281.
85. *Vide supra* p. 45 and *infra* p. 124 and note 345. On the ghetto, see the diaries by Kaplan, *Scroll of Agony* (translated and edited by Abraham I. Katsh), London, 1966; and by Adam Czerniakow, *Warsaw Ghetto Diary* (ed. by Nachman Blumental, Nathan Eck, Joseph Kermish and Aryeh Tartakower), Jerusalem, 1968.
86. Herzog, *Hechal Yizhak*, I, no. 31. See also Hilberg, *Destruction of European Jews*, p. 148; Poliakov, *Harvest of Hate*, p. 86.
87. R. T. Tabyomi, *Erez Tobah*, I, no. 60.

56 *The Nazi Holocaust*

DEPORTATION

As we have seen deportation was the stage following forced emigration. The first deportation occurred in October 1938, when Jews of Polish nationality were deported to Zbonszyn. The next deportations were those in pursuance of the plan to settle the Jews in eastern Poland to where Jews from Stettin, Czechoslovakia and Vienna had been taken.[88] None of these deportations was intended to be for extermination. They were to serve only as a means to free the Reich of Polish Jews and the annexed territories of Jews in general.

With the decision of the final solution[89] taken at the Wannsee Conference deportation adopted a new meaning, i.e. extermination, to implement the will of the Führer to exterminate the Jewish race.

Deportations are often mentioned in the *Responsa*. There were deportations of Jews to transit camps (in Belgium, France and Holland) or to ghettos. This applies particularly to Jews living in small communities. From there the victims were deported either direct to extermination camps or to labour camps from where they had then to be taken to the extermination camps when they had become unfit for work.

'I was informed,' writes Chief Rabbi Herzog in one *Responsum*,[90] 'that in the first years the Germans used to make an "aktia" immediately, i.e. to carry out an extermination at once. However, much later they changed their method. They used to set up a ghetto in the town first and from there they deported the inmates to the extermination camps where a "selection" took place, who should go to the crematorium and who to labour. (But also with regard to those who had been separated and sent to the right side (for forced labour) there is an assumption (*hazakah*) that the great majority died within a few years.)'[91]

After much discussion which followed the German invasion of Russia (22 June 1941) Göring (fieldmarshal) charged Heydrich (head of the National Security Office, deputy protector of Bohemia and Moravia) with 'bringing about a complete solution of the Jewish question in the German sphere of influence of Europe' (31 July 1941).[92] It was not before 20 January 1942, that Heydrich convened a conference at Am Grossen Wannsee.[93] Even before the Wannsee Conference

88. *Vide supra* p. 42.
89. On the final solution *vide infra*.
90. *Hechal Yizhak*, II, no. 15, p. 65.
91. On deportations *vide infra* Part III, chapter 4.
92. On the text see Manvell and Fraenkel, *Incomparable Crime*, p. 35; Hilberg, *Destruction of European Jews*, p. 262.
93–95. On the final solution and the Wannsee Conference, cf. Hilberg, *Destruction of European Jews*, pp. 264ff.; Reitlinger, *The Final Solution*, pp. 98ff.; Papadatos, *Eichmann Trial*, pp. 8ff.; Hausner, *Justice in Jerusalem*, pp. 93ff.; Manvell and Fraenkel,

deportations (death-marches) of Jews from Germany and Austria began and by November 1941, they had reached the Minsk, Riga and Lodz ghettos which were doomed to destruction.[94] Eventually a criminal plan came into operation. It was the so-called 'Final Solution' to the Jewish question which was tantamount to mass murder—and the complete extermination of the Jewish race.

THE FINAL SOLUTION

The Wannsee Conference had the most tragic consequences for the Jewish people as it amounted to a death-sentence passed on a person by the highest tribunal.[95] The conference was attended by fifteen high-ranking officers representing the most responsible sections of German government. Heydrich who opened the conference spoke of the final solution, i.e. the annihilation of the Jews, which was to include also those of England, Portugal, Turkey, Switzerland, Sweden, Spain and the whole of U.S.S.R.; a total of eleven million Jews. This was to be achieved as follows: the Jews would be deported to the East. The able-bodied would be used for forced labour in road building, the sexes separated, whereby a great number would die from natural causes and the surviving remnant would be 'treated accordingly', because those Jews could rebuild Jewish life should they be allowed to go free. These ominous words showed what the Nazis had in mind by speaking of 'the final solution'.

The final solution was carried out in extermination camps at first by shooting, later by the use of poisonous gases, particularly Zyklon B gas, which proved more efficient. The first method was common also in ghettos.

With the final solution the stage was reached when in general there was no alternative for the Jews but to die.[96] This form of death amounted to the highest degree of piety known as *kiddush ha-Shem*, i.e. death in the sanctification of the Name of God which is the greatest *mizvah* (fulfilment of one's religious duty) incumbent on every Jew.

Maimonides gives the following ruling:[97]

All (members of) the House of Israel are commanded to sanctify this Great Name as it is said 'But I will be hallowed among the children of Israel' (Lev. xxII 32). They are cautioned not to profane it as it is said 'And ye shall not profane My holy Name' (ibid.).

The Incomparable Crime, pp. 45ff.; Morse, *While Six Million Died*, pp. 307f.; Höhne, *Order of the Death's Head*, p. 392; Wiesenthal, *Murderers Among Us*, pp. 232, 297; Krausnick, in *Anatomy of the SS State*, pp. 59ff., 82ff. On the expression 'Final Solution' see Nahman Blumental, 'Le Mishmaatho U-le-Tephuzatho shel Ha-Bittui Ha-Germani "Endlösung der Judenfrage"', in *Jubilee Volume in Honour of Dr N. M. Gelber*, Tel Aviv, 1963, pp. 29. ff.
96. On means of escape, *vide infra*.
97. *Mishneh Torah, Hil. Yesode Ha-Torah*, V, 1ff.

F

How is this *mizvah* to be applied? Should a non-Jew arise and coerce a Jew to violate any of the commandments mentioned in the Torah, otherwise he would kill him, the Jew should transgress (the law) and not be killed as it is said concerning the commandments 'which if a man do, he shall live by them' (ibid. xviii 5), i.e. 'he shall *live* by them and not die by them'. And if he suffered death and did not transgress the law, he himself is responsible for his death.

This applies to all the commandments except the prohibition of idolatry, unchastity and murder. Concerning these three if a Jew is told to transgress one of them otherwise he would be put to death he should suffer death and not commit the transgression. The above distinction applies only if the non-Jew's motive is personal advantage; e.g. if he forces a Jew to build him a house or cook for him on the Sabbath . . . but if his intention is to coerce a Jew to violate the ordinances of his religion, then if this takes place privately and ten Jews are not present, the Jew should commit the transgression and not suffer death. But if the non-Jew forces him to commit the transgression in the presence of ten Jews the Jew should suffer death and not commit it even if the non-Jew's intention was to make the Jew transgress one of the other commandments.

All these rulings apply to a time free from religious persecution. But in the time of a religious persecution . . . when Israel is forced to abolish their religion or one of the precepts then it is the duty of the Jew to suffer death and not violate even any of the other commandments, whether the coercion takes place in the presence of ten Jews or in the presence of non-Jews.

If one is enjoined to transgress and not be put to death and suffers death one is responsible for one's death. If one is enjoined to die and not to commit the transgression and suffers death and did not transgress behold he has sanctified the Name of God. If he does so in the presence of ten Jews he sanctifies the Name in public, like Daniel, Hananiah, Mishael and Azariah and R. Akiba and his colleagues. These are the martyrs above whom no one can rank. About them it is said 'But for Thy sake we are killed all the day; we are accounted as sheep for the slaughter. . . '.

The entire history of the Jewish nation throughout the centuries is but a long chain of such cases of religious persecution and martyrdom. Whenever a Jew suffered martyrdom for his religion rather than save his life by embracing another religion and was put to death Judaism honoured him as a martyr by calling him *Ha-Kadosh* (the holy one) (or in the case of a woman, *Ha-Kedoshah*) adding to his (or her) name, in an abbreviated form, 'H.Y.D.', *Hashem Yinkom Damo* (*Damah*) (may the Lord avenge his (her) blood).

Most cases during the Middle Ages concerned the martyrdom of the Jews either in Roman Catholic or Greek Catholic countries. Baptism and practice of Christianity were required—some action was obligatory in case of conversion.

What is the position of a Jew who could save his life by a mere declaration without any action and yet refused to do so; if he was put to death was he to be regarded as a *Kadosh*? In his *Iggereth Ha-Shemad*[98] Maimonides deals with the persecution under the Almohades when people were forced to acknowledge the supremacy of Mohammed but were not forced to perform any act contrary to the Jewish religion. The Arabs demanded only lip-service and they themselves were aware that the Jews who had said they believed in Mohammed did not really mean it. The Jews were forbidden to observe Jewish practices in public only (but not in secret). Through their declaration of their belief in Mohammed they sought to save their lives. With regard to such persecution Maimonides declares the following: 'If somebody is put to death because he did not express his belief in the mission of Mohammed he has done what is right and good and has a great reward from God. His rank is of the highest among the martyrs. However, if a person comes and enquires whether he should let himself be killed or pay lip-service (literally: acknowledge) we advise him to acknowledge and not to let himself be killed, though he should not remain in that kingdom but should stay indoors until he can leave the country.' Maimonides remarks that 'hitherto we have never heard of such an extraordinary persecution where Jews are not forced to perform any action except make a declaration . . .'.

We who experienced the persecution under the Nazis about 800 years after that by the Almohades can paraphrase Maimonides' words 'we have never heard of such an extraordinary persecution when the Jews were not forced to do any action or make any declaration' to save themselves. During the Nazi persecution being a Jew was sufficient grounds for one's being killed. The very fact that one belonged to the Jewish race made a person die for *kiddush ha-Shem*. Although knowing there was no escape the victims nevertheless proudly bore all humiliations and died like R. Akiba with the *Shema* on their lips. Boys of fourteen years of age recited *viddui* (confession of sin) in front of the gas-chambers together with their fellow-prisoners and sanctified the Name of God.[99]

When led to their execution the Rabbis usually walked in front of

98. 'Iggereth Ha Shemad', in *Iggroth Ha-RMbM*, Mosad Ha-Rav Kook, Jerusalem, 1960 (vol. XX), pp. 61f.

99. See evidence of Nahum Hoch, at the Eichmann trial, session 71 (8.6.61), *infra* p. 119.

their congregants and heroically bore all insults on the way.[100] Here mention should be made of the case of R. Yizhak Zebi Efrati, Rabbi in Glina, who hid with some Jews in a bunker and was discovered by the Germans who led them all to be executed. On the way they sang 'Ani Maamin Be-Biath Ha-Mashiah'.[101] His brother R. Bezalel Efrati had been killed by the Germans beforehand, his prayer-shawl stained with blood being found by his brother R. Simon Efrati, the writer of this report. He had worn it during his execution. In it a letter was wrapped which he had received from R. Yizhak Zebi before the latter was executed. It contained Abravanel's explanation of Num. xxiv 23 that a strong wicked man would arise to whom kings would bend their knees, whose name would begin with the letter 'aleph' and that of his mother with the letter 'lamed'. This he said referred to Hitler whose name (Adolph) began with 'aleph' and whose mother's name (Lotte) began with 'lamed'. 'But in the end he would be defeated and the sunlight would shine upon us.'[102]

It is here that we must mention the heroic stand and self-sacrifice, the *kiddush ha-Shem* of the last three great Rabbis of the Warsaw Rabbinical Council, R. Menahem Ziemba of Praga and his younger colleagues R. Samson Stockhammer and R. David Szapiro. On the morning of 19 April 1943, they were summoned to appear before the head of the Catholic Church in Warsaw. When they arrived they were kept in an antechamber and received the following ultimatum: the Roman Catholic Church had decided to save their lives provided they would leave the ghetto within twenty-four hours. They were given one hour to consider the suggestion. The decision of the Rabbis came from the youngest, R. David Szapiro who maintained that the Jews could not be abandoned. Although no material help could be given to them they should not be left without spiritual encouragement. In view of that the offer of the Church was declined.

The ultimate fate of the three Rabbis is known to us. Only R. David Szapiro survived. R. Samson Stockhammer was killed by an American shell two days before V.E. Day. R. Menahem Ziemba was killed on the fifth day of Passover, 5703, while crossing the road, by a Nazi.[103]

---

100. Much has been written on the noble attitude of the Rabbis. See particularly Ungar, *ADMORIM She-Nispu Ba-Shoah.*

101. Reported by his brother, R. Simon Efrati, *Mi-Ge Ha-Haregah*, no. 3.

102. Efrati, *Mi-Ge Ha-Haregah*, p. 12. Abravanel's explanation is said to be found in his work *Mazmiah Yeshuah*, cap. VII. Unfortunately I was unable to find such an explanation given by Abravanel nor a book with this title. Furthermore, Num. xxiv 23, refers, according to Abravanel (ibid.), to Nebuchadnezzar.

103. R. I. Elfenbein, 'Menahem Ziemba of Praga', in *Guardians of Our Heritage*, ed. by R. L. Jung, New York, 1958, pp. 612ff. On Rabbi Ziemba, see also R. Simhah Elberg in *Elleh Ezkerah*, published by the Research Institute of Religious Jewry, New York, 716, II, pp. 39ff.; *Arim Ve-Immahoth Be-Yisrael*, ed. by R. J. L. Fishman, Jerusalem, 708. vol. III, pp. 276ff.

There were many other cases of Rabbis who refused to forsake their flocks and seek refuge. The Rabbis were frequently the first to be arrested by the invaders.[104] The attitude of the religious leaders when facing the Nazis forms a glorious chapter in the martyrology of our people. It shows that their attitude was by no means different from that of the martyrs of previous centuries. We possess an authentic book written on the Hasidic Rabbis of various dynasties who died martyrs during the Nazi holocaust.[105] The same fate was shared by hundreds of other Rabbis.[106]

The Rabbis bore their humiliations at the hands of the wild soldiery with great dignity. They suffered torture from their tormentors without complaint and often marched to the pits in front of their faithful ones wrapped in prayer-shawls or shrouds to be shot, or to the crematoria chanting 'Shema Yisrael' or 'Ani Maamin Be-Biath Ha-Mashiah'.[107] One author when writing on the bitter end of the members of the Hasidic dynasty of Bojano states: 'The last members of the Bojano dynasty marched from their houses to their death. They walked erect, clad in their best clothes holding the Scrolls of the Law in their hands. Those who stood by, Jews and Christians alike, were deeply moved at this sight.'[108] The greatness of the Rabbis thus became particularly apparent in times of distress and danger. Little wonder such an attitude made a great impact on the Jews and exerted a strong influence on their co-religionists.

How great this influence was on the masses can be seen from the questions put to the Rabbis. Thus one Jew asked the Rabbi for the correct version of the benediction one should recite when about to sanctify the Name of God. When the Rabbi told him the version he memorized it and taught his fellow inmates the benediction.[109]

Even those who either had been baptized and thus were able to live among non-Jews or had long since lost any connection with Judaism were deeply moved and 'returned to the fold' willing to share the fate of their Jewish brethren. This is illustrated in the following two *Responsa*.

Immediately the Germans had entered Lithuania on 28th Sivan 701 (23 June 1941) they began to torture and massacre the Jews. Among their first victims was a family of whom the husband and his wife were

104. On this and on what follows see Ungar, *ADMORIM She-Nispu Ba-Shoah*, pp. 34, 152, 243, 244; Mordecai Eliab, *Ani Maamim*, p. 19.
105. Ungar, *ADMORIM She-Nispu Ba-Shoah*.
106. Cf. e.g. Hillel Seidmann, *Ishim She Hikkarthi*, Jerusalem, 1970; see also *supra* notes 100, 101, 104.
107. See Ungar, *ADMORIM She-Nispu Ba-Shoah*, pp. 11, 34f., 227, 259; Eliab, *Ani Maamin*, pp. 14, 18f.; Efrati, *Mi-Ge Ha-Haregah*, p. 12.
108. Nathan Getzler, 'Tagebücher aus Czernowitz und Transnistrien', in *Geschichte der Juden in der Bukovina*, ed. by Hugo Gold, II, p. 57.
109. See R. Oshry, *Mi-Maamakkim*, II, no. 4.

killed on the same day. They left a son aged sixteen who was saved by their gentile maid who hid him. Having in mind what had happened to his parents and entire family he lived in constant fear of being handed over to the Germans. When after a long time she was unable to hide him any longer fearing her action might be made known to the Germans she took the young man to the local priest who baptized him. The lad was then 'safe' and could live in peace among the non-Jews.

However, in his heart a terrible struggle raged which gave him no rest as he remembered the fate of his parents and of his people. One day he left his 'home' and came to Kovno Ghetto wishing to share the fate of his fellow-Jews even if it meant dying with them. He repented the sin he had committed by living among non-Jews and behaving like one of them and regretted it deeply.

R. E. Oshry was asked whether the young man could be counted in the quorum for public prayer and, as he was a *kohen*, whether he could be called up to the Torah first and recite the priestly blessing. Both questions were answered in the affirmative.

The young man shared the fate of all inmates of the ghetto; when it was liquidated in 1944 he was killed with all the others.[110]

There was a family in Kovno which had assimilated to such an extent that there was no difference between them and non-Jews. As they tried by all means to sever the bond between themselves and Judaism they did not even circumcise their son. However, when in 1941 the Germans issued a decree that all those left alive had to leave Kovno and be shut up in the ghetto in the area of Slobodka this family too had to move there. The head of the family was killed cruelly and his wife and children had to share the bitter fate of all other inmates of the ghetto. Their fate was tragic, as they felt the humiliation severely. They asked themselves, 'why are we smitten? Are we not like our Christian neighbours?' This question stirred their son who was uncircumcised and created in him so strong an affection for his unfortunate people that he earnestly wished to be one of them. It exercised his mind: if in my death I am not separated from my people and my fate is like theirs why should I be apart from them during my lifetime? Why should I not have the seal of Abraham on my body? These thoughts impelled him to be circumcised. Unfortunately there was no observant *mohel* in the ghetto to circumcise the man, who was about twenty-seven years old, but only a Jewish doctor who used to desecrate the Sabbath in public. R. Oshry was asked whether this doctor could perform the circumcision as time was pressing and the young man was very anxious to be accepted in the covenant of Abraham. The Rabbi permitted the doctor

110. Ibid., no. 2.

to perform the operation as it was a time of great emergency 'people being taken out daily to be killed and the young man was crying bitterly saying if he is to die he wished to die for *kiddush ha-Shem* like all his brethren . . .'.[111]

To these lovers of Judaism the saying of the Talmud (*Ab. Zarah* 18a) applies: 'It is possible for one to acquire one's world (to come) in one hour.' When one Rabbi expressed some doubts as to the fitness of witnesses in a matrimonial matter (following the war) another Rabbi retorted, 'In our days, a time of general extermination, when many of the martyrs gave their lives for *kiddush ha-Shem* by reciting *viddui* and died with the "Shema" on their lips one must not have such fears'.[112]

While the term *kiddush ha-Shem* retained its original meaning viz. martyrdom for the sake of God, the attitude required of the victims towards their tormentors differed in the Nazi era. We possess two most interesting reports to this effect. One of them reminds us of the meeting which took place in the Upper Chamber of Nitzeh in the time of the persecution following the Bar Kochba uprising where the Sages discussed the question of one's attitude in the time of the persecution and took a vote afterwards on it.[113] We hear of a similar meeting which took place concerning the attitude of the Jews towards the Nazis. On 14 January 1943, the communal leaders assembled in the record office of Warsaw to decide what action should be taken in view of the imminent catastrophe. Among those present was the famous Rabbi and scholar R. Menahem Ziemba of Praga. After some discussion R. Menahem gave the following decision:[114]

We must resist the enemy on all fronts. We shall no longer heed his instructions. Henceforth we must refuse to wend our way to the *Umschlagplatz*, which is but a blind and a snare—a veritable stepping-stone on the road to mass annihilation. . . . As it is now, we have no choice but to resist. We are prohibited by Jewish law from betraying others nor may we deliver ourselves into the hands of our arch-enemy. . . . Sanctification of the Divine Name manifests itself in varied ways. Indeed, its special form is a product of the times we live in. During the First Crusade, at the end of the eleventh century, *Halachah*—as an echo of political events of the time—had determined one way of reacting to the distress of the Franco-German Jews, whereas in the middle of the twentieth century, during the rapid

111. Ibid., I, no. 8.
112. Breisch, *Helkath Yaakob*, I, no. 21.
113. *Sanhedrin* 74a.
114. Elfenbein, 'Menahem Ziemba of Praga', pp. 611f.

liquidation of the Jews in Poland, *Halachah* prompts us to react in
an entirely different manner. In the past during religious persecutions,
we were required by the law 'to give up our lives even for the least
essential practice'. In the present, however, when we are faced by an
arch-foe, whose unparalleled ruthlessness and total annihilation
purposes know no bounds, *Halachah* demands that we fight and resist
to the very end with unequalled determination and valour for the
sake of sanctification of the Divine Name.

> At once all debates ended. The Gaon of Praga had the final say.
> The *pesak-din* of the Warsaw Beth Din, issued in 1943 . . . was
> unanimously accepted by Polish Jewry. *Kiddush ha-Shem* is more
> than a free-will offering of the select few above. It is the paramount
> duty . . . incumbent upon all of us.

In the second report a distinction is made by R. Yizhak Nissenbaum
of Warsaw (who later died a martyr) in an address to his fellow inmates
of the ghetto. We are told that:

> Addressing his fellow victims in the ghettos he (Rabbi Nissenbaum)
> said that the *mizvah* of *kiddush ha-Shem* has different meanings in
> different ages. During the Middle Ages the *mizvah* required martyr-
> dom. Why? The enemy wanted to conquer the souls of Jews. He had
> no intention of massacring—only of converting to Christianity.
> Therefore Jews were to frustrate him by making it impossible for
> him to achieve his purpose. If Jews committed suicide, or allowed
> themselves to be slaughtered, they thereby made it impossible for the
> enemy to capture the souls of our people. However, Hitler and his
> cohorts wanted to destroy the Jewish body—to annihilate us
> physically. The *mizvah* of *kiddush ha-Shem*, therefore, required that
> he be frustrated by our survival. Jews should do everything—by
> flight or bribery—to live.[115]

Indeed the will to survive even under the most terrible conditions is,
as we shall see later, one of the characteristic features of the Jews of the
east European countries under the Nazi heel.[116]

In the same way as those who were led to the gas-chambers sanctified
the Divine Name so did those who fought for their survival in order to
frustrate the enemy's plan of total extermination.

115. Rabbi Dr Emanuel Rackman, 'The New "Jerusalem Programme"', in *Dispersion
and Unity*, no. 11, Jerusalem, 1970, quoted in *Jewish Review*, 31 March 1971, p. 6. On
Rabbi Nissenbaum, see also *Arim Ve-Immahoth,* etc., III, pp. 278ff.; *Elleh Ezkerah*,
I, pp. 309ff.

116. *Vide infra* on the difference between the Polish and the German Jews in their attitude
towards suicide.

ESCAPE FROM NAZI PERSECUTION

There were many Jews who tried to escape the Nazis by various means: entering neighbouring countries (Switzerland, Hungary, Rumania) illegally, or fleeing to Russia or into the woods of Poland and joining the partisans; hiding in bunkers; change of identity, and committing suicide.

Entering neighbouring countries illegally, fleeing to Russia or into the woods of Poland and joining the partisans

Illegal immigration which was already hazardous before the war became more perilous after fighting had started and various countries had been occupied by the Germans. Sometimes the escape proved fatal. A typical example is the following.

A young man from France left the country with his young wife who was twenty-two years old and their baby for Switzerland in Tebeth 5703 (December to January 1942–43) because of the German occupation. Whilst wandering through the high mountains they suffered from the cold and became very tired. The wife went on a little ahead to seek a place of shelter for the child. The husband with the baby in his arms sat down on a stone to rest. When after a while his wife did not return he began to shout fearing that something may have happened to her. The shouts were heard by the Swiss frontier guards who came to him and were informed what had happened. They went out to look for her; however, no trace could be found as on that day much snow fell covering the mountains and valley. The husband and child succeeded in entering Switzerland and were admitted to the refugee camp but nothing was known of the fate of his wife, despite a thorough search by mountain guides for a corpse. It was only in the following Sivan (June 1943) that a corpse was found. The authorities informed the husband immediately who went to identify her. However, because of his great distress he was unable to look at the body. He identified only her garments, the bracelet and ring she wore and her coat which was lying nearby. He asked the persons standing near him to see whether fifty dollars could be found sewn in the coat. Indeed these were; however, they had rotted from the damp. The authorities who had a photograph of the woman maintained that the photograph was that of the corpse. They assumed she had slipped while descending from the mountain near a river and had broken her arms. She was later covered by snow. According to the Swiss authorities the husband was registered as a widower.

The question was whether the husband might re-marry. Although he did not wish to do so then because of his great distress and could find no comfort, his relatives, however, wished to have the Rabbi's decision should the young man change his mind. Furthermore, they wanted to know whether a tombstone should be erected, etc.

After a lengthy discussion the Rabbi decided that the husband could re-marry, a tombstone ought to be erected and *kaddish* recited.[117]

The escape from the Nazi hell was in some cases made possible by illegally crossing the frontiers to Hungary, Rumania, etc., by bribing officials and non-Jews acting as guides.[118] While the *mizvah* of redeeming prisoners is regarded in Jewish law as the greatest merit,[119] helping to escape the Nazis was considered higher still. This can be seen from the following decision given by the Rabbi of Belz on saving Jewish lives.[120]

On his miraculous escape[121] from Poland to Palestine during the war the most famous 'Belzer Rav and Zaddik,' R. Aharon Rokah arrived in Hungary on the 14th of Iyyar 703 (19 May 1943) and stayed in Ungvar. On the 33rd day of the (Counting of the) Omer (23 May 1943) he reached Budapest where he stayed until the 21st of Tebet 704 (17 January 1944) when he left for the Holy Land. It was before his departure that leaders of the community assembled in the house of the *askan* (communal worker) R. Hayyim Rath to discuss assistance to refugees. There the 'Belzer Rav' announced the following decision which was to be put into practice (*le-halachah ve-la-maaseh*):

In normal times one must set aside one tenth of one's wealth for charity,[122] and even if a person wishes to spend liberally for charity he should not spend more than one fifth of his wealth.[123] Furthermore, concerning the ransom of captives our Sages decreed that they should not be ransomed for more than their value.[124] These laws applied when they affected only individuals, and when captive Jews were regarded by their captors as human beings of equal standing

117. Breisch, *Helkath Yaakob*, no. 146. The unoccupied zone of France was seized by the Germans on 11 November 1942.
118. On refugees in Hungary, see Introduction to *Yerushath Peletah;* Livia Rothkirchen, 'Hungary—An Asylum for the Refugees in Europe', in *Yad Vashem Studies*, VII, Jerusalem, 1968, pp. 127ff. On crossing the borders into Rumania with the help of paid guides and bribery, see R. Aharon Zimetbaum 'Maaseh Nissim', in *Dibre Pinhas*, pp. 173ff.; Weiss, 'Pirsume Nissa', in *Minhath Yizhak*, I, pp. 270f.; on boats from Bucharest to Palestine and the loss of one boat, see ibid., p. 272.
119. Maimonides, *Mishneh Torah, Hil. Mathnoth Aniyyim*, VIII, 10; *Shulhan Aruch Yoreh Deah*, cap. CCLII, no. 1.
120. 'Derech Kedoshim' in *Ha-Derech*, ed. by A. Lebowitsh, no. 1, Budapest, Adar 704 (February-March 1944), p. 22, and at length ibid., pp. 11ff.
121. On the Rabbi's escape see the report taken from Mosheh Yehezkieli, 'Hazzalath Ha-Rabbi Mi-Belz Mi-Ge Ha-Haregah' in *Beth Jacob*, no. 4, Jerusalem, Ellul, 715, p. 9, nos. 15–16, Ab-Ellul, 720, pp. 17 ff.; Ungar, *ADMORIM She-Nispu Ba-Shoah*, p. 255 referring to Nathan Ortner, *Debar Hen*, Tel Aviv, 1963.
122. See *Tosaphoth* on *Taanith* 9a *s.v. asser*, quoting *Sifre; Shulhan Aruch, Yoreh Deah*, cap. CCXLIX, no. 1; R. Joseph Hahn, *Yosiph Omez*, pp. 306ff.
123. *Kethuboth* 50a; *Beth Yoseph* and Isserles on *Shulhan Aruch, loc. cit.*
124. *Kethuboth*, 52b; *Gittin* 45a, in order to discourage the captors from capturing people.

(*shivvui ha-erech*) but who were in captivity suffering affliction. Therefore they had to be redeemed for a price equal to their value. Even in the Middle Ages when people were savage and lacked culture the captives could still live though amid difficulties and had to bear their yoke. But nowadays when 'culture' has spread and 'civilization' 'enlightened' the world, when human rights are trampled down, when Jews are not sold as slaves but led like sheep to the slaughter-house, when young children are taken to the gas chambers and furnaces and millions of Jews die martyrs . . . when it is a time of trouble affecting the whole of Israel, when the captives are constantly in danger of life and limb these laws do not apply. In such a time of danger every person is compelled to spend even his entire wealth to save lives and rescue families. As one would give away all one's possessions to save one's own life so one is bound to act likewise for every Jewish life. Moreover, one would not fulfil one's duty by spending one's own wealth alone—one must endeavour by all personal effort to try and save Jews from destruction and danger of annihilation which hovers over them at every moment. For that reason do hurry and hasten to help . . . .

We must now mention those *Responsa* which deal with the Jews who tried to escape the Nazis by fleeing to Russia (where one even joined the Red Army) or by joining the partisans or by being sheltered by Christians.

Although the refugees had to suffer much in Russia often being sent to Siberia or other places where they lived under difficult conditions at least they knew they were spared the cruelties and massacres their brethren in German captivity had to suffer. We are even told that when after the Germans had occupied Warsaw and began maltreating the Jews R. Yerahmiel Taub was asked by his young Hasidic followers whether they may flee from the ghetto to the Russian side where they would have to profane the Sabbath and eat non-kosher food. He replied that they may do so. He himself did not wish to leave the ghetto so that he could remain with the other Jews. He was later sent to Treblinka (1942) where he died a martyr after his whole family had been exterminated by the Germans.[125]

The following are practical instances of flights to escape the Germans.

In a letter of 22nd of Sivan 711 (26 June 1951)[126] addressed to R. Shlomoh Schleifer, Chief Rabbi of Moscow, Chief Rabbi Herzog of

---

125. Cf. Ungar, *ADMORIM She-Nispu Ba-Shoah* p. 94.
126. Herzog, *Hechal Yizhak,* II, no. 13.

Israel asked him for his help in the following matter (this case had been submitted to him by R. Unterman, Chief Rabbi of Tel Aviv-Jaffa):

In the year 1940 Mrs. R. K. and her children had been saved by the Russians and brought to Siberia. Her husband entered the Russian army. In 1945 the woman received official information from the Russian authorities that her husband was missing or had been lost without any trace at the front of Tiraspol in 1942. She says that all the time she had been in Russia she had received a widow's pension. She has since emigrated to Israel. A worthy proposal of marriage had recently been made to this unfortunate woman. She approached the Beth Din (in Tel Aviv) in tears for sympathy. The Chief Rabbi of Tel Aviv, R. I. J. Unterman, seeing that from the *halachic* point of view granting permission for re-marriage would be very difficult and sincerely wishing to help her turned to the Chief Rabbinate of Israel in Jerusalem for a solution. Thereupon Chief Rabbi Herzog wrote to Chief Rabbi Schleifer as follows:

'Will you, our friend and learned Rabbi, seek the Government's good-will in helping this unfortunate woman by replying to the following questions: (1) Has it yet been clarified that the husband was killed in the battle or is he still assumed to be "lost" or "missing"? (2) Is it possible he may still be alive and could be traced? If so, could you, most learned Rabbi, arrange for him, if he cannot come to Israel, to write a *get* and forward it to us or send us an authorization for the writing of the *get* which would be carried out in Tel Aviv? (3) Perhaps there exists a record in the military archives of the battle in Tiraspol in 1942 stating that most soldiers among them the husband of the above-mentioned woman had been killed. This is an important point which would be of special value in our case.'

Earlier in his reply to Chief Rabbi Unterman, Chief Rabbi Herzog tells him of his intention to write to the Chief Rabbi of Moscow (as he had done once before with success). 'And it is not improbable that Heaven will grace us that the Russian authorities will be willing to reply to the Chief Rabbi of Moscow as to any definite information on the death or whereabouts of the husband. When we receive such a reply I shall agree with your consent and with that of your Beth Din to permit the woman to re-marry. Should it, however, turn out that the husband may still be alive then we shall endeavour (to contact him if it is impossible to bring him here) to make him send a *get* or an authorization to write a *get*. If they (the Russian authorities) refuse to reply for whatever reason then we shall act wisely and consider the matter. In any case, we shall be considerate and try to relieve her from her unfortunate situation. May God have mercy upon our sister and take her forth from darkness to light. . . .'

A young man who was the *hazzan* (reader) of the local synagogue, approached his Rabbi asking for permission to re-marry.[127] He gave him the following story:

During the great massacre of 1941 he fled from Riga (Latvia) together with his wife and three of his children to escape death 'at the hands of the German murderers'. They headed for a town which was under Russian rule. *En route* they became faint and weary and could walk no further. They saw a carriage with Russian soldiers passing and asked for assistance. The soldiers permitted only the wife and children to board their carriage but not the man. The latter, although he felt it very difficult to part with his wife and children, nevertheless agreed that they go with the Russians. During all his wanderings until that day all his endeavours to trace his family had been in vain. All the societies whom he approached for assistance replied that they had no information concerning his wife and children. Seven years had elapsed since he had last seen them. He was lonely and still young and sought permission from the Beth Din to re-marry. The Rabbi replied that in his view re-marriage was permitted.

There are several cases mentioned in the *Responsa* of men and women who escaped the Nazis and were sheltered by Christians, with whom they later associated. Some men joined the partisans; women had in a few cases to pay with honour—this raised problems after the war. In one *Responsum*[128] we are told of a young man who had become engaged to marry a girl who had been brought up in an orthodox institution. However, before the marriage he learned that her mother was a proselyte and for this reason he wished to terminate the engagement, since he regarded marrying such a girl a disgrace to his family.

After some investigation it was discovered that her father had been a partisan who in the Nazi period had hidden in the woods of Poland. Her mother was a non-Jewess who had endangered her life to save him by providing him daily with food during those years. After the liberation they had lived as husband and wife after a civil marriage. On their emigration to Israel they stayed in a refugee camp and the woman who was pregnant, together with a young child embraced Judaism. They conducted themselves as strictly religious Jews keeping the Sabbath, observing the dietary laws and family purity. The children received a religious education. It appears that as far as the fiancée is concerned she was certainly conceived while her mother was still a gentile. She had, however, received a strict religious education and to that day did not know that her mother was a proselyte. The governess of the

---

127. R. S. M. Levin, *Minhath Shelomoh*, I, no. 53.
128. Aronzon, *Yeshuath Mosheh*, no. 66.

institution maintained that she had given the fiancé some vague indication before the *tenaim* (engagement contracts) were written that there were grounds for apprehension. However, he claimed he did not understand its significance.

The Rabbi decided that there was no question of discredit to the man, who was not a *kohen*, or to his family.

A young girl named 'Rachel Kohen' of Smyrna was in Belgium during the war and among those ordered to be expelled. To avoid expulsion which entailed danger to life, she had no alternative but to become the mistress[129] of a Belgian Christian (without any civil or religious ceremony). She gave birth to a boy whose father died in hospital in Elisabethville. The civil authorities knew the woman under the name of Rachel Kohen and regarded her son as a child born out of wedlock. His mother wished him to be circumcised and brought up according to traditional Judaism. R. Benzion Uzziel,[130] Sephardi Chief Rabbi of Israel, shows us that a child born of a Jewish mother and non-Jewish father is a Jew, but can claim no priestly privileges through his mother (who came from a priestly family). In order to avoid his being regarded as such, he should not be called 'Kohen' but 'Israel'.

Hiding in Bunkers

Some Jews tried to escape the Nazis by going into hiding in underground shelters or bunkers. They could go out only when there was no danger of being discovered.[131] Sometimes a non-Jewish friend helped.[132]

The fear of discovery was great. R. Meir Meiri (Feuerwerger) who for two years (1942–44) was in hiding writes:[133]

Those who were in the camps did not suffer as much as those who were in hiding, in caves or in cellars. For the inmates of the camps were already in the hands of the enemy and had come to terms with death. Those, however, who were outside the camps fought a great inner battle, every moment they were in fear and despair. Indeed, it happened very often that people could no longer live under such terrible stress and handed themselves over to the demons (*malache habbalah*, angels of destruction) or committed suicide.

---

129. For other cases see Oshry, *Mi-Maamakkim*, II, nos. 24, 25.
130. *Mishpete Uzziel*, Y.D., I, no. 45.
131. Weiss, *Minhath Yizhak*, I, no. 92.
132. Cf. e.g. R. M. Steinberg in his Introduction to *Mahazeh Abraham*, 2nd Part p. 5; Zimetbaum, 'Maase Nissim' in *Responsa Dibre Pinhas*, p. 171; Oshry, *Mi-Maamakkim*, III, no. 8.
133. *Ezrath Nashim*, I, p. 8.

R. Meiri tells us of a narrow escape he had when he was one day alone in the house and suddenly heard the door-bell ringing which could only have been done by the Nazis. As there was no reply they broke down the door and went from room to room searching for people. They had opened the door of the adjacent room and the Rabbi standing in prayer thought he would soon be in their hands. How great was his surprise that they had overlooked the door and entrance to his room. He had taken upon himself to perpetuate this in a book and to thank God in public for his salvation. 'And now I have fulfilled the vow I made at the time of distress.'[134]

A Rabbi who himself spent some time hiding in a bunker deals with an *agunah* (a woman whose husband disappeared) in one *Responsum*. The circumstances of the case illustrate the conditions.

It was submitted to R. I.J.Weiss by R. Hayyim Meir Hager of Vischnitz[135] and concerned an *agunah* who was young and anxious to marry and had met a man willing to marry her. However, *halizah* (cf. Deut. xxv 5ff.) was still required. Her levir was at that time in another country but could still perform *halizah*. If the matter were to be delayed the levir might leave for a place where the performance of *halizah* would be impossible and his sister-in-law would remain an *agunah* all her life. Furthermore according to the assertion of her relatives she might marry illicitly without *halizah*. Because of that it was a great *mizvah* (meritorious deed) to deal with the matter as soon as possible.

Evidence: R. Mosheh Wiesel of Apse came before us when the court (Beth Din of Grosswardein) was in session. He was the paternal uncle of Sarah, daughter of R. Eliyahu Yehudah and wife of R. Israel Glück of Apse and gave the following evidence:

'He was in Pest during the persecution in "Védett Ház" (Shelter House). He feared he might be taken by the Nyilaases[136] to the ghetto. Therefore the son-in-law of his brother (i.e. Israel Glück) sent for him to come to the bunker in Benczur Street. There were two bunkers at a distance of about fifty metres apart. In the bunker where his brother's son-in-law was there was no room for more than the six persons already there. In view of that the nephew placed his uncle (i.e. the witness) in the other bunker and promised to visit him every night and to look after him and provide him with food. This he did on the first night. The former visited him and cooked his supper there, as in his bunker there was no facility for cooking. On the second

---

134. Ibid., p. 9.
135. Weiss, *Minhath Yizhak*, I, no. 92.
136. Members of the Arrow Cross party, the Hungarian Nationalist party, see Reitlinger, *Final Solution*, pp. 456, 479f., 486; Hausner, *Justice in Jerusalem*, pp. 133, 152.

night, however, the uncle waited in vain, so did the other inmates of
the bunker who had expected their friends to visit them. They did not
come the following night either. The inmates of the bunker sent a
messenger to bring some news. He found the other bunker empty.
There was no one there, only some clothes with papers in them and
the purse belonging to the son-in-law of R. Wiesel's brother. The
supper (which had been cooked in the other bunker and brought
from there) was still untouched. When afterwards the inmates of the
second bunker had no food they sent a messenger to buy some bread.
It took about two days until he returned full of fear and reported
what had happened to him. He had been caught by the murderous
Nyilaases who, it is well known, caught hundreds and thousands of
Jews in those days and took them to the Danube where they were
killed and thrown into the water. The messenger too was taken there.
He was tied with a rope together with other men; however, the rope
was not strong enough and broke. He was therefore able to escape
and ran straight to the bunker and gave them an account. He reported
to his fellow inmates that he had overheard the murderers talking to
each other secretly that they had caught six persons in the bunker in
Benczur Street and killed them. The above-mentioned witness said that
he was well acquainted with Benczur Street and knew exactly that
apart from these two bunkers there was no other. There were only
the bunker in which he was and the bunker occupied by the son-in-law
with five others. From that time on nothing was heard of those six
people. Furthermore, his brother's son-in-law was a very able man
who had he been alive would have been able to escape from wherever
he was being held. Moreover, he was happily married. The witness
added that the city of Pest was at that time surrounded on all sides
so that no one could come or leave.[137] The enemy took no Jews outside
the city.

The above evidence was given on Thursday *Parashath Noah* (4th
Heshvan) 706 (11 October 1945) in Grosswardein.

Rabbi Weiss permitted the young Sarah Glück to re-marry provided
she would go through all formalities including *halizah*. His view was
shared by another Rabbi.[138]

Another tragic case involved a young baby. Many Jews were hiding
in a bunker to escape death. During one of the searches organized by
the evildoers a child in the bunker began to cry. It was impossible to

---

137. Soviet troops surrounded Budapest on 24 December 1944. On 18 January 1945, Pest
   was liberated and on 12 February 1945 Buda (the section of the capital on the right
   bank of the Danube) was liberated. For the dates see Jenö Levai, *Hungarian Jewry and
   the Papacy*, p. 119.

138. See Weiss, *Minhath Yizhak*, I, no. 92.

quieten it. Had it been heard outside the bunker all the Jews hiding there would have been arrested and killed. The question arose whether it was permitted to place a pillow over the baby's mouth to quieten it, an action which would have caused its death. Before it was decided someone placed a pillow over the child's mouth. When the Germans had passed it was removed. The child had been smothered. The Rabbi[139] questions whether such action was justified from the religious point of view in order to save the other Jews hiding in the bunker and whether the man who caused the death, albeit unwittingly, need make atonement. The Rabbi states that those who had objected to the placing of the pillow over the child's mouth did indeed sanctify the Name of God, but the man who smothered the baby needed no atonement since he had acted in accordance with the law to save the lives of many persons.

The same Rabbi tells us of a similar case in Glina where his brother R. Yizhak Zebi Efrati, who was Rabbi there, and his family were hiding in a bunker and during a search a baby began to cry. The Rabbi, who used to encourage his congregants not to despair quoting the saying of the Talmud 'Even when a sharp sword is lying over a man's throat he should not refrain from seeking mercy (from God)' (*Berachoth* 10a), had to decide whether to smother the baby in order to save his family. He did not hesitate for one moment to forbid anyone doing so. Consequently all of them were discovered by the Germans who led them away to be massacred. They went to their fate (*akedah*) with great and wonderful devotion chanting the song of the hope for redemption: 'Though he (the Messiah) tarry, nevertheless I do believe.'[140]

A tragic case of smothering a baby was reported some time ago in the Jewish and non-Jewish press.[141] It was in the year 1943 when forty-seven Jews were hiding in a village of Dolhinov near Vilno in a bunker. Among them was Joseph Kramer (the builder of the bunker), his wife and eighteen-month old son David. The Germans were hunting down the Jews in the village shooting them on sight. When the Germans approached the hideout the child began to cry. After fruitless attempts to stop the baby crying he smothered the child to save the others. They indeed escaped death and some of them joined the partisans and a number eventually reached Israel. The tragic action of the father gave him no rest ever since. Some time ago—twenty-nine years after the event—a *Sepher Torah* was presented to the suburban synagogue of Ramath Yoseph in Bath Yam (Israel) in memory of the child. The presentation was made in front of a large congregation among them former occupants of the bunker. When the scroll was

---

139. Efrati, *Mi-Ge Ha-Haregah*, no. 1.
140. Ibid. no. 3.
141. See *Ha-Zopheh*, 13th of Kislev, 732 (1 December 1971), p. 6; *Jewish Chronicle*, 10 December 1971, p. 4; *Evening News*, London, 2 December 1971, p. 7.

G

placed in the holy ark the father broke down and wept recalling the tragic dilemma he once had to face.

Two other cases of smothering babies occurred during an 'action' in Warsaw on 19 January 1943, and in Kovno on 27 March 1944.[142]

Change of identity

In their despair many Jews tried to save themselves by changing their identity. This was done by (a) change of name; (b) baptism; (c) acquiring certificates of baptism without having been baptized; (d) acquiring certificates with the initials 'R.K.' (*Römisch Katholisch*); (e) acquiring Aryan certificates; and (f) declaring onself a Karaite.

(a) Change of name

Some Jews obtained forged papers with non-Jewish names and were able to live freely and to avoid persecution. One Rabbi even relates that he and the members of his family had each two passports: one made out in German names and another in names of non-Jews from Hungary. He brought over Jews from Poland to Hungary under non-Jewish names. However, once on being asked whether he was a Jew or not, he replied he was a Jew and was taken to a camp near Budapest but was later released.[143]

Many Jews went to live with their non-Jewish friends, changed their names and pretended to be Christians. It happened that after the liberation some did not want to return to their former status and to their wives.[144]

Women were often saved by pretending to be Christians and taking up service in non-Jewish households. One woman was for years employed in Bergen-Belsen[145] and two women pretending to be Polish were maidservants even in the houses of Nazis.[146] One of them afraid that the shape of her nose would betray her as a Jewess performed an 'operation' on her nose with a crude knife.[147]

Cases of changing one's identity occurred in many countries under the Nazis. When Italy was about to enter the war some Jews tried to conceal their identity from the authorities. When the Germans entered Italy some Jews pretended to be Christians and were thereby saved.[148]

142. See Wdowinski, *And We Are Not Saved*, p. 87; Garfunkel, *Destruction of Kovno's Jewry*, pp. 178f.
143. Zimetbaum, 'Maase Nissim', pp. 165, 170.
144. Efrati, *Mi-Ge Ha-Haregah*, no. 13.
145. T.J. Tabyomi, *Erez Tobah*, I Jerusalem, 1947, no. 61.
146. Efrati, *Me-Emek Ha-Bacha*, Jerusalem, 1948, no. 8. One woman a member of a famous Rabbinic family 'was in the service of a wicked Nazi in Germany for several years', R. Joseph Thumim, *Nehamath Yoseph*, Introduction, New York, 1950, p. 5.
147. Efrati, *Me-Emek Ha-Bacha*, no. 8.
148. See Breisch, *Helkath Yaakob*, I, nos. 6, 17; Herzog, *Hechal Yizhak* II, nos. 71ff., 88f.; Efrati, *Mi-Ge Ha-Haregah*, no. 13.

In this connection mention should be made of the following questions discussed by one Rabbi in the Kovno Ghetto from the religious point of view. Is it permitted to flee to Christian clergymen and to live with them as a non-Jew, to act only outwardly as a Christian, e.g. to wear a cross and to attend church, etc.? Is that considered as acknowledging the non-Jewish faith (*ke-modeh be-AKUM*)?[149]

May a Jew flee to a non-Jew and work for him and tell him he was a non-Jew and conduct himself as a Christian in the matters mentioned before?[150]

Is it permitted to hand over children to non-Jews to be looked after until the end of the war and Hitler's defeat as it is doubtful whether their parents will survive? The children might then remain with the non-Jews and follow their way of life.[151]

(b) Baptism

Although according to the Nuremberg laws baptism did not change the status of a Jew we can see that Jews in various countries embraced Christianity hoping through such action to avoid the miseries which befell their former co-religionists. While the Catholic Church was reluctant to accept such converts[152] the other Churches accepted the newcomers although they were aware that the conversion was not motivated by sincere conviction of the truth of the Christian faith.[153] Sometimes the change of religion proved of benefit to the converts. Much light on such conversions is shed in the following *Responsum*.

On the 21st of Ellul, 702 (3 September 1942) the Rabbi of Neutra (Nitra, Slovakia), R. Samuel David Ha-Levi Ungar, inquired of R. Simhah Nathan Grünberg, Rabbi of Kezmark, what attitude he should adopt towards those who abandoned the Jewish religion, i.e. by renouncing it completely or by obtaining certificates of baptism. What should happen if their wives or children did so in order to protect their parents? What is the position of those parents: have they to be

---

149–150. The Rabbi (R. E. Oshry, 'Kuntras Me-Emek Ha-Bacha' in *Dibre Ephraim*, no. 3) replied that a Jew may flee to non-Jews and work for them in order to save his life. He may not follow Christian practices (i.e. to perform an action, 'kum va-aseh', e.g. wearing a cross etc.) or say he was a Christian. He may only give the appearance of being a non-Jew by remaining passive.
151. Oshry, *Dibre Ephraim*, no. 5, who shows that there are reasons for adopting a lenient view. It is of interest that the Jews hoped that Hitler would soon be defeated. The question is dated: 'During the massacre, 3–4 Nisan 704 (27–28 March 1944) in Kovno'. See also Garfunkel, *Destruction of Kovno's Jewry*, pp. 181f. On the date see p. 80. On a similar attempt to save children following the *Kinderaktion* in the Ghetto of Shavli, see ibid., pp. 152ff.
152. But see Johan M. Snoek, *The Grey Book*, Assen, 1969, p. 26 (concerning the Jews in Slovakia). For the reluctance of the Catholic Church towards baptism, see Hilberg, *Destruction of European Jews*, p. 466.
153. Ibid.

kept distant from any matter connected with religion (*dabar she-bi-kedushah*) or not? Are they fit to be appointed to any communal office and is one allowed to marry such people?

The Rabbi deals at first with the question of the person who had renounced his religion, whether he should be regarded as having been forced by circumstances or as a proper disbeliever.

> The position of the Jews nowadays is well known. Because of fear of being deported many think that leaving the Jewish religion would help them . . . as a result a number severed their ties with Judaism entirely and others procured for themselves certificates of baptism[154] but observed the Jewish religion secretly.
>
> In fact many act unwittingly thinking that they do not thereby transgress the Jewish law. Such people should be compared to the Marranos who were regarded by various Rabbis as Jews.[155] Hence, those who nowadays behave as Jews in secret and are careful not to transgress the law are not to be alienated. . . .

The Rabbi shows the difference between those who were forced to renounce their religion and those who were not. The latter was the case of the Jews currently when the government opposed conversion of Jews to Christianity. However, it was not quite clear whether or not the conversion could be considered as having taken place under duress. Nevertheless, the Beth Din was entitled to introduce an extraordinary measure to check lawlessness (*migdar miltha*).

With regard to the parents it was the duty of the Beth Din to curb this practice as otherwise the breach would widen, parents would tell their children to renounce their religion in order to save them (the parents).

The Rabbi says that in order to intimidate the members of his own congregation (Kezmark) he made an announcement that those who renounce their religion would be separated from the whole community in every respect. Indeed his words made a great impression. He advised the Rabbi of Neutra to publish a proclamation (*kol kore*) in both German and the vernacular calling upon people to repent, particularly those who had left Judaism.[156]

At first glance the statement in the *Responsum* concerning the parents appears obscure. How could children by embracing Christianity save their parents? Why should parents be punished for the conversion of their children? However, the situation becomes clearer when we consider the conditions of that time. The *Responsum* dealing with the

154. On such cases *vide infra*.
155. See Zimmels, *Die Marranen in der Rabbinischen Literatur*, Berlin, 1932, pp. 21ff.
156. Meisels, *Mekaddshe Ha-Shem*, I, no. 92. On the action taken by the Rabbi of Neutra, see *Elleh Ezkerah*, II, New York, 1957, p. 258.

life of the Jews in Slovakia was written at the beginning of September 1942. A few months earlier (15 May 1942) the Slovak government had issued a decree concerning the deportation of Jews from Slovakia.[157] This decree contained some exemptions from deportation. Thus, e.g. those converts who could prove that they were baptized before 14 March 1939 (i.e. before the founding of the Slovak state) were not to be deported. Furthermore, the exemption of the convert was automatically transferred to the other members of the family: spouse, children and even parents. Consequently by proving (by an antedated certificate) one's baptism to have occurred before 14 March 1939, not only the convert and his children but also his parents could be saved from deportation. Hence the strict view adopted by the Rabbi particularly towards the parents who tolerated the conversion of their children and derived benefit from it.

(c) Certificates of Baptism

There are questions in the *Responsa* whether a Jew is permitted to obtain a certificate of baptism to save his life. In fact the holder of such a certificate had not been baptized, nor did he declare 'his willingness to do so'. In different countries (Poland, Slovakia-Hungary, Lithuania)[158] at different times during the war Rabbis were asked the same question: 'May a Jew obtain a certificate of baptism to save his life?' It appears from some *Responsa* that many Jews obtained such certificates without even asking the Rabbi beforehand.

One author[159] in his attempt to show the attitude of the Protestant and Orthodox Churches and their leaders in various countries towards the persecution of the Jews in the Nazi holocaust, quotes cases under the heading 'Mercy-Baptisms', where the churches were willing to assist Jews in that respect although their action involved great personal danger.

'Out of noble feelings and not in order to receive a reward, the priests also distributed baptismal certificates to Jews who had never attended a church service . . .'[160]

Of course the Nazis were not aware of this trick. When they learned of such conversions in Slovakia nine pastors were sent to the concentration camps in Germany; one minister perished in the camp.[161]

---

157. See Hilberg, *Destruction of European Jews*, pp. 466f.; Reitlinger, *Final Solution*, p. 420.
158. *Vide infra.*
159. Snoek, *Grey Book*, pp. 26ff.
160. Michael Molho and Joseph Nehama, *The Destruction of Greek Jewry*, Jerusalem, 1965, p. 142, quoted by Snoek, *Grey Book*, p. 28.
161. For references see Snoek, *Grey Book*, p. 27.

Poland Rabbi Dr Jacob Avigdor (Chief Rabbi and Ab Beth Din of Drohobycz and Boryslaw) who spent five years (1940–45) in concentration camps and was released only at the end of the war tells us how the Germans after shutting up the Jews in the ghetto were waiting for an opportunity for open rebellion by the Jews in order to have reason to attack and exterminate them. The leaders of the community knowing this tried by all means to restrain the youth from any such action. Being thus unable to oppose the Germans openly they tried to do so by passive resistance and in secret. The Rabbi relates that his Beth Din had to deal with the question, asked by many religious Jews, whether they were permitted to use documents certifying the holders to be Christians and to disguise themselves as Christians. Similarly, Jewish girls asked whether they might take refuge in Christian homes. This question affected the basic principles of Judaism (idolatry, immorality) for which one must sacrifice one's life and not transgress (*yehareg ve-al yaabor*). More than once did they sit for many hours perplexed, unable to solve the problem. In fact, according to the *halachah* it was difficult to give a decision. However, all of them felt that they were living in completely different conditions and that the law of *yehareg ve-al yaabor* would therefore not apply. This law applied when the enemy came and demanded that a Jew transgress the prohibition of idolatry, murder or immorality, and if the latter should not do so he would be killed. In such a case the Jew must give up his life and refrain from complying with the order of the enemy. (In the time of a religious persecution one must resist even the changing of the shoe-strap to hide one's Jewish identity, see *Sanhedrin* 74b.) But as far as they were concerned, the matter was quite different. The Germans on no account wanted the Jews to use such certificates, they even prohibited genuine baptism under pain of death.[162]

On the other hand, if a Jew was living in the ghetto and did not rebel and did the work imposed on him—in those early days he was not

162. I could find no reference to the fact that Jews who embraced Christianity were punishable with death. Among other inquiries I made of the *Institut für Zeitgeschichte* in Munich I sought confirmation of the Rabbinic source that baptism to avoid persecution was punishable with death. I received the following reply (dated: 21 August 1972):

   Unter Punkt 4 schneiden Sie eine interessante Frage an: Im Generalgouvernement z.B. war es den Juden verboten, sich taufen zu lassen; es ist uns allerdings nicht bekannt, dass Verstösse gegen dieses Verbot mit dem Tode bestraft wurden. Möglich, von uns jedoch nicht nachzuweisen ist, dass lokale Machthaber mit dieser Strafe drohten. Da aber bekanntlich auf dem Verlassen des Ghettos die Todesstrafe stand, kann davon ausgegangen werden, dass man Juden, die mit der Absicht, sich taufen zu lassen, aus dem Ghetto flüchteten, hingerichtet hat, wobei dann aber nicht die Tatsache der Taufe, sondern vielmehr das Verlassen des Ghettos Strafgrund war.

I wish to point out that our Rabbinic source refers indeed to the *Generalgouvernement* which included the Ghettos of Drohobycz and Boryslaw, both in Galicia, where Rabbi Avigdor was Chief Rabbi.

removed to be killed. But if a Jew was caught having a certificate stating he was a Christian he was even at the beginning of the Nazi rule immediately killed. The order was given: if a Jewish man or woman be found in possession of false documents (documents stating that the holder was a Christian) he or she would be put to death at once without trial. Hence, if after that order had been issued, a Jew acquired such a certificate, his action entailed great self-sacrifice. Many people were most anxious to obtain such certificates in order not to comply with the German decree and to rebel at least by that action against the wish of the enemy. How could they, the Beth Din, decide that it was forbidden to hold such a certificate? By giving such a ruling, they would have strengthened the order and the decree of the Nazis. A similar decree was issued against Jewish girls who hid themselves in houses of non-Jews. If any Jewish person was found hiding in a non-Jewish house, then the non-Jew as well as the Jew would be killed. This had happened more than once. When despite the order a non-Jew took in a Jewish girl the latter was making a sacrifice by transgressing the order of the Germans. The girl had a feeling of strength and rebellion by utterly disregarding the wishes of the enemy. Had the Beth Din forbidden such action they would have assisted the Germans by enforcing their rules and helped them accomplish their desire.[163]

Slovakia and Hungary A similar question 'concerning buying a *Taufschein* (certificate of baptism) during the persecution to save one's life' is found in a *Responsum* from another country.

The Beth Din in Pressburg (Bratislava, Slovakia) decided not to call up to the Torah people who had acquired certificates of baptism in order to save themselves from the Nazis.[164] As a result of this decision, quarrels broke out and the Rabbi of Pistiani, R. Isachar Shlomoh Teichthal (author of *Responsa Mishneh Sachir*), was asked about the matter. The Rabbi replied that when the practice of buying certificates of baptism spread because of the severe persecution, he immediately denounced it in public showing the stringency of the prohibition and the implications and that according to Jewish law buying such a certificate falls under the ruling that one should suffer martyrdom rather than transgress the prohibition. The acquisition of such a document indicates that the holder recognizes another faith and it is as if he would declare explicitly that he were a non-Jew. However, the Rabbi points out, although it is quite clear that this practice was prohibited, the holders

163. R. J. Avigdor, *Helek Yaakob*, II, Mexico, 1956, pp. xif.
164. On the number of converts in Pressburg (Bratislava) in the years 1940–43, see Snoek, *Grey Book*, pp. 26f. where also the conversions in some other places are mentioned. Cf., however, the estimates quoted by Hilberg, *Destruction of European Jews*, p. 654, concerning conversions in Slovakia.

of such certificates who had been unable to withstand the temptation
and acquired them should not be excluded from the congregation. One
should remain passive. Similar cases occurred in his own community[165]
where some people who were said to have acquired certificates of
baptism had been called up to the Torah in his presence. The Rabbi
remained passive and did not seek to interfere despite complaints from
others. He based his decision on the view that if a person had been
forced to transgress the prohibition of idolatry, he is exempt from
punishment as he had acted under duress and had transgressed only
the law of *ve-nikdashti* (Lev. XXII 32). Similarly, in our case since he
continues to conduct himself as before he should be regarded as a
proper Jew and may be called up to the Torah. One should also bear in
mind that excluding such people might lead them to renouncing their
Jewish religion completely as such cases did happen 'nowadays'. As long
as no evidence was given at the Beth Din in his presence that he had
acquired a certificate, the holder could not be regarded as unfit in religious matters. Therefore the principle 'sit and do nothing' (*Erubin* 100a)
should be applied. Furthermore, since the certificates were bought to
be shown only on demand and at that time no ten Jews would be
present he would fail to comply with the commandment of Deut. VI 5
but would not be regarded as a non-Jew.[166]

Lithuania On the 1st of Nisan 702 (19 March 1942) R. E. Oshry was
asked by an inmate of the Ghetto of Kovno whether one was allowed
to save oneself by buying a certificate of baptism (*Taufschein*) having
thus the possibility of fleeing into the forests and joining the partisans.
The answer was in the negative.[167]

During the *Kinderaktion* in the Ghetto of Kovno on 27–28 March
1944, when parents tried to save their children from the hands of the
Germans the same Rabbi was asked the following questions. Some
parents had obtained birth certificates for their children from non-Jews
and left their children with their certificates in front of a Christian
orphanage so that the Christians would think the 'abandoned' children
were non-Jews. Is this permitted?

Other parents handed over their children to clergymen and wrote to
them that their children had been baptized. Is this permitted?[168]

(*d*) *Certificates with the initials 'R.K.'*

Slovakia A Jew had to go to Hungary urgently but no visas were given

165. Pistiani.
166. *Yerushath Peletah*, no. 27.
167. *Mi-Maamakkim*, I, no. 15, where the reason for his decision is given.
168. Oshry, 'Kuntras Me-Emek Ha-Bacha', no. 5. The first question is left undecided while
    with regard to the second question he is inclined to decide in the negative.

to Jews, only to non-Jews. He then asked the Rabbi whether he might acquire a certificate bearing the initials 'R.K.' (i.e. *Römisch Katholisch*). The Rabbi tried to adopt a lenient view as the letters 'R.K.' could be interpreted differently. He quotes a similar case. However, he is hesitant in deciding the question put to him without the consent of other great Rabbis.[169]

Lithuania A Jew has a name which is common to Jews and non-Jews 'as is often found among Jews of Germany'. He holds a passport from before the war, may he now in time of danger insert the letters 'R.K.' to be regarded as a non-Jew? Does such an action involve the prohibition of idol worship?

Reply:[170] this may, perhaps, be permitted as these letters can be interpreted differently and when writing them, he can have the intention to write the letters with that meaning. The Rabbi quotes the same case mentioned in the previous *Responsum* to support this.

(e) Aryan certificates

The Jews soon found out that holding a certificate of baptism did not give immunity from being deported by the Germans. Hence they tried to furnish themselves with documents stating that their holders were pure Aryans in the same way as they obtained certificates of baptism by paying large sums. This happened not only in Poland[171] but also in Italy. The number of 'Falsified "Aryan" certificates, granted by corrupt Fascist bosses to enable one to evade the regulations, rose to unbelievable heights'.[172] In Poland some Jews retained their certificates even after the liberation. The question was asked: is a person who holds a certificate that he is an Aryan (but not that he is a Christian) to be regarded as *modeh be-AKUM* (acknowledging idolatry)?[173]

(f) Declaring oneself a Karaite

There is an unusual case, unique in Rabbinic literature, from which we can see that a Jew could save his life by alleging he was a Karaite. He could even acquire a scroll of the Law from the Nazis. Thus we are told: 'During the Nazi holocaust a Jew saved his life by saying he was a Karaite and not of the Jewish (*sic*) race. He later bought a scroll of the Law from the wicked ones while all other scrolls were burned. After the war a relative of the original owner appeared, recognized the scroll and sought its return. The buyer, however, refused to comply with his

169. *Yerushath Peletah*, no. 27.
170. Oshry, 'Kuntras Me-Emek Ha-Bacha', no. 4.
171. Kaplan, *Scroll of Agony*, translated by Abraham I. Katsh, London, 1966, pp. 229f.
172. Cecil Roth, *The History of the Jews in Italy*, p. 538.
173. *Vide infra*.

request.' One Rabbi discussing the case decided that the relative's claim was justified but the latter should refund the buyer the sum he had paid the Nazis.[174]

At first glance it may appear rather strange that a person could be spared by the Nazis by claiming to be a Karaite. Were not the Karaites members of a *Jewish* sect? Were they not descendants of those who had broken away from Judaism in the eighth and ninth centuries rejecting the Oral Law?

However, the matter becomes clear when we consider the legal position of the Karaites in Lithuania, the Crimea and in other areas in the eighteenth and nineteenth centuries under Russian rule.[175] When those countries had been incorporated into Russia (1783, 1795) the Russian government drew a distinction between the Rabbanites and the Karaites (1795). While the former were oppressed and subjected to discriminations and restrictions, the latter were in the course of time exempted from various laws applicable to the Rabbanites (e.g. double taxation, prohibition of acquiring land, military service) until they attained full civil rights (1863). In their appeals and memoranda the Karaites always stressed that they were different from all other Jews particularly since they did not accept the Talmud. Instead of Jews-Karaites they were first called 'Russian Karaites of the Old Testament Faith' and later 'Karaites'.

The Germans followed a similar course in their treatment of the Karaites. They too regarded the Karaites as distinct from Jews and as belonging to a different race. According to some sources the Karaites were regarded by the Nazis as being 'Tartars but Jewish by religion' and were to be spared. Indeed orders were given to the *Einsatzgruppen* to spare the Karaites who were well treated by the German authorities and even given positions under Nazi rule.[176]

Committing Suicide

The question of the permissibility of committing suicide to avoid torture which could lead a person to giving up his religion has been dealt with by the Rabbis of various periods. Their views are divided.[177]

---

174. See R. A. Katz, *Leket Ha-Kemah He-Hadash,* Part III, on *Orah Hayyim,* cap. CXXXV, no. 16**, p. 10. From the text it appears that the man was not a Karaite, but only pretended to be one: *hizzil azmo ehad be-omro she-hu Karai.*

175. Cf. S. Dubnow, *Geschichte des jüdischen Volkes,* VIII, pp. 48, 349f.; *Encyclopaedia Judaica,* vol. 10, pp. 773ff.

176. Quoted by Reitlinger, *Final Solution,* p. 257. See also *Encyclopaedia Judaica,* p. 776.

177. See R. J. Caro in *Bedek Ha-Bayyith* on *Beth Yoseph Tur Yoreh Deah,* cap. CLVII; R. I. Untermann, *Shebet Mi-Yehudah,* I, p. 43; R. Z. Sorotzkin, *Moznayyim La-Mishpat,* II, no. 12; R. S. Engel, *Responsa MhRS,* vol. VIII, ed. by R. E. Halpern, London. 1955; Oshry *Mi-Maamakkim,* I, no. 6. See also Zimmels, *Ashkenazim and Sephardim,* p. 263 and the sources quoted there.

A different outlook on suicide in general can be found in the era of the Nazi holocaust. Humiliation, fear of torture and starvation produced two diametrically opposed feelings among the Jews living under the Nazi heel. These feelings had great consequences in their attitude to life. One was pessimism, resignation, despair and abandonment of any hope for the future, leading to suicide. The other was optimism, a strong will to survive and to bear patiently all sufferings and hope for a change for the better. The former view was shared mainly by the Jews of Germany and Austria, while the latter attitude can be found among the Jews of Poland and the other eastern territories.

It is of great interest to know that this observation was made by lay writers[178] as well as by Rabbis. Indeed, one Rabbi tells us that even the German tormentors wondered why the Jews of Poland and Lithuania did not follow the example of the Jews in Germany in committing suicide.[179]

As far as the Jews of Germany and Austria are concerned, we have reports that many Jews indeed committed suicide to avoid falling into the hands of the Nazis and being deported. Already in 1933, German Jews committed suicide by the hundreds.[180] When deportation started 'there were in fact about twelve hundred suicides in Berlin alone', declared one witness at the Eichmann trial.[181] With regard to the Jews of Austria we are told that after the Nazi invasion of Austria a flood of suicides began and was to continue until the final destruction.[182] This attitude of the Jews of Germany and Austria was unlike that of the Jews of the eastern countries among whom only individual cases of suicide occurred.[183]

The action of the president of the Jewish Council of Warsaw where there was the greatest ghetto of Jews, Adam Czerniakow, who committed suicide because he did not wish to sign a deportation order for 'resettlement to the east'—which was tantamount to being sent to extermination —is praised by one author.[184] A similar tragic act was the suicide committed by the president of the Jewish Council of Kolomyja.[185] Otherwise,

---

178. Kaplan, *Scroll of Agony*, pp. 112f.; L. Poliakov, *Harvest of Hate*, p. 99; Hausner, *Justice in Jerusalem*, p. 104.

179. *Vide infra* note 187.

180. Poliakov, *Harvest of Hate*, p. 13.

181. Quoted in Hausner, *Justice in Jerusalem*; cf. also Reitlinger, *Final Solution*, p. 91, concerning the suicides committed by victims during transportation from Berlin to Poland.

182. Norman Bentwich, in *The Jews of Austria*, ed. by J. Fraenkel, p. 468. See also A. D. Morse, *While Six Million Died*, p. 204; Hugo Gold, *Geschichte der Juden in Wien*, p. 89.

183. *Vide infra* note 187.

184. See Kaplan, *Scroll of Agony*, p. 303.

185. Hausner, *Justice in Jerusalem*, p. 197.

suicide of an individual is seldom mentioned, let alone mass suicide. When danger arose and imminent torture and deportation to the extermination camp was feared suicide appeared the only alternative. Nevertheless, people still refused to commit suicide and in their despair came to the Rabbi and sought his advice. The following moving story is reported.[186]

When during the German occupation, a few people of Kosice learned of the purpose of the transport to Auschwitz, etc., some Jews gathered in the *Beth Midrash* of R. David Halpern which was on the boundary of the ghetto and considered the possibility of escape (Nisan-Sivan 5704 = 25 March—20 June 1944). They decided to ask the famous religious leader the Gaon R. Hanoch Enoch Pak (who later died a martyr) for permission to commit suicide should they not succeed in escaping rather than 'come between the teeth of the cursed ones'. A committee of three Rabbis (R. Abraham Zebi Klein, R. David Halpern and R. Yizhak Klein) was formed to put that question to R. Hanoch Enoch Pak. When they arrived at the anteroom of the Rabbi's home they saw his son R. Menahem Mendel Pak (who later died a martyr) deeply absorbed in the study of the Talmud. They then entered the Rabbi's room and found him reciting Psalms. The Rabbi apologized that he was unable to concentrate and give his customary lecture on Talmud and codes owing to great sorrow and distress. He was, therefore, reciting Psalms. When they put their question to him the Rabbi burst into tears and said courageously: 'My friends, according to the Law I would be able to permit such action. However, our sages have told of the greatness of those who accept upon themselves the decree of Him, whose Name be blessed, and who are killed for the sake of the sanctification of the Name of God. No one can be superior to them . . . . Therefore, accept, I pray, the decree of Him, whose Name be blessed and sanctify His Name.' They departed from the Rabbi and accepted his words. Next morning, they complied with the Rabbi's decision. . . .

Another case was the following.[187] On the 6th of Heshvan, 5702 (27 October 1941), two days before the great *hurban* (destruction) of the Ghetto of Kovno at a time when about ten thousand people, men, women and children, were led to the slaughter before our eyes and every inmate of the ghetto was waiting for his bitter end an honourable man from the town came to me crying bitterly that he was afraid he might be forced to see his wife, children and grandchildren being slaughtered before his eyes in order to increase his suffering. The murderers used to take pleasure in seeing the suffering of their victims

186. R. E. Halpern, Introduction to *Responsa MhRS* by R. Samuel Engel, vol. VIII, p. 187.
187. Oshry, *Mi-Maamakkim*, I, no. 6; Garfunkel, *Destruction of Kovno's Jewry*, p. 248, who states that also cases of nervous breakdown seldom occurred. On this persecution and date *vide supra* pp. 50f.

and therefore killed children in front of their parents, wives in front of their husbands and after that they tortured and killed the head of the family. As he could not stand such suffering (he was sure he would die of a heart attack), he inquired as to whether he was permitted to commit suicide, to be spared the torture and be buried in a Jewish cemetery in the Kovno Ghetto . . . . After examining the question from different angles, the Rabbi who is inclined to adopt a lenient view remarks *inter alia:*

> One can be sure that he will be subject to terrible sufferings. Nevertheless one is certainly not permitted to declare it in public as a clear decision that one may commit suicide in such circumstances as through this action support is given to our enemies, who many times wondered why the Jews did not commit suicide as the Jews of Berlin did. Such an action is a *hillul ha-Shem* (profanation of the Name) because it shows that the Jews do not trust in God to save them. . . . It should be noted with pride that in the Ghetto of Kovno there were no cases of suicide save in three instances. All the other inmates of the Ghetto believed with perfect faith that God would not forsake his people . . . .

It appears indeed[188] that this difference in their attitude towards a new way of life was in the majority of cases the outcome of their position in the pre-Hitler period. In Germany where the Jews played an important part in all spheres of life, scholarship, science, theatre, film, commerce, industry, etc., and regarded themselves as part of the German nation, this sudden change meant catastrophe, the collapse of their world. It seemed to them that they had lived all their years in a dream and had become awakened to a life of reality without any prospect of survival. This attitude was unlike the position of the Jews in Poland where a majority of them had always felt a gulf dividing them from their Polish neighbours. Apart from that, the religious feeling was much stronger among them than among the German Jews (of course this did not apply to the entire German or Polish Jewry, but only to the majority). When then the Jews of Poland became engulfed by Nazism, their sufferings although to some extent greater than those in Germany, did not break their spirit but on the contrary gave them strength drawn from resources inherent in their nature.

Perhaps one can see a parallel to this phenomenon in the history of Jews in Spain and Germany in the Middle Ages. When the great catastrophe of expulsion befell the Jews of Spain the number of those

188. See also Poliakov, *Harvest of Hate,* p. 99.

leaving the country was naturally high. But 'the majority of those (almost all of them) adherents of philosophy embraced Christianity; however, women and the common people sacrificed their lives and possessions for the sanctification of their Creator'.[189] There were also two Rabbis who turned their backs on their religion (Don Abraham Senior and his son-in-law). The Jews of Spain were bound up with the country and had made great contributions to all branches of learning and in spite of the agitation of the Church the Jews were still admitted to high positions. This was in contradistinction to the position of the Jews in Germany in the Middle Ages. Hardly had they organized the communities and established the schools of Torah than a wave of persecution swept over them. The first Crusade left its mark on them as did the persecutions during the subsequent centuries. Their hearts were steeled against any attack and they drew their courage and strength from their deep religious feeling. The number of converts to Christianity during persecutions was negligible. Martyrdom and suffering were the hallmarks of Ashkenazi Jewry.

CONCENTRATION AND EXTERMINATION CAMPS

The first concentration camp was set up in March 1933 in the vicinity of Dachau, near Munich, and was destined to house Communists and Social Democrat officials. The concentration camp was intended to be a special protective custody quarter separate from the police prisons and those of the minister of justice.[190]

The number of concentration camps increased in the following years. Between August 1937 and July 1938 there were four concentration camps on Reich territory: Dachau, Sachsenhausen, Buchenwald and Lichtenburg.[191] During those years the concentration camps were used also for the detention of 'anti-social elements' and criminals, etc. The number of the concentration camps increased, particularly after the outbreak of World War II when camps were erected on Polish soil.

With the final solution some of the concentration camps became extermination camps. Apart from various methods of killing individuals mass murder was carried out, often also outside the camp, by: (1) Mass shooting; (2) gassing; (3) injections; (4) exhaustion, hunger and disease.

1. *Mass shooting* The victims were put into a mass grave often dug by

189. H. Graetz, *Geschichte der Juden*, VIII, p. 347, note 4, quoting R. Joseph Jabez, *Or Ha-Hayyim*, pp. 5a, 12a.
190. For the reason, see Martin Broszat, 'The Concentration Camps 1933–45', in *Anatomy of the SS State*, London, 1968, p. 405.
191. Ibid., p. 445.

themselves beforehand. Mass shooting took place in Lithuania, Poland, Ukraine and Rumania.[192]

It was not difficult to carry out mass murder. The Jews were told to assemble at a special place under the pain of death. The reason for such parades differed often from place to place. All of them had this in common that they were based on lies and deception. In Kovno, 26,400 Jews assembled at the place they were told in order that those unfit for work could be sent elsewhere. In fact about ten thousand inmates were led away to be killed in cold blood.[193] In another case, thirty-four thousand Jews were murdered, having assembled at a place where they were supposed to present themselves for registration and subsequent accommodation.[194] In Kiev, the Jews were ordered to present themselves for resettlement. More than thirty thousand appeared with the result that they were led to execution.[195] The ravine Babi Yar near Kiev is the mass grave of thousands of victims murdered by the Germans.[196] In Sokal on Bug (Galicia) several thousand Jews deported from the neighbouring area were murdered first, followed by two thousand Jewish inhabitants of that town (22nd Iyyar 5703, i.e. 27 May 1943).[197]

Very often, the victims had to dig their own graves and in many cases were still alive when they were buried. R. Shlomoh David Kahana, Jerusalem, head of the section dealing with *agunoth*, tells us that his office is in possession of evidence given by people who had been buried alive and were saved.[198] R. Isachar Beer Halpern, who spent several years of the war in various Nazi camps, reports that he witnessed the soil covering thousands of victims who had been shot moving as they were

---

192. Cf. Oshry, *Mi-Maamakkim*, I, nos. 3, 7, 23; II, no. 5; III, no. 4; Efrati, *Me-Emek Ha-Bacha*, no 5; *Mi-Ge Ha-Haregah*, no. 11; R. B. Stern, *Be-Zel Ha-Hochmah*, I, nos. 14ff.; see also Reitlinger, *The Final Solution*, London, 1968, pp. 218ff., 248f.; A.Anatoli (Kuznetsov), *Babi Yar*, pp. 91, 96f., 110. (In May 1971, it was reported that three former Nazi police officers went on trial in Regensburg charged with the murder of 33,771 Jews at Babi Yar in 1941. See *Daily Telegraph*, 4 May 1971, p. 4). According to another report which appeared in the press, mass graves had been discovered in the Ukraine with remains of 1,480 prisoners murdered by the Nazis. See *Jewish Chronicle*, 8 January 1971, p. 4. In the Ninth Fort in Kovno forty-five thousand people, Jews and non-Jews, were shot by the Germans. See Garfunkel, *The Destruction* of *Kovno's Jewry*, Jerusalem, 1959, p. 158. See also ibid., pp. 71f., 76f., about the massacre called 'the great *actia*' of 28–29 October 1941.

193. Garfunkel, *Destruction of Kovno's Jewry*, p. 158; Oshry, *Mi-Maamakkim*, I, nos. 7, 23; II, no. 5; III, no. 4; Breisch, *Helkath Yaakob*, II, nos. 31f.

194. Höhne, *The Order of the Death's Head*, London, 1969, pp. 360f.; Reitlinger, *Final Solution*, pp. 247f.

195. Ibid.

196. *Vide* note 192.

197. Breisch, *Helkath Yaakob*, title-page. Among the victims were members of the Rabbi's family.

198. Breisch, *Helkath Yaakob*, I, no. 21.

still alive, while the murderers were standing nearby enjoying themselves.[199]

Another Rabbi[200] gives a similar account of mass murder in Poland. It happened, he says, in various places in Poland that the murderers, instead of deporting their victims to the extermination camps, led them to an open space and ordered them to dig pits with their own hands. The Jews had to lie on the ground and were shot. Some victims were not hit. Afterwards, a second group was ordered to enter the pits whilst those of the first group were still struggling in agony between life and death. The *Shema Yisrael* of the latter mingled with the groaning of the wounded 'and blood touched blood' (Hosea, IV 2) so that the pit became filled with layers of people wallowing in their blood half alive. Their murderers then covered them with earth and the ground shook with screams.

In many places the so-called sardine-method was used.[201] After the victims had dug a large pit one group entered it and was shot. It often happened that not all of them were dead yet soon afterwards those of the second group entered the pit and lying down in such a way that their heads fronted the feet of the first group, they were shot. This happened several times until the pit was full, when earth was put on top.

As a matter of fact, the Nazis were not the only ones to use the sardine-method in mass killings. In a report which appeared some time ago in the press[202] under the heading 'Bodies like Sardines in Tin at Katyn Killing, said British Envoy' we are told of this method used at the massacre of over ten thousand Polish officers in the Katyn wood in May 1940. The Germans claimed that the Russians were responsible for this mass killing while the Russians blamed the Germans for the crime. Among the 1943 official documents deposited in the Public Record Office under the Thirty Year Rule a confidential dispatch is contained written by the British ambassador to Poland in May 1943 in which he calls the attention of the foreign secretary to grave issues involved. We learn from this report that the Russians were responsible for that killing.

At any rate this does not exclude the possibility that the Germans had used the sardine-method first, as immediately after the outbreak of World War II they overran Poland and with their *Einsatzgruppen* (special squads carrying out liquidations in occupied territories)[203] massacred Jews by shooting.

199. *Mishneh La-Melech, ad fin.* Introduction.
200. Efrati, *Mi-Ge Ha-Haregah,* no. 11.
201. On this method, see Hilberg, *The Destruction of the European Jews,* p. 209.
202. *Daily Telegraph,* 5 July 1972, p. 5.
203. See 'Glossary'.

2. *Extermination by gassing.*[204]

3. *In Dachau sick persons were killed by injections.*[205]

4. *Exhaustion, hunger, disease* The Jews of Rumania and Bessarabia were driven into Transnistria where they perished in the marshes.[206]

The extermination camps were supplied with victims brought in by deportations from invaded towns, ghettos and transit camps. This was arranged by train, horse-box or cattle-trucks[207] and marches.[208]

As far as journeys by train are concerned, we hear in the *Responsa* of attempts made by individuals to escape; however, most such attempts proved fatal. This can be seen from the following texts.

Mr . . . , husband of Mrs . . . , was arrested in France in the year 702 (1942) and handed over to the Germans. He was in Drancy. In his last letter from there at the time of *Sukkoth* he wrote that no food parcels should be sent to him any more as he had been transported to Germany. One (religious) man gave evidence before the Beth Din that Mr . . . of Marseilles reported to him that he journeyed together with the husband and knew him and his wife very well from the time they had been living in Marseilles. Both (the husband and the man who reported) had been transported together in the same carriage to Germany. During the journey the witness saw that the husband mentioned above had broken a board of the carriage when they stopped in the middle of the road, in order to escape. However, when he put his head out of the carriage a soldier standing there hit it with his metal-covered rifle-butt. The witness saw the man struggling in convulsions for a time and he died later. The corpse lay in the carriage for about six hours and was thrown out by the other passengers lest it contaminate the air, as it is well known the carriages were very overcrowded.[209]

The following question was sent by R. Gurwitz in Melbourne to Chief Rabbi Herzog in Jerusalem.[210] A husband, his wife and two sons were

204. There were various methods of gassing: mobile gassing vans and gas installations in chambers, see Reitlinger, *Final Solution*, pp. 147, 258, 390f.; Hilberg, *Destruction of the European Jews*, pp. 65ff.

205. R. Aryeh Leb Grossnass, *Leb Aryeh*, London, 1958, no. 45.

206. *Vide infra s.v.* 'Camps'.

207. Cf. e.g. Herzog, *Hechal Yizhak*, I, no. 31; Weiss, *Minhath Yizhak*, II, London, 1958, no. 64; R. J. Klein, *Atereth Shlomoh*, Budapest, 1946, p. 83; Breisch, *Helkath Yaakob*, no. 15. (The terms used are: *rakaboth, keronoth massa behemoth, Wagen*.)

208. *Vide infra*.

209. Breisch, *Helkath Yaakob*, I, no. 15. The *Responsum* is dated: 8th Sivan 707 (27 May 1947).

210. *Hechal Yizhak*, I, no. 31.

H

deported by the Germans by train from the Warsaw Ghetto to the death camp in Maidanek, in April 1943. *En route* they jumped from the train in the following order: first, the younger son; then the father, followed by the elder son and then his mother. She immediately met on the track two Polish railway workmen who told her that they had found six bodies on the track. The bodies were those of a woman, three men and two children. They described their faces and the clothes they were wearing. From this description she concluded that her husband and two sons were among those killed. Their clothes had been correctly described as those which they wore before they jumped from the train. After the war the woman returned to Warsaw and made inquiries at various offices but her husband's name did not appear on the list of survivors. No one knew anything about him.

The Rabbi was of the opinion that the woman might re-marry. The matter was very urgent as a worthy proposal of marriage had been made to her and she wished to marry as soon as possible. Chief Rabbi Herzog decided she might re-marry. From his *Responsum* we see that 'it was customary among the wicked Germans to give orders to search the track every day to see whether any dead people had been found'.

Concerning marches on foot, the 'Death-March' of the Hungarian Jews is well known.[211] Such death-marches occurred very often with the advance of the Allied armies. They are described in the following two *Responsa*.

In their fear of the advance of the American army the Nazis forced the remaining victims to proceed willy-nilly to other places in order that they should not fall into the hands of their pursuers. Everyone who became weak on the way and was unable to continue marching was shot on the spot. Such a march was termed *Toten Marsch*. From time to time, the Nazis permitted the Jews to rest for a few minutes and to sit on the road-side. Very often if one of the wretched people had a little nap or fell into a deep sleep, owing to fatigue and weakness, so that when the order came to march again he did not awake, the murderers approached him and killed him immediately without saying a word. Because of that the unfortunate ones walked in company together and when they sat down to rest, one would awake the others.

A man came before a Rabbi[212] asking whether he need atone for the following:

When he was marching with his younger brother, they sat down to rest. He told him he could sleep a little and he would watch and rouse him when the order to resume the march was given. However, as the

211. See *The Times*, 19 April 1961, p. 10; *Jewish Chronicle*, 21 April 1961, pp. 15f.
212. Breisch, *Helkath Yaakob*, II, no. 143.

rest was prolonged, he himself fell asleep and suddenly the order 'forward march' ('*Los! los!*') was given. In confusion, he ran to the place where his friends were standing although he was not quite aware of what he was doing. They immediately began to march and when he remembered his younger brother it was already impossible without danger to his own life to return. Since then, he had not heard of his brother who, no doubt, was murdered. For thirteen years, he had had a troubled conscience and wished to know whether he required atonement or not. The Rabbi decided in the negative; however, he advised him to perform some meritorious deeds and to refrain from putting people to shame which counts as murder. He should try to bring up an orphan in his house and support those who study Torah, etc.

Another case was the march from the ghetto in Grosswardein.

Statement of evidence. When we three judges were in session Mrs. Reizel Reich, aunt of Mrs. Sheva Engel, came before us and gave the following evidence.

'I, and my brother's daughters, Sheva and Zierel Reich of Grosswardein, were together from the very first day of our exile. Sheva was the wife of Gershon Meir Engel. From the time we entered the ghetto we stayed together until the end, i.e. from May 26, 1944 till January 27, 1945. Whilst on the march on the 27th of January, we entered a stable to sleep. Sheva fell ill, fainted and we revived her. She did not sleep all night. In the morning we had to set off. In the afternoon she felt ill, the first time we succeeded in reviving her but a few minutes later she collapsed and her sister and I held her but unfortunately she could not stand. We were about ten metres behind the others. The guard approached us and we pleaded that he spare her life and that we would soon follow. He, however, ordered us to march, and if not he would have shot all three of us.

We went three or four steps further when he shot her. I stood still and saw him shoot again. We had to move on. She remained lying in the road.

One or two days later, a girl arrived with whom we had been together in the camp and who had hidden herself but was discovered and sent on. She reported she had seen the woman lying dead.'[213]

The aunt added that she had seen the murderer shoot his victim at point-blank range.

The question was whether the 'widower' might marry her sister. The Rabbi[214] decided in the affirmative.

213 The original evidence was given in Yiddish.
214. Weiss, *Minhath Yizhak* II no. 62.

Extermination camps

There were six extermination camps constructed in Poland.[215] 'There was much competition', one author points out,[216] 'among German companies for contracts in the construction of these extermination centres. In submitting their tenders for the building of crematorium ovens, the firm C. H. Kori, for example, assured the S.S.: "We guarantee the effectiveness of the crematorium ovens, as well as their durability, the use of the best materials and our faultless workmanship".'

The following camps[217] are mentioned in the *Responsa:*

AUSCHWITZ (OSWIECIM), thirty-seven miles west of Cracow, was set up in May 1940. In order to expand the camp, the adjacent town Birkenau (or Brzezinka) was added in October 1941. The latter was also called Gypsy Camp (*Zigeunerlager*)[218] because gypsies were housed (and exterminated) in one of the compounds there, or Auschwitz II, while the former was known as Auschwitz I.[219] 'Auschwitz-Birkenau was the peak of horror.'[220] In the indictment against Eichmann, the following is said about this camp: 'millions of Jews were exterminated in this camp from 1941 until the end of January 1945 in gas chambers and in crematoria, and by shooting and hanging. The accused directed the commanders of that camp to use gas known as Zyklon B . . .'.[221]

Gassing began on 3 September 1941, as an experiment and from then onwards it became a 'factory of death'. Three and a half million people were put to death in three years.

Death transports arrived from Poland, Upper Silesia, Greece,

215. See Hilberg, *Destruction of European Jews*, p. 555.
216. Robert Goldston, *The Life and Death in Nazi Germany*, p. 165.
217. Of the vast literature on the camps (particularly on Auschwitz) the following books were consulted:Broszat, 'The Concentration Camps', pp. 421ff.; H. G. Adler, *Theresienstadt 1941–1945;* Hilberg, *Destruction of European Jews*, pp. 555ff.; Reitlinger, *Final Solution* pp. 110ff., 120ff.; Poliakov, *Harvest of Hate*, p. 200; Lord Russell, *The Scourge of the Swastika*, p. 165; Bernd Naumann, *Auschwitz*; Hannah Arendt, *Eichmann in Jerusalem*; M. Mavis Hill and L. Norman Williams, *Auschwitz in England;* Hausner, *Justice in Jerusalem*; Manvell and Fraenkel, *The Incomparable Crime*; Michael Bar-Zohar, *The Avengers*; Simon Wiesenthal, *The Murderers Among Us*; O. Kraus and E. Kulka, *The Death Factory*; 'Indictment against Eichmann' (copy in the Wiener Library) also reproduced by Peter Papadatos, *The Eichmann Trial*, pp. 111ff.
218. 'It is known that her husband was in Birkenau called "Zigeunerlager", among the first to be exterminated', writes one Rabbi (Breisch, *Helkath Yaakob* II, no. 20; see also Kraus and Kulka, *Death Factory*, p. 164). On the extermination of the gipsies and the liquidation of the gipsy compound (31 July 1944) see Naumann, *Auschwitz*, p. 256; Poliakov, *Harvest of Hate*, p. 265.
219. In fact, there was a third camp known as Monowitz-Auschwitz III or Buna which served as a labour camp. In all, Auschwitz comprised thirty-nine camps divided into three main groups. On this see Kraus and Kulka, *Death Factory*, pp. 8ff.; Arendt, *Eichmann in Jerusalem*, p. 4.
220. Hausner, *Justice in Jerusalem*, p. 169.
221. 'Indictment', p. 2.

France, Holland, Belgium, Norway, Hungary and Germany, etc. In addition, more than seventy thousand Russian prisoners of war were put to death. During the period of the camp's existence there were prisoners of twenty-seven different nationalities.[222] Auschwitz was evacuated in January 1945.

Joseph Mengele, the chief doctor of Auschwitz, in whose hands the fate of the arrivals lay, used to say jokingly[223] in front of the crematorium: 'Here the Jews come in by the door and go out up the chimney.'[224]

BELZEC, situated in the then Lublin District. From the indictment against Eichmann we hear that 'this extermination camp was operated from the beginning of 1942 until the spring of 1943, and poison gas, among other means of extermination, was used therein'.[225] Six hundred thousand Jews were put to death there. There were no survivors.[226]

BERGEN-BELSEN, situated north-east of Hanover, was established in 1943. It too was in line with the other camps in its harsh treatment and torture of inmates. There were no gas chambers at Belsen but thousands died of disease and starvation. There were cases of cannibalism in the camp.[227]

BUCHENWALD, situated six miles from Weimar, opened in summer 1937. The inmates were experimented upon for medical purposes and the skin of the tattooed corpses of prisoners was used for making lampshades, book covers, etc.[228]

CALAIS, north-east of France, seems to have been either a labour or a transit camp. A Jew from Antwerp, Belgium, who had been taken by the Germans with many other Jews from Belgium in 1942 to Calais for hard labour was deported to Auschwitz-Birkenau in 1943.[229]

CHELMNO or KULM (KULMHOF AM NER), situated sixty kilometres north-west of Lodz, started its operations in December 1941 and continued until the beginning of 1945. Here the victims were killed by exhaust

---

222. Kraus and Kulka, *Death Factory*, pp. 206, 252.
223. See Bar-Zohar, *Avenger*, p. 234.
224. Auschwitz-Birkenau is often mentioned by the Rabbis; cf. e.g. Breisch, *Helkath Yaakob*, I, no. 17; II, no. 33; Efrati, *Mi-Ge Ha-Haregah*, no. 11; Klein, *Atereth Shlomoh*, p. 83; Waldenberg, *Ziz Eliezer*, III, no. 25; Weiss, *Minhath Yizhak*, I, no. 1; II, no. 64. See also *OzarHa-Posekim* on *Eben Ha-Ezer*, XVII, no. 36 (pp. 248, 250).
225. 'Indictment', *loc. cit.*
226. This camp is mentioned by R. M. Rath, *Kol Mebasser*, I, no. 84.
227. Hausner, *Justice in Jerusalem*, p. 160. This camp is mentioned by Avigdor, *Helek Yaakob*, p. 79; R. T. Tabyomi (Guttentag), *Erez Tobah*, no. 61; Klein, *Atereth Shlomoh*, p. 83.
228. This camp is mentioned by Avigdor, *Helek Yaakob*, p. 79; Jeruchem, *Birkath Hayyim*, no. 42; Aronzon, *Yeshuoth Mosheh*, no. 61, p. 240 (who mentions the making of various articles from the skin of the victims); *Ozar Ha-Posekim*, p. 252, quoting *Nezer Ha-Kodesh*, no. 11. See also Lord Russell, *Scourge of the Swastika*, p. 181.
229. Breisch, *Helkath Yaakob*, II, nos. 29f. (*vide infra* Part III, p.271.)

gas in gas vans (mobile gas chambers). R. Aronzon, Rabbi of Sanok, tells us that the Jews of the ghetto, among them members of his family, were taken to Chelmno on the eve of the new moon of Iyyar, 702 (16 April 1942) where they were exterminated.[230]

CZESTOCHOWA is mentioned by one Rabbi as an extermination camp.[231]

DACHAU, situated about twelve miles from Munich, was the first camp to be established (March 1933). Originally intended as a prison camp for political prisoners, it soon became a concentration camp for other 'offenders'. Medical experiments were carried out there on the inmates, with the result that many died.[232]

DRANCY (on the Seine), served as a transit camp for French Jews from where they were later deported to Auschwitz for extermination. There were four thousand children of two to fourteen years of age deported there. Their parents had been sent there previously.[233]

GUNSKIRCHEN (Austria) is mentioned by one Rabbi as a concentration camp, 'worse than any other camp'.[234] It was a sub-camp of Mauthausen.

GROSS-ROSEN (in Lower Silesia) was set up as a camp in 1940. When Auschwitz had to be evacuated because of the advance of the Russian armies in January 1945, sixty-four thousand prisoners who could not be exterminated were marched to Gross-Rosen. In February 1945, many inmates of Gross-Rosen were sent to Buchenwald.[235]

KONIN, a labour camp, is mentioned by one Rabbi.[236]

'KOVNO K.Z. LAGER.' This name is found in a *Responsum* of a Rabbi who himself was in the Ghetto of Kovno.[237] In September 1943, the Ghetto of Kovno was turned into a concentration camp. The administration was no longer in the hands of the S.A. but was taken over by the SS. The *Ältestenrat* lost its significance. People were taken

230. *Op. cit.,* no. 61, and p. 306, note 37.

231. R. Beer Halpern, *Mishneh La-Melech,* Introduction, p. 12. As a labour camp it is mentioned by Reitlinger, *Final Solution,* p. 324; Hilberg, *Destruction of European Jews,* p. 342.

232. This concentration camp is mentioned by Avigdor, *Helek Yaakob,* II, p. 79; Jeruchem, *Birkath Hayyim*; Waldenberg, *Ziz Eliezer*; Grossnass, *Leb Aryeh,* no. 45.

233. This camp is mentioned by Breisch, *Helkath Yaakob,* I, no. 15; R. A. Rapoport, *Kuntras Be-Inyan Agunah*; Weiss, *Minhath Yizhak,* II, no. 64. See also Hausner, *Justice in Jerusalem,* pp. 106f.

234. Meisels, *Binyan Zebi,* II, no. 66 (*infra* Part III, no. 14).

235. This camp is mentioned in the *Responsa* of Avigdor, *Helek Yaakob,* p. 79; Breisch, *Helkath Yaakob,* I, no. 17. See also Broszat, 'The Concentration Camps', p. 476; Bar-Zohar, *Avengers,* p. 219.

236. Aronzon, *Yeshuoth Mosheh,* no. 38, p. 306, who refers to his diary on the life in Konin.

237. Oshry, *Mi-Maamakkim,* II, no. 18. (The abbreviation K.Z. stands for *Konzentrationslager*).

to places far from Kovno for forced labour, men separate from women.[238]

MAIDANEK, in the neighbourhood of Lublin, operated from autumn 1941. Jews from Warsaw and Lublin Ghettos as well as from other places were deported there. In Maidanek, the Germans established, close to the concentration camp, also a death camp with a total of about three hundred thousand Jews from Poland and other countries of occupied Europe. At the liquidation of the camp and the surrounding labour posts on 2 and 3 November 1943, eighteen thousand Jews were shot.[239]

MALIN (MALINES?) in Belgium served as a transit camp from where the Jews were sent to Auschwitz.[240]

MAUTHAUSEN, near Linz in Austria, was established after the annexation of Austria in March 1938. Thousands of opponents of the Nazis were sent there 'since both Dachau and Buchenwald were brimming over'. In February 1941, Jews from Holland were sent there.[241]

MILLES (LES MILLES), situated in the 'Free Zone' of France (near Aix-en-Provence), served as a transit camp.[242]

OHRDRUF, south-west of Buchenwald, is mentioned by a Rabbi who was an inmate of this camp and gives us a description of the conditions there. This was one of the camps to where prisoners from evacuated camps like Auschwitz and Buchenwald had been taken in view of the approaching Allied armies.[243]

ORANIENBURG, near Berlin, was founded in 1933. In 1936 the concentration camp was transferred to nearby Sachsenhausen, the original site becoming the seat of the Inspectorate.[244]

---

238. For particulars see Garfunkel, *Destruction of Kovno's Jewry*, pp. 148ff., 156. On massacres in October 1941, see Oshry, *Mi-Maamakim* II, nos. 5f.; III, no. 4; Garfunkel, *Destruction of Kovno's Jewry*, pp. 71ff.; Reitlinger, *Final Solution*, p. 230. On deportations of Jews from the Greater Reich, from Berlin, Hamburg, Düsseldorf, Prague and Vienna to be massacred, see ibid., p. 96; Oshry, *Mi-Maamakkim*, I, no. 30; II, no. 21.

239. This camp is mentioned as a concentration camp and extermination camp by Meisels, *Kuntras Takkanoth Agunoth*, no. 37, p. 13; Breisch, *Helkath Yaakob*, I, no. 17; Herzog, *Hechal Yizhak*, I, no. 31; Waldenberg, *Ziz Eliezer*, III, no. 25. For particulars, see Papadatos, *Eichmann Trial*, p. 112; Hausner, *Justice in Jerusalem*, p. 188; Helmut Krausnick in *The Anatomy of the SS State*, pp. 99f.

240. See *Ziyyun Le-Menahem* of R. Menahem Kirschbaum, ed. by R. Yehudah Rubinstein, p. xi. On Malines, cf. Hilberg, *Destruction of the European Jews*, p. 387; Reitlinger, *Final Solution*, p. 369.

241. Mentioned by Avigdor, *Helek Yaakob*, p. 79. On Mauthausen, cf. Evelyn Le Chene, *Mauthausen*, London, 1971.

242. This camp is mentioned by Rapoport, *Kuntras Be-Invan Agunah*; Weiss, *Minhath Yizhak*, II, no. 64. Les Milles was in the Free Zone of France while Drancy (*q.v.*) was in the Occupied Zone, Reitlinger, *Final Solution*, p. 77.

243. Mentioned by Avigdor, *Helek Yaakob*, p. 79.

244. Ibid.

PLASZOW, near Cracow was a labour camp. According to one *Responsum* some Jews were transferred to Gross-Rosen.[245]
RAVENSBRÜCK, near Fürstenberg in Mecklenburg, was established as a concentration camp for women in May 1939.[246]
SACHSENHAUSEN, see ORANIENBURG.
SOBIBOR (am Bug), about 120 miles to the south-east of Warsaw. This camp figures among the extermination camps enumerated in the indictment against Eichmann. 'This extermination camp was operated from March 1942 until October 1943 and there were erected there, among other buildings erected for the purposes of extermination, five stone gas chambers.'[247]
STALF (?). In one *Responsum*,[248] the 'slave-labour camp of Stalf' is mentioned which was near the concentration camp of Stutthof. The writer could not identify this place.
STUTTHOF, near Danzig was set up as a concentration camp in September 1939.[249]
TRANSNISTRIEN (TRANSNISTRIA), derived from *Transdnietrien, Trans-Nistrului, Trans Dniester*, i.e. beyond (the other side of) the Dniester.[250] This name was given to the territory between the Dniester (Nistru) and the Bug in the southernmost corner of the Ukraine. It had been taken from the Russians by Rumania and was decreed into existence after the treaty between the latter and Nazi Germany on 19 August 1941. It lasted for two years and seven months (19 August 1941–20 March 1944) when it was reconquered by the Russians. At first the Jews from Czernowitz were deported there. Later transports came from Bessarabia and other places. The Germans employed a different method from that in Poland and Germany. No crematoria

245. Breisch, *Helkath Yaakob*, I, no. 17; Halpern, *Mishneh La-Melech*, p. 12.
246. Mentioned by Klein, *Atereth Shlomoh*, p. 83.
247. The quotation is taken from the 'Indictment', p. 2. Soap is said to have been made from the fat of the victims at Sobibor, see Alexander Pechersky, 'Revolt in Sobibor', in *They Fought Back*, ed. by Yuri Suhl, London, 1968, p. 73. This camp is mentioned by Herzog, *Hechal Yizhak*, II, no. 79 and in *Ozar Ha-Posekim*, XVII, no. 36, p. 248.
248. See Breisch, *Helkath Yaakob*, I, no. 18.
249. This camp is mentioned twice by Breisch, *Helkath Yaakob*, I, no. 18, where it is once called 'Struthof Pommern' and another time 'Stuthof Pommern'. The latter spelling is the correct one. However, it should be spelled with double 't' (Stutthof). I found, however, the name 'Struthof' mentioned in *Beth Jacob*, Jerusalem, 1965, no. 70, p. 11, where a photograph is reproduced showing a poster over the gate of the camp entrance 'Konzentrationslager Struthof-Natzweiler'. Natzweiler, however, is in Alsace. (The word 'Struthof in Pommern' in R. Breisch's *Responsum* should be corrected to 'Stutthof in Pommern' as it is indeed spelled later.) I was told by Prof. E. J. Cohn that the first word in 'Struthof-Natzweiler' is not the name of a locality but denotes a place 'The Struthof' in Natzweiler.
250-51. Cf. Manfred Reifer, 'Geschichte der Juden in der Bukowina (1919–1944)', in: Hugo Gold, *Geschichte der Juden in der Bukowina*, II, pp. 22f.; Hermann Sternberg 'Die Tragödie der Bukowiner Juden', ibid., p. 52; Nathan Getzler, 'Tagebücher aus

were put up, but they let the Jews die of cold, starvation, typhoid and exhaustion in the deep marshes. 'Transnistria became the cemetery for more than 200,000 Jews.'[251]

TREBLINKA, near Malkinia on the River Bug. 'This extermination camp was operated from July 23, 1942, until November, 1943. Also in this camp poison gas among other means of extermination was used.'[252] Himmler's chief of staff boasted that five thousand Jews were being sent daily to Treblinka. Every week two suitcases with eight to ten kilogrammes of gold taken from the teeth of corpses[253] used to be sent out from Treblinka. Treblinka is called by one Rabbi 'mizbeah ha-damim ha-anaki she-hekim ha-rozeah ha-Ashmodai' (the gigantic altar of blood erected by the murderous Ashmodai).[254]

WESTERBORK (Holland) served as a transit camp from where Jews were deported to Auschwitz and Sobibor.

Transports from the camps of Westerbork (Holland) and Drancy (France) to Auschwitz were sometimes split at the railway station at Cosel (eighty kilometres from Auschwitz). Males under fifteen and over fifty years of age as well as women and children and sick persons were sent to Auschwitz for gassing while all those fit for work were sent to forced labour camps.[255]

Arrival at the camp

Recruits for the extermination camps consisted mainly of people taken from the various ghettos and transit camps. These newcomers had been either forced to set out on their journey or were lured into making it by various promises and deceptions. Sometimes, as we have seen, a roll-call was arranged and afterwards the Jews were herded into cattle-trucks; on other occasions the *Ältestenrat* had been compelled to provide lists of names. There were instances when the victims were told to come with luggage not to exceed fifty kilogrammes as they would be resettled in

Czernowitz und Transnistrien (1941–1942)', ibid., pp. 58ff.; Menasheh Ungar, *ADMORIM Shenispu Ba-Shoah*, pp. 125, 160; Julius Fisher, *Transnistria: The Forgotten Cemetery*, London, 1969. The quotation is taken from Fisher's Introduction, p. 10. Deportation of Jews from Czernowitz is mentioned in the Introduction to the *Responsa* of R. Shmuel Meir Ha-Kohen Holländer, *ShM Ha-Kohen*, Part I: 'Friday night almost the whole town was sent to Transnistria' and the Rabbi escaped through a miracle. On Transnistria, see also Weiss, *Minhath Yizhak*, I, no. 93.

252. The quotation is taken from the 'Indictment' against Eichmann, p. 2.

253. Hausner, *Justice in Jerusalem*, pp. 130, 169.

254. Efrati, *Me-Emek Ha-Bacha*, no. 1; *Mi-Ge Ha-Haregah*, no. 4. See also ibid., no. 11; Breisch, *Helkath Yaakob*, no. 17. On Treblinka as 'one of the worst camps', *vide infra* p. 285.

255. On Westerbork and the transports from there to Poland, cf. Herzog, *Hechal Yizhak*, II, no. 79; Dr J. Presser, *Ashes in the Wind*, London, 1968, pp. 406ff., 482ff. On Drancy, cf. Weiss, *Minhath Yizhak*, II, no. 64.

an area under better and healthier conditions. Some Jews even took books for themselves for their new homes. Thus books of Jews from Hamburg appeared in Kovno while their owners were taken to be exterminated. At the end of November 1941 not less than thirty thousand Jews were brought to Kovno from Frankfurt am Main, Berlin, Vienna, Breslau, Hamburg, etc., under the pretext of being resettled in the Baltic States. Similarly, two thousand Jews of the ghettos of Drohobycz and Boryslaw who were to be 'resettled' were all exterminated.[256] Every journey took place under difficult conditions owing to lack of food, water and air. They lasted several days or even weeks. However, in most cases families were still united.

On arrival at the camp the passengers were driven out from the trucks with blows from rifle-butts and with lashings. The procedure which followed was not the same in all camps.[257] In Treblinka, Belzec, Sobibor and Chelmno, the new arrivals were immediately, almost without exception, exterminated. In Auschwitz, newcomers had to parade in front of the camp doctor who was standing on the platform. He then pointed his thumb 'right' or 'left'. By this the fate of the victim was decided. Right meant to live for slave labour, left meant death, i.e. the crematorium.[258]

Naturally, great excitement and confusion arose on arrival after several days' journey. Men and women (often even members of a family of the same sex) were separated.[259] One Rabbi, an inmate of the camp, tells us that 'although men and women were placed in different rows, the two rows were near each other so that each could see what happened to the other'.[260] 'Furthermore, the Jewish guards called "Canadas" who accompanied the row of people to the crematorium could inform those who were to live about this.'[261]

Pregnant women were immediately sent to the crematorium. It also happened (most probably when pregnancy was not noticed on the woman's arrival) that soon after giving birth both mother and child were sent to the crematorium.[262]

Fitness for work was not always the criterion for a person's being spared, i.e. to be sent to the right side (the labour camp).

---

256. *Vide* Avigdor, *Helek Yaakob*, p. xiii (*infra* p. 126); Oshry, *Mi-Maamakkim*, I, no. 30; Garfunkel, *Destruction of Kovno's Jewry*, pp. 122f.; (*vide* also *supra* p. 54).
257. For particulars, see Hilberg, *Destruction of the European Jews*, pp. 625ff.; Broszat, in 'The Concentration Camps', pp. 483ff.
258. Evidence about seeing a man being sent to the right or the left side played an important part, as we shall see later (p. 227).
259. See Klein in his additions to his father's (R. Shlomoh Zalman Klein), *Atereth Shlomoh*, p. 83 (also quoted by Waldenberg, *Ziz Eliezer*, III, no. 25).
260. Meisels, *Kuntras*, no. 149, p. 36.
261. Ibid. On *Canadas* see 'Glossary'.
262. Meisels, *Binyan Zebi*, II, no. 45.

Everyone who was in Auschwitz knows that among those sent to the left were even many men still fit for work. Usually he who appeared to be over forty,[263] although still fit to work, was not sent to the labour camp at all. Many times only a small proportion of the transport was sent to the labour camp.[264] It happened that mothers with children or carrying babies were sent to the left side. Some mothers not knowing this handed over their babies to their daughters or other relatives. While the former passed the selection and were directed to the right side, those carrying their babies were sent to the left side.

One Rabbi tells us that he himself witnessed such a case of a mother of his community. *Canadas* would often warn mothers beforehand and tell them to abandon their children and thus the mothers were saved.[265]

It is well known to everyone who has been in Auschwitz that there were many separate camps for men and women, and in most cases the transport was not admitted into one camp. Many times the Germans led some of the victims to the town of Auschwitz and they did not remain in Birkenau. Furthermore, those who had been admitted into one camp were distributed among various blocks. Many times new arrivals with the same transport from the same town went into the labour camp and in spite of that met each other only after some days. Hence the fact that a person was not seen in the labour camp is not definite proof of his having been sent to the left side.[266]

On their arrival at the camp the victims were ordered to hand over all their belongings. Prayer books, phylacteries and other religious articles such as *shopharoth* and *lulabim* were confiscated and placed in the store-rooms. It was through the help of the *Kapos* or by 'stealing' them themselves that the inmates of the extermination camps succeeded in obtaining those religious articles. In one case even an Ukranian *Kapo* 'sold' a pair of phylacteries to Jews and the agreed price was one ration (or two rations) of bread![267]

It is interesting that the inmates of Auschwitz extermination camp were still in possession (in 1944) of their jewellery and money which they had hidden and with which they tried to bribe the *Kapos* and

263. On the age limit of the deportees from Holland, *vide supra* p. 97.
264. Meisels, *Kuntras*, no. 38, p. 13; no. 135, p. 33.
265. Ibid., no. 144, p. 35; *Binyan Zebi*, II, no. 38, p. 58; no. 45, p. 63; no. 56, p. 73.
266. Meisels, *Kuntras*, no. 150, p. 36.
267. *Beth Jacob*, no. 22, Jerusalem, Adar 721, p. 3.

'redeem' their children and in one case a Rabbi about to be sent to the crematorium.[268]

There are various reports by the Rabbis about the fate of the new arrivals at the camp. They discussed these cases for they play a most important part in post-war history when questions of *agunoth* (i.e. wives whose husbands had disappeared) arose and every point, however irrelevant it appears, often served as a piece of evidence to permit or to disallow the woman re-marrying.

Thus one Rabbi makes the following statement:

> As is known to us, the order of murder was as follows: At first the greatest part (of a transport) was selected for death. The small part left was distributed in camps. From time to time selections for death were made in the camps.[269] Furthermore, in the camps themselves people were killed by various unnatural methods (*mithoth meshunoth*). The remaining few were deported. They were usually driven on foot so that most died on the way. The very small minority of those left went 'from exile to exile'. Every time they mingled with other people. The majority died and only a small minority was left.[270]

Another Rabbi who had been in Auschwitz and experienced the stay in the death camp states the following facts:[271]

> We know certainly that all men and women who had been led to the left side were burned in the crematorium as it had become clear to us when we were at Auschwitz and saw that whenever a transport arrived flames ascended from the crematorium. Thousands of people entered that Gehenna simultaneously and we did not see even one leaving. When the transports ceased the flames ceased too. This is clear proof of the fate of those who entered the crematorium. . . . Since it is clear that every one sent to the left side was burned, hence, if there is one witness to that effect, the wife of such victim may re-marry. This idea occurred to me at Auschwitz when I was standing very close indeed to the crematorium. . . .
>
> I have seen a letter from a great scholar who lives in Jerusalem in which the view is expressed that the fact of being led to the left side is equal to that of a person who had fallen into waters the shores of

---

268. *Vide infra.*

269. 'As is known from the phraseology of people who had been in Auschwitz only those who had been directed to the left immediately after their arrival are called "persons sent to the left". Those, however, who were later selected for extermination are called "selektiert"'. Weiss, *Minhath Yizhak*, I, no. 96.

270. Ibid., no. 2. Cf. also Avigdor, *Helek Yaakob*, pp. 78ff.

271. On what follows, cf. Meisels, *Kuntras*, no. 1, p. 5; no. 8, pp. 7f.; no. 9, p. 8; no. 78, pp. 21ff.; no. 82, p. 23. See also no. 38, p. 13. On his classification and summary, see also *infra* Part II, pp. 227f.

which cannot be seen in which case his wife must not re-marry (in the first instance), as sometimes he may have been rescued. Similarly a person sent to the left (i.e. to be killed) may have escaped and survived. In my view it is quite true that a miracle of a chance to escape could have occurred. When I was at Auschwitz on *Sukkoth* 250 young men were led from the labour camp to the gas chambers. After two hours fifty of them returned and told me the reason for their being saved from the gas chambers (see p. 118). If such a thing occurred all the inmates of the camp knew about the miracle. It is clear as daylight that he who had arrived at Auschwitz and had been put on the left side had no chance in the world of escaping to freedom since the camp was surrounded several times with wire charged with electricity and guards were standing all round. If a person fled from the left to the right side he had to come to the labour camp and joined those sent to the right. Consequently everyone would have seen him as there was no other place of refuge but the labour camp. Hence if people saw a person sent to the left and he was not seen in the labour camp it was obvious that he had been taken to the gas chamber and burned in the crematorium. . . .

With regard to people about whom there is evidence that they had been seen in the labour camps and not afterwards one must take the following facts into consideration.

Those who had been in the camps for forced labour consisted, as is well known, of three groups: One group did light work being employed in the kitchen, bath-house, etc. They had enough to eat so that if it was certain that they had worked there until the end of the war their *hazakah* (presumption) of being alive is still valid.

A second group did hard labour and was subject to beatings and sufferings from hunger and thirst until they became weak called 'Mussulmänner',[272] and it is known that whenever the cruel ones made a 'selekzie' they chose those weak people who were no longer fit for hard work and sent them to the crematorium. A third group who lay in the camp hospital after becoming weak and sick were the first ones during 'selekzies' to be taken from the hospital to the crematorium. This is known to anyone who has been in a *Konzentrationslager*.

Whenever healthy people and skilled workers were selected for work outside the camp also some of those who had been employed in the kitchen were taken with them. Sometimes a person would be sent to hard labour for the slightest reason or fault, e.g. he had not worked fast enough . . . .

272. On this expression, cf. 'Glossary'.

Those victims who had been sent to the right side were to be spared for the time being.[273] They were to be employed not only for forced labour but many of them served as guinea-pigs for various medical experiments, as has been mentioned above ('Introduction').

One such experiment was sterilization which served a double purpose: as an experiment, and also as a means of exterminating the Jews in 'a natural way'. Chief Rabbi Unterman of Israel deals with the question whether sterilizations performed by the Germans on their Jewish victims fall under the prohibitions of Deut. xxiii 2.

What are of interest for us, apart from the *halachic* aspect, are the methods used by the Germans, which show their cruelty and guile. In the *halachic* works the following is recorded:

There were two methods of sterilization: (1) an operation was performed within the body, cutting through the spermatic duct. 'The wicked', Chief Rabbi Unterman writes, 'added sin to their guilt by cutting off a piece of the duct in most cases so that the two ends of the duct could not join together again and heal'; or (2) the victim was led into a room and placed before a partition in which there was a lattice. They were asked to complete a questionnaire while standing before the lattice unaware that on the other side of the partition a Roentgen (X-ray machine) had been placed which emitted rays directed towards the genitals. The time required for answering the questionnaire sufficed for the rays to have their effect. The Chief Rabbi shows that the prohibitions of Deut. xxiii 2, do not apply to those victims.[274]

According to some reports[275] sterilization performed by X-rays constituted an advanced second stage in the process against the Jews. At first sterilization was carried out by a drug which proved impracticable. For that reason sterilization by X-rays was suggested by a Dr Brack. With twenty such machines three to four thousand people could be sterilized daily. 'Happily', remarks one author, 'the fortunes of war did not allow the Nazis to carry out this particular programme of scientific genocide'.[276] It should be pointed out that from the evidence of a prisoner at Auschwitz from August 1940–January 1944, given at the libel action (in 1964) brought by Dr Wladislaw Alexander Dering against the author and publisher of *Exodus* (written by Leon Uris), we

---

273. The life expectancy of the men and women selected for work was two to three months; see Filip Friedman, *This was Oswiecim*, p. 36; Naumann, *Auschwitz*, p. xxi. According to another author (see Kaplan, *Scroll of Agony*, p. 279) survival of more than one month would be beyond human strength. (No doubt, both views are right: the 'length of life in the camp' depended on the circumstances and conditions of the prisoners.)

274. *Shebet Mi-Yehudah*, 1st Part, Jerusalem, 1955, IV, pp. 286ff.; cf. however, Breisch, *Helkath Yaakob*, II, no. 145.

275. Hilberg, *Destruction of the European Jews*, pp. 604ff.; Jacques Delarue, *The History of the Gestapo*, London, 1966, pp. 308ff.

276. Delarue, *History of the Gestapo*, p. 309.

learn that sterilization of both men and women was often performed by radiation and operations. Sometimes both methods were used on an individual and young girls and boys of various ages were subject to the sterilization process fully conscious of what was being done.[277]

The Nazis were not satisfied with exploiting the living by forced labour and using them as human guinea-pigs, but exploited the dead also. All new arrivals had to hand over all their possessions[278] and the garments particularly of those going to the gas chambers were sorted and sent to Germany. The Nazis sought even, as mentioned above, to utilize the corpses or parts thereof for their advantage and pleasure.

A section in the Seventh Count of the Indictment of Eichmann (b) (6) runs as follows:

> During the Second World War and up to a short time before its conclusion, freight trains containing the movable property of persons murdered in extermination camps, concentration points and ghettos were run month by month from the occupied districts in the East to Germany. This property also contained vast amounts of parts of the bodies of the murdered persons, such as hair, gold teeth, false teeth and artificial limbs; all other personal effects were also taken from the bodies of the Jews before their extermination or thereafter.[279]

In the *Responsa* the following items are mentioned and dealt with. The questions concerned (a) their being kept as they might require burial, (b) their disposal, and (c) whether they defile a *kohen*.

Hair

After the entry of the Allied Army a huge pile of women's hair was found in one of the camps, of which a great part had previously been removed to that despicable country (*erez ha-tumah*) Germany. One of the survivors of the holocaust who had to attend to the hair[280] testified that most of the hair had been taken from the corpses of the victims who had been brought to the gas chambers. The air-vents were later opened and the corpses were removed. Afterwards those given the task had to perform a 'selection'. Then they had to cut off the hair[281] and extract gold teeth, etc., before the corpses were taken to the furnace.

---

277. See Hill and Williams, *Auschwitz in England,* London, 1965, pp. 142ff.
278. Cf. however, *supra* p. 99 where some victims succeeded in hiding jewellery and money in spite of that.
279. 'Indictment', p. 10. See also Papadatos, *Eichmann Trial,* p. 120.
280. Usually done by Jewish prisoners; see Manvell and Fraenkel, *Incomparable Crime,* p. 71.
281. It often happened, however, that the victims had their hair shorn immediately on their arrival at the camp. 'We screamed', declared one witness at the Auschwitz trial, 'because we didn't recognize ourselves.' Naumann, *Auschwitz,* pp. 128, 222.

The question was asked whether the hair had to be buried. The Rabbi decided that it had to be buried. 'If these martyrs had not the merit that their bodies should be brought to a Jewish grave and their ashes were used for manure, at least their hair should be buried . . .'[282]

What did the Germans do with the hair? It served various purposes. Some hair was steamed and packed in bales and sent to Germany where it was used for the manufacture of mattresses and slippers. When the Soviet troops liberated Auschwitz they found seven tons of human hair which according to the estimate of specialists had come from 140,000 women.[283]

Gold teeth

Although the extraction of gold teeth from the victims is mentioned only incidentally in the *Responsum* quoted above, the gold the Germans robbed from the victims in such a way played an important part in the German economy. Colonel Burton C. Andrus, commandant of Nuremberg prison, related the confession made to him by Walter Funk, president of the German Reichsbank, during the trial at Nuremberg that he had been personally responsible for having Jewish prisoners murdered so that gold could be taken from their teeth without trouble.[284]

Dr Robert M. W. Kempner, formerly deputy chief U.S. prosecutor at Nuremberg, declared that nothing in the whole of his long legal career (in Germany and the United States) shocked him so much as the sight of the victims' gold-filled teeth locked away in the safe of the Reichsbank.[285]

Skin, bones and ashes

Human skin removed from corpses was treated and used for making household articles.[286] In a *Responsum* one Rabbi[287] speaks of the 'work

282. Efrati, *Mi-Ge Ha-Haregah*, no. 10.

283. Delarue, *History of the Gestapo*, p. 258; Lord Russell, *Scourge of the Swastika*, p. 243; Hilberg, *Destruction of the European Jews*, p. 614; Max Weinreich, *Hitler's Professors*, New York, 1946, p. 199.

284. Colonel Burton C. Andrus, *The Infamous of Nuremberg*, London, 1969, p. 55.

285. See his Prologue to Levai's *Hungarian Jewry and the Papacy*, p. ix. For further references see Hausner, *Justice in Jerusalem*, p. 168; Naumann, *Auschwitz*, pp. 105, 190, 252, 267, 330; Delarue, *History of the Gestapo*, p. 257; Lord Russell, *Scourge of the Swastika*, p. 170. According to Anatoli, *Babi Yar*, pp. 17, 374, people dug for gold where victims had been resting. They were called 'prospectors', or *Goldsuchers* by the Germans. In one *Responsum* (see Oshry, *Mi-Maamakkim*, II, no. 18) the question is discussed whether one may have benefit from the gold teeth (bridges, crowns, dentures, etc.) from persons who died in their hiding places and bunkers after the Germans had set them on fire. The decision was that no benefit may be derived therefrom.

286. See Manvell and Fraenkel, *Incomparable Crime*, p. 85 and note 26; Lord Russell, *Scourge of the Swastika*, pp. 181ff.

287. Aronzon, *Yeshuoth Mosheh*, p. 240.

of mockery' (*maase tathuim*, on the expression see Jer. x 15) 'of the cursed German Nazis who have made various articles from the sheets of Torah scrolls during the years of the terrible holocaust 700–705, as they have made various articles from human skin in the death camp of Buchenwald as is known to us from the time when "our soul cleaved to the dust" (cf. Ps. cxix 25) in the lowest section of the valley of the shadow of death'.

In one *Responsum*[288] the following case is reported:

A *kohen* received non-religious books from Germany which were bound in human skin taken from those who had been killed in the extermination camps. The questions were:
(i) May he keep them in his house, as the skin may defile?
(ii) May he sell those books, as no benefit may be derived from a corpse or part of it?
(iii) Has he to bury the skin?

Answer: the *kohen* may not keep such books in his home. The skin being part of a corpse must be removed from the books and buried; one may have no benefit from it.

At the Nuremberg trial Rudolf Höss, commandant of the Auschwitz Camp, gave evidence that from 1943 the Germans began to utilize the unburned bones of the victims for practical purposes. The bones were ground and the powder was sold to the firm Strem for the making of superphosphate. This was confirmed in documents found in the camp.[289]

According to some authors ashes of the victims were used as fertilizer. There was, one author says, a special brigade called 'the gardeners' who scattered ashes over vegetable gardens.

In one *Responsum*[290] written immediately after the war the question is discussed whether a *kohen* may transfer the ashes of martyrs to Israel as otherwise they would be used by the local inhabitants for fertilizer.[291]

Fat

While the misuse of the victims' gold teeth, skin, bones and ashes is undisputed a difference of opinion exists concerning the utilization of their fat for the production of soap. There are three different views on this subject: (1) the fat of the martyrs was indeed used for the production of soap; (2) it is doubtful whether such fat was ever used; (3) it was

288. Grossnass, *Leb Aryeh*, no. 36, pp. 88f.
289-90. See Weinreich, *Hitler's Professors*, p. 199; Friedman, *This was Oswiecim*, pp. 64f.; *Beth Jacob*, no. 84, Adar 726, May 1966, p. 19; Delarue, *History of the Gestapo*, p. 257; Anatoli, *Babi Yar*, p. 376.
291. Efrati, *Me-Emek Ha-Bacha*, no. 2. See also *Mi-Ge Ha-Haregah*, no. 10 *ad fin*.

I

only a rumour that human fat was used for the production of soap, a rumour, which is nowadays not taken seriously.

1. The fat of the martyrs was indeed used for the production of soap. One of the first Rabbis to deal with this question was R. Shmuel Meir Ha-Kohen Holländer (Rabbi in Rumania and later in Israel).[292] He discusses the question whether 'one needs to bury the soap which had been brought from Germany and which bears the initials ד.י.פ (R.J.F.) being an abbreviation of the words "Reines Juden Fett" (pure Jewish fat). This soap was made, as is well known, from the fat of our brethren, the martyrs, which also contains ashes and small fragments of bones. Does it convey uncleanliness to a *kohen* by contact (*magga*) or over-shadowing (*ohel*)?'

His decision was that the soap required burial and as far as the ashes and splinters of bones are concerned they conveyed uncleanliness to a *kohen* by contact only . . . (the *Responsum* was written in 1948).

The Rabbi submitted his question to Chief Rabbi Ben Zion Meir Hai Uzziel of Jerusalem concerning 'the soap made by the Germans from the bones (and flesh) of the Jewish martyrs who had been killed and burned by them. The imprint of the bars of soap shows clearly that they had been made from Jewish martyrs as the letters imprinted in Latin characters "R.J.F." are an abbreviation of "Reine Jüdische Fette". Must this soap be buried? Does it defile a *kohen*?'

Answer: as far as uncleanliness is concerned the answer is in the negative. With regard to the question of burial, the Chief Rabbi decided that this should be done.[293]

The production of soap is mentioned by two composers of *kinoth* (dirges).[294]

A memorial stone has been erected in Nahariah, Israel, at the grave of the soap alleged to have been made from the fat of the martyrs. It bears the following inscription (in Hebrew):[295]

Here Lies
THE SOAP PRODUCED FROM THE CORPSES OF THE
MARTYRS OF OUR PEOPLE
'Remember what Amalek did unto thee'[296]
By murdering six million Jews

292. *Responsa SheM Ha-Kohen,* I, Jerusalem, 1952, no. 15.
293. Chief Rabbi Ben Zion Hai Uzziel, *Mishpete Uzziel,* 2nd ed., Part III, *Yoreh Deah,* vol. II, no. 116.
294. On these *kinoth, vide infra,* p. 159, nos. (i) and (ii). On soap-making, see R. M.Weiss-mandel, *Min Ha-Mezar,* p. 28.
295. A photograph of this memorial stone appeared in *Haarez,* 17 December 1972, to which my attention was drawn by Mr Harry Sapir LL.B., Jerusalem, who sent me a copy of it.
296. Deut. xxv 17.

in the years of the Holocaust of World War II
'For He doth avenge the blood of His servants and doth render
vengeance to His adversaries.'[297]
May Their Souls be bound up in bond of everlasting life.[298]

According to various reports the soap was even exported after the
war and found its way to different countries. Thus we read in the press
that 'the Canadian Jewish Congress reports that a bar of soap
"produced" by the Nazis from Jewish corpses was forwarded to them
by a resident of a smaller Jewish community in Canada. After consulting Rabbinic authorities it was decided to arrange for the burial of
the bar of soap by the Cemetery Department of the Baron Hirsch
Institute of Montreal.'[299]

In the middle of 1968 'fifty bars of German soap suspected of being
made from the remains of prisoners in wartime Nazi camps' were
seized by police in Italy.[300]

As late as December 1970 a report appeared in the Jewish press that
'a number of packets, each containing ten bars of soap made by the
Nazis from human fat taken from Jewish victims, had been found in a
carton in a Jewish Agency storeroom. They were buried in the cemetery
on the Mount of Olives where a special memorial was to be erected'.[301]

Where was this soap produced? According to several reports a factory
producing soap from human fat and bones existed in Danzig. One of
them is the evidence given by the mayor of Danzig (5 May 1945) who
claimed that in the Danzig Institute of Hygiene a soap factory was
discovered in which human bodies from the Stutthof camp near Danzig
were used. Three hundred and fifty bodies of Poles and Soviet prisoners
and a cauldron with the remains of boiled human flesh were found.
There was also a box of prepared human bones, and baskets of hands
and feet and human skin, with the fat removed.[302]

Another report is the description of the National Museum in Warsaw
opened in 1946. 'Other exhibits depict the manufacture of soap from
human remains. A human soap factory was discovered near Danzig.
Some half-made soap was found together with some of the finished
product. All the gruesome processes of manufacture, from the chopping

297. Ibid. xxxii 43.
298. Usual phrase on tombstones taken from I Sam. xxv 29.
299. *Jewish Chronicle,* London, 17 February 1961.
300. *Sunday Telegraph,* London, 28 July 1968, p. 3.
301. *Jewish Chronicle,* 18 December 1970, p. 2.
302. Friedman, *This was Oswiecim,* p. 64, quoted also by Hilberg, *Destruction of European Jews,* p. 624, note 21.

up of the human bodies, the cutting off of their heads and so on, until the soap was produced, are shown in all their ghastliness.'[303]

2. It is doubtful whether human fat was ever used.

This doubt can be found mentioned in two *Responsa*.

(a) In a communal courtyard (the name of the community is not mentioned) the soap called ד.י.פ (R.J.F.) was buried which had been brought from Germany and which, according to reports, was made from fat of the Jewish victims. Ashes brought from the crematorium of Auschwitz were buried there too. Are *kohanim* allowed to walk over that place of burial?

R. I.J.Weiss (till 1948 Rabbi in Grosswardein, later in Manchester, now in Jerusalem) who was asked about this matter gave a ruling that the soap should be covered with earth in such a way so that no defilement should be conveyed. At the end of his *Responsum* he quotes the view according to which the soap does not defile by 'overshadowing' (*be-ohel*).[304]

Two important points are mentioned by the Rabbi. (i) The ingredients consisted of at least sixty per cent fat (according to the statements made by experts); however, sometimes the soap contained only forty per cent fat and was made for washing oneself (not for clothes and linen). (ii) It is not certain that all the fat was of human origin. 'As it is well known, it has not been agreed upon by everyone that this soap (R.J.F.) has been made from human fat.'

(b) A similar doubt about the use of human fat for soap production is found in a *Responsum* by R. Eliezer Waldenberg (Ab Beth Din of Jerusalem). He was asked by the Rabbi of Acre in 1958 (i) whether it was permitted 'to transfer the coffin containing soap made from bones and fat of the martyrs of our people, from the place where it had been buried to a more spacious place at the same cemetery where a memorial

---

303. *Jewish Chronicle*, 28 June 1946, p. 9. On other reports on Danzig, see the references quoted by Hilberg, *Destruction of European Jews*, p. 624; Weinreich, *Hitler's Professors*, p. 200. On soap alleged to have been made from human fat in Sobibor, *vide supra*, note 247. In a report prepared by an anti-Nazi officer attached to the German High Command of the Armed Forces, which through intermediaries reached the representative of the World Jewish Congress in Switzerland, it was stated that 'there were at least two factories processing Jewish corpses for the manufacture of soap, glue and lubricants . . .' Arthur D. Morse, *While Six Million Died*, New York, 1968, p. 15. If we believe the assurance of Anatoli, 'A Word from the Author', that everything he had written in *Babi Yar* had really happened and nothing had been invented (see *Babi Yar*, p. 294) then we must take for granted what he says about a building constructed in great secrecy in Babi Yar which turned out later to have been intended as an experimental soap factory for the production of soap from corpses. However, it was not completed. *Babi Yar*, p. 304.

304. *Minhath Yizhak*, I, no.30.

stone and an *ohel* (mausoleum) could be erected', and (ii) whether such soap and ashes of martyrs required burial. With regard to the first question R. Waldenberg decided that it was not permitted to transfer the coffin for various reasons. He also mentions the doubt expressed by the questioner that it was not certain that the soap had been made from the bones and fat of the martyrs. The second question is decided in the affirmative.[305]

(3) 'The assertion of the production of soap from Jewish corpses is, as far as we know, not upheld seriously any more.'[306]

Considering all the views mentioned and the relevant sources available, it appears that one has to make a difference between the 'proof' of the production of soap from human fat, which is based on the interpretation of the alleged letters 'R.J.F.' imprinted 'in Latin characters'[307] on the soap cakes and the evidence given in connection with the soap factory in Danzig.

As far as the imprint is concerned it appears rather strange that the Germans who tried to conceal their criminal actions in the extermination camps should have put the imprint R.J.F. (*rein jüdisches Fett*) thus advertising their evil deeds. In fact the letters which appear on the cakes of soap are 'R.I.F.' being an abbreviation, as several scholars have pointed out,[308] of 'Reichsstelle für industrielle Fettversorgung' (or,

305. *Ziz Eliezer*, VIII, no. 35. On the whole problem, cf. Hilberg, *Destruction of European Jews*, pp. 614, 624.

306. Quotation from the letter of the *Institut für Zeitgeschichte*, vide infra note 308.

307. This spelling is found in a *Responsum*, vide supra, note 293.

308. In his reply to my inquiry Dr Herbert Rosenkranz, first assistant to director of *Yad Vashem* in Jerusalem, pointed out to me that the letters imprinted on the cakes of soap were R.I.F. (Indeed from a photograph taken by a friend of mine of the cakes of soap exhibited in 'Marteph Ha-Shoah' before I had received Dr Rosenkranz's reply I could see that this was the case.) Dr Rosenkranz included an off-print of his article 'RIF' which appeared in *Die Gemeinde*, Vienna, 30 October 1965 in which *inter alia* he states that 'die richtige Lesung der Abkürzung war "Reichsstelle für industrielle Fettversorgung", schon im September 1939 mit dem Sieg über Polen durch das sich auf einen langen Krieg vorbereitende Deutschland eingeführt. Seit damals kamen diese Seifenstückchen zur Verteilung, schon 1940 in polnischen Ghettos . . .'

I received a similar reply from Dr I. Arndt of the Institut für Zeitgeschichte: 'Die Abkürzung "RIF" steht für "Reichsstelle für industrielle Fettversorgung" (oder auch für "Reichsstelle für industrielle Fette und Waschmittel", vgl. das Abkürzungslexikon von Paul Spillner, Ullstein Taschenbuch Nr. 2604/4, 1967); diese Reichsstelle war für die Zuteilung von Seifenerzeugnissen und Waschmitteln zuständig und gehörte zum Geschäftsbereich des Reichwirtschaftsministers. Die sogenannte Rif-Seife gab es schon bald nach Kriegsbeginn und dem Volksmund dürfte die im Kriege geläufige Interpretation "*raus ist's Fett*" zuzuschreiben sein, nicht ganz von der Hand zu weisen ist u.E. die Vermutung, dass der Volksmund auch die Version "reines Judenfett" erfunden hat, ob noch im Kriege—als trotz der Geheimhaltung der Judenvernichtung Kenntnisse darüber in die Bevölkerung durchsickerten—oder nach dem Kriege, ist kaum festzustellen. Die Behauptung der Seifenherstellung aus jüdischen Leichen wird, soweit uns bekannt ist, nicht mehr ernsthaft aufrechterhalten.'

'Reichsstelle für industrielle Fette und Waschmittel'). That government department (*Reichsstelle*) was responsible for the distribution of soap and washing products. The so-called R.I.F.-soap was already in use soon after the outbreak of the war, and people later took the abbreviation as standing for *Rein Jüdisches Fett* disregarding completely the fact that the middle letter of the abbreviation was 'I' (and not 'J').

On the other hand, one has to admit that the reports concerning the production of soap from human fat in the laboratories in Danzig cannot be ignored.[309] Hence the writer shares the view expressed by other scholars[310] that, while the letters R.I.F. cannot serve as evidence of soap production from human fat, attempts were made in Danzig by the Germans (who had misused parts of the corpses of their victims, their hair, skin, gold teeth, bones) to produce soap from the fat of the prisoners. As the camp of Stutthof[311] near Danzig housed also Jewish prisoners there is little doubt that bodies of Jewish victims too were used. The production was still in an initial stage and did not assume large proportions owing to the defeat of the German armies.

The following suggestion could perhaps explain the R.J.F.-soap production. In his attempt to whitewash the Nazis soon after they had come to power and to show that the alleged atrocities were pure inventions Jakov Trachtenberg quotes (in his book which appeared in 1933, *vide supra* p. 4) Dr. Max Naumann, Honorary President of the Association of National German Jews (p. 77) who maintained:

'I regard it merely as a new edition of the war time tales of "frightfulness" spread against Germany and her Allies during 1914–18. Even methods and details are identical with those told of . . . the use of human fats as substitute for other animal fats.'

While as far as World War I is concerned such an allegation was indeed nonsense the idea remained dormant and was not forgotten. With the appearance of the soap marked "R.J.F." the imagination influenced by the rumour spread in 1914–18 regarded "R.J.F." as the abbreviation of 'Reines Juden Fett". Eventually the Nazis indeed put this idea into practice: they began to produce soap from the fat of their victims.

Life in the death camp

It may sound rather paradoxical to speak of 'life' in the 'death' camp. Yet we have ample evidence of the high spirit, the deep devotion to religion and the positive attitude to life in face of death at Auschwitz

309. For references, *vide supra*, notes 302 and 303.
310. See e.g. Herbert Rosenkranz, *Die Gemeinde*, Vienna, 30 October 1965.
311. On Stutthof, *vide supra* pp. 96, 107.

shown by young people in spite of the fact that their parents had been exterminated and they themselves were about to be sent to the crematorium. Were these reports not written by a Rabbi, renowned for his scholarship and piety, who himself was at that time in Auschwitz[312] one would regard them as invented or at least as exaggerated. In fact the purpose of recording these events in his *Responsa* was truly 'for the sake of sanctifying God's Name'.

Many cases are recorded by various authors of how the inmates of the camps tried to observe the law. Thus in one case they baked *mazzoth* for *Pesah*,[313] and refrained from eating *hamez*. A special prayer was composed for those who had to infringe the prohibition of *hamez*.

It was to be recited with great devotion before eating *hamez*. It runs as follows:

> Our Father in Heaven! It is revealed and known to Thee that it is our wish to fulfil Thy will and celebrate the *Pesah* Festival by eating *mazzah* and keeping the prohibition against eating *hamez*. But our heart is pining because the enslavement prevents us (from doing so) and we are in danger of our life (*va-anahnu be-sakkanath nephashoth*). We are ready and prepared to fulfil Thy commandments 'one should live by them' (Lev. xviii 5) and not die by them (*Yoma* 85b), and to beware of Thy prohibition 'Take heed to thyself, and keep thy soul diligently' (Deut. iv 9). Therefore we pray to Thee to keep us alive and preserve us and redeem us speedily so that we can observe Thy statutes and do Thy will and serve Thee with a perfect heart. Amen.[314]

One Rabbi reports that 'although there was no possibility of taking into the camp of Auschwitz any article or book as they have taken from us everything *tallith* and *tephillin* included, there were still small editions of Psalms with the commentary "TephillahLe- Mosheh" by R. Mosheh Teitelbaum to be found'.[315] As we shall see (p. 116) they had a *shophar* as well as an *ethrog* and an old *lulab* brought by the Jews of Lodz who had been deported from the ghetto to Auschwitz. They had no myrtles, while the willows could be taken from the trees growing near the river which flowed through the camp. Also a small *sukkah* was erected at a corner of a workshop where furniture was repaired and a few boards were available. However, sitting in the

---

312. He was R. Zebi Hirsch Meisels, formerly Rabbi in Neumark and later in Waitzen (Vac), after the liberation Chief Rabbi of the British Zone in Bergen-Belsen. Of late Rabbi in Chicago.
313. See *Beth Jacob,* Jerusalem, No. 71, Nisan 725 (April 1965), p. 16.
314. The Hebrew text of the prayer is in the possession of the Beit Lohame Haghetaot (Ghetto Fighters' House), Kibbutz Lohame Haghetaot, Galilee, Israel. I made use of it by kind permission of Mr Zvi Shner on behalf of the Ghetto Fighters' House.
315. Meisels, Introduction to *Mekaddshe Ha-Shem,* I, Chicago, 715 (1955).

sukkah involved great danger as the SS often passed to supervise the Jews' work. Anyone found who did not belong there was subject to severe punishment. Indeed the Rabbi's son who was found eating a *ke-zayith* of bread (size of an olive) in the *sukkah* was beaten mercilessly.[316]

Another Rabbi tells us how they succeeded in Auschwitz and in other camps in studying the Torah by heart or from books which they possessed by a miracle. This was done in company with other Rabbis before many people, during working hours as well as in free time. They tried to encourage people, to instruct them and show them the right way of life and how to fulfil the commandments by various devices as far as possible.[317]

Special mention deserves to be made of the following event witnessed by R. Z.Meisels:[318]

On the eve of *Rosh Ha-Shanah*[319] about 1,600 young men up to the age of eighteen who were living scattered about and unnoticed in the camp of Auschwitz were rounded up by the Nazis and their accomplices and taken to a place at the back of the blocks where the commandant of the camp appeared. He ordered that a pole be placed in the ground and a board be nailed horizontally on top. Each boy had to pass under that board and he whose head touched the board would be spared and sent back into the camp (i.e. he was fit to work), the others who did not reach the required height were to be taken to a closely guarded block to be killed. As the boys knew that if they did not reach the board they would die, they tried to walk on their toes as they passed under the board. When the commandant noticed this he would knock the boy over the head with his truncheon, so that the boy fell to the ground and wallowed in his blood and did not rise again . . . or the boy was taken to the crematorium . . . fatally wounded . . . this happened to several boys.

After this examination and selection about 1,400 boys remained in the open place from where they were later taken to a specially closed block, to be kept there until the following morning when their fate was to be decided. Neither food nor drink was given them. *Kapos* were placed at the gates and no one could enter or leave.

On the following morning, the first day of *Rosh Ha-Shanah*, great

---

316. Meisels, *Mekaddshe Ha-Shem*, pp. 10ff., 14.
317. R. Yehezkiel S. Lipschitz-Halberstam of Stropkow, Introduction to *Dibre Yehezkiel*, 1st Part, Jerusalem, 1956.
318. Meisels, *Mekaddshe Ha-Shem*, p. 7.
319. The year is not mentioned. A similar selection was made in Auschwitz on the eve of *Yom Kippurim*. See the evidence given at the Eichmann trial by Joseph Zalman Kleinmann, Session 68, p. 7.6.61. FL IEM (copied from the copy in possession of the Wiener Library).

confusion and consternation prevailed when the rumour spread that the boys would be taken to the crematorium towards evening. No one was taken to the crematorium during day time only at night. During that day many fathers who had been left with only one son who had been seized and relatives and friends ran around the block in confusion. They hoped they might be fortunate enough to save their dear ones before sunset. But the *Kapos* took no notice of the fervent supplications and cries to release boys who had been locked up. 'As it is well known, most of those *Kapos* were wicked men, hard-hearted, the dregs of the people.' In that case, however, their argument appeared justified, since they were responsible for the number of children who had been put in their charge and had to hand over the exact number to the SS towards evening. If one child was missing the *Kapos* would suffer the same fate and would be taken to the crematorium, 'life for life'.

Eventually, after much endeavour and bargaining greed prevailed and the *Kapos* consented to free a lad after receiving great sums. They immediately seized another boy who had been released the day before (as he had attained the required height or had hidden himself) and he was taken to the block, so that the number remained unaltered.

Many people had still money or jewellery hidden in their shoes or in other places, or collected sums from their friends and therewith redeemed their child from sure destruction. This kind of trade—'bring and buy sale'—continued openly all the day of *Rosh Ha-Shanah* as the SS did not patrol the inner part of the camp during day-time which was in the charge of the Jewish *Kapos*.

There were, however, many people, men of conscience, who did not want to redeem their son at the expense of the life of another child, applying the Talmudic doctrine (*Pes.* 25b) that one must not save one's own life at the expense of that of another person as the latter's life is no less valuable than one's own.

The Rabbi then continues: 'I shall never forget the terrible case which my eyes saw and my ears heard concerning the matter mentioned above, a fact which is a symbol of the holiness of the children of Israel and their sincere devotion to the ways of the holy Torah, even at a time of trouble and terrible suffering.'

A Jew who did not seem exceptionally learned, and who came from Oberland,[320] approached him and asked the following question:

'Rabbi, my only son, who is dearer to me than the apple of my eye, is among the boys destined to be burned. I have the possibility of redeeming him; however, as I know the *Kapos* would, no doubt, seize another boy in his place, I ask you, Rabbi, to give me a decision

320. Part of Slovakia occupied by Hungary.

in accordance with the Torah whether I am permitted to redeem my son. Whatever your decision, I shall comply with it.'

When I heard that question trembling took hold of me. I had been asked to decide a matter involving life and death. I replied: 'My dear friend, how can I, in my position, give you a clear decision on this question, seeing that also in the time when the Temple was standing a question concerning capital cases had to be brought before the Sanhedrin? I am here in Auschwitz without any books on *halachah* (Codes), without any other Rabbis, without peace of mind, owing to the travails and troubles . . .'

The Rabbi considering the case thinks that, if the wicked *Kapos* were first to release the boy and afterwards seize another victim, one might perhaps be inclined to permit the redemption of the boy. The *Kapos* would from the religious point of view be prohibited from seizing another (innocent) boy as it would contravene the ruling 'one has to give one's own life and not transgress'. Perhaps at the last moment their Jewish conscience would make itself felt and they would refrain from doing that.

However, the method of the *Kapos* was different; they first seized the 'substitute' and later released the boy who was to be redeemed. There was therefore no need to discuss the matter.

The father who had approached the Rabbi urged him to give a decision. The Rabbi pleaded with him that he did not want to answer such a question. However, the father did not stop repeating his request despite the assurance of the Rabbi that he could give no decision either way. Then with great emotion and enthusiasm the father said:

'Rabbi, I have done what the Torah commands me to do, i.e. to ask a Rabbi for a decision, and there is no other Rabbi here whom I could consult. If you cannot give me a reply whether I may redeem my child, it appears you yourself are not certain that I may do so, for were it permitted, without doubt you would have told me so. Therefore I take it for granted that the decision is I must not do so according to the *halachah*. This is sufficient for me. Therefore, my only child will be burned according to the Torah and *halachah*. I accept this with love and joy. I shall do nothing to redeem him, because the Torah has so commanded me . . . .'

All my words that I did not wish to have the responsibility remained fruitless. He was adamant and did not redeem his son. The whole day of *Rosh Ha-Shanah* he walked about happy, repeating to himself that he had the merit to offer his only son to God, although he had a chance to redeem him . . . . His attitude would be highly valued by God like the binding of Isaac which also took place on *Rosh Ha-Shanah*.

Another case was the following.[321] Among the boys doomed to die was one of the Rabbi's pupils, a young man of about twenty years of age. His name was Mosheh Rosenberg from Hungary. He was learned and God-fearing and, as he was not sufficiently tall, was among those to be burned. On the other hand, a boy of fourteen or fifteen who had 'passed the test' was not taken to the death block. It then happened that a boy of about fifteen years whose name was Akiba Mann, son of the head-teacher of Waitzen, R. Baruch Mann (who died a martyr) approached the Rabbi and asked: 'Rabbi, what will happen to Moshehle?' The Rabbi replied: 'What can be done? Is there any possibility of saving him?' He repeated the question adding, 'Is it right that Moshehle be burned and we be silent?' 'I replied again,' says the Rabbi, 'is there a way of saving him?' 'Yes,' he replied, 'I have enough money to redeem him.' 'But surely you know that redemption must be at the expense of the life of another boy? Who can take upon himself such a responsibility?' 'I have a plan for this too,' he replied, 'I shall take his place, I'd happily do that . . . .' When I heard that, I rebuked him, telling him that I could not permit that under any circumstances as in such a situation the Talmud clearly rules (*Baba Mezia* 62a) 'Your life has preference to that of your fellow man'. He left the Rabbi, but after a short while returned.

'Rabbi,' he said, 'I can find no rest if Moshehle is burned and I who can by no means be compared to him would remain among the living. I have decided to let myself be exchanged for him and to take his place, even if you do not give me explicit permission. However, I would like you to give me an assurance that my action would not be regarded as suicide.' I again rebuked him, and after much argument, he left me very sad, as I did not give him permission.

Saving a great Rabbi

One of the inmates of the camp of Auschwitz was Rabbi Menahem Mendel Karader, Dayan and head of the *yeshibah*, of Miskolcz (Hungary).[322] All the inmates of the camp had to shave every morning. R. Menahem, however, did not wish to do so during the days of *selihoth* (the days preceding *Rosh Ha-Shanah*) and consequently, at the *appell* (roll-call) on *Rosh Ha-Shanah* morning white hairs of his beard were visible. The wicked Nazi became very angry when he noticed that. He took hold of R. Menahem and put him in the block together with the boys destined for death (see *supra* p. 112.) and he was to be sent to the crematorium with them. However, that Nazi was not in charge of

---

321. Meisels, *Mekaddshe Ha-Shem*, p. 9.
322. Ibid., p. 10.

the transport of the boys who were under the authority of other members of the SS. It was therefore thought that R. Menahem could be redeemed from the *Kapos* without needing a 'substitute' (see *supra* p. 114). The Rabbi writes that he immediately began to negotiate his release with the *Kapos*, but they were afraid that R. Menahem would be recognized outside the block by his white beard, and that the SS officer who had sent him to the block would recognize him after some days. The *Kapos* would then bear the responsibility.

As far as the transports from Auschwitz were concerned from time to time transports of hundreds or thousands of inmates would be sent to other camps or to forced-labour camps. On *Rosh Ha-Shanah* a transport of about a thousand people was to be sent to a certain place. R. Meisels made arrangements with a Jew, who was among those to be sent with the transport on *Rosh Ha-Shanah*, to change places with R. Menahem, so that R. Menahem would join the transport while he would remain in the camp. The Jew agreed to this proposal. R Meisels immediately returned to the *Kapos* and urged them to agree to that too and after much bargaining and a promise to pay a large sum of money, they consented to that exchange. However, they stipulated that R. Menahem shave off his beard before leaving the block to avoid attracting attention. It was explicitly arranged that the *Kapos* were not to take another Jew in place of R. Menahem.

R. Meisels tells us that he spoke to R. Menahem from a distance and explained the whole position and that in his view shaving off the beard on *Rosh Ha-Shanah* would be permitted in view of the danger to life. R. Menahem accepted that and replied immediately that the Torah tells us 'Joseph Ha-Zaddik shaved himself' (see Gen. xli 14) and according to our Sages (*Rosh Ha-Shanah* 10b) that too happened on *Rosh Ha-Shanah*. 'I wish not to be regarded as more righteous than he[323] and am ready with all my heart to do so.'

The Rabbi collected money to redeem R. Menahem and when that was accomplished, he joined the transport and left Auschwitz while another man originally destined to be sent away remained in Auschwitz.

Blowing the Shophar

R. Meisels tells us[324] that he succeeded in obtaining a *shophar* before *Rosh Ha-Shanah* and that he went from block to block on that day and blew the required hundred sounds about twenty times in spite of the great danger involved of being noticed by 'the Nazis and the wicked *Kapos*'. The Rabbi points out that the hearing of the *shophar* served as

323. See, however, Meisels' note ibid.
324. Ibid., pp. 10ff.

comfort and raised the spirit of the unfortunate souls. They had been able to hear the sound of *shophar* even in Auschwitz.

When those Jews who had been in the transport due to be sent away on that day learned from R. Meisels who had come with R. Menahem to make the exchange (see *supra* p. 116) that he had a *shophar*, they were thrilled and asked the Rabbi to blow the *shophar* for them. The Rabbi did so and when, before blowing the *shophar*, he heard the names of notes read by the famous *hasid*, R. Joshua Fleischmann of Debreczen (who later died a martyr) in a trembling and sighing voice and the bitter cries of the assembled inmates, R. Meisels says he could hardly concentrate.

When the boys who had been shut in the block to be sent to the crematorium (see *supra* p. 112) learned that there was a *shophar* in the camp, they began to cry and shout from the block that the Rabbi should come to blow the *shophar* for them. The Rabbi tells us of the great danger that was involved in such an attempt and he succeeded in fulfilling the wish of the unfortunate boys (the Rabbi adds that his action involving danger to his own life was not in accordance with the *halachah*).

He then tells us of the address he delivered to them before blowing the *shophar* and of the heart-rending words of the boys when he left them. One of the boys got up and cried out: 'My dear friends, the Rabbi has spoken words of encouragement and quoted the saying of our Sages that "even when a sharp sword is lying over a man's throat he should not refrain from seeking mercy (from God)" (*Berachoth* 10a). I wish to tell you (he spoke in Yiddish): we can hope for the best, but we must be prepared for the worst. For God's sake, brethren, let us not forget in the last minute to cry out with devotion (*kavvanah*) "Shema Yisroel".' Thereupon they all raised their voices and shouted 'Shema Yisroel'. When the Rabbi was about to leave, several boys approached him with the request to provide them with a *ke-zayith* (size of an olive) of bread so that they could fulfil the duty of having a meal on *Rosh Ha-Shanah*, as they had had nothing to eat or drink since the previous day when they were shut up in the block. Unfortunately, the Rabbi could not comply with their request to return to the block, and so all the lads were led fasting to the crematorium.

The miraculous escape of fifty boys

More fortunate were the last fifty boys rounded up in the camp who had been taken to the crematorium during the night which happened to be the night of *Simhath Torah*.[325] Rabbi Meisels reports that they were ordered by the Nazi murderers to take a bath and be clean 'for

325. Ibid., pp. 14ff.

this was the manner of the Nazi murderers to deceive the martyrs so as to give them the impression they would be set free.'[326]

The boys knew of the trick and their situation. After overcoming their emotions one of them rose and called out: 'My dear friends (*haberim*), today is *Simhath Torah*, it is true we have no Torah here to dance with, but the Master of the Universe is with us. Let us dance with Him before we are burned.' Hardly had he finished his words and all began to sing and dance, reciting the well-known song 'Ashrenu mah tob helkenu . . .' and also 'Ve-taher libenu . . .'. The enthusiasm of the young lads overstepped all bounds.

When the Nazi guards standing in the adjacent room heard the noise they burst in with anger. They were surprised to see boys who were on the threshold of death, having the courage to sing. They inquired the reason for the merriment. When the boys told the SS commandant the reason, that they were glad to depart from this low and despicable world where cursed and ugly people ruled and that furthermore they were soon to have the opportunity of being reunited with their parents who had been murdered he became enraged and ordered the boys to be taken back into the block where they would have to stay until they were punished severely.

A miracle then occurred. The following day a big transport of inmates from Auschwitz was to be dispatched to various labour camps in Germany early in the morning. A large number of the fifty boys (*rubba de-rubba*) succeeded in infiltrating into the crowd sent to the labour camps and were thus able to leave Auschwitz. The few who were left dispersed to the various blocks of the camp in Auschwitz and mingled with the other inmates so that they would not be recognized. In this way, all fifty boys were saved. This was regarded as a wonder throughout the camp.

A similar event is mentioned in the evidence [327] of a survivor of the death camp at the Eichmann trial in Jerusalem.

The witness, Nahum Hoch (born in Transylvania in 1928 today an architect in Haifa) was one of the thousand boys who had been put into blocks eleven and thirteen which were notorious for being the last stage for those going to the crematorium. He described in detail the events of the last three days after the boys (all of them between the age of fourteen and sixteen) had been selected, how they had attempted a

break out from the blocks but were then rounded up, and how they had been led to a big hall that looked like a bath house. On the walls

326. On the deception of being sent for a bath and disinfection, see also Poliakov, *Harvest of Hate*, pp. 205f.
327. I am quoting from the copy of the minutes of the session 71, 8.6.61., Iil ff. of the Eichmann trial in the possession of the Wiener Library, London. The case is reported by Hausner, *Justice in Jerusalem*, pp. 173f., where the fact of 'singing' has been omitted.

all around us there were hooks, and on each hook there was a serial number. They ordered us to hang our clothes on the hooks and to remember the serial number . . . . They told us when we would come out, we could tell where to take our clothes from. Of course this was deception and we knew that. We undressed and we threw the clothes on the floor in the middle of the room. Later we were put in columns, rows of five . . . . One of the *Sonderkommando*[328] there came up to us and said: 'Hebrah, boys, at least don't show that you are worried. Sing . . .' He was a Jew. He said it in Yiddish. He said: 'Hebrah, sing. Boys, sing.' I don't know the exact words . . . he told us to sing . . . Some of us were frozen—we could not utter a word . . . . Others began reciting a confessional prayer, and others sang. . . . They took us into a dark hall and shut the door behind us . . . after some time . . . they opened the door . . . the Camp Commandant selected fifty strong boys (among them the witness) and we were ordered to dress . . . and were taken out of the camp to the railway station. There we were ordered to get into freight trucks loaded with potatoes and empty the wagons—take the potatoes off and bury them in the ground. Then we knew—why we had been taken out—because there was a shortage of manpower for unloading these potatoes . . . .

It would appear that Hoch's case is identical with that mentioned by Rabbi Meisels as there are three points they have in common: the day when they sang and left the closed block (*Simhath Torah*), the number of the boys saved (fifty), and the order to sing.

However, there are several differences between the two reports. Thus e.g. according to the first report, it was one of the boys who asked the others to sing as it was a day of rejoicing; according to the second report it was one of the *Sonderkommando* who did so, to show they were not afraid. He did not belong to the group of boys as he remarked, when the boys were taken out: 'This is the first time I've encountered here people taken out of the gas chambers alive. I wish I were as safe as you are.' (Such words could have only been spoken by one of the *Sonderkommando* who used to accompany the inmates to the gas chambers and after a few months' work were themselves killed as they knew too much.)

The main difference, however, is the reason for which the boys were saved. According to the Rabbi's report, it was *the singing* which caused the boys' death to be postponed so as to punish them; according to the witness's report the saving of the boys was due to *the shortage of manpower*.

328. See 'Glossary'.

In order to solve this contradiction, the writer contacted the witness Mr Hoch and mentioned the points both reports had in common and also the contradictory facts. In his reply[329] Hoch pointed out that, as is well known, apart from the camp of Auschwitz, in that town there were another five camps on the one side of the road in Birkenau-Auschwitz and also on the other side there were camps and gas chambers. He draws attention to the fact that in his evidence he reported that the incident happened on the *day* of *Simhath Torah* at noon while in the Rabbi's report this happened on the *night* of *Simhath Torah*. He is therefore of the opinion that there were two different miraculous events in two parts of the Auschwitz camp: 'I do not call in question the Rabbi's report; there were, no doubt, other miracles in the camp and crematoria in Auschwitz . . . .'[330]

It appears indeed that this suggestion is correct. There were two different events in different places of the same camp in Auschwitz in one and the same year. This is proved by the following fact. From the evidence given by another witness named Joseph Kleinmann who had been deported from the Carpatho-Russian district (and who happened to be together with Hoch) we learn that there were two selections: one selection *without* yardstick on Friday (three days before *Rosh Ha-Shanah* which happened to be on Monday and Tuesday)[331] and another *with* the yardstick on the eve of *Yom Kippur*. With regard to the selection on the Friday before *Rosh Ha-Shanah*, the witness said: 'We were taken—this was in the gipsy camp—it was a transit camp for Hungarian Jews and also for the Jews from the Lodz Ghetto, later; in the barracks there, there were 3,000 children and boys—special barracks, called 'Kinderblocks' (Children's blocks)—it was the Friday before the Jewish New Year, which was on Monday and Tuesday that year. Mengele[332] appeared with his deputy, Dr Thilo[333]—it was on a Friday, at sundown—at parade time—and he went into the 'Kinderblocks' and made a selection. He ordered us to undress the upper part of our bodies and said—we were the last barracks in that line, in the line of the Children's block.'

329. Dated: 9th of Ab 731.
330. On my recent visit to Israel I had an opportunity of seeing Mr Hoch who repeated his suggestion to me.
331. During World War II *Rosh Ha-Shanah* fell on Monday and Tuesday only twice: on 22 and 23 September 1941, and 18 and 19 September 1944. The incident the witness reported could have happened only in September 1944. *Vide infra.* See also Hausner, *Justice in Jerusalem*, p. 173.
332. Josef Mengele was the most cruel and infamous doctor at Auschwitz. The new arrivals had to parade in front of him, and he by a mere pointing with his thumb 'right' or 'left' decided the fate of the victim. Millions of people perished through him. At the end of the war he fled to South America and lived in Paraguay.
333. On him, see Reitlinger, *The Final Solution*, p. 566.

From these reports (by R. Meisels and both witnesses) we learn that the boys had been deported from Hungary, Transylvania and the Carpatho-Russian district. Deportation from these countries did not commence before April-May 1944. The liberation of Auschwitz by Soviet troops occurred on 26 January 1945. *Rosh Ha-Shanah* between the deportation and the liberation fell on Monday and Tuesday (18 and 19 September 1944)[334] agreeing with the witnesses' statement. The selection without yardstick mentioned by the witness could have taken place on Friday three days before *Rosh Ha-Shanah* which fell on the following Monday and another selection with a yardstick took place on the eve of *Yom Kippur* while the selection mentioned by R. Meisels occurred *with* a yardstick on Sunday, eve of *Rosh Ha-Shanah*.

This shows us clearly that selections were made before *Rosh Ha-Shanah* on two different days (Friday and Sunday) with and without the yardstick. This must have taken place in two different compounds. Hence two miracles happened on *Simhath Torah*.

The Kapos

The behaviour of the Jewish overseers called *Kapos* (sing. *Kapo, Kamp Polizei*) was in contrast to the noble attitude shown by some people in the camps.[335]

As during the bondage in Egypt, the taskmasters appointed officers from the children of Israel who were responsible for seeing that the daily work was done, so the Germans appointed *Kapos* from the Jewish and non-Jewish inmates of each concentration camp, who were in charge of their fellow-sufferers. The role the Jewish *Kapos* played was unfortunately different from that of the officers in Egypt. While the latter suffered with and showed sympathy for their fellow Jews (see Ex. v 14ff.) the former sought to please their overlords by often displaying cruelty to their brethren denouncing them to the Gestapo and ill-treating them severely. A Rabbi when speaking about them remarks that 'it is well known that most of the *Kapos* were wicked, hard-hearted, the dregs of the people'. They were cruel towards their own brethren, robbed them, beat them without mercy. They kidnapped young people for gain and acted like slave-dealers.[336] Even in the last hours before the liberation, the *Kapos* did not want to give up their role as overlords. They robbed their fellow men and treated them badly. A Rabbi reports[337] the following event: When he was deported to Auschwitz he took the *tallith* with an *atarah* (crown) on it, which had belonged to

---

334. Cf. r 31.
335. On the *Canadas, vide supra* p. 98 and 'Glossary'.
336. *Vide supra* p. 113 and *infra*, pp. 175f.
337. Meisels, *Mekaddshe Ha-Shem*, pp. 15ff.

K

his grandfather the saintly Rabbi of Sziget, the author of *Yitab Leb*,[338] R. Jekuthiel Tietelbaum. It had been given to him as a present, 'it was sure that this *tallith* would serve as a kind of protection'. When he arrived at Auschwitz all belongings were taken away and the Rabbi had to be parted from his *tallith*. He managed, however, to be employed in the garment sorting office. The good clothes had been made ready for dispatch to Germany. Whilst working there, he found his *tallith* which he retrieved. To avoid suspicion when wearing the *tallith* which was large, he cut it up and made a small *tallith* (*tallith katan*) from it. Wearing even the small *tallith* brought him once into great danger when it was discovered on him by the chief bath attendant 'Phoenix', who had been a Communist, and sent to the concentration camp for life. The Rabbi tells us his ordeal with the *tallith katan*. Eventually, he had it returned to him.

It happened during the final weeks, before the liberation by the American (*sic*) troops, that the inmates of the camp, about fifteen hundred Jews, were moved from place to place in order to prevent their being freed by the Americans.[339] On the last Sabbath they heard the sound of guns and bombardment which indicated that the Americans were nearby, a fact which raised high hopes in their hearts. Suddenly, they were ordered to move elsewhere. This order caused them great fear and anxiety. They feared they would be taken to a crematorium in accordance with Hitler's wish to exterminate the Jews.

During the transports, the *Kapos* used to search the prisoners for anything valuable which, if found, was confiscated. In that way, they robbed the prisoners of their shoes and garments, the last things they possessed. When the Rabbi was searched and nothing, except the *tallith katan*, was found, *Kapo* 'Willy' became very angry, tore it off and threw it into the fire. This act caused the Rabbi great consternation. He burst into tears crying continuously as his last protection which had proved so successful till then in the time of trouble, had been taken from him at a time when he required more help than ever.

The prisoners were taken to the freight-train station and were loaded into cattle-trucks, which were densely crowded, without any food or drink in a suffocating atmosphere, as was usually the case with such transports.

During the night, they tried to sleep a little, each man's head resting upon the shoulder of his neighbour. The Rabbi's head rested upon the

338. On Torah, 2 Vols., Sziget-Lwow, 1875–80. See Walden, *Shem Ha-Gedolim He-Hadash, s.v.*
339. Meisels, *Mekaddshe Ha-Shem*, pp. 16ff. On *Kapos* after the liberation, *vide infra* pp. 175f.

shoulder of his son. But after the Rabbi succeeded in falling asleep, he was awakened by his son (who was then fourteen years old) who said: 'Father, I have such pain I can't stand it any more' and he asked his father to put his head on his neighbour's shoulder sitting on his other side. The son acted similarly. But suddenly the noise of heavy bombs was heard from a squadron of aeroplanes led by Americans who were watching the train thinking German soldiers were in it and were trying to bomb it. There was a deafening noise, and suddenly, a fragment of a bomb passed between the Rabbi's head and that of his son just through the gap where, a few minutes before, the former's head had lain. The fragment fell on the hands of the *Kapo* who was lying comfortably on a bench in the middle of the carriage and blew them off. Naturally, he began to shout for help and implored those present to save him from death. People saw it as a punishment for his having torn away the Rabbi's *tallith katan*. He asked the Rabbi for forgiveness and to pray for his life.

Not always were the inmates of the camps moved by train. One witness[340] at the Eichmann trial testified that when news came of the approach of the Russian troops, the order was given (on 5 January 1945) that all inmates of Auschwitz and all its subsidiary camps numbering 54,651[341] prisoners march westwards. A great number did not survive the march and those who remained were distributed among various camps inside Germany.

There are two *Responsa* in which such death-marches are mentioned.[342]

WHY DID THE JEWS NOT RISE AGAINST THEIR TORMENTORS?
REPLY BY RABBIS

One often comes across the question why the Jews in the ghettos and camps did not rise against their tormentors.[343] Why did they allow themselves 'to be led like sheep to the slaughter'?[344]

340. See Hausner, *Justice in Jerusalem*, pp. 174ff.
341. No doubt, the report of the Rabbi and his figure mentioned before refer to a section only.
342. *Vide supra.*
343. Cf. e.g. Hausner, *Justice in Jerusalem*, p. 176; O. Kraus and E. Kulka, *The Death Factory*, pp. 250f.; Garfunkel, *The Destruction of Kovno's Jewry*, pp. 263ff. and the latter's reply.
344. On this phrase, *vide* 'Glossary'. There were, however, as is well known, acts of resistance on various occasions. Apart from the heroic uprising in the ghetto of Warsaw, the Jews tried whenever they had the opportunity to fight the Nazis. Not only did they join the partisans (also mentioned in the *Responsa, vide infra, supra*) but even boys of the age of fourteen to sixteen years shut up in the death block tried to defy the Nazis by breaking out and singing Hebrew songs before entering the gas chamber (*vide supra* p. 118 and the evidence at the Eichmann trial, session 71, 8.6.61, LII). On cases of revolt and resistance, cf. particularly the work edited and translated by Yuri Suhl, *They Fought Back*, London, 1968; Poliakov, *Harvest of Hate*, pp. 224ff.

Several Rabbis who were inmates of the ghettos and concentration camps and had first-hand experience of the diabolical methods of the Nazis protested independently against those who reproach the inmates of the ghettos for not having resisted the Nazi atrocities with force.

One of them was Rabbi Dr Jehiel Jacob Weinberg, head of the Rabbinical seminary in Berlin, who had spent some time in the Warsaw Ghetto. 'One cannot describe', he writes,[345] 'what happened within the walls of the ghetto. There the German beast showed itself with all its ferocity, violence and cruelty never seen or heard since the heavens and earth have been created . . . . *Ereh be-nehamah* "May I not live and see the consolation of Zion" if I have not seen men, women and children thrown to the ground and trampled by people fleeing for fear of death, or persons having collapsed from hunger and cold and murderous blows. They lay on the ground helplessly and breathed their last with no one to bring them to burial . . . . It was a daily occurrence for German soldiers and officers to roam the streets equipped with iron bars and knock down everyone who came their way.' After describing this, R. Weinberg raises a bitter accusation against those writers, 'the heroes of the pen' (*sopherim gibbore et*) as he calls them, who blame the unfortunate inhabitants of the ghetto for not having rebelled against the German sadists, for having remained passive whilst standing at the entrance to destruction and for not having followed Samson's example 'Let me die with the Philistines' (Jud. xvi 30), i.e. by sacrificing their lives killing their tormentors. 'Those who complain about this', R. Weinberg says, 'do not know the diabolical method of the Germans, of their systematic actions which took place gradually until at the end not men but shadows, wrecks of Jews were left, full of despair and having one desire to give up their lives soon.'

Another Rabbi, Dr Jacob Avigdor (Chief Rabbi of Drohobycz and Boryslaw, after the war in the U.S.A.) spent all the war years in ghettos and camps.[346] He too tries to show how wrong it is to reproach the Jews for not having resisted the Nazis with force.[347] 'The Nazis did everything leading to the liquidation of the Jews secretly and methodically. The extermination began in 1942 after the Germans had established themselves as masters of the conquered countries. The first action of the Germans against the Jews was the decree to wear a badge[348]

345. *Yad Shaul, Sepher Zikkaron al Shem Ha-Rab Dr Shaul Weingorth*, ed. by R. J.J. Weinberg and R. Pinhas Biberfeld, Tel Aviv, 1953, p. 9; see also Weinberg, *Eth Ahai Anochi Mebakkesh*, pp. 34f. Introduction to *Seride Esh*, I, p. 1.
346. See his *Helek Yaakob*, Mexico, 1956, pp. xiiif.; 67f.; 78f.
347. Ibid., pp. ixff.
348. The *Judenstern* (badge of the six pointed star) was introduced in Wloclawek on 28 October 1939, in Cracow on 18 November 1939 and throughout occupied Poland on 23 November 1939. See Gerhard Schoenberner, *The Yellow Star*, pp. 31, 216. A similar

of identification on the right arm so that they be distinguishable as
Jews from afar. Who would have thought that that would eventually
lead to extermination? All Jews knew that similar orders had been in
force in the Middle Ages.[349] The Germans had even given their reason,
that they looked upon the Jews as their enemy and feared that their
troops might be misled by Jews. It was for the purpose of identifying
the Jew so as to prevent deception by and communication with him.
Did this decree in itself constitute sufficient grounds for a rebellion
against German troops?'

The Rabbi explains that there was no reason to rise against the
Germans when a few months later they ordered all the Jews to move to
a special quarter as similar directions were given to the Ukrainians,
Poles and Germans. Hence the decree was not originally aimed especially at the Jews. 'If the former did not rise against the Germans but left
their houses to live in their quarters, how could the Jews alone rise
against them?'

The Rabbi tells us of the great plight of the Jews, how the Germans
were anxiously awaiting signs of slightest provocation from the Jews,
how the leaders of the Jewish community were anxious to get the
Jewish youth to restrain themselves, how the Germans were disappointed that the Jews were bearing everything in patience. 'Perhaps',
the Rabbi says, 'this was the reason for the lengthy process of extermination. Had the Jews rebelled, not one Jew would have been left alive.'
'From this point of view, one should not ask why did the Jews not
rebel but one should rather seek explanation for the great power of
self-restraint which prevailed among the Jews.'

'When then the Jews were enclosed in the ghetto, the conditions of
life were so difficult that one wonders how we could survive. The famine
was terrible, the death-rate was sometimes twenty times more than
normal. Various epidemics raged, the healthy people were subjected all
day to hard labour and when they returned to the ghetto they were
without food, fresh air and medicaments, and were shirtless; in spite
of all this, everyone wished to suffer and live contrary to the wish of
the enemy whose desire it was that the Jew should die or commit
suicide . . .[350]

'This chapter has not yet been written and not expressed at all.'

---

decree was issued against the Jews in Germany on 1 September 1941. *Vide infra*
'Glossary', p. 365. See Bruno Blau, *Das Ausnahmerecht für die Juden in Deutschland
1939–1495*, p. 89, no. 329.

349. 'All Jews knew that such a decree was not new as it had been current in many countries
in the Middle Ages.' R. J.Avigdor, *Helek Yaakob*, p. x. The yellow badge was introduced by Pope Innocent III at the Fourth Lateran Council in 1215 and subsequently
by the rulers of various Christian countries.

350. On this intention of the Germans, see also *supra*, note 187.

Rabbi Avigdor relates that after the Jews had moved into the ghetto, the first order given by the Germans was that a thousand Jews were to prepare themselves to leave it. They were allowed to take with them a bundle not to exceed fifty kilogrammes each. The reason for this move was given by the Germans as an attempt to move a thousand Jews elsewhere to a place with improved sanitary conditions.[351] No one would have thought that they were taken to be killed. Consequently a thousand Jews of Drohobycz and a thousand of Boryslaw left the ghetto together on the 5th of Nisan 702 (23 March 1942) and all were sure that they were going to travel to a better place so much so that the inmates of the ghetto got together for two consecutive days to bake *mazzoth* for them.

We were afraid there might be no possibility of baking *mazzoth* at the place of their arrival. Hence on the 5th of Nisan they moved their lodgings wholeheartedly.

The first attack on the ghetto came on the 26th of Ab 702 (9 August 1942) when for the first time about 10,000 Jews were removed by force from Drohobycz and Boryslaw and sent to the gas chambers of Belzec. This was the first[352] killing in the countries of Europe, but then there was no possibility of revolt, for at that time we were strictly enclosed in the ghetto.

When even under such conditions, in spite of being shut in, in spite of affliction, famine and disease, many hundreds of Jews succeeded in digging deep pits in the ground, canals, pipes, conduits, and in spending months there—this is nothing but supernatural strength. Also in this respect we are distinguishable from all the other nations upon earth and there is no nation in the world which would be able to survive under such conditions . . . .[353]

SERVICES OF INTERCESSION

It was still during the war that world Jewry learned of the terrible sufferings of their brethren under the Nazi heel. There were many

---

351. On a similar deception of the Jews of Hamburg, Frankfurt, Berlin, Vienna, Breslau, etc., cf. Oshry, *Mi-Maamakkim*, I, no. 30 and Garfunkel, *Destruction of Kovno's Jewry*, p. 122.

352. On the date of the opening of the extermination camp at Belzec, cf. however, *supra* (p. 93); Hilberg, *The Destruction of the European Jews*, pp. 311, 563; Helmut Krausnick, 'The Persecution of the Jews', in *Anatomy of the SS State*, pp. 98f.; Poliakov, *Harvest of Hate*, p. 114.

353. See also the reply given by R. J.M.Aronzon, quoted by Mordechai Eliab, *Ani Maamin*, pp. 81f.

families who had left some near or distant relatives in the *erez ha-damim* (the land of blood) whose fate was unknown. There was thus personal and collective concern felt by the Jews in the free countries. In their state of helplessness they employed the method used by their forefathers in times of distress. They turned to the God of their fathers for mercy. Orders for prayers for our brethren in Germany and Italy to be read after the prayer for the King and the Royal Family were issued by the Office of the Chief Rabbi (London) as early as 1939 to 'hearken to our prayers on behalf of our brethren given over to hate and oppression in Germany and Italy', and to 'nullify all cruel decrees against them'.[354] In the order of service entitled 'The Nazi War, a Service of Prayer and Intercession in connection with the Anniversary of the Outbreak of Hostilities' held on 8 September 1940,[355] there occurs a prayer on behalf of the British Army for those fallen in battle. There is also a phrase 'those of our brethren whose blood was spilt like water in Poland'.

A memorial prayer recited on *Tishah Be-Ab* 5702 (1942) and on the succeeding Sabbath for the victims of the massacres of Jews in Nazi-occupied lands contains the phrase, on behalf of our brethren 'who have been murdered, slaughtered, suffocated in multitudes with appalling cruelties, and whose blood was spilt like water in Poland, Rumania and other countries under the sway of the God-less enemy'.[356]

In the orders of service on the fourth and fifth anniversaries, the phrase referring to the victims of the Nazis does not mention victims of specified countries but contains the words 'of all lands under the wicked rule, under the heel of the arrogant iniquity'.[357]

In the order of service of Praise and Thanksgiving for the Victories of the Allied Nation, in the year 5705—1945, the memorial prayer for the victims of the mass massacres was on behalf of our brethren 'who were murdered, slaughtered and suffocated in vast multitudes and with appalling cruelties. Shuddering seizeth us when we remember the annihilation of hundreds of holy communities, and recall the murderous decree to destroy, to slay, and to cause to perish all Jews, both young and old, women and little children, in the lands that are under the heel of arrogant iniquity.'[358]

Special significance has to be given to the order of service on the day of fasting, mourning and prayer for the victims of mass massacres of Jews in the Nazi lands on the 5th Tebeth 5703 (13 December 1942).

354. Published by the Office of the Chief Rabbi, 5699-1939, p. 1.
355. Ibid., 1940, p. 4.
356. Ibid., 5702-1942. A similar prayer is found in the 'Order of Service on the Third Anniversary of the Outbreak of Hostilities, Thursday, September 3, 5702-1942, p. 4.
357. Ibid., 1943, p. 6; 1944, p. 6.
358. Ibid., 1945, p. 10.

The service was held in the afternoon (*minhah*) and was a *taanith zibbur* (public fasting) when the reading of the Law (Ex. xxxii 11–14 and xxxiv 1–10) took place. Of the prayers recited mention should be made of Ps. cxxx, last part of the *tahnun* recited on Mondays and Thursdays, various verses from the Bible, memorial prayer for the victims of the mass massacres of Jews in Nazi lands, selected parts from the *selihoth* of the *Yom Kippur Neilah* service, *Abinu Malkenu* and blowing of the *shophar*. There was also an address.[359]

The heroic uprising of the Jews of the Warsaw Ghetto was commemorated at 'A Service of Mourning and Prayer on the First Anniversary of the "Battle of Warsaw", on Monday 29th Iyyar, 5704— 22nd May, 1944' when two memorial prayers were recited: one for the martyrs of Warsaw 'the brave and devoted men and women who laid down their lives and died the death of martyrs in Warsaw, the City of Slaughter. They were swifter than eagles, they were stronger than lions. A spirit of zeal from the Lord of Hosts clothed them, and they gathered themselves together to stand for their lives, and render retribution upon thousands of the inhuman enemy. The battle was long: till weapons failed the heroes and they perished to a man. Their righteousness shall endure for all time, and the distant generations shall recount their glorious deeds'. The second prayer was for the victims of the mass massacres of the Jews in Nazi lands.[360]

It was still during the war when the leading Rabbis in the Holy Land met (among them were R. I.Z.Melzer, R. E.J.Finkel, R. J.Sher, and R. J.Sarna) on the 22nd of Heshvan, 5705 (8 November 1944) and decided to convene a general assembly in *Erez Yisrael* for 'wailing and repentance' which was to take place first in Jerusalem and afterwards in other Palestinian towns from which a full awakening should emerge embracing all spheres of life of Torah, *mussar*, charity and loving-kindness. This assembly was to take place on Monday, the 18th of Kislev, 705 (4 December 1944).

A special appeal for 'weeping, wailing and repentance' was issued. The order of the day was as follows: on Monday the 18th Kislev, 705 (4 December 1944)

1. People should assemble in the '*Hebron*' *Yeshibah* in Jerusalem at noon to study *mussar*.
2. At 12.30 p.m. a procession to the Western Wall should take place.
3. At 4 p.m. *hespedim* should be delivered at the above mentioned *yeshibah*.
4. Adoption of resolutions and various *takkanoth* in connection with the position of our people.

359. Ibid., 1942.
360. Ibid., 1944 pp. 6f.

On the appointed day, there was a large attendance and eleven resolutions were adopted to strengthen the fear of God, to study Torah and *mussar* and to learn at least two *mishnayoth* each day in memory of the martyrs, etc., to fix times to study Torah every day, at least for one and a half hours; in addition no less than twenty minutes be devoted to *mussar*. Everyone was to take it upon himself to do good deeds in accordance with his standard and his position, to practise loving kindness, in particular to send parcels to refugees, etc.

Similar meetings took place in other towns of Palestine.[361]

361. *Tebunah*, Jerusalem, Kislev, 3–(49), pp. 28ff. Adar 6–(52), 705, p. 67

4

The Aftermath—Reconstruction

When soon after the war details of the atrocities committed by the Germans were known some Rabbis in the Holy Land suggested at a conference that a ban (*herem*) against entering Germany should be proclaimed. However, one Rabbi was of the opinion that, although from the political, logical and moral point of view such action would be justified, it would be against the *halachah*. He then tries to prove his view.[1]

Although the oppressed Jews regained their freedom and were happy to have survived the ordeals of five years' slavery their happiness was not complete. Some did not leave the camp. Death took its toll even after the liberation. One Rabbi describing the conditions in the camp under the Nazis relates also the fate of some who regained their freedom. 'It is well known that the majority of those doing hard labour died from various causes, some called "mussulmänner" from the hard work and beatings and great starvation and thirst. Thousands—nay myriads died from severe diseases which raged in the camp, e.g. typhoid and other stomach disorders, etc. Even after the end of the war it was not possible to provide the inmates with sufficient medicines.'[2] 'Others were so emaciated and weak that medicines and cures were of no avail. In e.g. Bergen-Belsen about 20,000 people died in the first month after their liberation.'[3]

Conditions in other liberated camps were similar. In Gunskirchen, 'the worst of all camps', all inmates were ill and very weak because of the numerous sufferings of the past. To avoid the severe famine, the inmates went into the forests and villages to find some food to save themselves from death. One day, a great epidemic broke out, typhoid and other diseases. The American military authorities did not have enough medical supplies to save them all. Within a few days the great majority of the inmates died. Of the original thirty thousand inmates a mere thirteen thousand survived. One could see the American soldiers carry away literally thousands of dead for burial.[4]

Wherever the survivors turned, they could see Jewish communities

---

1. See R. Meshullam Rath, in *Sinai*, vol. VII, nos. 11–12, 1945, pp. 232ff. (*Kol Mebasser*, I, no. 13). See also *Ha-Pardes*, XIX, 1945, nos. 6–7. The president of the Board of Deputies of British Jews stated in a public speech that the Jews should impose a *Herem* on resettling in Germany or entering the country. See Cecil Roth in *Le Judaisme Sephardi*, XV, London, October 1957, p. 675.
2. R. Z.H.Meisels, *Kuntras Takkanoth Agunoth*, Bergen-Belsen, 1946, no. 80, p. 22.
3. Ibid., no. 12, p. 9. On the number, see *Binyan Zebi*, II, no. 66. A description of the plight of the Jews after their liberation is given by Karen Gershon, *Postscript*, pp. 30ff.
4. *Vide infra* Part III, no. 14. See, however, the figure given by Evelyn Le Chêne, *Mauthausen*, p. 146.

gone to rack and ruin. There was no one who had not lost some or all his relatives. Searches began for missing relatives and very often they could not be traced. Towns were deserted and once flourishing Jewish communities no longer existed. Places could be found where thousands (in one place ten thousand Jews) had been massacred and hardly buried. From under the thin surface of sand, limbs were protruding some of them in tattered garments with the 'star of David' on them.[5] In one place there was a woman's skull, the shoe of a young child nearby.[6]

Another Rabbi[7] describes the scene which met the eyes of those who, after the liberation, left their hideouts in Lithuania. The Jews attended to the burial of the dead. Skeletons, skulls, bones and limbs were lying scattered on the fields. The site where the infamous *Kovner Kazet Lager* had stood was an awesome picture. All that could be seen were the charred remains of houses which had been set on fire to kill any Jews who had been hiding in dug-outs underground. The Rabbi and other Jews were searching for bodies at the places called 'Block A.B. and C.' where mostly Jews had been confined, so that they could bury them. Among the human remains the body of a woman was found who was still holding her two little children in her arms. 'It is difficult to put into writing', he says, 'the terrible sight and the horror which unfolded itself before our eyes whilst we were gathering the bones. Still today my hands tremble when writing these lines. From the depths of my heart the cry breaks forth: Why O God, have You done this to us? Why and for what have we been handed over to slaughter like sheep?'

Non-Jews were digging out parts of corpses and searching for gold teeth.[8] Ashes of the martyrs were lying about like sand or heaped up to be used as fertilizer.[9] The attitude of the local population was disappointing. They did not receive the liberated Jews kindly. They looked askance at the returning Jews. They were astonished to see them emerge and wondered how they had survived. The Poles and Lithuanians were even aggressive[10] and on one occasion a young man took revenge. After the Germans had been driven from Lithuania, he shot a Lithuanian as he was angry that the Lithuanians had killed his entire family.[11]

5. R. Shimon Efrati, *Me-Emek Ha-Bacha*, no. 5.
6. Ibid.
7. R. E.Oshry, *Mi-Maamakkim*, II, no. 21.
8. Efrati, *Me-Emek Ha-Bacha*, no. 2.
9. Ibid., and *Mi-Ge Ha-Haregah*, no. 10; Jacques Delarue, *The History of the Gestapo*, p. 258.
10. Efrati, *Me-Emek Ha-Bacha*, no. 4; Oshry, *Mi-Maamakkim*, nos. 24, 25; R. A.Zimetbaum, 'Maaseh Nissim' in *Dibre Pinhas* by his father R. P.Zimetbaum, Brooklyn, p. 178; R. M.Steinberg, Introduction to *Mahazeh Abraham*, by his grandfather R. A.Menahem Steinberg, II, p. 6.
11. *Shomere Ha-Gaheleth*, ed. by R. Z.H.Harkavy and R. A.Shauli, Jerusalem-New York, 5726, pp. 69f., quoted also in *Noam*, XI, p. 268.

The roads were dangerous, journeys were hazardous and Jews were taken out from trains and murdered. Pogroms re-occurred (in Cracow, Kielce and Czestochowa); this time not by the Germans but by the Poles who had themselves suffered and once again innocent Jewish blood was shed on Polish soil.[12] In Kielce alone thirty-six Jews were murdered on 4 July 1946, 'in the biggest and most savage pogrom that has taken place in liberated Poland'.[13] Pogroms also occurred in Hungary and Slovakia.[14]

A terrible picture of the position of the Jews in post-war Poland is given to us by Rabbi Efrati who after his return from the forests of Siberia to Poland was appointed Rabbi of the Jewish community of Warsaw.[15]

I tried to gather those who had been dispersed and to organize the communal life of the remnants. However, outside there were still those at work who looked on with satisfaction and pleasure at the destruction of Polish Jewry, the élite of the Jewish nation, and looked askance at the return of those saved from Treblinka, Oswiecim, Belzec and Maidanek. Their strong desire was to destroy the remnants of the tribe of Israel. The life of the Jews who survived became intolerable. Pogroms took place and rivers of blood began again to flow on Polish soil. I was an eyewitness to the riots which occurred, beginning with the murder of four *haluzim*, members of the *Ha-Poel Ha-Mizrahi*, on their way to a conference in Cracow, culminating in the pogroms in Kielce. I shall not forget that bitter night which I spent by the bodies of those four martyrs of *Ha-Poel Ha-Mizrahi* who had been crushed by those cruel tearing beasts. However, while these had the merit of being brought to a Jewish grave in Lodz, this was not quite the case of the 17-year-old orphan, Yankele, who had a pale face and black eyes in which grief and love were reflected. (He was the only son of the Birnbaum widow.) He was travelling in search of the place where his father had been massacred. He was dragged from the wagon and killed, his body having been torn to pieces. With difficulty, the greater part of his body could be collected and brought to a Jewish grave. I was then asked whether it was the duty of his relatives and friends to search for the missing limbs . . . .

But even in Germany life was unsafe. In summer 1946 two displaced

12. *Vide infra*; see also Steinberg, *Mahazeh Abraham*, p. 6. One Rabbi (R. Hayyim Yizhak Wohlgelernter), who during all the years of the war had lived in a bunker, was murdered by a Pole after the liberation when he emerged from his hiding-place; see M. Ungar, *ADMORIM Shenispu*, p. 120.
13. *Jewish Chronicle*, 12 July 1946, p. 1.
14. Ibid., 31 May 1946, p. 10; 7 June 1946, p. 9.
15. Efrati, *Mi-Ge Ha-Haregah*, no. 8.

persons were found murdered in a wood near Munich,[16] and in 1947 journeys were still dangerous as can be seen from the following *Responsum*:[17]

The members of the Chief Rabbinate of Haifa, R. Baruch Marcus (chairman) and R. Nissim Chana submitted the following case to Chief Rabbi Herzog on the 29th Tebeth, 710 (18 January 1950).

Mrs A.K. approached us with the request to look into her case and find permission for releasing her from her *iggun* status.

This woman is still young, aged 24, she has a child, and is a new immigrant lacking means.

According to the evidence submitted to us, the case is as follows: Her husband travelled with merchandise about three years ago from the American Zone to the British Zone in Germany. Afterwards, there was no trace of him. His family made enquiries through the Jewish committees in both Zones but without success. It is well known that in general Jews were killed by the Nazis also after their defeat not in an organized manner but by individual Nazis . . . .

The cemeteries were lying desolate.[18] The fences had been removed, the graves trodden down. They were used as pasture land by the local people or cow-sheds were built thereon. Tombstones of the old cemetery of Salonica, the resting place of great men of many generations, were desecrated and were used for pavements, bathing pools, to repair houses and walls.[19] Such desecration also happened in Lithuanian towns.[20] Thus we are told in a report which appeared in the Jewish press that 'Tombstones from the Jewish cemetery in former Shaval, a small town in Lithuania, have been used to pave one of its streets, Kaliniukas Street . . . . The Jews of the town protested, but their protests were rejected.'[21]

One Litnuanian Rabbi[22] reports that when the walls of the ghetto were broken down and the captives regained their freedom, they were shocked to see the terrible destruction the enemy had wrought at the cemeteries, where famous scholars, great rabbis and *Zaddikim* and heads of *yeshiboth* were resting. Most painful was the sight of the

16. *Jewish Chronicle*, 5 July 1946, p. 9.
17. Chief Rabbi Yizhak Herzog, *Hechal Yizhak*, II, no. 10.
18. *Vide infra*. This applies not only to the Eastern countries but also to other countries under the Nazi heel.
19. *Beth Jacob*, Jerusalem, nos. 50–51, July-August 1963, p. 25.
20. Oshry, *Mi-Maamakkim*, II, no. 20.
21. See *Jewish Chronicle*, 10 July 1970, p. 14.
22. Oshry, *Mi-Maamakkim*, II, no. 20.

134 *The Nazi Holocaust*

streets paved with stones upon which names of the Jews were engraved and inscriptions which testified to their uprightness and great righteousness.

The Rabbi was then asked as to the *halachic* nature of these stones. Was it permitted to walk in those streets and tread upon those stones?

The Rabbi shows that according to some authorities no benefit must be derived from tombstones. Treading upon the stones would be a great insult to the dead, adding contempt to what had been done by the wicked ones who had removed them. The Jews should try to obtain permission from the authorities to remove those stones from the pavements and collect them in a safe place, as they could not be returned to the cemeteries for their location was in most cases no longer known, the non-Jews having ploughed up the graveyards for pasture ground for their cattle. Only in those towns where the cemeteries had been preserved and were provided with fences should the stones be taken back.

He then advises that no money and effort be spared to transfer the stones from the cemeteries of the Lithuanian towns to Kovno where the cemetery remained intact and to place them at a special site. 'These stones should serve as a memorial for generations of what the wicked have done to us . . . .'

There had been great havoc in Austria. In Vienna[23] the Jews had been forced to sell the cemeteries of Florisdorf and Grossenzersdorf and to exhume the bodies from the cemeteries in Währing (district of Vienna) within three months. One hundred and eighty-eight bodies were removed in 1942 and ninety graves were opened for the purpose of 'anthropological studies'. Eight hundred and eighteen tombstones of the old cemetery in the Seegasse were removed by the end of 1943.

The cemetery in Salzburg was desecrated and a cowshed was built on it. After the war, the Jews burned it down and prevented the American fire brigade from extinguishing the fire.[24]

In Hungary, it was a daily occurrence for non-Jews to steal tombstones from cemeteries of places where Jews were no longer living. Even the stones of the walls surrounding the cemeteries were taken away.[25]

The cemetery of Kiev at the top of Babi Yar was completely destroyed.[26]

Synagogues and houses of study were either destroyed, standing dilapidated or had been taken over by the local authorities and used

23. On what follows, cf. Herbert Rosenkranz, 'The Anschluss and the Tragedy of Austrian Jewry 1938–1945', in *The Jews of Austria*, ed. by Josef Fraenkel, London, 1967, p. 523.
24. Hugo Gold, *Geschichte der Juden in Oesterreich*, Tel Aviv, 1971, p. 79.
25. Rath, *Kol Mebasser*, II, no. 9.
26. Anatoli, *Babi Yar*, p. 456.

as stables, storehouses or clubs.²⁷ In one house of study a visiting Rabbi noticed the walls were stained with blood.²⁸

While in Germany, questions were raised before *Kristallnacht* concerning synagogues no longer in use owing to the emigration of the Jews, such questions were not asked in Poland in connection with synagogues still standing or the ground of destroyed synagogues. This was owing to the fact that Jews did not return and claim them.

In pre-war Poland there were more than a thousand Jewish communities, each of them having synagogues and several houses of study and prayer. Almost all were destroyed by the Nazis. Those left by the Germans were used by the Poles as store-rooms e.g. in Razienow and Radimno (Redem, Galicia). The synagogue in Lenczyca (district of Lublin) served as a club house.²⁹

Questions concerning synagogues were, however, raised by Jews returning to Czechoslovakia, Hungary and Memel (Klaipeda). Thus, e.g. R. Mosheh Nathan Schick, Rabbi of Miskolcz, head of the Rabbis in Hungary, was approached concerning the synagogues in Hungary. In one *Responsum*³⁰ he writes that it had already been decided that it was permitted to sell the synagogues through the seven elders even if they should be used for non-religious purposes (*li-debar hulin*), since they were no longer used for prayer.

However, in practice, if it was certain that the synagogue was to be used for a profane purpose, e.g. as a church or theatre, it was better to destroy it so that through such action it would lose its holy character. The Rabbi adds that the matter still required consideration.

R. Zebi Pesah Frank, Chief Rabbi of Jerusalem, was asked whether the synagogue in Prague and other synagogues in Czechoslovakia could be sold. The alternative was that they might be taken over by the church or by the authorities without payment. There was no prospect of the synagogues being used again as there were no Jews in the entire neighbourhood and no Jews were expected to settle there in the future.

The answer was in the affirmative, if they were not used on the Sabbath and festivals and it was probable that the authorities would take possession. The money should be used for religious purposes, e.g. for building a *Talmud Torah* and for support of those studying the Torah.³¹

27. Cf. e.g. Rath, *Kol Mebasser*, I, no. 6; R. I.J.Weiss, *Minhath Yizhak*, I, no. 118; Oshry, *Mi-Maamakkim*, I, no. 24; II, no. 23; R. Bezalel Stern, *Be-Zel Ha-Hochmah*, I, no. 29. See also *infra*.
28. *Vide infra*, p. 174.
29. See *Beth Jacob*, no. 90, November 1966, p. 25; nos. 106–7, March-April 1968, p. 4; *Jewish Chronicle*, 21 June 1946, p. 9.
30. In *Shomere Ha-Gaheleth*, ed. by R. Dr Z. Harkavy and R. A.Shauli, Jerusalem-New York, 1966, p. 44, no. 9.
31. R. Z.P.Frank, *Har Zebi, Orah Hayyim*, no. 80.

A similar question was addressed to Rabbi Frank from the community of Memel (Klaipeda). The question was whether one may sell the synagogue as the non-Jews may take possession and use it as a church. The answer was that it was permitted to sell it.[32]

In a *Responsum* by Rabbi Duschinsky to the Rabbi in Szerdahely (Hungary), we are told that the synagogue there had suffered at the hand of the Nazis. The question of selling the synagogue was discussed. R. Duschinsky is of the opinion that the ladies' gallery could be reduced in size and the money received for the wood and stones should be used for the repair of the synagogue.[33]

Torah scrolls had disappeared. Many of them had been hidden by the Jews in order to avoid their falling into the hands of the Nazis. Even recently a report appeared in the Jewish press of twenty Torah scrolls found hidden beneath the floor boards of a fifteenth century synagogue in Lichtenstadt, near Karlsbad.[34] Who knows how many Torah scrolls are still hidden which cannot be recovered?

Most scrolls found by the Nazis were either destroyed or used for making various articles (bags, wallets, shoes, etc.). As illustration the following cases deserve to be mentioned.

The question was asked whether a purse made from the sheets of holy scrolls containing eighty-five letters[35] and the Holy Name may be kept under glass in a well-guarded and holy place and be preserved for many days in order that later generations could know what the Germans had done to our people and to our Torah during the holocaust or must it be buried in an earthenware container near a scholar?

The Rabbi tries to prove that it does not require burial but *genizah* (removal, hiding). It should be kept hidden in a holy place and only on the days of remembrance be shown to pious people to rouse them to *teshubah* (otherwise it should be buried).[36]

It was in the labour camp of Konin in Lithuania in 1942 that a certain man, R. M.Bibergel of Gembin (who later died a martyr) came to the Rabbi trembling. He had been told by his employer, a German shoemaker, to make shoes from sheets of Torah scrolls given to him. He was to cut the scrolls to size and then stitch the finished article. If he refused he would be killed. He was ready to die rather than desecrate the scrolls. The Rabbi concludes that he had divine inspiration

---

32. Ibid., no. 81.
33. R. J.Zebi Duschinsky, *Responsa MhRIZ,* I, Jerusalem, 1956, no. 16. The *Responsum* is dated: 26th Tishri 708 (10 October 1947). For further cases, see Part III, no. 22.
34. Cf *Jewish Tribune*, London, 1 October 1971, p. 7, and 15 October 1971, p. 1.
35. A Torah scroll or fragment thereof containing at least eighty-five letters is to be regarded as holy. See *Tur Shulhan Aruch Orah Hayyim*, cap. CCCXXXIV, no. 12.
36. R. Y.M.Aronzon, *Yeshuath Mosheh*, no. 61, Tel Aviv, 1967. The *Responsum* was first published in a short form in *Kol Torah*, Jerusalem, Kislev-Tebeth 714, VIII (25) no. 3–4, pp. 12ff. There it is said that the Rabbi received the purse from a non-Jew in Austria.

of a means of disobeying the German order yet succeeding in avoiding death.[37]

The writer once saw in the possession of Professor Cecil Roth, a pair of soles made from parchment of a scroll he had brought from a country which had been under Nazi rule (Greece?).

In Grosswardein (Rumania) R. I.J.Weiss[38] found after his return synagogues and houses of study destroyed, pieces of Torah scrolls and holy books scattered in the streets.

In Kovno, about five hundred Torah scrolls, some of them brought from the neighbouring communities had been burned. Consequently, after the liberation there was not even one Torah scroll to be found in Kovno, except the one kept by R. Oshry.[39] It also happened, even before the end of the war, that Torah scrolls (or part of Torah scrolls) were offered for sale by non-Jews. This can be seen from the following *Responsum*.[40] A non-Jew brought two Torah scrolls from Bessarabia offering them for sale. One of the scrolls was incomplete, i.e. the books *Bamidbar* (Numbers) and *Debarim* (Deuteronomy) were entirely missing. The other scroll was complete but many lines in various columns had become unintelligible and it appeared that they had been covered by water. Hence both scrolls were certainly unfit to be used in the service. A religious Jew was willing to redeem the scrolls from the hands of the gentile but on condition that he might make one scroll from the two, which would be fit for the service. (There was no doubt, the Rabbi remarks, that the scrolls had been written by a Jew. All communities in Bessarabia and in other places had been completely destroyed and non-Jews had taken possession of all property of Jews, even of the holy articles, e.g. scrolls. Therefore the scrolls had belonged to Jews and had been written by Jews.) The question with which the Rabbi dealt was the following: Was it permitted to comply with the condition stipulated by the prospective buyer as (1) the scrolls were not of the same size, the sheets of one were five centimetres longer than those of the other, and (2) although the number of lines of both was the same, the script of one was bigger than that of the other. Thus when joining two sheets of the different sized scrolls, although the first lines of both sheets would begin with the same line, the bigger sheet would protrude as its last line would extend below the neighbouring sheet.

When dealing with cutting the margins of the one scroll to adjust it to the size of the second, the Rabbi remarks: 'Although in a case like ours one should wait until the end of the war when parchment would be available to complete both scrolls so that cutting the margins (which

37. *Yeshuath Mosheh*, p. 296, 'Addenda', no. 61.
38. 'Pirsume Nissa' in *Minhath Yizhak*, I, p. 273.
39. Oshry, *Mi-Maamakkim*, II, no. 14.
40. Stern, *Be-Zel Ha-Hochmah*, II, no. 51. The *Responsum* is dated: Ab 703 (August 1943).

L

was prohibited) to make one scroll would not be required, this would apply only if the scroll could be well-guarded until it could be repaired. In our case, however, cutting the margins must be permitted, as the scrolls would remain in the hands of the gentile and may be used for profane purposes. It may not be possible to trace and redeem the scrolls after the end of the war.'

We are even told that on 4 March 1941, *Sturmführer* Erwin Klassen offered two Torah scrolls for sale and mentioned the price to be paid for them. The Rabbi who was consulted about this offer replied that according to the Law it was a duty to redeem the scrolls,[41] but in that particular case, it was prohibited to do so, because if the sum demanded were paid, the Germans would take scrolls from other places and extort money from Jews.[42]

Sacred articles from synagogues, if they had not been looted by the Germans, were spoilt by the local non-Jews. In Hungary, shopkeepers hung curtains of the Holy Ark over their shops as sun blinds.[43] In Kovno, after the liberation, no curtain was available for hanging on the Holy Ark and no cloth could be found as everything had been seized by the Nazis. 'However, a Jew came and reported that he had seen a curtain which had belonged to the "Synagogue of the Merchants" in the house of a non-Jew and it was being used as a bed-spread.' (The Rabbi[44] was asked whether it was permitted to acquire the curtain from the non-Jew and use it again as a curtain. The answer was in the affirmative.)

Twenty years after the war, antique shops belonging to Polish Christians offered for sale to tourists Jews' goods, e.g. lamps, *kiddush* cups, spice-boxes and articles once belonging to synagogues, e.g. candelabra and ornaments of Torah scrolls.[45]

Archives and libraries had also been destroyed or confiscated. Particular mention should be made of the archives of the Jewish communities in Greece which were destroyed, so that no statements could be checked.[46]

Precious books, too, had been burned or confiscated and sent to

41. See *Tur Shulhan Aruch Yoreh Deah,* cap. CCLXXXI, no. 1.
42. Quoted by Ungar, *ADMORIM Shenispu,* p. 98. On a Torah scroll sold to a Karaite, *vide supra,* p. 81.
43. Zimetbaum, 'Maaseh Nissim', p. 171.
44. Oshry, *Mi-Maamakkim,* II, no. 23. The greatest unbelievably-sadistic desecration was that perpetrated in the extermination camp of Belzec. There the doors of the gas chambers were covered with curtains taken from Holy Arks bearing the Hebrew inscription 'This is the gate of the Lord into which the righteous shall enter' (Ps. CXVIII 20). Hausner, *Justice in Jerusalem,* p. 167.
45. *Beth Jacob,* nos. 106–7, pp. 4f.
46. Chief Rabbi Ben Zion Meir Hai Uzziel, *Mishpete Uzziel, Eben Ha-Ezer,* nos. 44, 45; see also Michael Molho and Joseph Nehama, *The Destruction of Greek Jewry 1941–1944,* p. 114, *vide infra* 210.

Germany[47] or lay about in the streets and shops and were used for wrapping various articles.[48]

When[49] after the liberation attempts were made to rebuild the devastated communities, it became apparent that in a city like Kovno once famous for its scholarship, no Hebrew book, not even a prayer book, could be found. However, after a few weeks of thorough searching, boxes full of books which had once belonged to the Jews of Hamburg, were discovered in the store-room of the customs house. When the cursed Germans expelled those Jews from the town where they had dwelt for generations they deceived them by saying that they wished to settle them in the Eastern countries, like Lithuania, etc. They were therefore to take all their belongings with them. The unfortunate Jews, in their naivety, believed the words of the murderers and packed all their belongings among them their holy books and set out on the journey into exile. They soon discovered that the cruel Germans had misled them with their lies for they were all taken to the Ninth Fortress near Kovno to the infamous place where the blood of our brethren among them also that of the Jews of Hamburg and other places, was shed like water . . . while the books with the other belongings were taken to the customs house.

Naturally the Rabbi was very happy with his find when he discovered the books which he then took to 'Hausmann's Beth Ha-Midrash', that they should be accessible to all. Just when the books had been taken to that place the beadle appeared and cried bitterly. He reported that he had with his own eyes seen non-Jews in the market-place wrap fish, in pages torn out of Hebrew books, such as Talmud, Maimonides's works, *Tur, Shulhan Aruch*, etc., which had been taken there from the store-room of the Romm Press in Vilna.

The question arose: was it the duty of the Jews to redeem those pages from the hands of the non-Jews to avoid their being treated disrespectfully, and if the decision was in the affirmative, what was to be done with them, as they were loose pages and unfit to be used for study? Had they to be put away and hidden, and, if so, how was that to be done?

The answer was that the pages had to be redeemed from the hands of the non-Jews and to be put in sacks and buried in the cemetery in a grave surrounded by boards like a box.

The Rabbi tells us that when the Jews heard his decision rather than

47. *Vide infra* 204.
48. Oshry, *Mi-Maamakkim,* I, no. 30; Zimetbaum, 'Maaseh Nissim'; R. J.Avigdor, *Helek Yaakob*, II, 'Preface', p. xiv.
49. On what follows, see Oshry, *Mi-Maamakkim*, I, no. 30.

spend the last coins they possessed on food, they spent them on redeeming the pages in order to bury them according to the Law.

When on 18 February 1942,[50] the Germans issued an order that all Jewish inmates of the ghetto had to hand over all their books, the Jews complied. Books were taken from synagogues and from private libraries and deposited in a certain place specified by the Germans. An officer of the Jewish police of the ghetto, Mr Yizhak Grünberg (who later died a martyr)[51] jeopardized his life by secretly collecting the most valuable books. He placed them in a box which he buried in a pit he had dug for that purpose. He did so in the hope that when the day of freedom came survivors would be able to recover the books. They were indeed found later, after the liberation.[52]

One Rabbi amid great danger and self-sacrifice succeeded in burying all his books, about eight thousand volumes including several of his own works, in a deep pit. 'Today I can reveal that that pit is under a house which stands in Szackiego Street in Drohobycz. But unfortunately there is no possibility of retrieving them as Drohobycz is under Soviet rule.'[53]

The dearth of Hebrew books was greatly felt particularly by the Rabbis, who had been appointed by the occupying forces to look after the religious needs of the inmates of the liberated camps and ghettos.

R. Avigdor, who had spent several years in various concentration camps and who after the liberation went to Belgium, was writing a *Responsum* on the *agunah* problem. He apologizes for daring to deal with such an important matter particularly as for almost six years he had not seen any book required for that subject and also in Belgium he lacked books and 'there is no workman without tools'.[54]

R. Zebi Hirsch Meisels who had been in the concentration camp of Auschwitz and after the liberation had been appointed by the British authorities Chief Rabbi of the British Sector in Bergen-Belsen, remarks in a letter about matrimonial matters addressed to Dayan Abramski in London that he had no books, not even a *Shulhan Aruch Eben Ha-Ezer*, at his disposal.[55]

R. Jonathan Steif, Ab Beth Din in Budapest, had to forward a question he was asked to R. Breisch in Zurich as he was without books.[56]

In a letter to R. Jeroham Wahrhaftig in Jerusalem, R. J.J.Weinberg thanks him for his book *Dibre Jeroham* he had received from him. He

50. On the date, *vide infra* p. 205, note 23.
51. On him, see L. Garfunkel, *The Destruction of Kovno's Jewry*, pp. 169, 174, 183f.
52. Oshry, *Mi-Maamakkim*, II, no. 8.
53. Avigdor, *Helek Yaakob*, p. xiv.
54. Ibid., pp. 67, 70.
55. *Binyan Zebi*, II, no. 33.
56. R. M.J.Breisch, *Helkath Yaakob*, I, no. 6.

was as happy with it 'as one that finds great spoil' (Ps cxix 162) for it was the first book he had received after he had left the concentration camp where he had been held prisoner during the war years. When he came to Montreux he did not have one of his books as all of them had remained in the Berlin library and were lost.[57] However, sometimes even during the war books appeared on the market. Thus the Slovak government was in possession of many thousands of books and Hebrew manuscripts pillaged during the war and offered them for sale. A Rabbi was asked whether a Jew might buy them. He decided that with regard to books the principle of *yeush* (renouncing ownership) does not apply. Hence one is not allowed to buy them. However, R. Breisch tries to prove that in our case the principle of *yeush* does apply and it appears that the buyer is not bound to hand over the books to the owner even if the latter wished to give the money paid for them. 'To our great regret, as we have heard, the owners were deported, deprived of everything, and we know what happened to books in other countries under the Nazis. They were burned in public with great contempt. Surely the owners had given up hope of recovering them. However, it appears to me that the Rabbis in Poland have in the past made an announcement or issued a ban prohibiting the purchase of books from *erez ha-damim* (the bloody country). One must consider whether that still applies. However, from the *halachic* point of view there is no doubt that one may buy the books.'[58]

Jews were moving across Europe. Many survivors wished to return to their homeland. This was particularly the case with Greek Jews who had been deported to the camps in Poland.[59] Many of the surviving Jews of Poland, Rumania, Lithuania and Hungary who had returned to their places of origin soon left disappointed with the conditions there.[60] The search for relatives and other survivors proved fruitless. Their homes had been occupied by others, the synagogues had been destroyed, the cemeteries lay deserted, the tombstones were in most cases removed and in addition to that the Jews were met by a hostile population, as we have already seen.[61]

They went to Germany which to them appeared safer than Poland

---

57. *Seride Esh*, II, no. 70. No date is mentioned but in R. Wahrhaftig's reply in the following *Responsum* the date is given as Thursday *Va-Yishlah*, 708 (27 November 1947).
58. *Helkath Yaakob*, I, no. 136. It appears that the prohibition referred to by R. Breisch concerned purchasing books brought from Germany after Hitler had come to power. I can recall that after World War I many Hebrew books appeared on the market in Vienna brought from Soviet Russia where many houses of study had been closed. There was a rumour that one should not buy those books to discourage the authorities from pillaging Hebrew books.
59. *Vide infra* Part III, no. 16.
60. Cf. Gershon, *Postscript*, London, 1969, pp. 36ff.
61–63. Ibid.; Leo Katcher, *Post Mortem*, London, 1968 pp. 2ff.; *supra* pp. 132, 133.

and Lithuania, although we are told that murder by individual Nazis was still possible in 1947, as mentioned above.[62]

Various camps for displaced persons were set up by the occupying authorities, some of them situated near the sites of the former concentration camps, which prepared the survivors for emigration to Israel (e.g. Bergen-Belsen, Landsberg, Föhrenwald, etc.).[63] Some of the emigrants boarded ships trying to enter the Holy Land, but met their death when their ships were wrecked.[64]

Much attention was paid also to the religious needs of the Jews. Ignorance prevailed among the masses. How great the ignorance was, e.g. among the Jews who returned to Holland, can be seen from a *Responsum* of Chief Rabbi Herzog in which he complains that the Jews (women) there do not know of the law of *yibbum* and *halizah*, although it is clearly mentioned in the Torah.[65] When the remnants returned to Salonica, which had suffered greatly through the Nazi invasion and deportations, no religious leader was available and Chief Rabbi Herzog expresses his regret for the community of Salonica, 'a city and a mother in Israel which through our sins has come down wonderfully' (cf. II Sam. xx 19 and Lam. I 9).[66]

In Munkatsch (Mukacevo), once famous for its piety and scholarship, no Rabbi was available in the first months after the liberation to warn men against marrying women who thought their husbands had been killed. In fact the latter were alive.[67]

Special care was taken of the displaced people living in the camps. Rabbis were sent by the religious authorities of Britain and America to give assistance to the survivors in their daily life. As mentioned above, among the former camp inmates there were Rabbis who were appointed by the authorities to look after the needs of the people. To mention only a few: R. Isachar Beer Halpern, formerly in Beitsch-Reischa, who went through many concentration camps and later came to Rome where he was appointed Rabbi and contributed greatly to the revival of Judaism there. He then emigrated to America.[68]

R. Ephraim Oshry, Rabbi in Kovno, who spent many years in the Kovno Ghetto where he played a leading part in the religious life of the Jews, succeeded in re-establishing the religious institutions, rescuing Jewish children and erecting an orphanage there. He then went to various refugee camps in Austria where he founded *yeshiboth*. From there he proceeded to Rome where he also established a *yeshibah*. He then left for Montreal where he was Rabbi and head of *yeshibah*

64. Efrati, *Mi-Ge Ha-Haregah*, no. 13, p. 106; Weiss, 'Pirsume Nissa', p. 272.
65. *Hechal Yizhak*, II, no. 81.
66. Ibid., no. 27 (*infra* Part III, no. 16).
67. Weiss, *Minhath Yizhak*, V, no. 47.
68. See the Introduction to his *Mishneh La-Melech*, New York, 1952, pp. 12f.

'Meor Ha-Golah'. He later moved to New York where he is at present Ab Beth Din of the Beth Ha-Midrash Ha-Gadol, President of the Vaad Ha-Rabbanim and head of the *yeshibah* 'Torah Ve-Emunah'.[69]

R. Joshua Mosheh Aronzon, formerly Rabbi in Sanok (Poland), who had been an inmate of various ghettos and camps was after the liberation appointed Chief Rabbi of several camps in the American Zone in Austria and various communities in Germany. He cared for the erection of *mikvaoth* and *kashruth* and for the study of the Torah, etc. He then emigrated to Israel where he has been appointed Rabbi and member of the Chief Rabbinate in Petah Tikvah.[70]

R. Simon Efrati, formerly Rabbi of Bendery (Bessarabia), was deported to Siberia. After the war he was appointed Rabbi of Warsaw and took great interest in helping *agunoth* (women whose husbands disappeared) to re-marry. He then left for the Holy Land where he is active as National Director of the Kashruth Department of the Chief Rabbinate in Israel.[71]

R. Zebi Hirsch Meisels who before the war had been Rabbi in Waitzen (Vác, Hungary) and who had been an inmate of Auschwitz extermination camp was appointed as mentioned above, by the British authorities Chief Rabbi of the British Zone and took up his appointment in Bergen-Belsen.[72] This camp for displaced persons had a Jewish population of twenty thousand[73] and became a centre of Jewish life.[74]

Various workshops were set up to prepare the inmates for emigration to Israel, children's homes were established and a printing press was erected. There R. Meisels, who was most active in assisting the displaced persons, printed his *Kuntras Takkanoth Agunoth* which deals with one of the most urgent problems of those days.[75]

There were other religious problems which had arisen, some caused by laxity in morals and religious outlook. 'To my great regret, most inmates of the camp openly smoke cigarettes on the Sabbath and have cut down the yoke of *mizvoth* and *derech erez*. Almost all tell me that before the war they did not profane the Sabbath and had kept the commandments. But the *zaroth* they experienced in the camps and the

69. See the Introductions to his works *Dibre Ephraim,* and *Mi-Maamakkim,* and the title-pages thereof.
70. See Introduction to his *Yeshuath Mosheh,* pp. 5f.
71. See title-page of his work *Me-Emek Ha-Bacha,* and no. 6, p. 68, and title-page of his work *Mi-Ge Ha-Haregah.*
72. Of late Rabbi of 'Sheerith Yisrael' in Chicago. See *Kuntras Takkanoth Agunoth* and title-page of *Binyan Zebi,* II, and nos. 33ff.; Introduction to *Mekaddshe Ha-Shem,* I, and 'Shaar Mahmadim', ibid., pp. 7ff.
73. Meisels, *Binyan Zebi,* II, nos. 35, 37, 38.
74. Cf. Gershon, *Postscript,* pp. 38ff.
75. *Vide infra.* Of books reprinted in Bergen-Belsen mention should be made of Heilprin's *Seder Ha-Doroth* and *Tanna De-Be Eliyahu.*

great *hurban* which they had witnessed with their own eyes have caused them to become lax.'[76]

Such laxity found its expression particularly in intermarriage which occurred when people returned home and did not find their families.[77] It was feared that some *agunoth* might enter into civil marriages or would cohabit if too great stringency were applied by the Rabbis in certain cases.[78]

The comings and goings in Bergen-Belsen after the liberation were called by one Rabbi[79] in connection with moral matters *androlemsia* (meaning: punishment of men, misery, confusion, misfortune). The same expression is used also by another Rabbi to denote the moral decay following the war. 'Surely in our time in consequence of the terrible holocaust which brought *androlemsia*[80] among Jewish families there are real *mamzerim* (illegitimate children) born to those who had remarried after rumours that their husbands had died but who later were found to be alive.'[81]

Families had been torn asunder, children grew up without knowing their origin and consequently questions concerning legitimacy arose. The following case is a typical example:

A religious young man, a scholar (*talmid hacham*) became engaged to a girl in one of the small towns of Europe. Afterwards, the rumour spread that there was a defect in her status of legitimacy (she was a *pegumah*). Rabbi Pollak, formerly of Grosswardein, later in Vienna, was asked by the young man to make enquiries in her birthplace Klausenburg, about her. The Rabbi learned, when looking at her birth certificate, that her mother's name was Sarah, which indicated she was a Jewess, while with regard to the father it was mentioned in Hungarian that it was not known who he was. In view of this, the girl had to be regarded as a *shetukith*, i.e. an illegitimate child of unknown fatherhood.

Rabbi Breisch who dealt with this case remarks: 'As, owing to our great sins, after the great destruction which befell the Jewish people, when many boys and girls became detached and uprooted from their homes and scattered over other places and grew up without

---

76. Meisels, *Binyan Zebi*, II, nos. 33, 37.

77. Weiss, 'Pirsume Nissa', p. 273.

78. On laxity in morals, cf. also Herzog, *Hechal Yizhak*, II, no. 79; Breisch, *Helkath Yaakob*, I, no. 18; II, no. 29; Meisels, *Kuntras Takkanoth Agunoth*, p. 17 *ad fin.* R. Meir Feuerwerger (Meiri), *Ezrath Nashim*, II, pp. 208, 211.

79. R. Jehezkiel Abramski in Meisels's *Binyan Zebi*, II, no. 36.

80. On the proper spelling and reading of this word the root of which is Greek, see *Aruch*, ed. Kohut, I, p. 143 *s.v.*; Jastrow, *A Dictionary*, etc. *s.v.*

81. Chief Rabbi I.J.Unterman, *Shebet Mi-yehudah*, Jerusalem, 1955, p. 284. On such a case *vide supra* (R. Oshry).

their parents, questions to the discredit of the family are very frequent it is most important that such matters be dealt with . . .'[82]

Of the problems which arose in Bergen-Belsen, mention should be made of the following:

Rabbi Z.H.Meisels reported to Dayan Abramski in London that the British authorities complied with his request and issued a decree that everyone who wished to live with a woman in one room had to bring a certificate from Rabbi Meisels that they were a married couple. Living together without such a certificate would make them liable to a penalty. It then happened that the Rabbi became aware of a couple of whom the husband admitted having had a wife before and five children who had been deported to Treblinka in 1942 where there was a crematorium. But the husband was sure that his wife had been burned and so he then married his second wife. The *kiddushin* (without *huppah* and *kethubah*) had been 'performed' by a *shohet* (slaughterer). They had then lived for about one year as husband and wife, but they parted later when sent to different places. They were reunited in Bergen-Belsen about three months earlier where they lived together. When the woman was questioned, she admitted that she too had been married before the war, but had no children. Her husband had two brothers. She met them in 1944 and they informed her that he had been killed in Auschwitz. About three months previously she had met the man with whom she was living. They had known each other for a long time from their home-town. They agreed to marry. They 'shook hands' and swore to marry each other. On account of that, they lived together and wished to marry according to the law of Moses and Israel.

The Rabbi was aware of all the difficulties involved in such a marriage and in his view they had to be separated. He wished to hear Dayan Abramski's view. (His reply was that they had to separate and no marriage was permitted.)[83]

Another problem which R. Meisels submitted to Dayan Abramski should be mentioned. The president (the Head of the Jewish Council) of the ghetto of Lodz was a Mr Hayyim Rumkowski.[84] He was a powerful, ambitious man. He even tried to assume the role of 'King'. He struck coins[85] and printed postage stamps with his own effigy describing

---

82. Breisch, *Helkath Yaakob*, III nos. 6–7. (R. Breisch came to the conclusion that she was not a *shethukith* and might marry the young man who was not a *kohen*).
83. Meisels, *Binyan Zebi*, nos. 33, 34.
84. *Vide supra* p. 53.
85. The pictures of ten- and five-mark pieces struck in Lodz are reproduced in the *Jewish Chronicle* of 19 November 1971, p. 19. They had been presented by a young Pole to a retail numismatist. However, we are told that the issuing of coins specifically for Jews' use in the ghettos was common practice under the Nazi regime (and not confined to Lodz only).

himself as 'Hayyim I' and performed about twenty to thirty wedding ceremonies every Sunday without *huppah* and *kethubah*. The man gave the woman a ring as *kiddushin* in front of two witnesses and uttered the usual formula 'Hare ath . . .' and a vessel was broken and the words 'Mazzal tob' were called out. No Rabbi was present at the ceremony.[86] 'Now,' says Rabbi Meisels, 'those couples come to me and ask for a certificate stating that they were married, so that they could live together in one room.'

Dayan Abramski replied that if the woman had been unmarried beforehand (*penuyah*) and two suitable witnesses (*ksherim*) were present and the man gave the ring for the purpose of *kiddushin*, she should be regarded as a married woman. Their marriage should be confirmed in writing in order to avoid their thinking that it were invalid. (However, says R. Meisels, not before a *huppah* is arranged and the seven benedictions are recited.)[87]

Finally, the following case should be quoted:

A man and a woman appeared before the Rabbi in Bergen-Belsen asking him to arrange *kiddushin* for them. When looking at the man, the Rabbi was very doubtful whether he was Jewish. He was unable to reply to the Rabbi's question whether he had learned 'Aleph Beth' and was astounded at it. The witnesses whom the couple had brought and who were supposed to know the man, contradicted each other. They could only testify that he was circumcised. What was to be done?

No reply arrived from Dayan Abramski to this question. However, in the following letter R. Meisels informed Dayan Abramski that he had been threatened by violent men should he not perform *kiddushin*. A further investigation revealed that the man was a non-Jew, one of the Moslems living in Yugoslavia who were circumcised. The man averred that he wished to become a Jew, The woman also told the Rabbi she was pregnant as she had thought he was a Jew. Dayan Abramski's decision was lenient, if R. Meisels was sure the man would keep the Jewish Law. However, R. Meisels had some reservations on this decision.[88]

In the cultural field the printing or reprinting or photostating of books became one of the foremost activities in the post-war period, particularly in Germany. Works of various branches of Jewish and Rabbinic lore were published.[89] Pentateuch with *Onkelos* and *Rashi*, Prayerbooks

---

86. It is of interest to mention that a photograph has been reproduced (by Isaiah Trunk, *Judenrat*, p. 190) of a wedding performed by Rumkowski. The couple is seen standing in front of a candelabrum placed on a table. Rumkowski is seated at the other side of the table and is reading from papers or a book. It was after the September action in 1942 when most of the Rabbis had been deported and the Rabbinical Association abolished that Rumkowski performed marriages; see Trunk, *Judenrat*, p. 193.
87–88. Meisels, *Binyan Zebi*, nos. 33–37.
89. Cf. also Philip Friedman, *Bibliography of Books in Hebrew on the Jewish Catastrophe and Heroism in Europe*, Jerusalem, 1960, pp. 155ff.

Hasidic and Midrashic works, *Responsa*, commentaries, *Pesah Hagga-doth*, Heilprin's historical work *Seder Ha-Doroth*, were printed or reprinted in photostat and it is most interesting that, as mentioned above, even in Bergen-Belsen works were published. Hebrew books appeared also in Landsberg, Munich and Föhrenwald. The Talmud tractates of *Kiddushin* and *Nedarim* were reprinted in 1946 and distributed among 'the remnants of Israel, houses of study and individuals who study the law'.[90]

Of other books which appeared in Germany, mention should be made of the following:

1. *Siddur* 'Beth Yaakov' by R. Jacob Emden, Augsburg, 1948.
2. *Bene Yissachar* by R. Zebi Elimelech of Dynow, Föhrenwald, 1947.
3. *Sepher Baal Shem Tob*, sayings and commentaries of R. Israel Baal Shem Tob, taken from works of various authors, Landsberg, 1948.
4. *Kizzur Shulhan Aruch* by Rabbi Shlomoh Ganzfried, Munich, 1947.
5. *Tanna De-Be Eliyahu*, reprinted by Nisan Lezer (of Briegel?) 'at present in Bergen Belsen Block 52', no year is given.
6. *Tiphereth Shlomoh* on Torah by R. Shlomoh ben R. Dob Zebi Ha-Kohen of Radomsk, Föhrenwald, no date is given.
7. *Responsa* 'Abne Hephez' by R. Aharon Levin, Munich, 1947 (1948).

A unique phenomenon and of great significance was the reproduction of the Talmud in Munich-Heidelberg in 1948 which is dedicated to the United States Army by the Chief Rabbi of the United States Zone in the name of the Rabbinical organization. The front page bears a picture of the rising sun with the inscription: 'From Servitude to Redemption, from Darkness to Great Light', and below it depicts the concentration camp with its huts and fences of barbed wire on both sides and two slave-labourers busy with their work. There is underneath the inscription taken from Psalms CXIX 87: 'They had almost consumed me upon earth; But as for me I forsook not Thy precepts.' The back of the page contains the following dedication (there is also one in Hebrew):

This edition of the Talmud is dedicated to the United States army. This army played a major role in the rescue of the Jewish people from total annihilation and after the defeat of Hitler bore the major burden of sustaining the DPs of the Jewish faith. This special edition of the Talmud published in the very land where, but a short time ago, everything Jewish and of Jewish inspiration was anathema, will remain a symbol of the indestructibility of the Torah. The Jewish

90. From the Foreword to the Talmud edition printed in Germany (*vide infra*).

DPs will never forget the generous impulses and the unprecedented humanitarianism of the American Forces to whom they owe so much. It is noteworthy that throughout the long exile of Israel it was not merely once that Jewish books were burned by the authorities. Non-Jewish governments had never replaced them. Now for the first time in the history of our people a government has assisted in reprinting the works of the Talmud 'which is our very life and the length of our days'. The U.S. Armies have saved us from death for life. They shield us even now in this land and it is with their help that the Talmud appears again in Germany.

It is a characteristic feature of the Hebrew Rabbinic books which appeared after the war that their authors (or those who reprinted Rabbinic books) or publishers have printed, either at the beginning or at the end, lists of relatives, fellow-citizens, Rabbis, etc., who died martyrs. The dates and the names of the extermination camps where they had died are usually mentioned. It resembles the revival of the martyrologies of the Middle Ages of which the best known is *Das Martyrologium des Nürenberger Memorbuches*, published by Siegmund Salfeld (in Berlin, 1898).[91] However, the object of compiling such lists of martyrs appears to be different. While the intention of the compilers of the martyrologies was to preserve lists with the names of the martyrs to be mentioned at the services held in memory of the deceased, the main aim of the authors and publishers of books after World War II was to perpetuate the memory of the martyrs, as no tombstones had been erected and that the dates of their death (if known) be remembered.

Another feature of the books published is that they contain letters of great Rabbis mentioned in the work or whose works were printed. Some of these letters are reproduced in facsimile.

The inclusion of photographs of the martyrs is very common and in not specifically Rabbinic books, photographs of the sadistic acts perpetrated by the Germans are added.

Less frequent are the artistic embellishments to be found in the books published after the war. Apart from the Talmud edition mentioned above, there are some books which bear pictures alluding to the Nazi holocaust. Thus e.g. a page of the work *Birkath Abraham* by R. Yizhak Klein (who died a martyr on the 13th of Sivan 5704)[92] depicts burning scrolls and letters in the form of pigeons ascending from them. Underneath there is the inscription taken from *Abodah Zarah* 18a: 'I see parchment burnt but the letters soar up.' (These words were spoken

---

91. On the martyrologies and the development of the memorial books, see *The Jewish Encyclopedia*, vol. VIII, pp. 456ff.; *Das jüdische Lexikon*, III, p. 1406; IV, pp. 82f.
92. Ed. by his son Shalom Klein, Montreal, 1969.

by the martyr R. Hanina ben Teradyon during his martyrdom under Hadrian when he was wrapped in a Torah scroll and burned.)

Finally, mention should be made of the fact that many collections of *Responsa* (and also some other Rabbinic books) contain either at the beginning or at the end biographies of the authors under the Nazis and their miraculous escape. This could be treated as a subject in itself by students interested in the Nazi holocaust.

Such biographical notes and reports about their experiences under the Nazis and their escape are contained, e.g. in the collections of *Responsa*:

R. Mordecai Yaakob Breisch, Introduction to *Helkath Yaakob*, Jerusalem, 1951.

R. Yizhak Yaakob Weiss, 'Pirsume Nissa' printed at the end of *Minhath Yizhak*, Part I, London, 1955, pp. 265ff.

Rabbi Dr Jacob Avigdor, Introduction to *Helek Yaakob*, II, Mexico, 1956.

Yerushath Peletah, Introduction, Budapest, 1946.

R. Zebi Hirsch Meisels, Introduction 'Shaar Mahmadim' to *Mekaddshe Ha-Shem*, 1st Part, Chicago, 1955.

R. Hayyim Yizhak Jeruchem, *Birkath Hayyim*, 'Alim Bochim', Introduction by his son, R. Aharon Jeruchem, New York, 1956.

R. Abraham Menahem Ha-Levi Steinberg, *Mahazeh Abraham*, 2nd Part, Introduction by his grandson R. Mosheh Ha-Levi Steinberg, New York, 1964.

Rabbi Aharon SGL Zimetbaum 'Kuntras Maase Nissim' in *Dibre Pinhas* of his father Rabbi Pinhas SGL Zimetbaum (who died a martyr), New York, pp. 165ff. (also in *Hasde David*, New York, 1965, pp. 165ff.).

R. Nathan Zebi Friedmann, Introduction to *Nezer Mattai*, Tel Aviv, 1957.

R. Yehezkiel Shraga Lipschitz-Halberstam of Stropkov, Introduction to *Dibre Yehezkiel Shraga*, 1st Part, Jerusalem, 1956.

R. Meshullam Rath, Introduction to *Kol Mebasser*, 1st Part, Jerusalem, 1955.

R. Bezalel Stern, Introduction to *Be-Zel Ha-Hochmah*, 1st Part, Jerusalem, 1959.

R. Jehiel Jaakob Weinberg, Introduction to *Seride Esh*, 1st Part, Jerusalem, 1961.

R. Yehoshua Mosheh Aronzon, Introduction to *Yeshuoth Mosheh*[4] and pp. 305ff., Tel Aviv, 1967.

R. Menahem Kirschbaum, *Ziyun Le-Menahem*, Introduction by the editor, R. Yehudah Rubinstein, New York, 1965.

R. Ephraim Oshry, Introductions to *Dibre Ephraim*, New York, 1959, and to *Mi-Maamakkim*, I–III, New York, 1959–69.

R. Simon Efrati, Introduction 'Ani Maamin' to *Me-Emek Ha-Bacha*, Jerusalem, 1948, pp. 10ff., and Introduction 'Be-Shaar Ha-Gai' to *Mi-Ge Ha-Haregah*, Jerusalem, 1961.

R. Shemuel Meir Ha-Kohen Holländer, Introduction to *Shem Ha-Kohen*, Jerusalem, 1952.

R. Pinhas SGL Litsh Rosenbaum, Introduction to *Elleh Dibre Shemuel* of his father R. Shemuel Shmelka SGL Litsh Rosenabum (who was burned in Auschwitz together with members of his family and congregation of Kleinwardein, Hungary, on 12th of Sivan 744, i.e. 3 June 1944), Jerusalem, 1961.

R. Meir Feuerwerger (Meiri), Introduction to *Ezrath Nashim* I, Frankfurt-Brussels, 1950.

THE PROBLEMS

The *Responsa* which deal with problems discussed by the Rabbis particularly after the war are of great variety. They range from replies to questions concerning the erection of monuments, museums, observing the laws of mourning, *Yahrzeit* (anniversaries of death) and re-interment, to returning to Judaism, embracing Judaism, *Kapos* and the two most important problems of rescuing Jewish orphans and the legal status of women liberated from the camps. The question of *agunoth*, i.e. women whose husbands cannot be traced, is the most important and frequent question discussed by almost all the Rabbis.

A selection of such cases is given below which throw light on the religious life of the Jews from various angles.[93]

Monuments

After World War II, Jews in various countries wished to perpetuate the memory of the victims of Nazism by erecting monuments. Does such an action infringe the prohibition of Deut. xvi 22 ('Thou shalt not set up a pillar') and Lev. xviii 3 ('Ye shall not walk in their statutes') and constitute a deviation from the usual practice of our forefathers not to erect monuments?

In 1947 the Ashkenazi Chief Rabbi of Israel, R. Isaac Halevy Herzog, and the Sephardi Chief Rabbi of Israel, R. Ben Zion Meir Hai Uzziel, were asked independently by R. Aharon Lastshaver, Ab Beth Din of Montevideo (Uruguay), concerning his community's intention to erect a monument in the cemetery in honour of those martyrs who had been killed during the last war and whose places of rest were unknown. The questioner sought approval for his view that such action was prohibited for the reasons mentioned.

---

93. On these and further problems, *vide infra* Part III.

Both Chief Rabbis were not in favour of erecting a monument, but not for the reasons which the questioner mentioned. 'If they would hearken to me,' writes Chief Rabbi Herzog,[94]

I would say to the members of the holy congregation: Brethren, it would be better if you do not introduce such an innovation. Who of our forefathers was not mindful of the honour of the dead and yet it never occurred to him to erect a monument. Therefore do refrain from doing so; you should rather found a school for children or a large Synagogue. This would be a merit for you and elevate the souls of the martyrs who would intercede for you in the Upper World. However, if you still insist upon your plan then you should erect a *mazebah* at the cemetery where similar stones exist and it should resemble a tombstone. You should try to obtain some ashes of the martyrs and bury the ashes there . . . . There is still another suggestion better than that of erecting a monument. One should erect at the cemetery an important and tall building like a tower, so that one could enter it, unlike a tombstone, and it should bear an appropriate inscription. In this building prayers for the dead should be recited . . .

After refuting the arguments of the questioner Chief Rabbi Uzziel[95] advises, to avoid any possible doubt, that one engrave the entire Psalm XCIV (which would serve as a disgrace, rebuke and warning to the enemies of Israel for future generations) in addition to the words of tribute to the memory of the martyrs. 'However, the erection of such a monument at the cemetery does not absolve us from our duty to erect public buildings dedicated to the study of Torah which is our primary duty in order to perpetuate the memory of our martyrs, rebuilding *yeshiboth* which have been destroyed . . . their ruins cry to us for their rebuilding—that has preference over silent monuments . . . .'

In the same year (1947) another Rabbi, R. Yizhak Yaakob Weiss, dealt with a similar question which was addressed to him by the leaders of the Orthodox Congregation of Grosswardein (Rumania). Many Jews wished to perpetuate the memory of the thousands of victims of that town. The community was divided as to where the memorial was to be erected. The freethinkers (*ha-hopheshim, Neologen*) wished this to be done only under their auspices while the Orthodox who feared that through that the influence of the *Neologen* would become stronger and

94. Printed in *Kol Torah*, Jerusalem, Iyyar 5707, see Zimmels in *Sepher Ha-Yobel Le-Rabbi Hanoch Albeck*, p. 422. Both Chief Rabbis' replies are given here in a very shortened form.
95. *Mishpete Uzziel*, 2nd ed., Part II, *Yoreh Deah*, vol. I, no. 22, where other reasons given by the questioner are refuted.

that their own power would weaken—a fact which would lead to difficulties in religious matters—sought everything in their power to have the memorial under their auspices. They intended to erect a large gravestone (*mazebah*) upon which the crimes committed by the Nazis on the local Jews were to be engraved.

The Rabbi said in his reply that such a plan was tantamount to the erection of a monument customary among non-Jews. 'Although I was told that this had been done in other places[96] possibly with some variations from the non-Jewish practice, nevertheless it is forbidden on account of Deut. XVI 22. The fact that this has been done in other places proves nothing, since Jews there might not have considered the stringency of the prohibition. Furthermore, another prohibition may be involved namely that of Lev. XVIII 3 (imitation of non-Jewish practices).' However, the Rabbi rejects the latter on the grounds of a *Responsum* of R. Joseph Colon (d. Padua, 1480) according to which the prohibition of Lev. XVIII 3 does not apply to anything done for honour. However, in order to avoid the infringement of Deut. XVI 22, the Rabbi suggested that the *mazebah* should be erected in the following way: soap bars 'R.J.F.' which according to reports were made from the fat of the victims,[97] and ashes brought from Auschwitz alleged to have been taken from the crematorium and pieces of Torah scrolls torn by the Nazis, which require *genizah* (removal, hiding), should be put together in one grave over which the *mazebah* should be placed, as is normally done at a graveside, with an inscription stating what had been done to the Jews by the Nazis.[98]

A Rabbi[99] tells us that he was asked by one of the esteemed Rabbis of the United States whether it was correct for a 'heap of witness' (*Galed*, cf. Gen. XXXI 47) to have been erected in a great city in memory of the martyrs where their ashes were taken and put into a glass case for display. The Rabbi replies that it was wrong to keep the ashes for display as they must be buried. (He quotes his *Responsum* in his work *Emek Ha-Bacha* (No. 2) where he proved that it was a duty to bury the ashes of the martyrs.) Although ashes do not convey levitical uncleanliness

---

96. E.g. in Copenhagen, Dachau, Belgrade and in Greece, see *Beth Jacob*, no. 130, 730 (1930), pp. 16ff.

97. See *supra* pp. 108ff.

98. *Minhath Yizhak*, I, no. 29. At the end of the *Responsum* a lenient view expressed by two Rabbis on the erection of a monument is quoted. One of them deals with the question of the erection of a monument in honour of those fallen in World War I. The other Rabbi refers to the victims of the Nazi holocaust. However, R. Weiss remarks that in view of the stringency of the prohibition involved his decision to erect a monument (*mazebah*) at the side of a grave where the ashes of the martyrs, etc., had been buried was accepted and he delivered a memorial address.

99. Efrati, *Mi-Ge Ha-Haregah*, no. 9.

one may still have no benefit from them (as in the case of a corpse). Both a corpse and ashes must be buried.

Ohel (mausoleum) on the graves

In one of the towns of Poland all Jews were taken to the field near the cemetery, massacred and buried. At the cemetery there rest great *zaddikim* of previous generations. It was not customary to erect an *ohel* (mausoleum) over the grave of a *zaddik*. It was planned to erect an *ohel* over the mass grave. It was feared if this were done it would reflect disparagingly on the *zaddikim* buried there. Was this fear justified?

The Rabbi's reply was in the negative. He remembered having seen a book where it was stated that this would not be regarded as disrespectful.

When he arrived in Jerusalem and was elected advisor in *halachic* matters in regard to the cemetery in Jerusalem, he was again asked that question and sought to elaborate. He decided that it was permitted to erect an *ohel* over the grave of a *zaddik* although there were no *ohalim* over the graves of other *zaddikim* buried there. 'There is all the more reason for this to be done over the place of execution of the martyrs of the wicked government. The martyrs are the pride of Israel (see *Baba Bathra* 10b) and none rank higher . . . .'[100]

Museum

A question was asked concerning the erection of a building (museum) on the site of mass graves in an extermination camp. It was intended that the museum contain the various sadistic instruments employed by the Nazis. Rabbi S. Efrati writes:[101]

I was asked the following question by two journalists when we were standing together on the hill of Treblinka at the threshold of the gigantic altar of blood which the murderer had erected to his idol Ashmodai,[102] in order to destroy Israel, where among the forests of Poland a great mass grave was dug in which victims from all parts of Europe lie, where the enemy has called for their own version of 'an ingathering of the exiles', to kill and strangle them, where the enemy had gathered those dispersed from Lwow, Warsaw, Kovno, Pressburg, from Amsterdam to Salonica, to this valley, the valley of

100. Ibid., no. 7.
101. *Me-Emek Ha-Bacha*, no. 1. See also *Mi-Ge Ha-Haregah*, nos. 4f., containing the comments of Chief Rabbi Uzziel and R. Efrati's rejoinder.
102. In *Mi-Ge Ha-Haregah*, nos. 4f.: 'erected by the murderous Ashmodai'.

M

Bacha.[103] The two journalists were *kohanim* and they asked whether they might tread on the holy soil moistened by the blood of martyrs buried there. My reply was in the negative. Then one member of the central committee turned to me with the request that I decide whether on that soil a building could be erected to house the horrifying pictures of the destruction of a third of our people which would be accessible to *kohanim* so that they too would be able to see what the enemy had done to us.

After careful consideration, the Rabbi gave instructions how to erect the building 'which should remain a sign of disgrace and an everlasting monument of abhorrence of the German people'.

This *Responsum* was sent by Rabbi Efrati to Chief Rabbi Uzziel for his comments.[104] The Chief Rabbi replied in a letter dated Kislev 708 (Nov./Dec. 1947).

Anniversaries of death (Yahrzeit)

As the exact dates of the massacres could not always be ascertained, many questions arose as to fixing the days for *yahrzeit*.

The writer himself had the following problem:[105] His parents left Vienna in 1939 for Holland, where a brother and a sister of his mother were living, who had obtained permission for them to immigrate. While his father died in 1942 his mother was deported by the Nazis. In reply to an inquiry made by the writer at the Tracing Department of the Jewish Refugee Committee in London, he received a letter (dated 14 January 1947) that 'according to information received by the United Kingdom Search Bureau, your mother Mrs Mindel Zimmels was deported to Sakrau on October 26, 1942'. He then observed the 15th of Heshvan which coincided with that date in 1942 as *Yahrzeit*. To a further inquiry the Tracing Department of the Jewish Refugee Committee replied (on 3 October 1947) that no additional information had come to hand.

Recently when he made inquiries about his relatives (of Dutch nationality) who had also been deported some time later, he received a statement from the Netherlands Red Cross (dated 8 February 1971) that his mother, Mrs Mindel Zimmels, had been taken to the concentra-

---

103. Cf. Ps. LXXXIV 7 where the word *Bacha* is either the name of a place or '(a vale of) balsam trees'. According to Rashi *ad loc.* it means: 'The vale of weeping, tears'. This is the meaning of the word here. Joseph Ha-Kohen (d. 1575) called his book dealing with the persecutions of the Jews *Emek Ha-Bacha*, an allusion to this meaning.

104. See *Mi-Ge Ha-Haregah*, nos. 4f. and *Mishpete Uzziel*, 2nd ed., Part III, vol. II, nc 117.

105 The writer thought it opportune to give prominence to this case as an expression of respect for his mother.

tion camp of Westerbork (Holland) on 24 October 1942, and from there to Auschwitz, on 26 October 1942, and 'is presumed to have died on October 29, 1942 in the neighbourhood of Auschwitz'. At the end of the letter, there was a note that the above information (concerning the death) was not based on the evidence of witnesses but on the fate of the entire transport. To further inquiries, the Netherlands Red Cross replied that a transport from Westerbork arrived in Auschwitz on the third day after leaving Westerbork and that on arrival, all men below fifteen and over fifty years of age as well as all women and children were gassed at Birkenau, which formed part of the camp of Auschwitz. They added that the information of the Refugee Committee about Sakrau was not correct.

It appears therefore that Mrs Zimmels was still alive on 26 October (15th of Heshvan 5703) and was murdered on 29 October 1942 (i.e. 18th of Heshvan 5703).

In view of that there was no doubt that the correct *Yahrzeit* was the 18th of Heshvan. Since, however, the writer had kept *Yahrzeit* on the 15th of Heshvan for so many years, he was in doubt whether in future years he had to keep both dates or could (by the means of *hatharath neder*) be absolved from keeping *yahrzeit* on the 15th of Heshvan. He put his case to Dayan I. J. Weiss on the latter's visit to Manchester (July 1971) and the Dayan said that the 18th of Heshvan should be kept as *Yahrzeit* and, although *hatharath neder* should be performed, *kaddish* should be recited after the study of *Mishnah* on the 15th of Heshvan as well.

Memorial days

Apart from questions sent by individuals to Rabbis concerning the observance of laws of mourning for their relatives killed by the Nazis, we find the Rabbis dealt with the fixing of days to commemorate the death of the martyrs generally, so that all Israel could honour their memory on a fixed day each year.

The author of the *Responsa Me-Emek Ha-Bacha*, R. S.Efrati, states that when he was Rabbi in Warsaw after World War II, it had been suggested that the great men in Israel should fix a special day in the year for mourning the victims and Jews in all places observe the laws of mourning by saying *kaddish*. A date had been suggested. 'Unfortunately till today nothing has been done.'[106]

However, when the 'Hazon Ish' was asked to join the *haskamah* to introduce mourning and a public fast for the victims of the Nazi holocaust, he refused to do so. He argued that all religious (*halachic*)

---

106. *Me-Emek Ha-Bacha,* no. 3, p. 32.

matters are fixed by the Torah. They have their root in the Written Law and are interpreted by the Oral Law. 'Not even a Prophet without support from the Torah is entitled to introduce a new practice. Just as a reduction of the Law is a deviation from the Torah, so too is any addition to the Law . . . .[107] The introduction of public fasts to be observed for all times would amount to introducing a law of Rabbinic significance which we are certainly not entitled to do.'[108]

However, days of remembrance have been introduced and observed in some countries often coinciding with other public fastdays.

(i) *Erev Rosh Hodesh Heshvan.* According to one report, a day of memorial was fixed for the Jews in Rome in 1944. We are told that on the Sabbath, the first day of the intermediate days of *Sukkoth* (16 October 1943) 1,100 Jews had been deported from Rome to Auschwitz and only twelve survived. In the following year after the liberation of Italy, the Chief Rabbinate of Rome fixed the Eve of *Rosh Hodesh Heshvan* which coincided with 16 October as a day of memorial.[109] However, from another source it can be seen that a day of memorial had not been fixed yet, as Chief Rabbi Prato of Rome inquired of Chief Rabbi Herzog of Israel on the 18th of Adar 707 (10 March 1947) whether it was right to fix a memorial day (*yom zikkaron*) for the saying of *kaddish* for those who perished in the terrible holocaust. In his reply, Chief Rabbi Herzog pointed out that it was difficult to advise on this matter as the wife of a missing husband might later rely on this and re-marry. He thinks that a day should be fixed for all Italian Jews to attend synagogue and recite *kaddish* for all martyrs and kindle lights in their memory. It should be publicly emphasized in the name of the Rabbinate that this in no way gives permission to *agunoth* to re-marry. It is a matter of a general nature since it is known that most of the victims had died. Should women ask for permission, written evidence should be submitted which would then be forwarded to the Chief Rabbinate in Israel who would give their decision in each case.[110]

---

107. One should compare the case of *Purim* which was instituted only after the contemporary scholars found an indication in the Torah. Cf. Talmud *Yerushalmi, Megillah* I, 7, 70d. See also Nahmanides on Deut. IV 2.

108. *Kobez Iggeroth me-eth Maran Baal Hazon Ish,* Part I, nos. 97, 101, Jerusalem, 1955; *Peer Ha-Dor,* Biographical Study on R. Abraham Yeshayahu Karelitz, ed. by R. Shlomoh Kohen, III, Bene Berak, 1970, pp. 123ff.

109. Dr Yom Tob Levinski, *Sepher Ha-Moadim,* vol. VIII, Tel Aviv, 1957, pp. 149f. quoting *Reshumoth,* new series, vol. II, pp. 25f. See also Raul Hilberg, *The Destruction of the European Jews,* p. 429 where it is said that the arrest of the Jews began during the night of 15–16 October and was finished in less than twenty-four hours. Of the people seized 'a total of 1007 were shipped off on October 18, 1943, to the killing center of Auschwitz'; cf. Roth, *The History of the Jews in Italy,* pp. 543f.

110. Herzog, *Hechal Yizhak,* I, no. 28.

(ii) 10th of Tebeth.   The 10th of Tebeth has been proclaimed by the Chief Rabbinate of Israel as an additional day of mourning and 'Yom Kaddish' in memory of the martyrs of the Nazi holocaust. On that day, *kaddish* is recited and *mishnayoth* are studied in their honour.[111]

(iii) 20th of Sivan.   It was for the third time in Jewish history that the 20th of Sivan was chosen as a day of fasting and mourning for the persecution of our people. The first time was in 1171 when R. Jacob Tam, the famous Tosaphist, decreed that this day be kept as a day of fasting because of the persecution of the Jews in Blois. It was observed by the Jews of France and England.[112]

About five hundred years later it was again the 20th of Sivan which was fixed as a fastday and day of mourning on the occasion of the persecution under Chmielnicki in Poland in the years 1648–49. It was chosen because the first persecution occurred in Nemirov on that day. Special *selihoth* are recited at the morning service.[113]

It was for the third time, in 706 (1946), that it was adopted as a fastday and a day of remembrance by the Hungarian Jews because of the persecutions in 701, and particularly in 704 and 705 (1941, 1944, 1945). There are special *selihoth* taken from the ritual of the Jews in Poland in 1648 and printed with regulations for the day. On the title page is stated:

> *Selihoth* for the 20th of Sivan fixed by the Geonim and saintly Rabbis following the massacres of the year 1648 in Poland have now been renewed with some alterations for the provinces of Hungary. They have been arranged with the authorization of the great Rabbis by the Central Office of the Orthodox Communities of our provinces following the massacres of our brethren there in the year 701 and subsequent years, particularly in 704 and 705, and the destruction of the Synagogues, Houses of Study, Torah Scrolls and other holy books.
>
> Budapest, 706.

In the Foreword is stated that the 20th of Sivan had been chosen, as on this month most of the massacres had occurred and it had also been observed as a fastday in Poland.

---

111. Cf. Dob Rosen, *Shema Yisrael*, Jerusalem, 1969, p. 83; R. Mordechai Ha-Kohen, *Pirke Shoah*, Jerusalem, 710, pp. 9, 11.

112. See Joseph Ha-Kohen, *Emek Ha-Bacha*, ed. Letteris, Cracow, 1895, pp. 49ff. and 52 and the editor's notes ibid.; S. Bernfeld, *Sepher Ha-Demaoth*, I, pp. 224ff. R. Tam died that year.

113. Nathan Hanover, *Yeven Mezulah*, Cracow, 1896, p. 56; Bernfeld, *Sepher Ha-Demaoth*, III, p. 133. For an additional reason for choosing this date, see R. Shabbethai Kohen (ShaCh) quoted by Bernfeld, p. 140. See also R. Abraham Gombiner, on *Shulhan Aruch Orah Hayyim*, cap. DLXXX *ad fin*.

Regulations are given for the fast which is prescribed for both men and women from fifteen years to fifty-five years of age. For those exempt non-observance of the fast was to be 'redeemed by charity'.

These regulations are followed by those dealing with the observance of *Yahrzeit* and *hazkarath neshamoth*. Of these the following should be mentioned:

If a person knows the day his father or mother was brought to Auschwitz and it is thought that they had been placed among those to be killed, he should observe this day as *Yahrzeit*. If they arrived in the evening at Auschwitz, the following day should be observed as *Yahrzeit*. He who does not know, the day when his parents and other relatives were brought to Auschwitz should observe the 20th of Sivan as day of *Yahrzeit*.[114]

The six orders of the *Mishnah* should be divided for study among the congregants and the *siyyum* should take place on the 20th of Sivan.

The order of the day's proceedings is then given followed by the prayer for the dead '*El male rahamim*' for the Jews of Hungary and other countries of Europe who had been killed for *kiddush ha-Shem*, '*Ab ha-Rahamim*'(in our Sabbath service), the *kaddish* similar to that found at the end of the Talmud editions, *selihoth* most of them taken from the *selihoth* for the 20th of Sivan and *kinoth* among them the famous *kinah* by R. Meir Rothenburg '*Shaali Seruphah*' composed on the occasion of the burning of the Talmud in Paris in 1242.

(iv) Thursday night of the week in which *Va-Yikra* is read is devoted to the memory of Jewish children massacred by the Nazis. During the service the first chapter of Leviticus is read which is usually the first portion a child learns when beginning the study of the Pentateuch.[115]

(v) The 27th of Nisan has been fixed by the Israeli government as a day of national mourning and as a memorial day of the uprising against the Germans.[116]

---

114. No *kaddish* or memorial prayer should be said for a missing man who has left a wife and no permission has been given to her by the Beth Din to re-marry.

115. R. Mordechai Ha-Kohen, *Pirke Shoah*, pp. 9, 11f. On other days of commemoration see ibid.

116. See the text quoted by Dob Rosen, *Shema Yisrael*, p. 73 from *Sepher Ha-Hukkim* 9th Nisan 719, and 18th Nisan 721; Levinski, *Sepher Ha-Moadim*, p. 158. The uprising of the Warsaw Ghetto began on 19 April 1943 which was the eve of *Pesah*. In order to prevent the observance of the anniversary from coinciding with *Pesah* the Knesseth designated 27th Nisan as the permanent date for the commemoration of the uprising. See also Robert Serebrenik, *The Warsaw Ghetto Revolt*, ed. by World Jewish Congress, 1956, p. 5, and Isaac Schwarzbart, ibid., p. 4. Cf., however, R. M. Ha-Kohen, *Pirke Shoah*, pp. 9, 12.

Kinoth (dirges) complaints

One Rabbi suggests that there be added with the consent of all the great men of Israel at least one strophe to the *selihah Elleh Ezkerah* (which deals with the Ten Martyrs and is recited on *Yom Kippurim*) in memory of the holocaust in the years 700–705 (1940–45).

He writes: 'We are more ashamed than any other generation that until today no Rabbinical institute (*mosad*) or religious composer (*mekonen*) who is known for his righteousness apart from his learning has composed a *kinah* to be recited on the 9th of Ab on the last *hurban* when millions of holy and pure people were cut down through the sheer wickedness of the world and the insolence of the nations who stood afar . . . .' (These words were printed in 1967.)[117]

A similar complaint was raised by another Rabbi. Of his complaint the following words should be mentioned:

Fasts and memorials have been fixed, *selihoth* and prayers of supplication have been composed to commemorate the *hurban* of the *Bathe Ha-Mikdash*, the persecutions in the Middle Ages of Worms and Speyer in 4856 (1096, The First Crusade), the persecution in 5408 (1648) on the 20th of Sivan (under Chmielnicki and earlier about the persecution in Blois in 1171). For the most tragic *hurban* in history, there is no fasting, no *kinah* (lamentation, dirge), no *piyyut* (poem) or prayer.[118]

These complaints, as far as the composition of a *kinah* is concerned, are no longer justified. In fact we possess several very moving *kinoth* lamenting all Jewish martyrs as well as individual personalities.

(i) The *kinah* composed by 'The Rabbi and Zaddik R. Michael Dob Weissmandel' (he died in 1958). He was a pupil and son-in-law of R. Shemuel Ha-Levi Ungar, Ab Beth Din of Neutra (Slovakia). It is included in his book *Min Ha-Mezar*, New York 720 (1960).[119]

(ii) *Kinah* 'Al Hurban Ha-Aharon' composed by R. Simon Schwab, New York, has appeared with an English translation (it is recited by the Reader at the Golders Green Beth Ha-Midrash Congregation, London, on *Tishah Be-Ab*).

(iii) R. Hayyim Yizhak Wohlgelernter lamented the death of R. Yehezkiel Holstuck of Ostrowca who died a martyr on the 10th of

117. Aronzon, *Yeshuath Mosheh*, no. 42, para. 3.
118. R. A.Jeruchem, 'Alim Bochim', Introduction to the *Responsa Birkath Hayyim* of his father R. H.Y.Jeruchem, New York, 1966, p. 33.
119. See also his *kinoth* in *Beth Jacob*, no. 24, Iyyar 721, p. 3 and nos. 123–24, vol. XI, 730, p. 3.

Tebeth 703 (1943). The composer himself who had survived the Nazi holocaust was killed by the Poles when he left the bunker. The *kinah* was written in Shebat 703 (December-January 1942–43), a ndwas found by his brother David Wohlgelernter.[120]

(iv) *Kinah* by Chief Rabbi Herzog on the ruins of the Warsaw ghetto on the occasion of his visit there.[121]

(v) R. Simon Efrati composed a *kinah Ani Maamin* which is printed in the Introduction to his collection of *Responsa Me-Emek Ha-Bacha*, 708 (1948) pp. 12ff.

(vi) *Kinah Eli Polin* by J. L. Bjaler printed in *Pirke Shoah* by R. Mordechai Ha-Kohen, Jerusalem, 1950, pp. 6ff.[122]

Return to Judaism, embracing Judaism

Cases of those Jews and Jewesses who sought shelter among non-Jews by changing their identity either by procuring Aryan papers or certificates of baptism raised various problems after the liberation. One Rabbi[123] gives us a vivid description of the survivors. He divides them into two groups: one group consisted of those who had returned from Russia. The other group were those who emerged from their hiding places and underground shelters as non-Jews. The former having always been in Jewish company had the sole desire to live again freely as Jews. Seeing, however, that this was far from easy, if not impossible, in Poland they started wandering again in search of safety. Some were unsuccessful and perished *en route*.

The second group consisted of those who had saved themselves by denying their Jewish identity. Many decided to remain in the country where they lived with their Christian friends. They continued to live under the names they had assumed. Various problems arose in connection with matrimonial matters. No doubt, their family life suffered. After much persuasion they came to the Beth Din to divorce their orthodox wives. 'We have done much for their wives, for the pious daughters of Israel.' Of the various problems with which the Rabbis had to deal the following cases should be quoted:

The relatives of a certain Miriam, known as Marisia Bondezdrow, approached the Rabbi with this request: her husband who was then in

---

120. Ungar, *ADMORIM Shenispu*, p. 120.
121. *Beth Jacob*, no. 120, vol. X, p. 12.
122. On the recital of the *kinah*, see R. M. Ha-Kohen, *Pirke Shoah*, pp. 6, 12. For a *Kinah* composed by Rev. A. Rosenfeld see *Seder Kinot Ha-Shalem*, London, 1965, pp. 173ff.
123. Efrati, *Mi-Ge Ha-Haregah*, no. 13.

Warsaw was one of those who had cast off the heavenly yoke and was about to marry a non-Jewess. If the Rabbinate should fail to persuade him to give his wife a *get* she would remain an *agunah* all her life. She was young and came from a great and respected family. During the Nazi holocaust she hid herself in a Christian home. If she received a *get* there was still hope she might return to her relatives (and to the fold of her people) who survived, and walk in God's way.

When the husband appeared before the Rabbi, he agreed, after great persuasion, to divorce his wife.[124]

R. Shlomoh David Kahana, formerly Ab Beth Din of Warsaw, later Rabbi in the Old City of Jerusalem, submitted the following case to the Chief Rabbi of Israel, R. Yizhak Herzog, on the 15th of Tebeth 710 (4 January 1950).[125]

He had been urged repeatedly by many of his acquaintances from Warsaw to assist a young woman who was an *agunah* and required *halizah* from her brother-in-law who had survived owing to his 'Aryan Certificate' (which he had obtained by stating that he was a non-Jew). His sister-in-law asked him to let her perform the ceremony of *halizah* but he refused to deal with this. All the endeavours of the Rabbis remained fruitless.

Three trustworthy persons who knew him very well testified that he had severed all bonds with Jews. He never met them, did not attend synagogue on any festival, desecrated the Sabbath publicly by doing prohibited acts (smoking and writing) and had not circumcised his son. In spite of the fact that most Jews had already re-adopted their Jewish names (even his sister who was with him had cancelled her Aryan Certificate) he was still known by his non-Jewish name.

The question was whether the brother-in-law could be regarded as an apostate (*mumar la-abodah zarah*) in which case a lenient view concerning *halizah* could be adopted. 'This question', remarks R. Kahana, 'is at present only theoretical and of no practical importance, since it may still be possible to influence him to perform the act of *halizah*. However, the main point of my remarks is that it is a duty to draw the attention of those who hold certificates testifying their holders to be non-Jews to exchange them for Jewish ones in order to avoid their being regarded as idol-worshippers . . .'

In his reply, the Chief Rabbi says that all endeavours should be made to enable *halizah* to be performed. He then considers the position of a *mumar* concerning *halizah* in general and that of that man in particular. There are some interesting points in the question and in the answer.

124. Ibid.
125. *Hechal Yizhak*, I, nos. 88ff.

We are told that there were some Jews (in Poland in 1950!) holding
Aryan documents who used to attend synagogues and refrain from
doing work on the Sabbath and from transgressing the dietary laws.
They retained their certificates either through 'fear' or 'laziness', which
the Chief Rabbi found very strange. He asks:

> Of what are they afraid, they are living now in free countries?
> Perhaps they have become confused and fear a re-occurrence of the
> fate of the Jews under the Nazis. If this were the case then he (the
> levir) should not be regarded as a proper apostate. This reason is
> far-fetched. Perhaps they hold their Aryan passports for the purpose
> of citizenship which they could not otherwise obtain. In reality, they
> regard themselves as proper Jews and observe the law. This would
> not apply to the levir who defies the law.

> To the best of my knowledge, those people made themselves Aryans,
> not exactly 'Christians'. Cannot 'Aryan' include atheist? If so, by
> calling oneself 'Aryan' I do not know whether such person could be
> described as 'an idol-worshipper'.

At any rate, the Chief Rabbi agrees with R. Kahana that they should
be told to change their Aryan Certificates for Jewish ones, in order
that their repentance should be complete.

It also happened that a man who had been saved by a woman,
became attached to her to such an extent that he wished to marry her.
The case was as follows:

R. Mosheh Aharon Krausz of Nagy-Bánya tells us that on his visit
to Csikszereda to attend his son's induction as Rabbi, he met one
among those who were present, who had been living together with
a non-Jewess for some years. He came from a respected and religious
(orthodox) family but was attached to the non-Jewess and unable to
leave her. The Rabbi tried to influence him to give up his association
with the woman but all his endeavours were in vain. All his wealth
and belongings, he maintained, came from her. She had saved him
from death and had done him many great favours. They were in love.
The man added that she had several times expressed her intention of
embracing Judaism and conducting herself in a religious way, but had
always been rejected. She came also before the visiting Rabbi wit
tears in her eyes, begged not to be rejected but to be accepted int
the Jewish fold. She would live as a religious Jewess.

Discussing the possibility of conversion to Judaism, the Rabbi is of
the opinion that his view be put before other Rabbis of the country
for their approval. He mentioned that he himself thought that the
woman could be accepted into Judaism on condition that the couple

promise to conduct themselves as religious Jews in every respect. Naturally, they would then have to undergo a religious marriage.[126]

Rescue of Jewish children

Jews living in the ghettos tried in despair before their deportation or during a *Kinderaktion*, when the children were taken away by the Nazis to be massacred, to hand them over to non-Jewish friends, monasteries and convents, to be looked after.[127] Their parents hoped to reclaim them after the war. However, in most cases, the parents had been massacred by the Nazis and the orphans were left with their non-Jewish foster parents (who had sometimes handed them over to monasteries or convents).

The rescue of Jewish children was one of the most important tasks of the Jewish leaders in the post-war period. Great efforts were made by the Chief Rabbi of Palestine, R. Yizhak Herzog. In January 1946 he left Palestine to visit various countries to save the children kept in non-Jewish hands. He had an audience with Pope Pius XII and with the heads of state of Italy, France, Switzerland, Belgium and Holland. He also visited Germany, Poland and Czechoslovakia. He succeeded in saving about twelve thousand Jewish children and brought them back to Judaism.[128]

The Chief Rabbi of the British Empire was Chairman and Dayan I. Grunfeld vice-chairman of the international organizational Commission on the Status of Jewish War Orphans in Europe. In Holland there existed 'L'Ezrath Hayeled', the Jewish organization for the rescue of war orphans. Its chief officer, Dr. L. Friedmann, reported in March 1953, that 'of the 1,750 Jewish war orphans, 500 were at present under Jewish guardianship, 393 were still with non-Jewish foster parents, the fate of 69 had not yet been decided, while the remainder were over 21 years of age.'[129]

Very active in the rescue of Jewish children as well as adults in Lithuania was R. Ephraim Oshry, Rabbi in Kovno. He tells us of the desperate attempts made by parents who lived under the Nazis, to save their children from destruction by removing them from the ghetto of Kovno and handing them over to non-Jews so that they should be looked after, until the time would come when the Merciful One would

---

126. *Yerushath Peletah*, no. 26.
127. Cf. e.g. Garfunkel, *Destruction of Kovno's Jewry*, pp. 152ff. on the conditions in Kovno. Cf. also R. Oshry *infra*.
128. See *Beth Jacob*, no. 120, vol. X, 1969, pp. 12f.; *Jewish Chronicle*, 4 June 1946, p. 9; 7 June 1946, pp. 1, 6; 28 June 1946, p. 7. His visit to Rome is also mentioned in *Hechal Yizhak*, II, no. 71.
129. *Jewish Chronicle*, 6 March 1953, p. 10.

have pity on His people and stop the destroyer from his destructive work.[130]

Similarly, many Jewish children were handed over to Christian priests to be kept in their monasteries and convents. The priests accepted them in the hope of converting them to Christianity. After the collapse of the Nazi regime the first steps made by the Rabbi[131] and other liberated Jews was to reclaim the children from the Christians and bring them back to their ancestral faith as soon as possible so that they would not become completely estranged from Judaism. As many children were in the hands of the priests, it was necessary to go to their private houses and monasteries. The Rabbi was asked whether it was permitted to do so from the religious point of view. He was also asked whether one may enter clergymen's private houses since religious objects were usually kept and religious ceremonies were performed there. The clergymen often denied keeping Jewish children at all. The children who had been taken there were not aware of their past. The question therefore arose, perhaps the assertions of the clergymen were true. If so, it would certainly be forbidden to enter their houses.

The Rabbi decided that since everyone knew that the purpose of entering the religious places of the non-Jews was not to worship but only to save the Jewish children in order to avoid their being brought up as Christians, therefore not even the principle of *marith ha-ayyin* (avoiding the semblance of wrong-doing) applied in such a case. Hence, every attempt was to be made to enter those places and search for the Jewish children to bring them back to the fold. 'It happened to me too', concludes the Rabbi in his *Responsum*, 'that I went to the Lithuanian priest and with the help of God succeeded in saving many children who are today in Israel and follow a Jewish life, keeping the Torah and the commandments in every respect. Many others did likewise and courageously saved children, captives of non-Jews and restored them to the fold of their people . . . .'

In two other *Responsa* R. Oshry[132] tells us of the great difficulties he had to encounter when he was on his way to trace Jewish children who were living among non-Jews or in monasteries and convents. Apart from the danger during journeys and obstacles created by the monks and nuns, they were dishonest. They agreed that it was their duty to return Jewish children, but on the other hand they assisted the gentiles in hiding the children and tried everything to prevent them from being returned.

130. Oshry, *Mi-Maamakkim*, I, no. 31; cf. also Garfunkel, *Destruction of Kovno's Jewry* pp. 152ff.

131. Oshry, *Mi-Maamakkim*, I, no. 31.

132. *Mi-Maamakkim*, II, nos. 24f. On the difficulties of tracing Jewish orphans and receiving them back, cf. also *Beth Jacob*, no. 24, Adar 721, pp. 20ff.; and nos. 57–58, Adar 724, p. 9.

The Rabbi tells us of a case which he himself calls unusual. A non-Jewish woman appeared before him and told him she was prepared to return to its Jewish relative a Jewish child that had been given to her by its mother. The relative, however, refused to accept the child.

On the Rabbi's request to give him some particulars about the case, she told him that the boy's mother had died shortly before the liberation after giving birth to the child whose father was a non-Jew who had hidden her from the Germans. However, before her death when she felt her end was near, she called her friend, the non-Jewess, and asked her to promise that immediately after the liberation she would return the child to one of the relatives of her (Jewish) husband. If she promised to do so, the mother would be able to die in peace, as she would know that 'there remained an offshoot of her family which had been cut down completely by the German murderers and of which no one was left'. The non-Jewess promised her Jewish friend who died soon afterwards to fulfil her last wish. After the liberation she hastened to keep her promise and after long investigations succeeded in finding the Jew to whom the child should be handed over in accordance with the wish of its mother. However, to her great distress and perplexity, he refused to accept the child, saying the boy was not a Jew as his father was a non-Jew. As the Jew did not want to accept the child, there was no alternative but for the non-Jewess to adopt the boy and bring him up as a non-Jew, which she did.

The non-Jewess added that after a certain time, the mother of the child appeared to her in a dream crying and asked her to go to a Rabbi and to tell him the whole story. This was the reason she had come to the Rabbi to find a way that the child could be a Jew so that the soul of her friend could rest.

After thanking her, the Rabbi called the relative who had refused to accept the boy. The relative told the Rabbi that what the non-Jewess had said was true. However, his refusal to accept the boy was due to the fact that he wished to avoid discredit to the entire family, which this matter would bring if it became public. The husband of the woman who was his relative was living in Minsk where he was practising as a physician. When the non-Jewess came to him for the first time he immediately informed the husband of the whole event, who, however, did not want to have anything to do with the child which was 'a child of harlotry' and in his (the relative's) view the husband was right as the child was a *mamzer*, since when the mother became pregnant by the non-Jew she had been a married woman as her husband was alive . . . because of that the relative too refused to accept the child as it would bring shame to the family. The Jew asked the Rabbi not to reveal this to anyone as his family was a well-known and distinguished one in Israel.

The Rabbi tried to show the relative that he was wrong in his assumption. Had the matter not been revealed he would have caused the loss of a Jewish soul, as the child was not a *mamzer* but was a proper Jew. He asked the relative that if he refused to accept the boy, he should give the Rabbi his consent to take the child from the non-Jewess and he, the Rabbi, would take care of it.

The Rabbi tells us that he was able to find a Jewish religious family which was willing to adopt the child.[133] The family later emigrated to London and the boy was studying in the *yeshibah* and distinguished himself in his studies . . . to the great joy of his 'parents'. (The Rabbi shows the legal background for his decision.)

R. Oshry[134] tells us also of the rescue of a Jewish girl who was about to be lost to Judaism.

On one occasion he came to the town of Zasliai. There he learned that in the neighbouring village a Jewish girl was living among non-Jews. He hurried there and found the Jewish girl. She told him she was from Kovno and that her family had been one of the most distinguished, wealthy and learned families of that town (the Rabbi confirmed this). She told him of the many troubles and adventures she had had. She had been saved from the Germans by the son of the non-Jewish care-taker of her father's house who had kept her in hiding. He had supplied her with all that was necessary and helped her to disguise herself as a non-Jewess. When the Rabbi asked her why she was still among non-Jews and had not returned to the Jews after the danger had passed, she began to cry and told him that the young non-Jew who had saved her had exploited her gratitude by having illicit relations with her and she had given birth to a son who was 'a proper non-Jew' (*goy gamur*) as his father was a non-Jew. The latter then left for Germany and she did not know where he was. As she loved her son very much she could not leave him among the non-Jews who were strangers to her. The Jews surely would not accept her son (the *goy*) and would keep aloof from him. Because of that, she said, she had to spend her life among the non-Jews against her will. To the Rabbi's question how she was so sure that her son was a '*goy gamur*', she replied she thought so. If the Rabbi were to circumcise her son and arrange to redeem her firstborn (*pidyan ha-ben*) and accept him in the Jewish community, she said, she would gladly leave the village with its non-Jewish inhabitants and return to live among her Jewish brethren.

The Rabbi promised to comply with her request. However, before doing this the Rabbi tells us he had to deal with the position of the boy

133. Circumcision was performed and also immersion took place in order to comply with all the views on the status of the child.
134 *Mi-Maamakkim*, II, no. 25.

from the religious point of view. Was he to be regarded as an un-circumcised Jew who required only circumcision or was he a subject for proselytization too? What was his position concerning *pidyan ha-ben*? May the mother redeem him or not? May the Beth Din do so? Some liturgical questions had to be discussed too.

After dealing with the case, the Rabbi tells us that the wish of the mother was fulfilled. She later married a strictly religious Jew and her son was successfully studying in one of the greatest *yeshiboth* in Israel and promised to become a *gadol be-Yisrael*.

The same Rabbi[135] tells us of difficulties of another nature, he encountered while rescuing Jewish children as many of them had not been circumcised by their parents who by such conduct had sought to conceal the children's Jewish origin. In addition, it was quite difficult for the children to endure the pains of circumcision apart from the fact that they were weak owing to the privations they had had to suffer.

However, all obstacles had been overcome. The children had been accepted into the covenant of Abraham. There was, however, one boy of about ten years of age who under no circumstances agreed to be circumcised unless he had an assurance that he would suffer no pain from the operation. The question was then raised whether anaesthetics could be used. The reply was in the affirmative, as the child might otherwise have wished to remain among the non-Jews with whom he had already mixed. The decision was carried out and the Rabbi informs us that the Jews were successful in circumcising about eighty children.

Unfortunately, the rescue work was not always easy. A typical case which caused a great sensation in 1953 in Jewish as well as in non-Jewish circles and which was described as 'much more horrible than the Dreyfus affair'[136] was that of the two Finaly boys. In 1944 the children's parents fleeing from Vienna settled in France as refugees. However, they were deported by the Gestapo and nothing more was heard of them. Before his arrest, the father, Dr Finaly, handed over his two boys to a Mlle Brun, director of the Municipal Créche at Grenoble. Mlle Brun baptized the boys and vowed to bring them up to enter holy orders.

After the war, the survivors of the Finaly family asked a friend, Mr Keller, of Grenoble to trace the children. When he found them Mlle Brun refused to hand them back, claiming that their father had asked her to bring them up as Christians in spite of the fact that the children had been born under the Nazis during the German occupation and had been circumcised. Legal proceedings began in 1946 and at the end the children were kidnapped and transferred to a monastery in Spain. After a hard struggle lasting eight years in which Rabbis and Jewish

135. Ibid., no. 15.
136. *Jewish Chronicle,* 12 June 1953, p. 12.

organizations as well as high Catholic dignitaries and non-Jewish politicians were involved, the children, twelve-year old Gerald and eleven-year-old Robert, were handed over to their aunt who took them to Israel to be brought up in Kibbuz Neve Ilan, in the Judean Hills, founded by French immigrants.[137] Most characteristic was the attitude of the Bishop of Bayonne which caused great indignation. When Mr Keller approached him for help, he dismissed the plea with the following words: 'After all, if the children had not been adopted by Mlle Brun, the Gestapo would have sent them to the crematoria.'[138]

An interesting case of a girl who had been baptized but later returned to Judaism is reported in the following *Responsum*:

A man married a woman who had been born in *erez ha-damim* (the land of blood) and escaped from the Nazis when she was five years old. She was brought up in the traditional way of life. She then married a religious man. Afterwards, she learned that after her birth she had been baptized by her parents under duress (*be-ones*) in order to be saved from the harsh decree issued against the whole community of Israel. She remained a 'Christian' all the years of the war until she was taken to this country (England?) and was brought up according to the Law of Moses and Israel. Her husband wished to know whether her baptism performed under duress during childhood had any bearing in respect to the *halachah* and if so what remedy was available.

R. I.J.Weiss[139] decided that when she immersed herself for marital life she should immerse once more and make a declaration, 'I immerse for the purpose of removing any "blemish" and draw upon my soul and spirit sanctity and purity like all religious daughters in Israel.' She should also make a donation to charity.

Unfortunately, there were some cases of estrangement from Judaism which occurred even after the war. Thus one Rabbi reports that many Jewish girls who had come to Stockholm after the war had intermarried.[140]

The same Rabbi tells us also of another strange story, how he had succeeded in rescuing seventy girls who had come from the Nazi camps and had been put into the care of the convent in Klausenburg.[141] The reason for this had been as follows. The members of the local Jewish committee belonged to the left wing of the political parties. After the arrival of the seventy girls, they informed the American Joint in Bucharest about this by telephone asking for the money needed for the

137. Ibid., 31 July 1953, p. 1.
138. Ibid., 13 February 1953, p. 13.
139. *Minhath Yizhak,* IV, no. 100.
140. Zimetbaum, 'Maaseh Nissim', in his edition of his father's *Responsa Dibre Pinhas,* p. 179; also in *Hasde David,* (by his brother R. David Zimetbaum), p. 179. See also the case mentioned above, pp. 160f.
141. Zimetbaum, 'Maaseh Nissim', p. 176; in *Hasde David,* p. 176.

girls' board and lodging. The Joint, however, was not willing to give such a large sum as demanded by the committee. In their anger, the members of the committee handed over the girls to nuns. On hearing this, the Rabbi got in touch with the convent office; however, without success. He then turned to the bishop, telling him: 'Millions of Jewish souls have been lost and you wish to take away another 70 souls?' These words, says the Rabbi, made an impression on the bishop who immediately got in touch with the nuns who replied that they had taken the girls in as they were homeless without food. The bishop then told the Rabbi that if the girls were taken into care and everything necessary for them was provided, they would be released. After some difficulties, the Rabbi succeeded in obtaining the girls' release from the convent and in their being put into the care of the Jews.

It is amazing that still today the rescue of young persons continues, some of whom have been baptized, who had been handed over by their parents to non-Jewish friends or sheltered in monasteries.[142] However, those persons are not young children as were those rescued immediately after the war and furthermore it is not 'we who were in search of these lost sons of the Jewish people; today it is they who try to establish contact with us'.

There exists an Association for the Return of the Victims of the Holocaust to the Bosom of Judaism centred in Tel Aviv and headed by Rabbi Yedidyah Frenkel. 'The Association has set itself the aim of tracing young Jews who in infancy were put under the care of Christian families and who do not know anything about their origins or about the ways and means of returning to their fold.' Very often those children learned of their Jewish origins when their foster parents revealed their secret to them before their death.[143] Whenever such persons are traced efforts are made to obtain information about their families and their past. Some cases have been successful and the young men and women have settled in Israel.

The opening of graves, exhumation and reburial

Another question often discussed by the Rabbis was that of exhumation and reburial particularly of martyrs.

According to Jewish Law,[144] it is forbidden to open a grave after it has been closed, even if the relatives so demand in order to examine the body to see whether the deceased had signs of puberty (legal competence to transact business).

142. What follows is based upon the article 'Seeking a Return to the Jewish Fold' by Haim Shachter, in *Jewish Review*, 5 November 1971, p. 7; *Jewish Tribune*, 12 November 1971, p. 5.
143. Cases are quoted in the article.
144. See *Shulhan Aruch, Yoreh Deah,* cap. CCCLXIII.

N

Similarly, exhumation is forbidden unless the original burial was intended as only temporary with the intention of burying the corpse elsewhere later. Only in exceptional cases is exhumation permitted, e.g. if it is for the benefit of the deceased to transfer the body to where the deceased's parents rest or if one fears that the grave (or cemetery) would be desecrated or ruined (by flood, etc.) or when the removal of the body is for the purpose of burial in Israel.

After the defeat of Nazism, various questions were raised in connection with these laws. Some of them had already been discussed before the war when the cemeteries could no longer be protected as the Jews had emigrated.

Questions which arose after the Nazi defeat concerned the following cases:[145] (1) The martyrs had been buried in unsuitable places likely to be treated disrespectfully. (2) Removal from a common grave. (3) The corpses of the martyrs (in Poland) which lay covered with a thin layer of sand to be transferred to Israel. (4) Jewish martyrs had been buried by the Germans in a common grave by the roadside and the question arose whether they should be exhumed and reburied at a Jewish cemetery. (5) Whether a Jewess who had saved herself by pretending to be a Christian and who had been buried in a Christian cemetery, could be exhumed and reburied in a Jewish cemetery. (6) Cemeteries could no longer be guarded and the people resting there had therefore to be reburied in the new cemetery. (7) Ashes of martyrs concerning interment and defiling a *kohen*. (8) Digging at a cemetery where precious religious articles were supposed to have been hidden.

The *Responsa* below illustrate some of these cases.

A question was addressed to R. Jonathan Steif of Budapest, by Jews in Rome on the following matter:

Three Jews and one Jewess were handed over to the Germans who tortured them to death and buried them not far from Rome in a common grave on a field near the road. At the burial some Jews were present who pretended to be Christians. A cross was placed at the graveside to indicate the grave. After the liberation the cross was removed. The question was asked: was one allowed to exhume the martyrs and rebury them in a Jewish cemetery? Several problems were involved.

R. Steif forwarded the question to R. Mordechai Breisch, who was inclined to permit this provided the Rabbi of Budapest agreed to the decision.[146]

---

145. On these questions, cf. Efrati, *Me-Emek Ha-Bacha*, nos. 2, 4, 5; *Mi-Ge Ha-Haregah*, nos. 9, 11; Breisch, *Helkath Yaakob*, I, nos. 6–7; Stern, *Be-Zel Ha-Hochmah*, I, nos. 14ff.; Oshry, *Mi-Maamakkim*, I, nos. 23, 25; II, no. 12; R. J.J.Weinberg, *Seride Esh*, II, nos. 127–31; R. S.Horowitz in *Hadarom*, no. 21, Nisan 5725, pp. 49ff.; R. Zebi Pesah Frank, *Har Zebi, Yoreh Deah*, no. 275; Rath, *Kol Mebasser*, II, no. 3.
146. Breisch, *Helkath Yaakob*, I, nos. 6ff.

A great sensation, re-echoed in the *Responsa*, was caused by the attempt of the French government to exhume remains from the Hohne cemetery at Bergen-Belsen where fifty thousand were buried (the number of martyrs at the cemetery at Bergen-Belsen is much higher, it is estimated that about 100,000 to 120,000 victims lie there).

According to a report which appeared in the Jewish press in London,[147] a French team came to Bergen-Belsen in April 1958 and intended to start exhuming the remains in order to identify the 139 (*infra*: 150) French victims and re-inter them in France. There was an immediate protest from Dr H. G. van Dam, the general secretary of the Central Committee of Jews in Germany, who after informing Dr Joseph Rosensaft, president of the World Federation of Bergen-Belsen Associations, together with Dr N. Goldmann, president of the World Jewish Congress, requested the late West German chancellor, Dr Adenauer, to call a halt to the disinterment of the martyrs. Dr Adenauer complied with their request.

Apart from the objections to the proposed exhumation from the religious point of view, there was evidence from scientific experts that, after so many years, it would be absolutely impossible to establish which of the bones of the nameless dead were French. A dispute arose between the French and German governments.

In order to settle it the matter was brought in summer 1966, before the international court of arbitration composed of three Germans, two Swedes (who acted as president and vice-president of the tribunal) and one representative each from Britain, U.S.A., France and Switzerland.

Two questions were dealt with: is the identification of the French war victims buried at the Hohne cemetery possible and are there reasons of such extraordinary importance as to justify the competent German authorities' refusal to grant permission for the exhumations planned by the French authorities?

In November 1969 the tribunal in Koblenz reached their decision. The first question was answered in the negative,[148] and the second in

---

147. *Vide infra.*

148. During the visit of the International Court of Arbitration to Belsen, a dramatic confrontation between the court and a group of survivors took place at the graves.

Mr Joseph Rosensaft, president of the World Federation of Bergen-Belsen Associations, told the Swedish President that even in 1945, when the remains of the martyrs were buried in the mass graves, they could not distinguish the identity of the skeletons, let alone their nationality. To assume that that could be done 25 years later, in the face of all scientific evidence, was totally unrealistic. He also explained to the court that, when burying the remains of the martyrs, medical staff poured into the mass graves large quantities of strong liquid disinfectant, as they were fighting a typhoid epidemic at the time. As a result of this, according to scientists, even the bones would have disintegrated by then. Identification in the circumstances was thus impossible. *Jewish Tribune*, London, 16 May 1969, vol. VII, no. 173, p. 5.

the affirmative. 'Belsen dead will rest in peace' was the heading of a report printed in the *Jewish Chronicle* of 7 November 1969.[149]

The Bergen-Belsen affair is discussed in a *Responsum*[150] of R. Zalman Sorotzkin dated 7th of Kislev 720 (8 December 1959) and addressed to Mr Aharon Goodman, Chairman of the European Vaad Ha-Poel of the Agudath Yisrael.

The following question was asked: The French government began to exhume the bones of our martyrs, victims of the Nazis, who had been buried in a common grave in Bergen-Belsen. Among them were also citizens of other nations France included. The French government wished to bury her citizens in her own land. For that purpose the bones of the victims were being taken to France where 'specialists' had boasted they know which bones are those of French citizens. Out of seven thousand five hundred victims they selected one hundred and fifty bodies and buried them in France. The rest were to be returned to Bergen-Belsen. The leaders of the Agudath Yisrael in Europe inquired whether it was their duty to prevent such action in future and to intervene with the governments concerned. This question was dealt with at a meeting of the Moezeth Gedole Ha-Torah of the World Agudath Yisrael and it was unanimously decided that it was forbidden to disgrace the bones of the martyrs in order to concede to the wish of the French government. The reply was forwarded to the governments of France and West Germany and the exhumations were stopped.

The Rabbi gives the various reasons for this decision. The Nazis used to bury thousands of victims in a common grave. Exhumation would disturb the bones, which is strictly prohibited. Apart from that the 'specialists' would handle the bones disrespectfully and let them remain unburied for some time.

In the following *Responsum*[151] the Rabbi tells us that the French, German and Austrian governments accepted the decision of the Rabbis of Agudath Yisrael and the exhumations ceased. As only one hundred and fifty bodies of seven thousand five hundred martyrs had been buried in France, and the remains of the other martyrs had been returned to West Germany and Austria and were lying in cellars, the question then raised was: what should happen to them? Should they be returned to Bergen-Belsen or might they be buried elsewhere? The Rabbi decided that they should be buried at the Jewish cemetery in Vienna where they were at that time and gives directions how the graves should be arranged. According to these two *Responsa* the question of exhumation has been settled.

However, as far as we can see from the reports in the press, no

149. P. 14; see also *Jewish Tribune*, 7 November 1969, vol. VII, no. 185, p. 1.
150. R. Z.Sorotzkin, *Moznayim La-Mishpat*, II, no. 15.
151. Ibid., no. 16.

exhumation has ever taken place. Hence the inquiry sent to the Rabbi as to what should be done to the bones 'lying in cellars in Vienna' appears rather strange. The writer made special inquiries about this matter and wrote to the honorary secretary of the Agudas Yisrael, Mr M. R. Springer, asking him (1) whether Mr Goodman's report was factually correct, i.e. that the corpses *were* exhumed and sent to Vienna, etc., and (2) on what information it was based. His reply was that there was no record about this and that he inquired of M. Muller in Paris and M. De Haas in Utrecht and both confirmed that no exhumation had taken place.

The writer wrote also to the Israelitische Kultusgemeinde in Vienna pointing out that such an important matter would, if it had occurred, be in the records of the community or of the *Hebrah Kadisha*. However, in a reply (dated 15 April 1971) signed by the president, Dr Anton Pick and the Amtsdirektor Reg. Rat Wilhelm Krell, he was told that corpses had never been brought from Bergen-Belsen to Vienna and the officials had never received a decision that the corpses from Bergen-Belsen had to be buried in Vienna.

After the liberation it came to light that graves of victims of the Nazi persecution had been desecrated and lay unprotected. In the Lithuanian town, Kupiskis for example, where more than three thousand Jews had been massacred, the martyrs had been buried by the Germans in the cemetery set aside for atheists. This cemetery had been dedicated by the Russians who had occupied that town before the German conquest. The number of people buried there had been small.

The following question arose: was it permitted to remove all the corpses from the place of the massacre and rebury them in a Jewish cemetery as there may have been among the remains, bones of non-Jews who had been buried there before or non-Jews executed by the Germans?

The decision was that the bones which no doubt were of Jewish victims had to be removed from there and reburied in a Jewish cemetery as, apart from other reasons, it would be a disgrace to leave them at a place dedicated to atheists. However, in accordance with the custom mentioned by one author, the remains were to be buried in a special place. The Rabbi also decided that a tombstone be erected at the cemetery to serve as a memorial to future generations.[152]

Of a different nature was the following question. After the liberation, a woman named Goldberg from Vilkaviskis[153] came to the Rabbi[154] and

---

152. Oshry, *Mi-Maamakkim*, II, no. 16.

153. The name of this town appears among the names of the large towns mentioned by Garfunkel, *Destruction of Kovno's Jewry*, p. 78, of which the entire Jewish population was massacred by the Germans in the winter of 1941 without having been closed in a ghetto first.

154. Oshry, *Mi-Maamakkim*, I, no. 25.

told the following story. During the Nazi holocaust, her daughter had
fled to non-Jews and pretended to be a gentile in order to escape death.
She went to church, ate and drank with them and wore a cross on her
neck—in short, she behaved like a Christian in every respect. She
fell ill and died and was buried in a non-Jewish cemetery. Her mother
strongly wished to remove her body from there and bury her in a
Jewish cemetery. Was that permitted?

The answer was in the affirmative, one of the reasons being that the
daughter who behaved like a Christian did so under duress in order to
save her life and because of fear of death. It would be a disgrace to her
to remain in the non-Jewish cemetery.

An interesting *Responsum* on the question of digging at the cemetery
for the removal of precious articles allegedly buried there is the following:

At the old cemetery of Regensburg there were some areas which
appeared not to have been used for burying the dead. However, the
possibility was not excluded that in the course of time the surfaces of
the graves disappeared and the graves were no longer recognizable.
According to the evidence of Christian neighbours, the Jews had buried
silver crowns of Torah scrolls and similar religious articles in that area.
A Rabbi[155] was asked whether one was allowed to search those empty
places for the religious objects. His decision could serve as a guide to
other towns where religious articles had been hidden. In fact, crowns
of Torah scrolls and jewellery had been found in the old cemetery of a
small town near Frankfurt am Main. The Rabbi decided in the
negative.

Ashes of martyrs with regard to their interment and defiling a *Kohen*

One Rabbi tells us about his visit to Kovel in Wolhynia after the war
which was once a place famous for its learning and Jewish life. He met
only destruction. The famous seat of the Rabbi of Turisk to whom
hasidim from all parts of Wolhynia and Poland used to come was
empty and waste. The *Beth Ha-Midrash* was closed and when he looked
in through the window he noticed with horror the walls of the building
were stained with blood. This showed that there the community of Kovel
had sanctified the Name of God. Suddenly the Rabbi was seized by awe
and trembling. In the north-eastern corner of the *Beth Ha-Midrash* he
noticed words written in blood: '*Nekom nikmath d* ...' (Revenge the
bl ...). It appeared that the writer expired while writing his last wish
with the blood of his heart.

On noticing this, the Rabbi says, he stood petrified. But then he felt
someone touch his shoulder and when turning he saw a Jew standing

155. Rath, *Kol Mebasser*, II, no. 3.

who was the only survivor in the town. He then asked the Rabbi the following question:

Before leaving 'the city of blood' (cf. Ez. xxii 2; xxiv 9; Na. iii 1) where all the members of his family were massacred and burned he sought to take some of the ashes of the martyrs who had been burned in the courtyard of the *Beth Ha-Midrash*. Among them were the members of his own family whose ashes he wished to take to the Holy Land where he desired to spend the rest of his life. However, since he was a *kohen* he wished to know whether he might take the ashes, which had been collected to be scattered over the fields and used as fertilizers for vegetables, to a Jewish grave in the Holy Land.

The Rabbi[156] decided in the affirmative and regarded such action as a meritorious deed. He proved that the ashes do not defile. He then appealed to the Jews in Israel and those outside Israel not to let the bones of the martyrs be dragged away by those dogs who exhume skeletons from the 'valley of slaughter' (Jer. vii 32) and search for gold teeth in jaw-bones. They are the most wicked among the nations who do not give rest to the martyrs whom they tortured and whose blood they shed. 'It is our duty to bring the martyrs' remains to *Erez Yisrael*, the aspiration of their hearts . . . .'[157]

Kapos

There were other disturbing problems which were raised after the war. They concerned former *Kapos* who had been recognized by inmates of the camps in countries to which they had emigrated. Thus for example we read, under the heading '*Kapo* in the Dock' of the trial in Haifa of Chaim Silberberg in June 1961; 'In the dock is Chaim Silberbert, aged 42, who is accused of causing grievous bodily harm to 13 fellow-inmates at Skerzisko camp, Poland. . . . One witness testified that in 1942 the accused volunteered to serve the Germans in a munitions factory, became a *Kapo* and was put in charge of discipline. The witness said Silberberg beat Jews and caused one to go partially blind. . . .'[158]

It even happened that the Israeli Chief Rabbinate had to intervene in one case. The reason was as follows:

A *herem* (ban) had been proclaimed in the Great Synagogue of Rio de Janeiro on 12 January 1947, on two brothers Abraham and Leibush Seifmann who had been *Kapos* in the labour camp in Ostrowiec

---

156. Efrati, *Me-Emek Ha-Bacha*, no. 2. On similar inscriptions (in pencil) in various languages found in the Ninth Fortress of Kovno, see Garfunkel, *Destruction of Kovno's Jewry*, p. 186.

157. For other *Responsa*, see R. Frank, *Har Zebi, Yoreh Deah*, no. 275; R. Shmuel Meir Ha-Kohen, *SheM Ha-Kohen*, I, no. 15; R. Uzziel, *Mishpete Uzziel*, 2nd ed., Part III, *Yoreh Deah*, no. 116; R. Breisch, *Helkath Yaakob*, I, no. 32.

158. *Jewish Chronicle*, 2 June 1961, p. 17.

(Poland) and were accused of having committed murder and assaults, of having extorted money and of having handed over partisans and Jewish children to the Nazis. For twenty years this *herem* was in full force so that when the wife of one of the brothers died she was buried in unconsecrated ground at the edge of the cemetery. The same happened when the child of one of the brothers died. However, the acceptance of the *herem* was not universal and the wife of the other brother succeeded in finding witnesses who refuted the evidence of the witnesses who had testified against the brothers. This resulted in the chief witness withdrawing his evidence and he was followed by the others. Eventually The Rabbinical Supreme Court in Jerusalem issued an edict that the *herem* was to be lifted on condition 'that the Seifmann brothers, in the course of the following year, set themselves on the right path and bring themselves nearer to the God of Israel, to His Torah and to the people of Israel'.[159]

In the *Responsa* the following cases are to be found:

One of the former *Kapos* (*noges, taskmaster*) was executed by the Germans. However, before he was taken to execution he confessed his sins and crying begged, in front of his fellow Jews, for forgiveness from God. The question asked later was: was it permissible to mention his name when his son was called up to the Torah as it is customary to call up a person by mentioning his father's name ('the son of ...'). As his father had been a wicked man his name ought normally not to be mentioned or did that not apply? Answer: since the father had repented and the 'office' had been forced upon him (as could be seen from the fact that he used to do good deeds for the benefit of the inmates and saved some from death) and he was killed by the Nazis and his son observes the Law, his name may be mentioned.[160]

Another *Responsum* concerned the question whether a former *Kapo* could act as a reader.[161]

There is still some confusion, writes one Rabbi, as to the attitude to be adopted towards former *Kapos*. Some regard it a religious merit to denounce them to the authorities; others maintain one should not look back to the past.

The Rabbi shows that even before the destruction of the Temple capital punishment was no longer administered to a murderer. The law concerning 'the avenger of blood' (Num. xxxv 19) was abolished too. Consequently it is not permitted to cause the death of a *Kapo*.[162]

---

159. Ibid., 1 August 1969, p. 14.
160. Oshry, *Mi-Maamakkim*, III, no. 12.
161. Ibid., no. 14. On other cases where *Kapos* are mentioned, *vide supra* pp. 112ff.
162. *Ha-Maor*, I, ed. by R. Meir Amsel, New York, 5727, p. 253.

RESTITUTION

Some *Responsa* deal with questions of restitution made by Germany. Concerning a declaration instead of an oath for the purpose of obtaining restitution, R. J.J.Weinberg tells the questioner that he himself had lost great sums of money by not making such declarations although they were true.[163]

A Rabbi was approached by several learned refugees who had escaped death whether they were permitted to accept restitution offered by the German government in respect of money and property of which they had been robbed. Would it be regarded as supporting the Germans to do a good deed and give charity which one should not accept from wicked people?

The Rabbi replied that this question had already been dealt with by great Rabbis, themselves refugees, and at the Agudath Yisrael conference in Jerusalem. His view was that the money could be accepted. The prohibition applies only to the acceptance of a voluntary gift from the donors (Germans) but not to restitution to which the victims were legally entitled. It was indemnity, not charity.[164]

'Is it a *mizvah* (meritorious deed) to give to charity a tithe of the money received by business men from Germany as compensation for confiscated property which had previously been tithed? Could it be regarded as merely "restoration of a loss" which would not have to be re-tithed?'

The answer is: 'The money should be tithed as the person who receives the compensation had given up all hope of recovering his property. Hence the money for restitution had assumed "a new face" (*panim hadashoth*), i.e. it counts as new gain.'[165]

A woman married an elderly invalid. She was busy both earning her livelihood and running the home and defraying the costs required for her husband's upkeep and treatment. She had received a sum of money from Germany as restitution for her having given up her living (*haphsakath parnasathah*) before her marriage. As she had no children and did not think she would have children she gave two thousand dollars to the Rabbi who asked the question and to the Rabbi's mother. One thousand dollars was to be distributed among the *yeshiboth* immediately, and the second thousand dollars after her death. The

163. Weinberg, *Seride Esh,* II, no. 161.
164. R. S.Y.Levin, *Minhath Shlomoh,* I, no. 29. Cf., however, the views in *Ha-Maor,* ed. by R. M.Amsel, New York, 5727, p. 254.
165. R. E.Waldenberg, *Ziz Eliezer,* VI, no. 27.

question was whether the money could be accepted from the woman as one may accept only small gifts for charity from a woman. If the money had already been accepted and distributed, had it to be returned?

Answer: the money the woman had received from Germany was to be regarded as *nichse melug* i.e. the capital belongs to the wife while the husband has the usufruct. She was therefore not entitled to give the charity without his consent, and it had obviously to be returned. However, the Rabbi makes a distinction whether or not the husband knew of any payment.[166]

Chief Rabbi Unterman[167] writes that many women appeared before the Bathe Din with the request for certificates confirming that they had lost their husbands as a result of the Nazi persecution. These certificates were needed to claim compensation from the German government. Very often those women declared explicitly before the Beth Din that they were not interested in re-marriage. They wished only to obtain compensation. Some women could not receive the required documents because of lack of evidence that their husbands' death was due to the Nazi persecution. Others, however, obtained them on the strength of evidence which was sufficient for their claim but which would not have sufficed for granting them permission to re-marry (e.g. the cases mentioned in the Talmud *Yeb.* 117a). After a certain time, these women appeared before the Beth Din asking for permission to re-marry adducing fresh evidence that they had heard from other people of the death of their husbands (which normally would suffice to grant them permission for re-marriage). However, an important point was involved. According to the *halachah* (*loc. cit.*), if a woman comes before the Beth Din maintaining her husband had died and asks for her *kethubah* she is not permitted to re-marry as her intention is only to collect her *kethubah*. Chief Rabbi Unterman discusses whether the original request for obtaining compensation does not put her in this category in which case permission for re-marriage is not to be given. He discusses various aspects but no final decision is given for practice.

The most important question, however, which has been discussed by the leading Rabbis of all countries as it affected thousands of our people who were in territories under the Nazi heel is that of the status of women whose husbands had disappeared (*agunoth*). Cases of men whose wives had disappeared have been dealt with too, and whether women liberated from the camps may marry *kohanim*.[168]

166. R. M. Feinstein, *Iggeroth Mosheh, Eben Ha-Ezer*, no. 103. The Rabbi deals also with the question if the money cannot be recovered whether the treasurers themselves are bound to repay it.

167. 'Be-Inyan Agunoth', in *The Memorial Volume in Honour of Chief Rabbi Yizhak Herzog* (Hebrew), ed. by R. S.Z.Zevin and Zerah Wahrhaftig, Jerusalem, 1962, pp. 68ff.

168. On these problems *vide infra* Part II, Chapters 3–6.

Part 2

Nazi Laws and their Consequences in the Light of the *Halachah*

INTRODUCTORY REMARKS

It has been pointed out[1] that on the basis of the so-called Enabling Act (*Ermächtigungsgesetz*) of 24 March 1933, Hitler and his cabinet were empowered to issue laws without Parliament, which might deviate from the constitution.

Needless to say ample use was made of that Enabling Act concerning the Jews as soon the Nazi machinery began to work. It did not commence with drastic measures applying to the whole or majority of the Jewish race, but was directed at first against selected professions and then went on to embrace all professions, segregating the Jews and forcing them to emigrate (later becoming deportation and eventually extermination).

We possess an informative book entitled *Das Ausnahmerecht für die Juden in Deutschland* 1933–1945[2] where all the laws can be found. It contains 430 laws, edicts and decrees beginning with the prohibition of acting as notaries in Prussia issued on 1 April 1933, and ending with the decree prohibiting Jews from using *Wärmeräume* in Berlin (13 November 1944). Unfortunately the book does not contain the laws the Nazis issued in the territories they invaded. The author intended to deal with them as well but was prevented by death from doing so.[3]

In 1956 a pamphlet entitled *Ausnahme-Gesetze gegen Juden in den von Nazi Deutschland besetzten Gebieten Europas* was compiled by the Wiener Library in London. Only those sources were used which were in the possession of the library. We can see from there that various authorities were responsible for issuing laws and that no uniformity in the legislation in the occupied countries or even towns and districts existed. Regional commanding officers and administrative chiefs as well as local rulers could give orders they had received from their superiors, but in addition they made decrees of their own applicable to the Jews under their administration. In both cases they tried to show their faithfulness to the Nazi doctrine by using more rigour and brutality than expected from them by their superiors.

In view of this we can understand some points in the legislation of the Nazis concerning the Jews in the occupied territories.

In addition to the anti-Jewish laws of the *Altreich* which were mostly introduced in the occupied territories as well, new decrees originated in

1. *Vide supra* p. xvi.
2. By Dr Bruno Blau, published in Düsseldorf, 1954.
3. See Foreword by Hans Erich Fabian.

179

the Nazi legislation of Poland aimed at the humiliation and exploitation
of the Jews. Curiously enough, some of these laws were later taken over
by the *Altreich* against the Jews there. Thus, e.g. the wearing of the
Judenstern was introduced for the first time in Wloclawek on 24 October
1939 at the order of a German town commissioner. A similar order
was given by the governor in Cracow on 18 November 1939 which
became law for the whole General Government on 23 November 1939[4]
and finally the wearing of the *Judenstern* was decreed for the Jews of
the Reich almost two years later (1 September 1941).[5] Similarly the law
of forced labour by the Jews issued in Poland in 12 December 1939,[6]
was decreed in the Reich on 7 March 1941.[7]

Sometimes a difference can be noticed in the Nazi legislation not
only between the Reich and the occupied territories but also between
places or towns of the countries overrun by the Germans. A classical
example is the prohibition of pregnancy under pain of death issued in
Kovno (Kaunas) and in Theresienstadt.[8]

Finally unlike the *Altreich*, the legislation in occupied territories
sometimes bears an anti-religious character. While all the Nazi laws
always affected the way of life of the Jews there were some specific
Nazi decrees to which great significance was attached in Rabbinic
circles. Of such decrees or their consequences mention should be made
of the following:

1. The prohibition of *shehitah*
2. Sterilization of insane people
3. The Nuremberg Law for the Protection of German Blood and
   German Honour
4. The confiscation of books
5. The prohibition of childbearing
6. The *Agunah* problem in the light of the final solution
7. How far can the Nazi persecution be termed *shaath ha-shemad*
   (religious persecution)?

---

4. See G. Reitlinger, *The Final Solution*, p. 55; Raul Hilberg, *The Destruction of the European Jews*, p. 145.
5. See Blau, *Das Ausnahmerecht*, p. 89, no. 329; Hilberg, *Destruction of the European Jews*, p. 121.
6. See Leon Poliakov, *Harvest of Hate*, pp. 38f.
7. Blau, *Das Ausnahmerecht*, p. 86, no. 305, who says: 'Auf Grund dieses Erlasses wurden dann die Juden unter erschwerenden und diskriminierenden Bedingungen zur Zwangsarbeit herangezogen.'
8. *Vide infra* pp. 212ff.

1
The Prohibition of *Shehitah*

In their propaganda against the Jews in the early stages of the spread of the Nazi movement its adherents took up an old accusation that ritual slaughtering was inhumane, causing suffering to the animal; hence *shehitah* should be banned.

In fact, attempts to prohibit *shehitah* had been made by various countries prior to the rise of National Socialism.[1] The agitation against ritual slaughtering originated in Germany in 1864 when a bill was introduced in the Landtag of Baden to the effect that animals should be stunned before slaughter. The proposal was defeated. It soon became known that the opponents of *shehitah* were motivated by anti-Semitic feelings. The agitation spread to other countries, however, with little success. From 1864 till the rise of the Nazis the prohibition of *shehitah* was imposed only in Switzerland (1893) and adopted, but subsequently repealed, in Saxony (1892–1910) and Finland (1902–3, 1909–13).

It was after the rise of Nazism that a campaign against *shehitah* was renewed. The reason given for this prohibition was that the method employed by the Jews was inhumane, the Jews themselves being regarded as barbarous and cruel. Thus the anti-*shehitah* movement became part of the Nazi propaganda.

From the year 1926 onwards when Nazism began to spread the ban on *shehitah* was debated in various Landtags. Bavaria (1930) was the first of the German states to ban *shehitah* without prior stunning. The Nazi agitation against *shehitah* influenced the people of Norway where a ban to that effect was introduced on 1 January 1930.

It was after Hitler had come to power that a decree signed by him was issued on 21 April 1933 forbidding *shehitah* without prior stunning, throughout the German Reich.[2]

From Germany the anti-*shehitah* movement spread to other countries and *shehitah* was prohibited: Sweden (1937), Hungary (1938) and Italy (1938). With the occupation of the countries by Hitler's armies in the years 1939 and 1940 *shehitah* was banned there as well. Those countries were: Bohemia-Moravia (prohibition issued on 27 March 1939), Poland (26 October, 1939), Slovakia (19 June 1940), Belgium (23 October 1940), Netherlands (31 July 1940), France (18 September 1940), Luxembourg (3 December 1940) and Alsace (10 April 1941).[3]

---

1. On what follows, cf. *The Jewish Encyclopedia*, XI, p. 612; *Jüdisches Lexikon*, V, p. 136; *Religious Freedom, The Right to Practice Shehitah (Kosher Slaughtering)*, by Rabbi Isaac Levin, LL.D., Rabbi Michael L. Munk, Ph.D., and Rabbi Jeremiah J. Berman, D.H.L., New York, 1946; *Encyclopaedia Judaica*, vol. 14, pp. 1340f.
2. *Vide infra.*
3. Cf. also *Ausnahme-Gesetze gegen Juden in den von Nazi-Deutschland besetzten Gebieten Europas*, published by the Wiener Library, London, 1956, pp. 9, 15, 19, 22. In Norway *shehitah* was prohibited in 1930.

At first the Jews in Germany tried to circumvent the prohibition by importing *kosher* (ritually slaughtered) meat from abroad (particularly from Denmark). However, soon the importation of *kosher* meat was forbidden.[4]

It is the greatest irony and unprecedented distortion of facts that the Nazis who committed the most callous and sadistic acts of cruelty to six million innocent people opposed *shehitah* ostensibly on the grounds of its causing suffering to animals. It is rather significant that as early as 12 March 1930, when in the Landtag of Baden one Nazi member brought a motion forbidding *shehitah* 'since this method is unworthy of a cultured state' a member of the Socialist party declared: 'This motion . . . is motivated . . . beyond doubt by race hatred directed against Jews.

'A party which declares as rightless a people because they belong to a distinct race is not entitled—in our opinion—to talk about protection of animals. A party which treats men brutally, and kills and murders them—to such a party we deny the right to discourse about kindness to animals. . . . Such a party comes here and proposes—for the protection of animals—*shehitah* prohibition. This is the height of effrontery and shameless pretense!'[5]

With the entry of Hitler's army into Poland the sadistic acts of cruelty against Jews by the Germans began at the same time the prevention of unnecessary suffering to animals was demanded. On 26 October 1939, the prohibition of *shehitah* was made legal.[6]

Under the influence of Nazi Germany the prohibition of *shehitah* without prior stunning was introduced in Hungary on 6 April 1938.[7] All the religious parties of Hungary (Orthodox, *Neologen* and members of the Status Quo communities) decided to object to the introduction of stunning before *shehitah*.[8] The idea was put forward that stunning by electricity *after shehitah* be suggested to the government. Should, however, the government not agree, stunning by a blow of a club after *shehitah* with certain qualifications could be suggested. Should also this suggestion not be accepted by the government who would insist on *Schuss Apparat* which causes perforation of the brain and instant death, then certain rulings (which the Rabbis mention) should be observed when employing that method.

As in Hungary the custom was current not to strike the head of the

4. See Levin *et al.*, *Religious Freedom*, p. 65, and *infra* p. 184.
5. Levin, *et al.*, *Religious Freedom*, pp. 63f., 93.
6. Ibid., p. 90. In fact various attempts to prohibit *shehitah* were made in Poland before the war. See also the correspondence in R. Z.H.Meisels's *Mekaddshe Ha-Shem*, II, nos. 22ff.
7. Levin *et al.*, *Religious Freedom*, p. 82.
8. On what follows, cf. Meisels, *Mekaddshe Ha-Shem*, I, p. 51, nos. 26f.

slaughtered animal as long as the blood was spurting forth (this was in accordance with the view of *Ture Zahab* on *Yoreh Deah*, cap. 67) the Rabbis of the *Vaad Ha-Merkaz* (Central Committee) discussed whether that custom could be altered.

Before approaching the government it was decided to hear the views of the great scholars all over the world, and the latter agreed to the suggestion of stunning the animal after *shehitah* in view of its being a time of emergency.

Unfortunately, the suggestion had no practical importance and the prohibition of *shehitah* without stunning beforehand remained in force. The life of the Jews in Hungary which was in the grip of the Nazis became more difficult from day to day.

After this historical review the reaction of the Rabbis to the prohibition of *shehitah* issued by the Nazis in Germany should be mentioned.

THE SLAUGHTERING OF QUADRUPEDS

The main spokesman of the Rabbis living in Germany at that time was R. J.J.Weinberg in Berlin. In the first volume of his *Responsa* collection *Seride Esh*[9] an historical introduction to the whole problem and the correspondence between him and the leading Rabbis from abroad are given. Some of them had their replies incorporated in their own *Responsa* collections. Also the views of religiously minded medical men were taken into consideration (e.g. Dr Lieben of Prague).[10] It was claimed that stunning would render the animal *terephah* before the act of *shehitah* had been performed, for the following reasons:

(i) *Nephulah*, the shock causes the animal to fall to the ground with force which would cause *rissuk ebarim* (internal injury). The latter may have already been caused by the electric current alone.

(ii) It was noticed that damage is done to the brain which constitutes in itself an act of *terephah*.

(iii) It was proved that damage is done also to the *sirchoth* (adhesions) of the lung which cannot be examined afterwards and affects the lung too.

(iv) The shock causes the blood to remain in the muscle preventing it from running out.

(v) When the bowels of animals killed after stunning were examined, effusions of blood were found on them, which indicated injury.

(vi) Blood was found also in the muscle of the heart, which showed damage to that organ.[11]

9. Mosad Ha-Rab Kook, Jerusalem, 1961.
10. *Seride Esh*, I, p. 4.
11. On the reasons, see also ibid., pp. 9ff., 44ff., 85ff., 102ff.

Various other suggestions and experiments were made but all the Rabbis strongly opposed the method of stunning the animal before *shehitah*.

Rabbi Weinberg adopted at first a lenient view; however, after reading the *Responsa* of the Rabbis among whom there were the most prominent scholars, he retracted and submitted to their decision.

In his introduction to the above mentioned volume *Seride Esh*, R. Weinberg tries to give an explanation for printing his treatise although it is no longer of practical value. He writes:

Many people will wonder and ask what has caused me to publish now my treatise on stunning written twenty-five years ago at a time when the decree against *shehitah* was issued by the arch-enemy Nazi Germany. Everyone knows that I refused to publish my treatise in spite of the request of many pious people. I did so for two reasons: (1) to avoid helping the enemy who opposed *shehitah*, and (2) to prevent those who are not so particular from finding a *hether* in a matter which had been prohibited by the great men of our generation. However, as a rumour has spread that I was—so to speak—(*kebeyachol*) among those who permitted stunning I wish to explain the entire matter for future generations.

I wrote my treatise at a time of terrible distress, at a time when a sharp-edged sword was lying over the neck of Israel, the wicked Nazi government having imposed a ban on *shehitah* if performed without stunning. At first the Jews helped themselves by importing meat from abroad (see also p. 182). Afterwards the Nazis prohibited with their cruel devices the import of *kosher* meat from abroad. They did not permit *shehitah* even for the sake of the elderly and dangerously sick. There was great danger that the majority would not withstand the temptation and would succumb to the prohibition of eating *nebelah*. In the meantime a rumour spread that the leaders of the Jewish Community of Berlin intended to introduce meat bought from non-Jewish butchers in its institutions, hospitals and homes for the aged, etc. The Governing Board of the Community, although it consisted mostly of Reform people, always complied in matters of *kashruth* with the Orthodox Rabbis. Now, however, they maintained that in a time of such emergency they were forced to use *nebelah* and *terefah* meat being advised by the doctors to do so. This rumour touched every soul. In our distress we decided to seek the advice of the great Rabbis of Lithuania and Poland whether in such circumstances stunning before *shehitah* was permitted. I went to Wilno, Warsaw and Lublin for that purpose. The *Geonim*, Rabbi

Hayyim Ozer Grodzinski of Wilno and R. Meir Schapiro of Lublin, asked me to write a *Responsum* on this matter.

I followed their advice. My *Responsum* included in this book is the reply to this problem. It is true that I inclined towards the lenient view. However, I knew beforehand that the *Geonim* of Lithuania, Poland and the leaders of orthodox Jewry in other countries would never agree to a change in the matter of *shehitah* which has been current from time immemorial. I myself hesitated to deal with a matter which is the foundation of the Jewish way of life. I spoke about this several times to the Rabbi, *Gaon* and *Zaddik* Ezra Munk, Ab Beth Din of the 'Adath Yisrael' of Berlin. (He was the head of the department dealing with the matters of *shehitah* in Germany and opposed the method of stunning by electricity.) I said that we must not seek *hetherim* to change the method of *shehitah*. The orthodox Jews will not listen to us. They will rather suffer hunger and afflict themselves and refuse to be defiled by eating meat of animals slaughtered according to the method decreed by the wicked enemy of the Jews, the head of the Nazi government. Our arch-enemy and many thousands like him will perish from the world, our holy Law, however, will endure for ever. The Jews in Germany must resist this temptation for the sake of the holy Law and for the sake of our brethren in other countries. If, God forbid, we are lenient in this method of *shehitah* we are certainly exposing to danger the Jewish method of *shehitah* in the whole world. We should rather show the world that we are ready to make sacrifices for our holy religion. Thus our enemies will see that by prohibiting *shehitah* they will not cause us to give up our faith. . . .

However, the words of my Rabbis and colleagues prevailed upon me to deal with the clarification of this stringent matter which because of its novelty had never been discussed and explained in Rabbinic literature. . . . This treatise on stunning which is printed in the volume was sent on advice of R. Hayyim Ozer to all great men of our people. Most of them prohibited stunning. Even those who originally were inclined to permit it because of time of distress and *pikkuah nephesh* (for the sake of dangerously ill people) later retracted their lenient view and also decided not to permit stunning. . . .

Of the letters of the Rabbis who prohibited stunning the following deserves mention as it is most moving. It is the letter by R. Hayyim Yizhak Jeruchem of Altstadt (who was then in Vienna). It contains the exhortation:

'To you, O men, I call. I beseech you, resist the temptation, show that you are of the descendants of those who had let themselves be stoned

o

and hanged because of our Torah.'¹² R. Weinberg continues: 'I myself realized that I did not succeed in clearing up all doubts and could not remove the suspicions connected with the performing of the stunning by electricity. I understand that the tests made with animals which after stunning remained alive, do not prove anything, as not all animals react in the same way. We have no means of proving that the electric current did not cause a lethal or *terefah* defect to one of the inner organs of the animal.'

'My treatise', writes R. Weinberg, 'is of no practical importance. The reason I publish it is my desire to explain some *sugyoth* of the Talmud which it contains and because of its great historical value.'¹³

The question of stunning was dealt with also by R. Menahem Mendel Kirschbaum, Rabbi and Ab Beth Din of Frankfurt am Main.¹⁴ When he went to visit his parents in Cracow in 1934 he was asked by R. Jacob Freimann, Ab Beth Din of Berlin, in his letter of the 17th of Tebeth 694 (4 January 1934) to discuss this matter with the great authorities in Poland. He consulted the Rabbis in Sosnowiec, Dombrowa, Reischa (Rzeszow), Przemysl, Lwow, Stanislawow, Monastarzysko, Tarnopol, Wilno, Brzesc Litewski, Lublin and Radomysl and the Hasidic Rabbis of Stucin and Belz.

THE SLAUGHTERING OF BIRDS (POULTRY)

At the same time as the Nazis issued a prohibition of slaughtering animals without prior stunning by electric shock they decreed that birds must be killed by instant severance of the head from the body ('schnelles vollständiges Abtrennen des Kopfes vom Rumpf').¹⁵ According to Jewish law¹⁶ the act of *shehitah* of birds is similar to that of quadrupeds: in either case both organs, the windpipe and gullet, should be cut through in the first instance. However, if, in the case of birds, only one organ or the major part of one organ and, in the case of quadrupeds,

12. Ibid., pp. 171f. I lived through this period and can recall the great consternation and horror which befell German Jewry and the sympathy shown by the Jews of other countries. On slaughtering fowls by severing the head from the trunk quickly and completely, *vide infra*.

13. *Seride Esh*, p. 7.

14. See his report in *Menahem Meshib*, II, no. 33, in *Ziyyun Le-Menahem*, ed. R. J. Rubinstein, p. 177. Some *Responsa* of the Rabbis are printed in *Kuntras Ha-Teshuboth* of R. Kirschbaum, in *Ziyyun Le-Menahem*, nos. 6, 8, 9, 10.

15. This phrase is found in R. M.S.Wassermann's *Responsa Sheilath Mosheh, Yoreh Deah*, no. 85. In a question addressed by R. Zuber of Stockholm to R. Yizhak Unna, *Shoalin Ve-Dorshin*, no. 19 with reference to a similar law in Sweden, it is said: 'Der Kopf muss getrennt werden vom Körper'. In fact the text as published in the *Reichgesetzblatt*, Part I, Berlin, 21 April 1933, no. 39, p. 213, runs as follows:
'Die Betäubung von Geflügel vor der Schlachtung ist nicht erforderlich, wenn das Schlachten durch schnelles, vollständiges Abtrennes des Kopfes vom Rumpfe erfolgt.'

16. *Shulhan Aruch Yoreh Deah*, cap. XXI, no. 1.

the major part of both organs had been severed the act of slaughtering has been properly executed. The cutting through of the organs followed by severance of the neckbone (nape)[17] renders the animal prohibited according to some authorities (among them Isserles) who decided that even if only the major part of the neck is cut through the *shehitah* is invalid. Other authorities (among them Caro) regard the act of slaughtering as having been properly executed.[18]

Naturally the Jews of Germany were very much affected by this harsh decree. In view of the great necessity three Rabbis independently tried to prove the permissibility of poultry whose head had been cut off immediately after the act of *shehitah*.

They sought to have the consent of the great authorities abroad (Poland, Lithuania) and wrote *Responsa* which they sent to those authorities. These Rabbis were R. J.J.Weinberg of Berlin, R. M.M. Kirschbaum of Frankfurt am Main and R. M.S.Wassermann of Breslau.

R. Weinberg[19] wrote a *kuntras* (treatise) in which he adopted a lenient view as it was a time of great emergency affecting all Jews living in the countries in which the act of *shehitah* of birds without cutting off the head was forbidden. It was to be feared that should permission for eating such birds not be found Jews might become involved in transgressing a greater prohibition: eating *nebelah* and *terephah* meat.

R. Weinberg handed his *kuntras* to the *Vaad Ha-Shehitah* (*Shehitah* Committee) the head of which was 'the Rabbi and *Zaddik* R. Esriel Munk', in Berlin who forwarded his *kuntras* to all great authorities abroad,[20]

asking them to express their view on such a difficult question which concerns *kashruth*, a matter for which the Jews of every generation had sacrificed their lives. It is natural that we living in Germany against whom this evil decree of the wicked government had been issued did not want to rely upon ourselves, for we had been affected. The cry of our brethren who tremble for the Lord and heed His Law reached our ears. Through this wicked decree food had been cut off from the young and the old and from the sick, who in the doctors' view cannot survive without meat. We have therefore thought it would not be right for us alone to decide this case but to approach the great authorities of our generation to show us the way we must

17. Ibid., cap. XXIV, no. 5.
18. See R. J.J.Weinberg, *Seride Esh*, pp. 173ff. where further references can be found.
19. *Seride Esh*, pp. 173ff.
20. Ibid. p. 182ff. note.

follow.[21] After a short time replies from the great men arrived. Most of them permitted the cutting through of the neck bone among them our teacher R. Hayyim Ozer (Grodzinski).

R. Weinberg writes[22] to his great regret much of this correspondence had been lost, only a few letters were left which he then presents to the reader.

He wishes also to mention that the first *kuntras* was written in a great hurry, at a moment of excitement because of the storm and anxiety caused by the wicked government's cruel decree. After the replies had come in, he composed another more comprehensive *kuntras* which also was lost, only fragments being left. He then reconstructs the text and presents it to the reader. It is more than a *Responsum*, it contains elucidation of many difficult problems and makes a fine contribution to Talmudical scholarship (it contains thirty-seven folios each of two columns).

As mentioned by R. Weinberg, almost all the authorities permitted the cutting off of the head after *shehitah*. But there were a few scholars who opposed it, and others who did not want to express their views.

The following are among the Rabbis whose replies R. Weinberg prints.[23] R. Hayyim Ozer Grodzinski, Ab Beth Din of Wilno. He permitted cutting off the head of the fowl after *shehitah* if no meat could be imported from abroad and gave some directives how to perform the act of slaughtering. This permission applied particularly to meat for the elderly and sick. It would be best if healthy people could abstain from eating meat; however, they may avail themselves of the permit until the indignation be 'overpast' (cf. Isaiah xxvi 20). (His letter was addressed to the *Vaad Ha-Shehitah*. A similar letter was addressed to R. Zebi Ha-Kohen Klein, Dayan of Berlin.) In another letter addressed to R. Jonah Zebi Ha-Levi Horowitz, Rabbi of the *Adath Yeshurun* in Frankfurt am Main, he says, 'since in your state unlike Baden,[24] the import of meat is not prohibited under no circumstances can the new method be permitted'. He then mentions the letter he had received from R. Wassermann of Breslau informing him of the newly invented machine[25] which could provide a solution.

R. Zeeb Zebi Ha-Kohen Klein, Dayan of the *Adath Yisrael*, Berlin, in his reply to Rabbi Weinberg, dated second day of *Rosh Hodesh Iyyar* 693 (27 April 1933), has some apprehension about permitting generally the cutting off of the head of the bird.

21. Ibid., p. 178.
22. Ibid.
23. On what follows, *vide* ibid., pp. 218ff.
24. *Vide supra* p. 182
25. On this machine *vide infra*.

R. Joseph Rosen, Ab Beth Din of Dinaburg, is against permitting the new method.

'Ha-Gaon Ha-Zaddik' R. Hayyim Eleazar Spira, Ab Beth Din of Munkatsch, did not want to express his view. However, at the end of his letter he makes a suggestion to which the wicked nation might agree: a small press (*Druck Pressel*) should be made like that used to emboss letters. The head of the bird should immediately after slaughtering be placed in that press which would affect the brain and 'kill' the bird instantly after *shehitah* and no separation of the head from the body would be required.

There are also letters from other Rabbis.

The second Rabbi in Germany to deal with this problem in *Responsa* was R. Menahem Mendel Kirschbaum (who later died a martyr). He tells us the following in a *Responsum* dated 'Friday, *Tasria-Mezora* 16th of Sephira, 693 (28 April 1933) Frankfurt am Main'.[26]

'In our country a decree has been issued forbidding the slaughtering of animals and fowls. However, as far as fowls are concerned it is permitted to slaughter them by performing the *shehitah* correctly provided that the head is cut off at the same time. I have heard in the name of a great Rabbinic scholar that he was inclined to permit this method to be used for fowls for hospitals even for those not dangerously ill. Is this correct?'

R. Kirschbaum decided that fowls slaughtered in such a way are forbidden even for those not dangerously ill.

Also several other Rabbis dealt with this problem.[27] While R. Nahum Weidenfeld, Ab Beth Din of Dombrowa, prohibited the cutting off of the head of the bird after the act of *shehitah*, R. Solomon Zalman Ehrenreich was inclined to permit the cutting off of the head after *shehitah* under certain conditions particularly for the use of sick people, but only with the consent of the Rabbi of Radomysl.

In the meantime, R. Mosheh Shimshon Wassermann, Rabbi in Breslau, approached R. Hayyim Ozer Grodzinski, Ab Beth Din of Wilno, concerning the problem of slaughtering fowls by cutting off the head immediately after the act of *shehitah* (Iyyar 693, May 1933).[28] He was of the opinion after consulting expert slaughterers that it was difficult in practice to slaughter in accordance with the law if the head were to be severed immediately afterwards with the slaughter knife. The matter was becoming very urgent as in some Jewish homes they had begun to

---

26. 'Menahem Meshib', II, no. 1, in *Ziyyun Le-Menahem*, ed. by R. Y.Rubinstein.
27. Ibid., pp. 399ff.
28. On what follows, cf. *Sheilath Mosheh* by Wassermann, nos. 85ff.

eat meat not ritually permitted. At first they might do so under duress but later it might be done willingly and in the end they would remain with this heavy sin.

As this was a time of great emergency—it affected thousands of families—one had to find a method of *shehitah* which would be permitted (from the religious point of view). Therefore he suggested the use of a machine invented by a religious doctor in Breslau called Dr Stark-Ethan, which cut off the head immediately after the ritual slaughtering had been performed. After the windpipe and gullet were ritually cut through the slaughterer or another person standing nearby pressed his foot on an iron lever and immediately a knife in the shape of an axe (the blade resembled a fine saw) would fall below the cut made during *shehitah* and cut off the head completely. The part where the cut of *shehitah* had been made, remained attached to the head and could be examined by the slaughterer as would normally be done.

He then tries to justify the use of this method. Perhaps the government would agree to the use of this machine as they merely demand that the head be cut off immediately.

R. Wassermann then received replies (written in May-June 1933) from various Rabbis agreeing in principle with the suggestion particularly if both gullet and windpipe were completely cut through and not merely the major part of each. Some Rabbis made suggestions concerning the examination of the slaughtered fowl. Among them were Rabbi Zebi Ha-Levi Horowitz of Frankfurt am Main; R. Hayyim Ozer Grodzinski (the Rabbi regards this method as excellent 'as through this our brethren would refrain from defiling themselves and infringing serious prohibitions'); R. David Menahem Munisch Babad of Tarnopol (if both organs, i.e. windpipe and gullet are completely cut through during the slaughtering process); R. Joseph Zebi Carlebach of Altona (he regards the suggested machine as excellent. 'Now it is up to you to obtain the permission of the authorities who are "hard opponents" (*baale din kashim*). But perhaps there is among your acquaintances "one Nazi" who would support you, not for our sake, but for his own sake so that the factory owners should benefit').

With regard to the meat I wish to inform you that there are here four or five importers who import meat from Denmark. Most of them sell the meat at a price of 1.15 (Mark) per lb. as the meat cannot be imported without the hind parts which require porging and as there is no one to do this those parts must be sold to non-Jews. The customer must therefore pay almost double. I later learned from one firm that it succeeded in importing the 'kosher' (ritually permitted) quarters without the hind parts. This firm promised me to sell the meat in Breslau at the price of 90 or 95 (Pfennige) per pound.

However, the meat purveyors of other towns refuse to co-operate with us and raise the price. In view of this I do not know whether the firm will keep its promise. . . . Just this moment I spoke again to Herr Magnus, the meat importer. He apologised that the meat in Denmark went up in price. He wishes to sell you meat at 1.08 per lb. *franco* (carriage paid to) Breslau.

In a letter[29] by Rabbi Zober of the *Adath Yisrael* Congregation in Stockholm addressed to Rabbi Unna in Mannheim the former asks the Rabbi to inform him of what he had heard from Dr Ehrenpreis in the name of Dr Hoffmann of Breslau, whether in Mannheim the Jews had invented a 'new knife' for slaughtering birds which cut off the head immediately following the act of slaughtering. R. Hayyim Ozer Grodzinski is said to have given his permission to use that knife. (A copy of that letter was in his possession.) R. Weinberg too is said to have permitted it. R. Zober asks R. Unna to reply as soon as possible as a question of *shehitah* was then being discussed by the government and according to the suggestion of the minister the head had to be cut off completely, 'der Kopf muss getrennt werden vom Körper'. He therefore requested more information about the knife and for a picture of it so as to be able to discuss it with the government.

In his reply R. Unna, who had in the meantime emigrated to Jerusalem, informs R. Zober that immediately after the prohibition of *shehitah* (in Germany) he suggested that the Rabbis find out whether in such an emergency it would be permitted to perform *shehitah* followed by cutting off the head. Some were inclined to permit it only for those who were ill and for others if meat could not be imported from abroad. No special knife had been invented; an order had merely been given for a knife to be made of specially hard iron in order to avoid a notch occurring in it when cutting the neck bone.[30] The Rabbi mentions some other regulations for those performing *shehitah*. These regulations were not satisfactorily observed in some places in Baden.

'At the end after all our efforts the government issued another decree prohibiting that method as well on the grounds of cruelty to animals (!). Stretching the neck was cruel and caused suffering (!) *vid.sap.*'

No date is given for the above. But the following letter (no. 20) also on *shehitah* sent by his nephew was written on the 9th of Ab, 698.[31] The next letter (no. 21) dated the 2nd of Shebat 698 (4 January 1938) and addressed to R. Hayyim Ozer Grodzinski of Wilno deals with a new

29. *Shoalin Ve-Dorshin*, Tel Aviv, 724 (1964), no. 19. See also the cases in nos. 20, 21.
30. It is rather strange that no mention is made of the machine invented by Dr Stark-Ethan of Breslau in 1939.
31. No doubt, it should read: 10th of Ab which was observed as a fastday, as the 9th of Ab 698 (6 August 1938) fell on a Sabbath.

method introduced in Sweden, i.e. stunning the animal with nitrogen before *shehitah*. In it R. Unna asks the Rabbi if that is permitted 'as hundreds and thousands defile themselves by eating meat of animals not ritually slaughtered. They are unable to live without meat and cannot pay the high price for *kosher* meat from abroad, the import of which is restricted by the government. Some invented a new term *neu kosher* (new *kosher*) i.e. they buy forbidden meat from the butcher, salt it and rinse it in remembrance of the matter.'

He had discussed this matter with leading Rabbis; however, all of them declared they would not agree without prior consent of R. H.O. Grodzinski. He therefore turns to him in this very important case. He adds that there are some Rabbis amongst them R. Munk of Berlin who object to stunning. He fears that if stunning in whatever form is permitted by the Rabbis in Germany it may be ordered by other countries. R. Unna, however, believes if the Jews show they are capable of dealing with all the hardships caused by the Nazis they will cease creating hindrances. Furthermore by permitting stunning many Jews would be prevented from eating *nebelah*.[32] No reply from R. H.O.Grodzinski is found in the book.

The question of stunning was discussed again in two countries later. In Hungary where the prohibition of *shehitah* was introduced on 6 April 1938, various suggestions were made to circumvent this prohibition. During World War II when, in summer 1940, the import of *kosher* meat to Switzerland was becoming difficult the question was discussed whether stunning the animal by narcotics (*narconal*) before the act of *shehitah* was permitted. The question was decided in the negative, and Rabbi Mordecai Breisch gave several reasons for this prohibition.[33]

As mentioned already, the reason given by the Nazis for the prohibition of *shehitah* without stunning i.e. to avoid unnecessary suffering to the animal was regarded even by some non-Jews as a mere pretext to annoy the Jews. The atrocities committed by the Nazis in the following years showed the whole world the true face of the 'superrace'. With bitter irony the Rabbis applied to the Nazis the verse taken from Hosea XIII 2: 'They that sacrifice men kiss calves.'[34] As far as the Jews in Germany are concerned who in such tragic times resisted all temptations and did not deviate from the tradition of their fathers it redounds to their honour that they followed their religious leaders. Today we know how right the latter were who encouraged German Jewry and

32. R. Y.Unna, *Shoalin Ve-Dorshin*, no. 21.
33. *Helkath Yaakob*, I, nos. 106, 107; cf. also the report of Weinberg, *Seride Esh*, p. 8, who refers to the book published by Dr A. Weil dealing with the whole matter.
34. Cf. e.g. the tragic case mentioned by R. Michael Dob Weissmandel, *Min Ha-Mezar*, p. 32.

maintained that, quoting the Talmudic phrase (*Kethuboth* 3b), 'A decree (of the enemy) is likely to be abolished, and therefore we do not abolish an ordinance of the Rabbis on account of a decree.'[35]

35. Cf. e.g. R. M.M.Babad in *Sheilath Mosheh* of Wassermann, no. 89; R. Yehudah Leibusch Babad in Weinberg's *Seride Esh*, I, p. 162; R. Joseph Rosen, Ab Beth Din of Dinaburg, ibid., p. 222 ('The decree will with the help of the Almighty soon be abolished'; R. A.Munk, ibid., p. 386); cf. however, R. Unna, ibid., p. 387.

2

Sterilization of the Insane

A law issued by the Nazis affecting the whole German nation was that of sterilization initiated by the 1933 Act for the Prevention of Hereditary Diseased Offspring.

By the outbreak of World War II, 375,000 people had been sterilized (including feeble-minded, schizophrenics, epileptics and alcoholics). The majority of them were sterilized involuntarily, i.e. under duress.[1]

Although this law was rather meant to apply to Germans, Jews also were affected by it as can be seen from two *Responsa* in which two Rabbis[2] dealt with the question whether it was permitted for a mentally ill woman to be sterilized. In one case[3] it is explicitly stated that the woman had been in a hospital and was not allowed to be taken home without having been sterilized. Both Rabbis decided that the sterilization of the women was permitted.

1. See Richard Grunberger, *A Social History of the Third Reich,* pp. 221, 225.
2. R. M.M.Kirschbaum, 'Menahem Meshib' in *Ziyyun Le-Menahem,* ed. by R. J.Rubinstein, No. 18 (the *Responsum* is dated: 2nd of Adar Sheni, 695, 7 March 1935); R. J.J.Weinberg, *Seride Esh,* III, no. 21 (the *Responsum* addressed to R. I.Unna in Mannheim is dated: 14th of Ab 697, 22 July 1937).
3. R. M.M.Kirschbaum, 'Menahem Meshib' who draws a distinction between the sterilization of women and that of men. In the former case it is permitted if fear exists that the children might inherit the disease, in the case of men sterilization is forbidden unless danger to life is involved. On sterilization of Jews by the Nazis in concentration camps *vide supra* pp. 102f.

3

The Nuremberg Law for the Protection of German Blood

As is well known, the notorious laws of Nuremberg issued on 15 September 1935,[1] contained 'the law for the protection of German blood and honour' (*Gesetz zum Schutze des deutschen Blutes und der deutschen Ehre*) prohibiting marriages and extramarital relations between Jews and Aryans on pain of imprisonment.

It is the greatest tragicomedy in the history of the Nazi holocaust that this decree turned out to be of great help for the Rabbis after the war when the camps were liberated and they had to deal with certain matrimonial cases. The law for 'the protection of German blood and honour' helped to protect *Jewish* blood and honour! The Rabbis were able to adopt a lenient view and to re-unite husband and wife and help unfortunate girls build up a house in Israel.

STATUS OF WOMEN LIBERATED FROM THE CAMPS

According to the Talmud and Codes a *kohen* must not marry a woman who has been a captive (unless there is evidence she had not been alone with a non-Jew). If a woman was raped she may stay with her husband only if he is not a *kohen*. If she yielded with her free will she must not stay with her husband even if he is not a *kohen*. Furthermore, if a woman was imprisoned by non-Jews for the sake of money she is permitted to live with her husband (even if he is a *kohen*[2] because we assume they fear they would lose their money if she were raped) and if for the purpose of taking her life (she had been condemned to death) but was saved afterwards she is forbidden to her husband (according to one view, even if he is not a *kohen*, because we are afraid she might have consented to have intercourse with the person who promised to save her).[3]

When the camps were liberated and husbands and wives who had been separated were re-united and similarly when young men who were

1. They were issued at the Reichstag at Nuremberg, hence the name the Laws of Nuremberg. On these laws, cf. *supra* Introduction pp. xvif. and notes 9–11. The Nuremberg Laws were introduced in Austria on 20 May 1938, see Hugo Gold, *Geschichte der Juden in Wien*, p. 84. They were not introduced in conquered countries the inhabitants of which were regarded by the Nazis as belonging to an inferior race. Cf. L. Poliakov, *Harvest of Hate*, p. 38. On the introduction of the Nuremberg Laws in conquered territories, see *Ausnahme-Gesetze gegen Juden in den von Nazi Deutschland besetzten Gebieten Europas*, by the Wiener Library, London, 1956, pp. 2, 6, 8, 15, 16, 23, 29.
2. This applies only to a place where the Jews are dominant.
3. See Maimonides, *Mishneh Torah, Hilchoth Issure Biah*, XVIII, 7ff., 17, 30; *Tur Shulhan Aruch, Eben Ha-Ezer*, cap. VII, nos. 1ff., 11 and Isserles ibid. where some differences of opinion are given; R. Meiri (Feuerwerger), *Ezrath Nashim*, III, pp. 83ff.

kohanim wished to marry girls who had been in a concentration camp
the following questions arose:

1. Is a *kohen* permitted to marry a girl who had been in a concentration
   camp under the Germans?
2. Are husbands, particularly *kohanim*, permitted to live with their
   wives who had been in concentration camps?
3. Are husbands, who are not *kohanim*, permitted to live with their
   wives who had been taken to 'houses of shame' and been tattooed (to
   be recognized and liquidated?) as they might have yielded with their
   free will? Or should their case be regarded as 'rape'?

Several Rabbis deal with these questions.

A *kohen* wished to marry a girl who had been in a concentration camp
but feared she was possibly forbidden to him because a woman who
had been in captivity must not marry a *kohen*. The Rabbi, however,
showed that the prohibition did not apply in this case. One of the
reasons was the decision laid down in the Codes that a woman who had
been imprisoned for the sake of money may return to her husband
even if he is a *kohen* since the non-Jews would not attack the woman in
case they lost the money through such action. 'How much less have we
to be afraid that this woman had been raped, for the cursed Germans
have in their arrogance prohibited intercourse between Germans and
Jews on pain of great penalty. This prohibition applied to anyone who
defiled their "chosen race" with the "low and degraded (*shaphel
ve-namuch*) race". . . . Furthermore, it is well known that the Germans
later killed those women and girls who were specially kept for immoral
purposes for soldiers in the battle field in order that their seed should
not remain in the body of Jewesses. . . .'[4]

It should be pointed out that another Rabbi, independently, gives this
as one of the reasons for permitting a *kohen* to marry a girl who had
been in a German camp. 'Furthermore, there is an additional reason
for permitting a *kohen* to marry a girl who had been in a German
concentration camp. As is well known intercourse with a Jewess was
"a sin worthy of death" (Deut. xxi 23) as the death penalty was meted
out. I heard from my friend Rabbi Snieg of Munich that he had been
present when one of the guards of the camp was hung for having had
intercourse with a Jewess. This is surely good reason for permitting the
girl to marry a *kohen*.[5]'

The latter Rabbi also dealt with the question concerning the wives of

4. R. M.J.Breisch, *Helkath Yaakob*, I, no. 16. Raping of girls by German soldiers who
   then killed their victims is mentioned by several authors, cf. e.g. note 11 and Anatoli,
   Babi Yar, pp. 112, 154.
5. Meiri, *Ezrath Nashim*, III, pp. 95f.

non *kohanim* and *kohanim* who survived the Nazi holocaust and traced their husbands, as to whether they were permitted to return to them.

He then proves that for several reasons the women are permitted to return to their husbands whether or not *kohanim* although in the latter case more stringency generally applies, namely they would become prohibited to their husbands even if they had been raped, a fact which would not make them prohibited to their husbands if not *kohanim*. One of the reasons he gave for his decision was the ruling quoted by Isserles[6] that the women who during the persecution in Austria (1420–21) had been forced to embrace Christianity and later returned to their ancestral faith might live with their husbands, even if the latter were *kohanim*. In addition some principles are quoted in support of a lenient decision.[7]

A decision about women released from the concentration camps was also given by R. I.J.Weiss in Grosswardein in 1946.[8] He was asked, should women liberated from concentration camps be regarded as 'captives', i.e. be unable to return to their husbands who are *kohanim*, or, if they are unmarried, be unable to marry *kohanim*? The questioner adds that he had been told that very often inmates of concentration camps would be able to testify to the fact that a woman did remain 'pure' (i.e. did not have intercourse with a non-Jew). However, one might not be able to rely on their evidence since those people might be disqualified from giving evidence as they were irreligious. The Rabbi nevertheless decided that the women may return to their husbands who are *kohanim* or marry *kohanim*. 'As the matter is of great urgency and is pressing (*ha-lahaz zeh ha-dehak*) affecting thousands of Jewish daughters and taking into consideration the leniency expressed by our Rabbis in such a case we are permitted to look for grounds to adopt a lenient view.' Among the various reasons was that the woman could not have saved her life by having intercourse with her captors as heavy punishment for infringing the *Rassengesetz* would have been imposed on those who had intercourse with a Jewess. Although they would not always have been killed they would have been removed from office or would have had other punishments and been in disgrace. 'Although they [the Germans] intended evil against us [by issuing the *Rassengesetz*], God meant it for good' (cf. Gen. L 20), i.e. this decree was now helpful in permitting the women to return to their husbands as well as *kohanim* marrying girls who had been in concentration camps under German rule.

With regard to the fitness of witnesses the Rabbi tried to show that

6. *Darche Mosheh* on *Tur Eben Ha-Ezer*, cap. VII, no. 13.
7. Meiri, *Ezrath Nashim*, III, pp. 83ff.
8. *Minhath Yizhak*, I, no. 87.

a lenient view can be adopted in this case. Two other Rabbis took a stricter approach.

Chief Rabbi Yaakob Mosheh Toledano[9] of Israel was hesitant in permitting the wives of *kohanim* who had been in German concentration camps to return to their husbands and similarly girls liberated from those camps to marry *kohanim*. On the one hand, a stringent view would have to be adopted on account of the various rulings laid down in the Codes. On the other, leniency could be applied in view of the reason quoted by the aforementioned Rabbis, i.e. the strict order given to the Germans by the authorities whose aim was to destroy the Jewish people, not to fraternize with Jewesses. 'The case has still to be considered.'

Although another Rabbi, R. Tobiah Tabyomi (Guttentag)[10] tries to prove that women who had been in camps may return to their husbands who are *kohanim* he is of the opinion that the matter ought not to be decided by an individual Rabbi even if he were a *mumheh* (expert) but had to be submitted to a group of great scholars. He expressed this view in connection with the following question sent to him by a Rabbi in whose neighbourhood a *kohen* was living. The wife of this *kohen* had returned to him from Bergen-Belsen after many years where she had been working as a Polish non-Jewess on account of false papers she had obtained. The husband was religious and a learned man. Was it the Rabbi's duty being the local Rabbi to draw the *kohen*'s attention to the religious implications of his wife's having been in the concentration camp, in view of the fact that the husband himself had not raised the matter? Has the woman the status of a 'captive' who is prohibited to live with a *kohen*? The local Rabbi added that from reports he had the woman was easily excitable and did not mention what she had gone through, not even to her relatives. Should anything be mentioned it could result in a great tragedy, so should the Rabbi rather keep silent?

R. Tabyomi regards that question, which is of a general nature, as most stringent. Such an apprehension (that the wife be regarded a 'captive') would affect all wives of *kohanim*, who had been in countries under German occupation. Furthermore, such a question would affect also unmarried women as to whether they could marry *kohanim*. 'As is well known, the non-Jews have raped and defiled very many women and girls,[11] all women who have been in the camps under German subjugation have the status of "captives of war" according to the view of all authorities. . . . However, we must try to find permission for all

9. *Bath Ami*, Tel Aviv, 1947, p. 66.
10. *Erez Tobah*, Part I, Jerusalem, 1947, no. 61.
11. Raping of women is mentioned by another Rabbi. See R. A.Zimetbaum, 'Maaseh Nissim' in *Responsa Dibre Pinhas*, New York p. 169. See also *supra*.

those unfortunate women who have suffered for so many years and who survived through a miracle and returned to their husbands. One must not increase the tragedy. Hence we have to see whether a lenient view could be adopted.' He shows that this was the case but the matter had to be submitted to a group of scholars. With regard to the question whether the Rabbi had to mention the implications to the husband, R. Tabyomi decided in the negative giving his reasons.

JEWISH WOMEN FORCED TO IMMORALITY WITH GERMAN SOLDIERS

There exists a difference of opinion as to whether women who had been taken to the 'houses of shame' and had been tattooed may return to their husbands who are not *kohanim*.

R. Oshry[12] tells us that immediately after the liberation of the ghetto he was asked a horrifying question which concerned not only the case submitted to him but also a great number of Jewish women who survived the terrible holocaust. The case was as follows:

A young woman coming from a most honourable family of Kovno approached R. Oshry crying bitterly. Like many other women she too had been seized by the cursed ones and used for immoral purposes. They had even tattooed on her arm the words, 'Harlot for Hitler's Soldiers'. After the liberation she succeeded in finding her husband alive and both intended to build up their house again as their children had been murdered by the Germans. However, the husband was startled when he noticed her tattoo. He realized he must first find out whether they were permitted to live together, as she might have agreed willingly to the Germans. In that case she may not live with her husband any more.

The Rabbi tried to prove that she could live with her husband (as he was not a *kohen*) and she was believed when she maintained she was forced. There was no reason to assume she might have submitted willingly to the Germans (in which case she would not be permitted to live with her husband even if not a *kohen*) since she knew what they had done to the Jews, men, women and children who had been mercilessly massacred. No doubt, the enemy was abhorrent in her eyes so that she would not have been enticed by him.

There was no reason to assume she might have yielded even to save her own life since the woman knew that the cursed wicked men killed these unfortunate women after a certain time. All the unfortunate women knew this hence none could have assumed that she would be able to save her life by yielding willingly. There was also the fact that

12. *Mi-Maamakkim*, 1, no. 27.

they were tattooed immediately after they had been seized in order to make them despicable for all time by being marked as harlots.

The Rabbi is of the opinion that by no means should those women remove the tattoo from their bodies since the inscription did not reflect any shame on their part but strength of character and self-sacrifice for the sake of God who will avenge the innocent blood.

It should also be pointed out, however, that from a statement made by the Rabbi we can see that there were cases where husbands divorced their wives when they learned that they had been used for immoral purposes. Indeed one Rabbi[13] decided that women who had been taken to 'houses of shame' must not return to their husbands even if they are not *kohanim.*

---

13. R. Y.M.Toledano, *Bath Ami*, p. 68.

4

Confiscation of Books

'Habent sua fata libelli.' This well-known proverb applies particularly to Hebrew books during the Nazi holocaust. In some places the books were burned or used as scrap paper, in others they were regarded as precious finds and sent to Germany like any other valuables.

The first reaction of the Nazis to books by Jewish authors came soon after they had come to power. They did not concern religious and Hebrew books. The desire of the Nazis to purge 'German cultural life of its Jewish manifestations found its most sensational expression in the huge bonfires of May 10, 1933, when thousands of volumes written by liberal, pacifist, socialist and Jewish writers went up in smoke. These carnivals took place in many of the larger cities of Germany and were organized and supervised by the student groups of the Nazi party'.[1] Among the books burned were those of Siegmund Freud, Emile Zola, Jakob Wasserman, Stefan Zweig, Thomas Mann.

The attitude of the Nazis towards burning Hebrew books found its expression for the first time on the day following the *Kristallnacht*. It was on that day that Hebrew books went up in flames.[2] The writer, then in Vienna, witnessed from behind the curtain of his flat in the house adjacent to the so-called 'Polish-synagogue' (in the Leopoldsgasse) the mob directed by the S.A. men, having destroyed the synagogue, collect all Hebrew books found there and in the other rooms of the building, pile them up in the street and, to the great joy of the spectators, light a bonfire.

The destruction of Hebrew books occurred later after the outbreak of the war in occupied Poland and Lithuania, etc. In February 1940, the library of the famous *yeshibah* of Lublin was burned. The fire lasted twenty hours.[3]

On the other hand, the value of the Hebrew books was soon recognized by the Nazis and the looting of libraries began. The confiscated books were (apart from their value in money) to serve to build up the High School (*Hohe Schule*), the centre for National Socialist research, teaching and training. As far back as 15 April 1939 Alfred Rosenberg founded the Institute of the National Socialist German Workers Party for Research into the Jewish Question (*Institut der NSDAP zur Erforschung der Judenfrage*). But it was not until 26–28 March 1941 that the institute was inaugurated as Institute for Research into the Jewish Question, Branch of the High School of the NSDAP (*Institut*

---

1. Jacob Marcus, *The Rise and Destiny of the German Jew*, pp. 19ff.
2. On the burning of Torah scrolls by the Nazis, *vide supra*, p. 137.
3. See *Beth Jacob*, no. 30, Jerusalem, Tammuz 722, p. 17.

P

zur Erforschung der Judenfrage, Aussenstelle der Hohen Schule der NSDAP) the seat of which was Frankfurt am Main.[4]

Curiously the first confiscation of libraries is not connected with Alfred Rosenberg who intended to use the books for his 'research' and to make new discoveries, but with Adolf Eichmann who was anxious to acquire libraries of great value as treasures for the Reich. Libraries and museums were his favourite subjects of interest.[5]

One of his first lootings of books took place in Vienna in 1938; the library of the *Israelitisch-Theologischen Lehranstalt* in Vienna, the private libraries of Chief Rabbi Taglicht and of Professor Samuel Krauss were loaded on trucks and taken away.

It was during the summer of that year that one day on the writer's visit to the library of the *Kultusgemeinde* (to whose committee he belonged) the librarian Moses Rath told him with some excitement that a few minutes earlier Eichmann had visited the library and warned him that he was responsible for every single book that had disappeared or might disappear. Looking through the list of 'accounts' including the writer's the latter noticed he had guaranteed for a student to borrow books all of which had been returned except one work, i.e. Richard Beer Hoffmann's *Jakobs Traum*. Unfortunately, the student could not be approached as he had been arrested by the Nazis. So the writer went out to buy the book and replace it, and after a long search succeeded in obtaining it in one of the bookshops. The bookseller looked at him with great curiosity when at that time, aware of the position of the Jews, he asked for that book. He must have noticed how happy the writer was to obtain it.

On 19 July 1938, the Amtsdirektor of the *Kultusgemeinde*, Dr J. Löwenherz, was forced by Eichmann to sign a declaration that he was surrendering the library of the *Kultusgemeinde* and its archives. Both the library and the archives were later transferred to Berlin. The matter was to be kept secret.[6] In reply to an inquiry the Amtsdirektor of the *Israelitischen Kultusgemeinde* in Vienna, Regierungsrat Wilhelm Krell, confirmed that the confiscated books had not been returned except for a small part which the *Kultusgemeinde* received back through the *Gewerkschaftsbund* from Germany. All the manuscripts have been lost.[7]

4. On the whole plan, Rosenberg's rival Walter Frank and Hitler's High School, see Max Weinreich, *Hitler's Professors*, New York, 1946, pp. 97ff. which deals with this at length.
5. *Vide infra.*
6. See Herbert Rosenkranz, 'The Anschluss and the Tragedy of Austrian Jewry 1938–1945' in *The Jews of Austria*, ed. by Josef Fraenkel, p. 494, also in *Reichskristallnacht*, Vienna, 1968, p. 66, note 14.
7. I can recollect the following fact dating from the time I studied at the *Israelitisch-theologischen Lehranstalt*. It was in the 'twenties when the financial position of the *Lehranstalt* was very critical (all money had been invested in War Loans which had become worthless) that the authorities of the *Lehranstalt* intended to sell the manuscripts to America. It was then (through the good office of Chief Rabbi Chajes?) that

The fate of the confiscated library of the *Israelitisch-Theologischen Lehranstalt* is unknown (letter of 3 December 1970). Similarly the confiscated libraries of Oberrabbiner I. Taglicht and Professor S. Krauss disappeared and cannot be traced.

Indeed this shows us clearly that the pillaging of the libraries in Vienna which took place before the *Kristallnacht* was the work of Eichmann. In 1944 he still displayed great interest in Jewish culture and books. On his first visit to Hungary (31 March 1944) he expressed his wish to the members of the Jewish Council to see the Jewish museum and library, matters which had interested him since 1934.[8]

The famous library of the *Jüdisch-theologischen Seminars*, Breslau, which included priceless manuscripts and printed works was destroyed in November 1938. After the war, the *Schweizerische Israelitische Gemeindebund* received many boxes containing books which had belonged to the library of the seminary. They were distributed among the libraries of the Jewish communities of Basle, Geneva and Zurich.[9]

The library of the Hildesheimer Rabbinical Seminary was confiscated by the Germans and later transferred to Prague. Some books were saved by a student who emigrated to Haifa, and he inquired of R. J.J.Weinberg whether he could keep them and use them. R. Weinberg tells us that he had lost all the books of his own library, having been unable to take a single book away.[10]

The looting of libraries of other countries occupied by the Nazis continued in the following years. About two months after the outbreak of the war the Nazis began to remove libraries from Warsaw. On 23 October 1939, they removed the most valuable books and manuscripts from the Tlomacka Library to some unknown place and in December 1939 the remaining books were taken away. 'In general, the conqueror displays a weakness for libraries. . . .'[11]

In the Kielce district, all the books of the Rabbis, synagogues and houses of study were confiscated by the Nazis and sent to Germany.[12]

Confiscations of books occurred in many other places, particularly

---

the *Kultusgemeinde* took over the manuscripts with the commitment to keep up the *Lehranstalt* for a certain number of years. These manuscripts (which had belonged to Adolf Jellinek, J.H.Schorr and Abraham Epstein) were then added to the manuscripts owned by the *Kultusgemeinde*.

8. Gerald Reitlinger, *The Final Solution*, p.456; Gideon Hausner, *Justice in Jerusalem*, p.137.
9. Lothar Rothschild, 'Die Geschichte des Seminars von 1904–1938' in *Das Breslauer Seminar*, Tubingen, 1963, p. 165.
10. R. J.J.Weinberg, *Seride Esh*, III, no. 71.
11. Chaim A. Kaplan, *Scroll of Agony*, the Warsaw diary of Chaim A. Kaplan, translated and edited by Abraham I. Katsh, London, 1966, pp. 39, 70f.
12. R. S.Huberband, *Kiddush Ha-Shem*, edited by Nahman Blumental and Joseph Kermish, Tel Aviv, 1969, pp. 98ff. The author remarks that in Warsaw the libraries of the synagogue, Professor Schorr (he later died a martyr), the community and private individuals were pillaged. See also note 15.

where *yeshiboth* existed. In order to steal a march on the Nazis some victims tried, as mentioned above,[13] to bury the books in the ground. In fact the pillaging of books in Poland was not confined to Jewish libraries. The various libraries in both the Government General and the Incorporated Territories[14] were confiscated. Similarly museums, public and private art collections, archives and scientific laboratories were plundered and sent to Germany.[15]

Who was responsible for that pillage? It appears that as far as the Government General is concerned Governor General Hans Frank had given the order to this effect, while with regard to the part of the Incorporated Territories called *Wartheland Reichsstatthalter* Greiser was in charge of the operation. It was he whose name appeared on the decree published in Posen on 15 December 1939, ordering the registration of all scientific and cultural books belonging to Poles. This registration had to be made at an address given in the decree preparatory to the collection of books owned by Poles.[16]

The name of Alfred Rosenberg[17] in connection with confiscation of books for his 'High School' appears for the first time on 1 July 1940. After the French defeat (25 June 1940) Rosenberg asked Hitler's permission to search the libraries and archives as well as 'ownerless Jewish cultural property' in France for valuable material. His request was granted and pillage of libraries began which did not remain confined to France but was also extended to other countries invaded by the Germans.[18] Thus not only the libraries of the *Alliance Israélite Universelle* and the *École Rabbinique* in Paris but also the libraries from Holland[19] were sent to Germany.[20]

On 1 March 1941, a new decree was issued by Hitler. It was an extension[21] of the previous one authorizing Rosenberg to confiscate

13. *Vide supra* p. 140.
14. Of the three territories into which Poland was divided the western provinces were incorporated into the Reich, the central territories formed the so-called Government General (under Hans Frank) and the eastern territories were taken over by the Russians. On the administration of the western provinces and the General Government, see Raul Hilberg, *The Destruction of the European Jews*, pp. 130ff.
15. See *The Black Book of Poland*, New York, 1942, pp. 473ff. where the various national, public and private libraries pillaged by the Germans are listed.
16. Ibid., pp. 474ff.
17. On Rosenberg, see Joachim C. Fest, *The Face of the Third Reich*, London, 1970, pp. 163ff., 172, and particularly Reinhard Bollmus, *Das Amt Rosenberg und seine Gegner*, Deutsche Verlags-Anstalt, Stuttgart, 1970.
18. Cf. Fest. *Face of the Third Reich*, p. 172; Bollmus, *Das Amt Rosenberg*, p. 238.
19. On Holland, *vide infra*.
20. See Weinreich, *Hitler's Professors*, p. 104.
21. Bollmus, *Das Amt Rosenberg*, p. 151: 'Der Auftrag Rosenbergs wurde von Hitler am 1. Marz 1942 noch einmal erweitert; er bezog sich nunmehr auch auf die "unter Zivilverwaltung stehenden besetzten Ostgebiete", ausgenommen das "General-gouvernement", und umfasste jetzt ganz algemein "Bibliotheken, Archive, Logen und sonstige weltanschauliche und kulturelle Einrichtungen aller Art." '

books and archives also in Eastern occupied territories which were under civil administration, except the Government General. It was addressed to 'all headquarters of the Armed Forces, the Party and the State'. It ran as follows:[22]

Jews, freemasons and the ideological opponents of National Socialism who are allied with them are the originators of the present war directed against the *Reich*. The methodological, intellectual fight against these powers is a task of military necessity. I have therefore authorized *Reichsleiter* Alfred Rosenberg to carry out this task with the consent of the Head of the supreme command of the armed forces. His *Einsatzstab* (squad) for the occupied territories has the right to search through libraries, archives, (Freemasons') lodges and other ideological and cultural institutions of all kinds for appropriate material and to order it to be confiscated for the ideological tasks of the NSDAP and the later scientific researches by the High School.

Subject to same regulations are the cultural valuables which are in possession of Jews or belong to them, or are ownerless, or the origin of which cannot be explained satisfactorily. The regulations concerning the execution of co-operation with the armed forces are issued by the Head of the supreme command of the armed forces with the consent of *Reichsleiter* Rosenberg. The necessary measures within the eastern territories which are under German administration are taken by *Reichsleiter* Rosenberg in his capacity as *Reichsminister* for the occupied eastern territories.

(Signed) Adolf Hitler.

Führer Headquarters, 1. March, 1942.
To all offices of the Armed Forces, the Party and the State.

There is, however, one point which, perhaps, still requires explanation. From Hitler's second decree (of 1 March 1942) it appears that only from then onwards Rosenberg was entitled to confiscate books in the occupied eastern territories. In fact we possess two *Responsa* from which we can see that already on 18 February 1942, an order was given in Kovno (Kaunas) to hand over all books, secular as well as religious works, to the central book storehouse which was in the care of Alfred Rosenberg.

'On the 1st of Adar 5702 (18 February 1942)[23] an order was given by

---

22. See German version of Document 149 PS (vol. XXVI, p. 135) in Bruno Blau, *Das Ausnahmerecht für die Juden in Deutschland 1933-1945*, no. 371, pp. 104f. and 'The Partial Translation of Document 149–PS' contained in *Nazi Conspiracy and Aggression*, vol. III, Office of United States Chief of Council for Prosecution of Axis Criminality, Washington, 1946, pp. 190f. (in possession of the Wiener Library, London).
23. According to L. Garfunkel, *The Destruction of Kovno's Jewry*, p. 127, the order was issued on 27 February 1942.

the cursed enemy to all inmates of the Ghetto that they hand over immediately all books, both sacred (Talmud, Rabbinic works, etc.) and secular, to a central store which was to be under the control of the staff of the "expert" for Jewish cultural matters the well-known enemy Alfred Rosenberg. For that purpose a special officer was sent from Rosenberg's office called Dr Bankrad to carry out the order.'

Dr Bankrad together with the ghetto commander Jordan[24] turned to R. E.Oshry who had been in charge of the book store and asked him to supply them with a copy of the old edition of the Talmud as they wished to know what it contained. They turned to R. Abraham Gerstein (who later died a martyr) to explain to them the first page of the text R. Oshry had given them. It happened to be the first page of the tractate *Zebahim*. R. Oshry was then asked by the Rabbi whether one was allowed to comply with their order and to teach them Torah for it was possible to evade that order though not easily.

R. Oshry tries to prove that great danger to life existed under the conditions of those days. Therefore teaching the non-Jews the Oral Law was not prohibited, particularly in view of the fact it was not a regular study but an occasional one and any refusal would have entailed great danger.

He himself, R. Oshry concludes, had been asked to explain the *Glosses* written by R. Yizhak Elchanan on the margin of the Talmud pages of his copy of the Talmud which had been brought into the book store. They wished also to have a *Responsum* of his explained which was bound together with his copy of the tractate *Berachoth*. It dealt with an *agunah*, Rachel, daughter of Abraham of Jezno.[25]

The second *Responsum* has been quoted above.[26] It deals with the books hidden by the Jewish policeman of the ghetto. They had been handed over by the Jews in compliance with the order given by the Germans on the 1st of Adar 5702 (18 February 1942).

As we can see, the looting of libraries in the countries under Nazi rule had taken place by Rosenberg (in Kovno) before Hitler's second decree. Hence the question arises: what was the purpose of the decree of 1 March 1942? The writer is unable to explain this.

How big the haul of the Nazis was no one knows.[27] Considering the

---

24. On him, see Garfunkel, *Destruction of Kovno's Jewry*, p. 215.
25. R. E.Oshry, *Mi-Maamakkim*, I, no. 14.
26. *Vide supra*, p. 140.
27. It should be mentioned that (according to Garfunkel, *Destruction of Kovno's Jewry*, p. 129) in the ghetto of Kovno alone more than 100,000 books were confiscated. According to a Nazi report dated 29 April 1943, about 550,000 volumes had been confiscated until that date. See *Ausnahme-Gesetze gegen die Juden in den von den Nazi-*

numerous public and private libraries of the vast number of scholars and Rabbis living in Germany and particularly in the eastern countries before the war, one can have some idea of the immense value of the books. Most interesting light is shed on the pillage of books in Holland by the report by the leader of the Working Group Netherland, 'On the activities of the *Einsatzstab* of the Bureau of the *Reichsleiter* Rosenberg in the occupied Western Territories and the Netherlands, Working Group Netherland'.[28] After enumerating the libraries and archives of about over sixty lodges and fifteen clubs in various parts of the country, which were 'screened' and 'packed' giving now and then a description of a pillaged library, the report tells us that:

The Working group took over the international Institute for Social History in Amsterdam with its library and archives, boxes of extraordinary value. It seems that this institute was founded in 1934 with the intention of creating a centre of intellectual resistance against National Socialism. Its employees were mainly Jewish refugees from Germany. . . . In the library there are about 160,000 books. . . .

The Libraries of the Societas Spinozena in Den Haag and of the Spinoza-House in Rijnsburg also were packed in 18 boxes, and they, too, contain extremely valuable early works of great importance to the Spinoza problem. . . .

For the coming months, action is planned on the following (mentions four different types of libraries and archives, the last one being) Jewish private libraries in Amsterdam, particularly:

(A) The Israelite Library Beth-Hamidrasch Etz Chaim Amsterdam, Rapenburgerstraat 109. This library, founded in 1740, contains about 4,000 volumes, particularly Jewish theology.

(B) Library of the Netherland Israelite Seminar, Amsterdam, Rapenburgerstraat 177. It contains 4,300 volumes of Hebraica and 3,000 volumes Judaica. At the time, it took over the library of the Jewish Society for Literature, Thoelet (1830–1837) and valuable Jewish private collections. Among other works, it contains precious old prints from the years 1480 and 1560 and some manuscripts.

(C) The Portuguese-Israelite Seminar, Amsterdam, Jonas Daniel Meyerplein 5. There are 25,000 volumes, 450 manuscripts, 600 prints

---

Deutschland besetzten Gebieten Europas, ed. by the Wiener Library, London, 1956, p. 24. However, the haul was much bigger. Leon Poliakov, *Harvest of Hate*, London,1956, p. 68, speaks of 'the concentration of a collection of nearly six million volumes in a chateau near Frankfurt'.

28. I am using a photostat of Document PS–176 put at my disposal by the courtesy of the Wiener Library in London. In it it is stated that 'The working group Netherland of the *Einsatzstab Reichsleiter* Rosenberg began its work . . . during the first days of September 1940'.

208 *The Nazi Holocaust*

(Inkunablen) and numerous Exlibris, coins and the like, and famous material on Talmudic Literature.

(D) The so-called Rosenthaliana, primarily a foundation by the Jew Rosenthal from Hanover. From there, it was at the time transferred and affiliated with the local university library. In the meantime, it has, on account of donations, grown considerably. Technically, it belongs to the Municipality of Amsterdam, but in the Catalogue of Libraries in the Netherlands in 1931, it is designated as 'Private'. According to the catalogue, it contains 25,000 volumes and 300 manuscripts. However, the number of volumes reaches 100,000.

The libraries mentioned specially under (A) to (D) ought to be of particular interest for the history of Western Europe. It is very likely that hitherto unknown facts may be brought into the open, on the era of Cromwell and that of the glorious Revolution of 1688 and the resulting personal union between England and the Netherlands. In particular, light may be thrown on Cromwell's attitude towards the Jews, possibly even on the Jewish influence on the development of the Secret Service.

The Nazis kept their word. The libraries mentioned in the report were pillaged and transferred to Germany. The writer made inquiries and received the following authoritative reports: the library of Societas Spinozana, The Hague, was confiscated by the *Einsatzstab* Rosenberg and 'probably the books were transferred to the Rosenberg Institute. The exact date of the confiscation was October 21, 1940. Most of the books were returned to Holland in Summer 1946; they are now again in the Domus Spinozana...' (Letter from the secretary of 7 September 1971).

With regard to the library of the Spinozana House in Rijnsburg he was told that 'the complete library, some reproductions and some minor objects, were confiscated in January, 1941, by order of a Dr. Schwier "Referent des Reichskommissars in den Niederlanden".' The books were sent to Germany: 'shortly after the capitulation of Germany nearly all the items were discovered in Frankfurt am Main, and they were replaced in our museum at Rijnsburg in 1946.' (Letter from the Secretary G. Van Suchtelen of 18 May 1971.)

Concerning Libraries (A), (B) and (D).[29]

(A) The librarian of the *Portuguees Israëlietisch Seminarium Ets Haim* sent me a report (published in 1966) according to which 'the Library consists of more than 25,000 books and 600 manuscripts. It is said to be the oldest book treasury in the world.' A history of the growth of the library is then given. In her covering letter of 7 February

29. I have not received a reply concerning (C).

1971, the librarian informs me that 'in 1939 valuable instruments of the Synagogue and the most valuable books of Ets Haim were brought to a strong-room in a bank in Amsterdam. In 1944 the Nazis found these treasures and through this discovery they found the library. The books were packed in boxes and sent to Rosenberg's Institute. However, on the way to this Institute the train, which contained the boxes, was surprised by a bombardment. The train was already in Germany and the Nazis brought the boxes to Offenbach, where they stayed till after the war. American soldiers found the boxes and brought them back to Amsterdam in 1945/6. Many very rare books were lost . . ., however, the greatest part of the collection has been returned. . . .'

(B) With regard to the library of the Netherland Israelite Seminary the writer received a reply from Chief Rabbi A. Schuster (since 1951 dean of the seminary) in which he writes that the entire library had been confiscated by the Nazis and sent to an unknown destination. 'Ultimately the library was returned, though heavily deficient.' (Letter of 2 July 1971.)

(D) Dr L. Fuks of *Universiteits-Bibliotheek van Amsterdam* of which *Bibliotheca Rosenthaliana* forms part, sent a printed report (which appeared in Amsterdam, 1967) with personal additions for this work. The relevant passage runs as follows:

The Germans closed the Library in the beginning of 1941 and deported the books (about 60,000) to Germany in 1944, where they were going to be partly destroyed and partly incorporated in Rosenberg's 'Institut zur Erforschung der Judenfrage'. These evil intentions were prevented from being put into practice by the German capitulation. Most of the bookchests were stacked in a convent near Offenbach, where they were found and shipped back to Amsterdam (April 1946). The keeper and his assistant with their families had also been deported, but they did not return home. . . .

Though several unique and rare books, the collection of Jewish coins and the 'objets d'art' were missing and the catalogue destroyed, the Bibliotheca Rosenthaliana could officially be reopened on September 1, 1946.

As far as Italy is concerned the Germans had no time to remove the books already packed in boxes from the Jewish library in Florence because of the collapse of their army on the Italian front.[30] However, they succeeded in pillaging the famous libraries of the community and of the Rabbinical Seminary of Rome, both rich in early prints and

30. See *Beth Jacob*, no. 91, December 1966, p. 5.

manuscripts. They were sent north to Munich and were not heard of again.[31]

The pillaging of books in Greece was very successful; in particular in Salonica where various communal and private libraries existed, rich in books on all subjects and particularly in *Responsa*. In the work *The Destruction of Greek Jewry* 1941–1944[32] there is a special chapter dealing with the pillaging of the libraries which fell victim to Rosenberg's greed. We also hear that archives,[33] Torah scrolls and other religious articles had been plundered. More than eight libraries removed by the Germans are listed. One library owned by R. Hayyim Habib, which was an old family collection containing eight thousand *halachic* books, was hidden together with the communal archive. However, they were discovered by the Germans who burned them completely. 'The community of Salonica famous for its spiritual treasures which had been collected for 500 years remained without books.'[34]

The consequences of the confiscations of books have been mentioned above.[35] A great dearth of books became apparent in all countries which had suffered under the Nazis. It often happened that they had taken away the most precious works and manuscripts only, while those needed by the Jewish masses in their daily religious life, e.g. prayerbooks, copies of the Bible, Talmud, Codes and Rabbinic books, often printed in Poland, Germany and in other countries, were taken to factories as waste paper (*Makulatur*), given to non-Jewish shopkeepers for wrappers or burned.

After the defeat of Germany many books were found which the Nazis had robbed from Jews in various countries. The military authorities handed over part to the American Joint Committee who shipped them to America and distributed them among the *yeshiboth*. A Rabbi reports that among the books given to his *yeshibah* were some which bore the names of synagogues and of private owners who were either still alive or whose relatives were known to be alive. The question was: was it legally obligatory to restore the books to their owners and was it permitted to use the books in the meantime? The Rabbi came to the conclusion that the books had to be returned to their previous owners or to their families, though one was allowed to use the books in the meantime.[36]

Some of the questions raised in the *Responsa* were:[37] is it a duty to

31. Cecil Roth, *The History of the Jews in Italy*, Philadelphia, 1946, p. 548.
32. By Michael Molho and Joseph Nehama, Jerusalem, 1965, pp. 112ff.
33. On the loss of the archives, *vide supra* p. 138.
34. Molho and Nehama, *Destruction of Greek Jewry*, p. 115.
35. *Supra* pp. 139f., 146ff.
36. R. M.P.Teif, in *Ha-Pardes*, vol. XXV, 3 December 1950 (Kislev 711), New York, pp. 5ff.
37. *Vide supra,* pp. 139f., 141.

redeem the torn and loose pages from the non-Jews to avoid their being used for improper purposes? Is it a duty to buy those books as the owner might not have given up hope of recovering them? Is it permitted to make use of the offer of the Slovakian government which is in possession of thousands of books taken from deported Jews? Another question concerns the claim to ownership of books buried and found after the liberation.

5
Prohibition of Childbearing

'And the Egyptians dealt ill with us, and afflicted us, and laid upon us hard bondage. And we cried unto the Lord, the God of our fathers, and the Lord heard our voice, and saw our affliction and our toil, and our oppression.' (Deut. xxvi 6–7.) These two verses which used to be recited in the prayer at the bringing of the first fruit to the Sanctuary have been incorporated into the *Haggadah* read at the *Seder* on *Pesah* night with the comments made by our Sages on each single passage. Thus the expression 'And saw our affliction' is explained as referring to the separation of husband and wife (the wife should not become pregnant) to avoid the boy born being killed,[1] or, according to another interpretation,[2] the Egyptians enforced the separation. 'And our toil'—this refers to the (drowning of the) male children.

These two charges are found in the register of the Nazi crimes. Separation of husband and wife was not carried out merely when families were sent to camps but an order was enforced to avoid or interrupt pregancy. The Fourth Count of Crime against the Jewish People of the indictment against Eichmann was that (a) 'as from 1942 the accused, together with others, devised measures the purpose of which was to prevent childbearing among the Jews in Germany and countries occupied by her', (b) 'The devising of such measures by the accused . . . was also designed to advance the "final solution of the Jewish problem".' (c) 'The measures referred to include:

(1) The instruction by the accused to Dr Epstein who was the Head of the Council of the Elders in the Concentration Camp of Theresienstadt during 1943/1944 concerning the forbidding of births in the camp and the interruption of pregancy by artificial abortion in all cases and at all stages of pregnancy;

(2) An order by the German police in the Baltic countries in 1942 against Jewish women in the Ghetto of Kovno forbidding birth and compelling such women to undergo operations for abortion at all stages of pregnancy.'[3]

What happened if this order had not been carried out and a woman became pregnant and no abortion had taken place? As far as the Jews in Theresienstadt were concerned bearing children was punishable with

---

1–2. See *Minhath Aharon* on the *Haggadah* (Podgorze, 1907, p. 70); *Sepher Abudarham, Seder Ha-Haggadah U-Perushah*, Jerusalem, 1963, p. 227, and particularly the references in *Haggadah Shelemah* by R. M.M.Kasher, Jerusalem, 1961, p. 41.
3. 'The Indictment' (copy of the Wiener Library, London, p. 7). The prohibition of childbearing is mentioned by Isaiah Trunk, *Judenrat*, p. 159, only with reference to Vilna and Kaunas.

deportation of father, mother and child, while in Kaunas (Kovno) the death penalty was imposed on father, mother and child.[4]

At first the order given in Kovno was not always taken seriously by the Germans. However, in July 1942 they repeated their order with a severe threat to persecute pregnant women. Therefore the *Ältestenrat* had to arrange abortions of pregnant women. In spite of the threat some women gave birth to their children secretly.[5]

A tragic case is reported in the following *Responsum*:[6]

On the 20th of Iyyar 702 (May 7 1942) the cursed Germans issued the order that any Jewish woman found to be pregnant 'there is only one law that she be put to death' (cf. Est. IV 11). It happened that on that day a pregnant woman passed by the Jewish hospital of the Ghetto. She was noticed by one of the German murderers who immediately shot her in great anger as she had transgressed their order. The woman fell to the ground and was brought in to the hospital by passers-by in the hope that her life might be saved. However, all was in vain. A Jewish doctor who was then at the hospital was brought in in the hope of saving the child as the woman was in the last days of pregnancy. The doctor was of the opinion that the child might be saved but an operation would have had to be performed on her immediately.

It so happened that R. Ephraim Oshry was present and he was asked whether the operation could be performed or whether it encroached on *nibbul ha-meth* (dishonouring the dead), as it was doubtful whether the child was viable. Furthermore, it was questionable whether the operation could have been performed immediately as the woman might then not have been quite dead. Perhaps by delaying the operation she might be able to recover, while if the operation was performed it would only accelerate her death.

The Rabbi decided that the operation could be performed. This was done and the child was saved. Unfortunately, all good intentions were in vain. 'The cruel murderers who with German thoroughness kept registers of those alive as well as of the dead recorded in detail the victims they had killed. These murderers came to the hospital to take the name of the woman. When one of the murderers saw the baby he took hold of it and smashed its head against the stones of the wall of the hospital.

Because of the prohibition of pregnancy the department for gynae-

---

4. R. E.Oshry, *infra* note 7; Gideon Hausner, *Justice in Jerusalem*, pp. 159, 213.
5. L. Garfunkel, *The Destruction of Kovno's Jewry*, pp. 130f.
6. R. E.Oshry, *Mi-Maamakkim*, II, no. 10.

cology of the Jewish hospital in Kovno was liquidated and arrangements for abortions had to be made.[7]

It appears that unlike in the ghettos of Theresienstadt, Kovno and Wilno the punishment of death was not imposed on a woman who was pregnant or gave birth to a child in another ghetto. However, we learn of one case where a baby born in a camp was taken away by the Germans a few days after birth and nothing more was heard of it.[8]

The second passage in the above-mentioned prayer 'And our toil' which refers to the drowning of the male children only was surpassed by the Nazis many times in a sadistic manner.

Not only were children of both sexes sent to the crematoria (in one *Responsum* we are told of 1,200,000 shoes of little children which had been found)[9] but babies were kicked to death or their heads smashed against the wall. This was one of the favourite sports of the Nazi sadists.[10]

In this connection mention should be made of the fact quoted above (p. 98) that mothers and babies were, immediately after their arrival at the camp, sent to the left, i.e. to be exterminated.

One Rabbi when speaking of the treatment of men and women by the Nazis says: 'As we know, the Nazis made no difference between killing men and women. Indeed they had more satisfaction killing women, particularly if they were pregnant, and when women were there with children they were dashed in pieces.'[11]

7. Garfunkel, *Destruction of Kovno's Jewry*, pp. 109, n. 14, 130. On questions addressed to Oshry, see *Mi-Maamakkim*, I, no. 18 (concerning the insertion of an absorbent), and no. 20 (concerning performing abortion).
8. Chief Rabbi Yizhak Herzog, *Hechal Yizhak*, II, no. 84. It is not mentioned what happened to the child. It should be pointed out that there was a 'market for children' in Lithuania where the Germans sold many children brought from Russia after their parents had been killed or deported to extermination camps. The Lithuanians paid five marks per child! Garfunkel, *Destruction of Kovno's Jewry*, p. 154, note 17.
9. R. Nathan Zebi Friedmann, *Nezer Mattai*, no. 39. In the massacre of children in Kovno by the Germans on 3rd and 4th of Nisan 704 (27 and 28 March 1944), which they called *Kinderaktion*, about 1,200 children were exterminated. See Oshry, *Mi-Maamakkim*, I, no. 16.
10. One SS officer specialized in this killing of children with one blow on the head against a wall. See Lord Russell of Liverpool, *The Scourge of the Swastika*, p. 243; cf. also Heinz Höhne, *The Order of the Death's Head*, p. 361; Bernd Naumann, *Auschwitz*, pp. 123, 133, 138, 199, 385.
11. R. J.M.Toledano, *Bath Ami*, p. 13.

6

The *Agunah* Problem in the Light of the Final Solution

The question most frequently discussed by almost all the Rabbis of various countries in connection with the Nazi holocaust is that of the *agunah*[1] cases. It is of great interest that the Rabbis tried to adopt an extremely lenient view within the limits of the law in matters concerning *iggun*. There are four aspects to be considered as far as the Nazi holocaust is concerned.

(1) If the husband disappeared whether and when his wife is permitted to re-marry. For if she re-marries and her former husband is found to be alive the greatest family tragedy occurs: she must not live with either man (both have to divorce her), and a child born from her second[2] husband is a *mamzer* (illegitimate).

(2) If the wife disappeared whether and when her husband may re-marry. If the wife be alive the husband would infringe the prohibition of bigamy issued by R. Gershom, the Light of the Exile (b. at Metz in 960, d. at Mayence in 1040).

(3) If a woman's brother-in-law disappeared, although there is sufficient evidence of her husband's death she must not re-marry without permission of the Beth Din, if she had no children from her husband, as *halizah* (see Deut. xxv 5ff.) is required. (A similar question arises if husband and child had been deported and killed by the Nazis and there is no evidence as to which of them, the husband or the child, had been killed first. In the latter case *halizah* would be required.)

(4) If the wife disappeared whether and when her husband may marry her sister. For were his wife alive he would infringe a Biblical prohibition of marrying two sisters while both are alive (see Lev. xviii 18).

It is therefore of paramount importance to ascertain whether the missing husband or wife (or brother-in-law) is alive or not.

The problem of *agunah* is not new. It has featured throughout the ages.[3] It occupies a peculiar position in the Jewish legal system. On the

1. The term 'iggun' which occurs once in the Bible (Ruth, i 13) means to 'shut oneself in (or, off)', ('Would ye shut yourself off for them and have no husbands?' Naomi asked her daughters-in-law) and in later literature it adopted (in its passive form) the meaning of a woman (or man) being tied to her (or, in case of a man to be tied to his) spouse.
2. See *Tur Shulhan Aruch, Eben Ha-Ezer*, cap. XVII, no. 56, where a distinction is made between the cases where the child was born before or after the first husband had given his wife a bill of divorce (in the first instance the child is a 'Biblical', in the second a 'Rabbinical' *mamzer*. If the first husband had intercourse with her before she had been divorced by the second husband the child born is a 'Rabbinical' *mamzer*.
3. See the literature mentioned by Yizhak Zeeb Kahana, *Sepher Ha-Agunoth*, Jerusalem, 1954. See also N. Z. Roth, 'Le-Hishthalsheluth Baayath Ha-Agunah' in *Ignace Goldziher Memorial Volume*, Jerusalem, 1958, pp. 59ff.

one hand, the Rabbis were lenient when dealing with *agunah*. Already in the Talmud[4] some rulings have been laid down which appear extremely lenient. Unlike the evidence required in criminal or civil matters, in cases of *agunah* the evidence of one witness is sufficient. Also a woman's evidence and that of a non-Jew (if he does not know that his statement serves as evidence) is admissible. Even hearsay evidence is valid. On the other hand, the evidence has to be perfect and straightforward testifying to the death of the husband so that no doubt should arise as to the possibility of a witness being mistaken in his statements. The rulings laid down about the identification of the person concerned are very strict. Death has to be proved without leaving any shadow of doubt. In the same way as our Sages wished to help the unfortunate woman they intended also to safeguard her against any calamity which might befall her later and cause the breaking up of her family—a great catastrophe in her life and in that of her husband.

In general, cases where there is evidence about the death of the husband are more straightforward, and do not present much difficulty. Not so, however, are the cases where the death of the husband is only probable. Here too, certain rules have been laid down in the Talmud and Codes. Of such rulings mention should be made e.g. of the following few given in the Talmud and *Shulhan Aruch* which were often quoted by the Rabbis dealing with *agunah* cases of the Nazi holocaust. Seeing a man fall into a lions' den cannot serve as evidence of his death since the lions might not have attacked him as they may not have been hungry. This is unlike falling into a pit of serpents and scorpions since through his fall he pressed against them and they therefore attacked and killed him.[5]

Another ruling given in the Talmud[6] the interpretation of which caused a great controversy for centuries and was quoted by almost all Rabbis dealing with the *agunah* problem of the Nazi holocaust is the following: if a man fell into the water which has no visible end (i.e. the shores cannot be seen in all directions by a person standing on the edge of the water) his wife must not re-marry (as it might be possible that the man had been rescued on another shore not visible from the place where the drowning occurred). One Talmud scholar tried to make a distinction by saying that the above ruling of the Rabbis applied only to an ordinary man but not to a learned man for had he come out of the water (i.e. had he been rescued) that fact would have become known. However, his view was rejected. There is no difference, says the Talmud, between an ordinary man and a learned man. *Ex post facto* (*di-abad*) the re-marriage of his wife is valid but *ab initio* (*le-chathillah*) it is forbidden.

4. *Yebamoth*, 122a.
5. Ibid., 121a; *Shulhan Aruch Eben Ha-Ezer*, cap. XVII, no. 29.
6. *Yebamoth*, 121a,f.

In the *Shulhan Aruch*[7] the following ruling is given to this effect: 'Being seen fall into the sea even into the great sea (ocean) cannot serve as evidence of one's death as one might have come out of the water from another shore. . . . Similarly a woman must not re-marry on account of evidence given by one witness that he had seen her husband falling into endless waters and not coming up and any memory of him has been lost (and his name has been forgotten). . . . (However,) if she had re-married (*be-di-abad*) she can stay with her second husband. . . .'

People in a besieged town which had been captured or in a ship which has been lost at sea, or a man who has been led out to be executed are to be regarded as possibly being alive[8] and, therefore, their wives cannot re-marry. Although in the Talmud,[9] according to one view, a difference is made with regard to the person led out to be executed by a non-Jewish court whether the verdict had been signed or not (in the latter case the condemned person might have been freed on account of a bribe while in the former the execution has taken place and his wife would be allowed to re-marry) the *Shulhan Aruch* and other authorities do not take this into consideration (even if t he verdict has been signed a strict view must be adopted. Hence the wife must not re-marry on account of such evidence alone).

All the above rulings play, as we shall see, an important part in the *agunah* problem of the Nazi holocaust.

Questions concerning *agunoth* can, as mentioned above, be found in every country and in every age. Two factors contributed to this. The role the Jews played as merchants and pedlars and their lack of rights which caused them to be exposed to danger more than their non-Jewish neighbours. This applies particularly to the Jews in Germany in the Middle Ages, but also in later centuries in Poland and in the vast Turkish empire where the Jews formed the middle class of the population (the upper classes of the Turks devoted themselves chiefly to military affairs, while the lower classes were occupied with agriculture) the conditions were not much different. The extensive journeys by land and voyages undertaken by Jews in Turkey brought about problems of *agunah* very often either as result of loss of life, when the ships were wrecked or when the Jews were murdered. Another factor responsible for the frequency of *agunah* cases was wars and religious persecutions. The massacre under Chmielnicki in the seventeenth century when thousands of Jews were killed or led into captivity even as far as to Egypt[10] and others fled to Austria, Moravia and Germany brought

---

7. Cf. *Shulhan Aruch Eben Ha-Ezer*, cap. XVII, nos. 32, 34.
8. *Mishnah Gittin* III, 4.
9. *Gittin* 28b. See *Beth Yoseph* on *Tur Shulhan Aruch Eben Ha-Ezer* cap. XVII, no. 36 and the views of the authorities quoted there.
10. See *Darche Noam, E.H.*, no. 5; Kahana, *Sepher Ha-Agunoth*, p. 26.

Q

problems of *agunah*. In this connection mention should be made of the
following fact reported by R. Jacob Emden (this case is quoted by a
Rabbi dealing with the questions of *agunoth* of the Nazi holocaust).
When speaking of the persecution under Chmielnicki, R. Jacob
Emden tells us of the fate of his grandfather R. Jacob, father of Haham
Zebi. In his haste to save his life he separated from his young wife who
remained with her father R. Ephraim Ha-Kohen (b. Wilno, 1616, Rabbi
in Trebitsch [Moravia] then in Ofen, d. 1678). While the family succeeded
in escaping to Moravia R. Jacob was caught by the hordes who had
killed many Jews. When they met R. Jacob the commandant ordered
him to kneel down to be executed. He did so ready to die for *kiddush
ha-Shem*. But suddenly the commandant had mercy on the young man
and instead of striking him with the blade of his sword he only felled
him with the blunt side of his weapon. R. Jacob remained lying on the
ground during day-time, leaving his place at night to seek some food.
When after eight days the hordes had left the place he ran away. Some
people who had hidden themselves and saw him being struck by the
sword thought he had been killed. When two of them came to Trebitsch
to where his father-in-law had fled they testified to the 'fact' that
R. Jacob had been killed. On account of this evidence given by two
trustworthy witnesses R. Joshua Heschel b. Jacob of Lublin permitted
the 'widow' to re-marry. However, the young woman refused to accept
any marriage proposal as she did not give up hope that her husband was
still alive. How great was the surprise of all when half a year later her
husband appeared. From then onwards R. Heschel refused to deal with
agunah cases of that period when there were so many *agunoth* seeing that
he had permitted a married woman to re-marry.[11]

The frequency of cases of *agunoth* caused some Rabbis to arrange
special sections of their *Responsa* dealing with that subject; e.g. those
of the sixteenth century written by R. David ibn abu Zimra.[12]

In fact there exists a list of works containing *Responsa* on *agunoth*.
There is almost no book of Rabbis who make decisions (*baale horaah
ve-yoshbe al midin*) in which one would not find *Responsa* concerning
agunoth.[13]

It is of great interest that almost all the Rabbis were very anxious to
permit an *agunah* to re-marry. A Sephardi Rabbi of the fourteenth and
fifteenth centuries (RIbS) R. Isaac b. Sheshet (b. Valencia, 1326,
d. Algiers, 1408) regards the Ashkenazi Rabbis as more lenient than the

---

11. R. J.Emden, *Megillath Sepher*, ed. by David Kahana, Warsaw, 1896, pp. 6f.; H.
Graetz, *Geschichte der Juden*, X, p. 75; cf. however, Y. M. Zunz, *Ir Ha-Zedek*, pp.
105, 111.
12. *Takkanoth Agunoth* in his *Responsa*, Leghorn, 1828, Warsaw, 1882.
13. See Kahana, *Sepher Ha-Agunoth*, pp. 8ff., 11.

Sephardi Rabbis in this respect.[14] Was this due to the persecutions to which the German Jews were subjected? 'It is fitting for every Rabbi', declared R. Asher b. Jehiel (b. in Germany *c.* 1250, d. in Spain, 1327), 'to investigate all sides to permit re-marriage'[15] and another Rabbi of the sixteenth century states that 'He who permits an *agunah* to re-marry (naturally on religious grounds) it is as if he would have rebuilt a ruin of Jerusalem'.[16] There are still more sayings of the Rabbis of various countries and ages to that effect (to help *agunoth* to re-marry) which show how much importance was attached to solving the problem of an *agunah*.

Quite a new chapter in the history of the *agunah* problem began with the Nazi holocaust. As we have seen above (Part I p. 32) Chief Rabbi Herzog foresaw in May 1939 the great catastrophe which would befall the Jews if war broke out and would affect 'the lives of myriads of the daughters of Israel'.

He then made a suggestion in connection with a conditional bill of divorce which is very old dating back according to the Talmud to the time of David or even, according to another view, to that of Moses.[17] However, there was one point which constituted a difficulty on which he had to consult R. Hayyim Ozer Grodzinski. A reply came only on 15 November 1939 when the war with Poland was over. In his letter R. Grodzinski refers to Chief Rabbi Herzog's 'prophecy' of last summer.

The first cases of *agunoth* of World War II were submitted to the Rabbis even before the end of the war. R. David Shlomoh Kahana (formerly Ab Beth Din of Warsaw, later Rabbi in the Old City of Jerusalem) wrote a pamphlet on the *agunah* question in 1944.[18] Another Rabbi to whom a case was submitted in May 1945 was R. Tabyomi.[19] It concerned a woman whose husband had last been seen in the Warsaw Ghetto during the uprising. The question was whether permission could be found for the woman to re-marry after the war when 'the whole of Germany would be conquered by the United States'. In his reply the Rabbi says, truly the matter was currently not topical but it concerned Torah which we had to study. He then continues that the woman could perhaps be permitted to re-marry only after Germany had been liberated by the Allied armies and all forced-labour camps had been freed and twelve months had elapsed and no news about the missing

14. *Responsa*, no. 378. See Zimmels, *Ashkenazim and Sephardim*, p. 223.
15. *Responsa*, LI, 1.
16. *Responsa Bayyith Hadash He-Hadashoth*, no. 64. See Kahana, *Sepher Ha-Agunoth*, pp. 41f.; Chief Rabbi Yizhak Herzog, *Hechal Yizhak*, I, no. 24.
17. See *Sabbath* 56a, *Kethuboth* 9b; Jacob b. Asher, *Baal Ha-Turim on Num*, XXXII, 21.
18. Quoted by R. Z.H.Meisels, *Kuntras Takkanoth Agunoth*, Bergen-Belsen, 1946, p. 27; R. M.J.Breisch, *Helkath Yaakob*, I, Jerusalem, I, no. 21; Kahana quotes also 'Kuntrasim' of Chief Rabbi Herzog dealing with *agunah* cases, ibid.
19. R. T.Y.Tabyomi (Guttentag), *Erez Tobah*, I, Jerusalem, 1947, no. 60.

husband had been received. The case would then have to be put before the great men in Israel to decide.

The great urgency of dealing with the problem of *agunoth* can be seen from the fact that Rabbis of various countries took up the matter independently immediately after the war and made suggestions to solve it. Two of those Rabbis had been inmates of concentration camps while a third had spent two years in a bunker. Soon after the liberation they regarded it as their sacred duty to devote themselves to solving *agunah* problems.

One of them was R. Jacob Avigdor.[20] He was asked to express his view on the *agunah* question and consequently wrote a treatise on *agunah* at the beginning of the year 706 (i.e. September-October 1945).

Beginning[21] of the year 706 (1945) 'And I was among the captives' (Ezek. I 1) 'a brand plucked out of the fire' (Zech. III 2) I wrote this *Kuntras* whilst in Belgium after I had left cursed Germany—after a period during which my eyes witnessed daily for five years the slaughter and destruction during the years 700–705 (1940–1945). I have been asked by my friends to look into the matter of the *agunoth* who remained after we had been liberated by the British and American armies and who are still in the various camps in Germany. The majority of them are almost certain that their husbands are no longer alive; however, there are no witnesses who could testify to this.

I know my worth after I had spent many years in thick darkness and have seen affliction by the rod of His wrath (cf. Lam. III 1). Naked I entered the Jewish quarter, and naked re-entered the Ghetto. I walked the route to the fiery furnace. I too lay among the dead. On scores of occasions I was saved by sheer miracle from various types of death and fatal diseases. On numerous occasions I myself with my bare hands buried hundreds of victims who fell as martyrs. I put into their graves bundles of scrolls which had been torn into pieces and rolled in the streets. . . This is not the place to speak about this, no ink or paper would suffice for that. But I wish only to point out that I know myself the circumstances as I was smitten with various diseases all over my body. The wounds, bruises and sores can still be seen on my body, I likewise fear that also my innermost soul, mind and spirit have been affected and are still sore, smitten and in pain. In such a state I am, no doubt, incompetent to tackle the complex problems which face the married women, particularly since for about the last six years I have not seen any of the books I would require.

20. 'Iggunah De-Iththa' in *Helek Yaakob*, II, Mexico, 1956, pp. 67ff.
21. Perhaps it refers to the week in which the portion of the Law *Bereshith* is read. In that case it was written between Sunday 30 September and Friday 5 October 1945.

Even here in Belgium I am short of essential books and 'there is no workman without tools'.

However, I must confess that I find no rest. In my opinion only those Rabbis and Talmudic scholars who themselves were in the siege and in straits (cf. Deut. xxviii 53) and drank the cup of staggering (Is. li 17) and who with their own eyes witnessed all are fit to be consulted but he who has not been amid the atrocities can by no means comprehend what happened. . . .

R. Avigdor deals with the problem and tries to prove that from his own knowledge a small percentage only could have escaped death and of the overwhelming majority any inmate who cannot be traced can be presumed dead. Those who survived had their names listed in the registers.

Summing up the points which should be considered the Rabbi says:

(1) All of us Jews of European countries who had been under the Nazi rule were condemned to death by the German government as if a verdict had been signed.[22] No bribe whatsoever could help save the victim as money had by then been taken away, the whole property of the Jews being regarded as property of the Germans.

(2) The transports which had been dispatched were destined for extermination. Hence, if one was sent with a transport it is comparable to a person who is going out to be executed, not having the slightest chance of escape, bribery too being of no avail. In order to reduce the severity of their actions the Germans claimed they were sending the Jews off to labour. To justify this claim they had to leave a small number of Jews alive. So the minority was taken to work while the great majority was led to the furnace or grave.

(3) Most of the minority left died from hunger and terrible sufferings.

(4) From 'the minority of the minority' left some died during the *liquidazie* and the liberation from the plague and evil disease (cholera?).

(5) The 'minority of that minority of the minority' (i.e. the slightest number left) wrote home (and if he did not do so it can be taken as an indication that he was no longer alive).

The other Rabbi, R. Zebi Hirsch Meisels, a former inmate of Auschwitz, published a treatise *Kuntras Takkanoth Agunoth* in Bergen-Belsen where he had been appointed by the British authorities Chief Rabbi of the British Zone. In his introduction he 'apologizes' for dealing with this difficult matter.

22. *Gittin* 28b. *Vide supra* p. 217.

When we were in the labour camp in Auschwitz and in great danger
I besought God that time that the merit of our saintly forefathers
should shield us and save us from the lions' dens, from the wicked,
cruel people and bring us out from darkness to light and that I should
still have the merit to study the Holy Law in quietude and safety and
to occupy myself to the benefit of our crushed brethren who are given
over to trouble. When God helped me to be 'a brand plucked out of
the fire' (Zech. III 2) 'I am among the captives' (cf. Ez. I 1) in Bergen-
Belsen. I hear the cry of the *agunoth* weeping with bitterness of soul.
My heart aches when I see their great grief particularly because I too
was in the labour camp and because my service was really near the
crematorium and I saw with my own eyes the disaster at the time
when our brethren were led to the crematorium, and the entire set-up
in the labour camp,—'hearing cannot be compared with seeing'
therefore new points came to my mind in favour of giving permission
to re-marry. . . . I therefore 'venture' to make suggestions in this
matter which should not be regarded as final. . . .[23]

At the same time and also in following years treatises appeared by
Rabbis on the *agunah* problem.

R. Meir Meiri (Feuerwerger) who had spent two years (1942–44) in
a bunker until the liberation[24] published as a member of the Beth Din
of Brussels a *Kol Kore* urging the Rabbis to deal with the matter of
agunah as it affected the lives of the people. Great dangers were involved
as the people might succumb to immorality (he reports two cases
which had come before him where such danger was imminent). For
that purpose, he wrote his work *Ezrath Nashim* consisting of three
volumes.[25]

R. Simon Efrati (formerly Rabbi of Bendery, Warsaw, at present in
Jerusalem) tells us that immediately after the end of the war, when he
was Rabbi in Warsaw, people came asking for permission to re-marry.
He and his Beth Din tried to search for people who knew the fate of
their fellow men. He published notices (reports) in the Yiddish press
which appeared in Lodz and obtained permission to speak on the
wireless requesting people to come forward with any information which
might be of relevance.[26]

---

23. *Kuntras Takkanoth Agunoth*, Bergen-Belsen, 1946, Introduction.
24. *Vide supra* p. 70.
25. *Ezrath Nashim, ve-hu Takkanath Agunoth*, vol. I–III, Frankfurt-London, 1950–55. On
the *Kol Kore*, see Introduction to vol. I.
26. See his *Responsa Me-Emek Ha-Bacha*, no. 6 (*Kuntras Agunoth*). He then deals with
the *agunoth* whose husbands had been taken to the extermination camps of Oswiecim
(Auschwitz), Maidanek and Treblinka and he adopted a lenient view. In his *Responsum*
consisting of twenty-seven (26) pages he discusses the problem from every angle. At

R. Yizhak Jacob Weiss (formerly Ab Beth Din of Grosswardein, Rumania, then Manchester, at present Ab Beth Din of 'Edah Haredith', Jerusalem) wrote a lengthy *Responsum* on the *agunah* question immediately after the war. It was addressed to the Rabbis who had taken part at a meeting held in Arad (Rumania) in summer 1945. At that time the question of *agunim*, i.e. men whose wives had disappeared during the Nazi holocaust, was discussed. At his suggestion a committee was elected *Vaad shel Hatharath Agunoth* to deal with the matter and their decisions would be final. However, they soon realized that no less important was the question of *agunoth*, i.e. wives whose husbands had disappeared and that of husbands whose wives had disappeared and who wished to marry their sisters. He then discusses these questions in his *Responsa*.[27]

R. Jacob Mosheh Toledano (Chief Rabbi of Tel Aviv-Jaffa), tells us in the Introduction to his work on the *agunah* problem *Bath Ami*[28] that he and the members of his Beth Din, R. Shmuel Yizhak Jaffe and R. Mosheh Shimshon Wasserman had dealt with more than two hundred cases of *agunim* (men whose wives were missing) and forty *agunoth* (women whose husbands were missing) during the last year. Similar applications were being submitted every week. Because of the variety of problems involved in such cases he composed his book in which he expressed his view and gave a summary of the laws which might, no doubt, be a helpful guide to other Rabbis who have similar *agunah* cases coming before them.

The work *Bath Ami* consists of six chapters each of them subdivided in sections (the first four chapters deal with *agunoth*; on chapters five and six—*vide infra*). These chapters are: (1) on evidence about the

---

the end of it he requests the Rabbis of Israel and diaspora to read his *kuntras* and apologizes for having dealt with that subject. He did it purely out of sympathy for the unfortunate daughters of Israel with whom he suffered together 'and nearly sank in the ocean of blood and tears of our Jewish brethren in the exile of Poland and Russia. My soul is fully sated (cf. Ps. cxxiii 4) after having seen with my own eyes their ascending the hearth to the fire of the Nazi inferno and their annihilation and destruction in Russia. . . .'

27. *Minhath Yizhak*, I, nos. 1ff. R. Weiss is of the opinion that every inmate of the ghetto before being deported to Auschwitz has had his presumption of being alive impaired. With regard to a husband who had been led to the crematorium there are two possibilities: either he had been seen having been put on the left side or he was not seen later by those who had been selected for labour and who met in the bath-house, etc., which indicates that he had been sent to the crematorium. Furthermore, the possibility of escaping by giving bribe does not apply in our case as the victims had been deprived by their enemies of everything the possessed. R. Yizhak Zebi Sopher of Temesvar agrees with him that being put in left side is equal to falling into a pit full with serpents and scorpions (*vide supra* p. 216) in which case the wife of the victim may re-marry on account of the evidence by one witness or permission may be given on account of the evidence of two witnesses to a husband who wishes to marry the sister of his wife who had disappeared in such circumstances.

28. Tel Aviv, 1947.

death of the husband and his being killed; (2) when there is evidence that the husband was only taken in the carriages (*keronoth*) to the gas chamber and to extermination (*hashmadah*) or that he was in the ghettos which had been destroyed by the Nazis and is still missing; (3) when evidence exists only that the husband was living in a country conquered by the Nazis during the war and it is not known whether he was taken to the extermination camp or was in the ghettos which had been destroyed, he cannot be traced and is still missing (when speaking about the fate of the inhabitants of the countries conquered by the Nazis he says that 'the majority of the non-Jews remained alive, while the majority of the Jews in most countries invaded, e.g. Belgium, Holland, Serbia, Greece, France, Austria, etc., were exterminated. Only in a few of the conquered countries, e.g. Tripolitania, Tunisia, Rumania and Hungary did the majority of Jews remain alive'); (4) when the *agunah* requires *halizah* and the fate of the levir is unknown.[29]

Mention should be made of two other treatises on the *agunah* problem which appeared in 1946, one written by R. Israel Yaakob Zuber in Stockholm[30] and the other by R. Klein in Budapest.[31] The latter's work is called *Atereth Shlomoh, Sepher Takkanath Agunoth shel Milhemeth Ha-Olam*. It deals with *agunoth* of World War I, to which the Rabbi's son, R. Yekuthiel Klein, made additions concerning *agunoth* of World War II. The Rabbi tries to adopt a lenient view but remarks that his statement should be regarded only as 'Theory' and not to be used in practice without consent of the great Rabbis. His son then adds his own suggestion concerning the *agunoth* of World War II since much more leniency could be applied as there existed great differences in favour of the present *agunah* compared with the *agunah* in previous years. These differences were due to the position of the Jews in political and social respects during World War I and World War II.[32]

The only Rabbi in our times who refused to deal with cases of *agunoth* was R. Joseph Zebi Duschinsky.[33] The reason was he was afraid that the permission given by him to re-marry might turn out to be wrong as happened with Rabbi Heschel (in connection with the Chmielnicki persecution in 1648).[34] Rabbi Duschinsky also reports a similar case after World War I concerning a woman whose husband was missing for fifteen years. On account of the evidence of a non-Jew she asked for permission to re-marry but he, R. Duschinsky, refused to

29. *Bath Ami*, p. 31.
30. Quoted by Meisels, *Kuntras Takkanoth Agunoth*, p. 31, no. 123.
31. Budapest, 1946.
32. On these differences, *vide infra* pp. 229f.
33. *Responsa MhRIZ*, Jerusalem, 1956, no. 126. The *Responsum* is dated: 5th of Sivan 706 (4 June 1946).
34. *Vide supra* p. 218.

consent to this; however, a great and famous Rabbi gave her permission to re-marry. She did so (against the will of Rabbi Duschinsky) on a Thursday and on the following day, on Friday, a message arrived that her husband was living in Moscow. She obtained a bill of divorce from him later. 'And now a similar, terrible, case has become known.' He therefore refused to deal with matters of *agunah*. In principle he objects to relying on the fact that being placed on the left side (*vide infra*, p. 227) should serve as grounds to give permission to the woman to re-marry. 'This is a weak proof, as I know several young men who stood on the left side and were saved. . . .'

He then quotes[35] *Sepher Ha-Mikzaoth* of R. Hananeel,[36] in connection with the women re-marrying whose husbands died as martyrs. According to this work, all Israel had to mourn the death of a martyr and his wife should never re-marry. Although R. Duschinsky does not regard it as a final decision (*pesak gamur*) he feels it must be duly considered.

There were also several other great Rabbis who dealt with the problem of *agunah*, e.g. R. Mordecai Jacob Breisch in Zurich, R. J.J. Weinberg in Montreux, R. Mosheh Feinstein in New York and Dayan Yehezkiel Abramski in London. However, the centre of activity of the Rabbis helping *agunoth* was Jerusalem. There had existed already from the time of World War I a special office devoted to *agunah* cases called *Ihud Rabbanim Ole Polin, Mahlakah Le-Inyane Agunoth Ha-Milhamah*. This office after World War II was under the administration of R. Shlomoh David Kahana. In a letter dated 22nd of Tebeth 708 (4 January 1948)[37] he writes that as far as World War II is concerned there were in his office about 1,800 statements of witnesses sent to him by Rabbis of the camps in Germany, Sweden, Cyprus and from other countries like Poland, Russia, etc.

On another occasion[38] he points out that during the war he had dealt with about 3,000 cases of *agunoth* which had been sent to him by all the Rabbis of the camps with their questions. In his replies he takes into account all the factors which were in favour of each woman in accordance with the statement of the witnesses answering sometimes more, sometimes less extensively 'and thank God till now no mistake (*michshol*) has occurred through me'. It did not happen even once that an *agunah* who sought permission to re-marry learned later that her husband was alive.[39]

35. From the *Responsa* of R. Hayyim Or Zarua, no. 14 *ad fin.*
36. Edited by R. Simhah Assaf, Jerusalem, 1947. On the author and the passage quoted, see ibid., no. 16, p. 10 and Introduction, pp. 9ff.
37. Printed in the *Responsa Helkath Yaakob* of R. Breisch, I, no. 21.
38. *Helkath Yaakob*, II, no. 30.
39. On his *kuntras* on *agunah* problems, *vide supra* note 18 and R. Eliezer Waldenberg, *Ziz Eliezer*, III, no. 26.

Many problems were solved by Chief Rabbi Herzog of Jerusalem. Some of his *Responsa* are contained in his *Hechal Yizhak*[40] but there are several comprehensive treatises still in manuscript which deal with the *agunah* question.[41]

R. Eliezer Waldenberg (at present Ab Beth Din of Jerusalem) wrote a *kuntras* on *agunoth* on 9 November 1947, in reply to a question submitted to him by R. David Gross, Ab Beth Din of Bratislava (later in Jerusalem).[42] Two factors make, as mentioned already, the problem of *agunah* caused by the Nazi holocaust quite outstanding: (1) the vast number of women affected (in view of the fact that a third of our people perished, the number of *agunah* cases caused by the Nazis amounts to tens of thousands) and (2) obtaining suitable evidence about the death of the husband. Unlike all previous persecutions, only in exceptional cases, could witnesses be found to testify to the death of a particular man, as those who witnessed his death were themselves executed afterwards.

These facts are often stressed by the Rabbis dealing with the *agunah* problems of the Nazi holocaust. It is rather significant that a special section in *Ozar Ha-Posekim* on *Eben Ha-Ezer*[43] is devoted to the *agunah* problem of the Nazi persecution which, as the editors remark, has not its like even in the darkest periods of our history. The Nazis used most cruel methods to exterminate our people. These methods varied from place to place and from time to time. Hence the treatment of this problem differs from the *halachic* point of view. Concluding their introduction, the editors refer to the significance of that section which, apart from practical importance, is of great value from the historical point of view. It serves as a holy memorial of the martyrs on the one hand, and as a monument perpetuating the disgrace of the murderers on the other.

As the circumstances under which the husbands disappeared differed in several respects the Rabbis who had to decide cases of *agunoth* were confronted with a formidable task. They tried to classify these cases. Chief Rabbi Herzog has made the following classification of the cases of *agunoth* in a *Responsum* written on the 25th of Tishri, 5706 (2 October 1945).[44]

(1) Cases where evidence exists that the husband had been taken to the gas chamber.

(2) Presumption. It is well known that in many instances the

40. Parts I and II, Jerusalem, 1960–67.
41. R. Kahana in Breisch's *Helkath Yaakob*, I, no. 22. However, this was written at the beginning of 1948.
42. *Ziz Eliezer*, no. 25.
43. On cap. XVII, Vol. 7, pp. 124a,ff.
44. *Op. cit.*, I, no. 24.

murderers divided the victims into two groups: those on the right and those on the left. The former were destined 'to live' (i.e. to forced labour), the latter 'to die'. It has been established that the majority of the first group did not survive, but with regard to the second group there is a clear presumption (*hezkath rubba de-rubba*) (a very great majority) that they were killed. Only in very rare cases was someone able to jump from the train and escape.

(3) Cases where the husbands were sent to extermination camps and their fate is unknown.

(4) Cases where the husbands were brought into forced labour camps and all memory of them has been lost.

(5) Cases of husbands who were in the zones of destruction and disappeared and nothing is known of the circumstances of their removal or what happened to them.

A similar classification is made by R. Zebi Hirsch Meisels in his *Kuntras Takkanoth Agunoth* written in Bergen-Belsen in 706. The Rabbi points out that his decisions are to be regarded as suggestions only and not as final. His classification is as follows:[45]

(1) Cases where evidence exists that the husband had been sent to the left side in Auschwitz, or to other places known as extermination camps. Permission should be given to his wife to re-marry.

(2) Where there is a witness that the husband had been deported with a transport to the camp where there were gas chambers, but the witness does not know to which side he was sent. There is also then a possibility of permitting his wife to re-marry.

(3) Where the husband had been seen in the labour camp of Auschwitz or similar camp. There are, as mentioned above,[46] three different possibilities: (i) either the husband had been seen employed in hard labour, or (ii) doing light work, e.g. being employed in the kitchen or bath-house, etc., or (iii) in the hospital of the labour camp being already weak and ill. In the last case (iii) there is also a possibility of permitting his wife to re-marry. In the first case (i), if he was in a good state of health, the Beth Din must investigate when the husband had been seen and whether from that time until the end of the war the majority of the inmates of that camp had died or been killed. Furthermore, his wife has to be questioned whether she had made arrangements with her husband in case they should be saved, to write to an agreed address to inform each other of their survival. The Beth Din must inquire whether the husband had lived in disharmony with his wife or whether there was any other factor which might have been the reason

---

45. Pp. 5, 38.
46. *Vide supra* Part I, p. 101.

for his not coming home. Naturally, the woman too had to declare that she was sure had her husband survived he would have come to her. If it turned out that the majority of the inmates of that camp had been killed or died after the husband had been seen, and his wife had made arrangements with him to get in touch with each other if they survived, and she was sure had he been alive he would have come home and she had made searches in newspapers and lists of survivors and also evidence of witnesses existed from which could be gathered that most of those who survived were known, there was also a possibility of permitting re-marriage. In case (ii) where the husband had been employed in the kitchen, etc., and in a good state of health the matter had to be considered very carefully.

(4) Where there is evidence that the husband had been seen in such a ghetto from where all inmates had been deported to Auschwitz (or to a similar extermination camp) but he was not seen in the transport the Beth Din had to take into consideration the eventualities mentioned in the previous case and there might be a possibility of being lenient.

(5) Where there is evidence that the husband was in the town when the enemy had entered it and he was not seen any more and the possibility existed that he might have fled before the ghetto had been set up, the Rabbi is hesitant in permitting re-marriage.

(6) In those towns from where the Russians had deported men, women and children to their country of whom 'at present little by little returned' there was no possibility of permitting the wives of the deportees to re-marry.

Similar but of greater variety are the cases dealt with in *Ozar Ha-Posekim*.[47]

In general, as we have seen, the Rabbis dealing with *agunah* cases showed great compassion for the unfortunate women left bereft of their husbands and in most cases, of all their families. They tried to be lenient because of one positive and of one negative factor. The former was due to trying to help the unfortunate women and to rebuild the people, the latter was to avoid the women succumbing to immorality[48] (or entering forbidden marriages, living out of wedlock, etc.) which would have disastrous consequences for their offspring.

Using as a heading the statement found in a *Responsum* of R. Joel Sirkes (d. 1640) that 'if one Rabbi permits an *agunah* to re-marry, it is as. if he had rebuilt one of the ruins of Jerusalem'[49] Chief Rabbi Herzog[50]

---

47. *Loc. cit.*
48. This reason is found already in a *Responsum* of R. Mosheh Trani (quoted by Kahana, *Sepher Ha-Agunoth*, p. 24) and was often stressed by the Rabbis dealing with the *agunoth* of the Nazi holocaust, *vide infra*.
49. *Vide supra* note 16.
50. Herzog, *Hechal Yizhak*, vol. I, no. 24.

in discussing the *agunah* problem says: 'Many thousand times more is it our holy duty to take pains to permit the re-marriage of the *agunoth* of the terrible destruction caused by the Nazi holocaust when a third of our people—about 6,000,000 among them 1,200,000 children—was exterminated. It is therefore our duty (great *mizvah*) for this reason, too, to seek permission for re-marriage within the regulations of our *halachah* in the hope that thereby a portion of our people will be rebuilt and the seed of our father Abraham will be revived. . . .'

Also the following statement of a Rabbi deserves to be mentioned here:

In his attempt to show the leniency which could be applied to cases of *agunoth* nowadays, a Rabbi[51] contrasts the conditions of the Jews under the Nazis with those during World War I when his father suggested that a lenient view be adopted subject to the consent of the great Rabbis. These differences are of interest from the historical point of view. The Rabbi points out:

(1) In former days, ten per cent of Jewish soldiers were killed—while now[52] about that amount survived.

(2) During World War I, Jews were enlisted as soldiers faithful to their country and birthplace being also protected by equality of rights. But now they have been taken as enemies for the purpose of extermination and not only were they not protected but all the endeavours of the officers of the army[53] were to kill and 'to give Jacob for a spoil' (cf. Isaiah XLII 24).

(3) In World War I it could have happened that some individuals in Russia during the revolution under Denikin[54] and Kerenski[55] went to Japan and China, etc., to places unknown where there were no Jews. But during the last war the camps of the Jews were closed from beginning to end to such an extent that one could very seldom escape from them and even in that case one put oneself in danger as no place of refuge could be found. Had a man survived he would have re-appeared and would have been registered in the official offices in Russia as well as in all other European countries, or at least one would have heard about him.

(4) Most of the people who returned had been enlisted in labour

---

51. R. Y.Klein in his 'Addenda' to *Atereth Shlomoh* by his father R. S.Klein *vide supra* (p. 224), Budapest, 1946, pp. 82ff.

52–53. The writer of this treatise was living in Hungary where Jews were taken into labour battalions, *vide supra* pp. 41,124 and *infra* p. 298. Perhaps the Jews in general are meant.

54–55. After the abdication of the czar on 15 March 1917 a provisional government was formed under Kerenski. On 7 November 1917, a Soviet Republic was established. This was followed by the civil war (1918–21) associated with the name of Denikin, one of the generals and organizers of the 'White Army' directed against the Soviet regime. Cf. S. Dubnow, *Weltgeschichte des jüdischen Volkes*, X, pp. 515ff.

camps. Those who had not returned from there had been killed at the end of the war in those dangerous days by the order of Himmler. Not the slightest minority (*miuta de-miuta*) could escape this fate unless one went into hiding or if a miracle happened that the Russian or American armies reached that particular place sooner than the Germans anticipated. In that case those who had escaped were immediately registered by the army who had liberated them and who cared for their safe return home. No one escaped our attention. This was not the case during World War I when people could hide themselves or were brought against their will to an unknown place.

(5) After World War I the prisoners could return home only after several years. Now all prisoners, particularly Jews, may return home without being hindered from the countries conquered by the Russians as well as from those conquered by the Americans, British and French armies.

(6) According to statistics, about thirty per cent more women than men survived,[56] this caused some laxity in morals. Hence if the Rabbis do not look into the matter and hasten to help, the women would sink into the abyss and they themselves would solve the problem.

As is well known, the matter of *agunah* is very complicated and many legal aspects are involved. Terms like *rubba* (a majority), *rubba de-rubba* (a majority of the majority), *tre rubba bau be-bath ahath* (two majorities occurring at the same time), *miuta* (a minority), *miuta de-miuta* (a minority of the minority), *hazakah* (presumption), *kabua* (fixed) and various other principles, particularly *umdana de-Rabbi Eliezer mi-Verdun* (the supposition, or estimation of R. Eliezer of Verdun): 'were the husband alive he would have come', or, *abad zichro* (all memory of him is lost) are often found.

How careful the Rabbis have to be when dealing with an *agunah* case can be seen from the following ruling: Permission for re-marriage, in cases which are not straightforward, granted even by the greatest scholar should be given only after he has consulted two other great Rabbis who agree with him. This ruling became general practice through all the ages.[57]

Mention should be made of some rulings of the Talmud and Codes in the light of the Nazi holocaust.

It has already been pointed out that, according to the Talmud and the *Shulhan Aruch*,[58] in three cases a person's death cannot be presumed so as to permit his wife to re-marry: a person in a town conquered by the

---

56. Cf., however, Karen Gershon, *Postscript*, p. 23, where it is said: 'As a result of the Nazi extermination policy, the majority of the Jewish survivors consists of young people. Men outnumber women. . . .'
57. Waldenberg, *Ziz Eliezer*, no. 25, p. 107, quoting *Aruch Ha-Shulhan*, cap. XVII, no. 255.
58. *Gittin* 28b; *Shulhan Aruch Eben Ha-Ezer*, XVII, no. 36 (*supra* p. 217).

enemy after siege, or in a ship lost at sea or a man who has been led out to execution, as they have to be regarded as possibly alive.

This ruling, says one Rabbi, does not apply to a person caught by the Nazis. In the instances enumerated above when a minority, however small, escaped, that minority could be regarded as saved and out of danger. But in the case of a Jew of whom we are sure that he had been in a special concentration camp (the Rabbi mentions the extermination camp of Gross-Rosen) where the majority of the inmates was massacred it could not be assumed that anyone escaped. Had he escaped he would have fallen from a trap into a pit as it is known that wherever the person who had escaped set his foot he was again in danger. This danger increased from day to day because of fear, hunger and physical weakness, etc. Even if he succeeded in hiding himself, which the Rabbi regards as almost impossible, the Germans employed all forces of science, technology, trained dogs and imposing the death penalty on a non-Jew for helping a Jew in any way (so his chance of survival was out of the question).[59]

Evidence about a person led out to be executed. It is of interest that the view that 'a person led out to be executed by a non-Jewish court (the verdict having been signed by the court) should be regarded as dead, as the court did not accept bribes' gained momentum during the Nazi holocaust. 'In our case the principle of the possibility of accepting bribes does not apply as they had been commanded "thou shalt save alive nothing that breatheth" (Deut. xx 16) and "they ordained and took upon themselves" (Est. ix 27) to carry out this order. . . .'[60]

A similar view was expressed by other Rabbis that in our case the fear of taking bribes does not exist as the victims had been deprived of everything they possessed and the intention of the murderers was to exterminate the Jews.[61]

The assumption of receiving a bribe indirectly, i.e. through relatives of the victims living in other countries, was dismissed since those carrying out the death sentence did so according to instructions they received from their superiors living in the capital of Germany. Hence bribing the murderers to change the verdict was impossible. Once the fate of the victim was decided not even the superior would have changed his mind.[62]

Referring to the ruling about the falling into a lions' den (see *supra*

59. See Breisch, *Helkath Yaakob*, I, no. 17, p. 42b.
60. Ibid. See also Meisels, *Kuntras Takkanoth Agunoth*, nos. 2, 125.
61. Weiss, *Minhath Yizhak*, I, no. 3; R. Shlomoh David Kahana in Breisch's *Helkath Yaakob*, II, no. 30; Rath, *Kol Mebasser*, I, no. 84; R. M.Feinstein, *Iggeroth Mosheh, Eben Ha-Ezer*, no. 44.
62. R. Yizhak Zebi Sopher in Weiss's *Minhath Yizhak*, I, no. 4.

p. 216) one Rabbi says: the whole reason why seeing a person fall into a lions' den cannot serve as evidence for his death is that the place is large and the lions may not have been hungry at that time and therefore they might not have attacked him. (By corollary, it appears if not for the reason they might not have been hungry, the above evidence would be acceptable.) Hence our case, where someone falls into the hands of those wild beasts in the form of human beings of whom we know that they were unquenchably thirsty for the blood of Jews, like one who drinks salty water which causes still greater thirst—a matter which is more obvious than the evidence of a hundred witnesses—the evidence given is acceptable as it is worse than falling into a lions' den or a pit of snakes.[63] This latter point is proved in the following way: With regard to the report about Joseph having been thrown into a pit (Gen. xxxvii 24) the Talmud[64] tells us that, although there was no water in it, serpents and scorpions were there. If so, why did Reuben who wished to save Joseph advise his brothers to throw Joseph into this most dangerous pit? Reuben thought, says the *Zohar*,[65] it was better to throw him there where, if he is a *Zaddik* (righteous man), a miracle could happen to him not to be attacked by the snakes, and not let him fall into the hands of his enemies who would show no mercy to him. How much more does this apply to a Jew who falls into the hands of an enemy who regards Jewish blood as cheap and no chance of survival exists?[66]

Evidence about a person having been sent 'to the left side', i.e. to be gassed, is tantamount to seeing someone falling into a pit of snakes which would suffice to permit his wife to re-marry.[67]

Great significance was attached to the decision of an Italian Tosaphist R. Eliezer[68] b. Samuel of Verona[69] in the case of an *agunah* whose husband had disappeared seven years earlier in endless waters (i.e. the shores of the water cannot be seen by a person standing on the edge).[70]

63. Breisch, *Helkath Yaakob*, I, no. 17. In this connection it is noteworthy to quote the following passage from the diary of an inmate of the Warsaw Ghetto (Chaim A. Kaplan, *Scroll of Agony*, p. 254, entry dating from 19 May 1942): 'The Nazi is not a normal human being, and it is open to question whether he is human at all. Perhaps he is nothing but the missing link between man and the animals. . . . The goring of Nazis is worse than that of a killer bull. People fear them as they would a lion. When a German appears in the streets of the ghetto, everyone crosses over to the opposite sidewalk just as he keeps his distance from a beast of prey . . .'. 'When one falls into the hands of the Nazis he falls into the abyss', ibid., p. 316, entry: 2 August 1942.
64. *Sabbath* 22a.
65. On Gen. xxxvii 26, pp. 185a,f.
66. Breisch, *Helkath Yaakob*; Meisels, *Kuntras Takkanoth Agunoth*, no. 27, p. 11; Tabyomi (Guttentag), *Erez Tobah*, I, no. 60, p. 185f.; R. H.M.Roller in *Responsa Nezer Mattai* of R. N.Z.Friedmann, no. 39.
67. Sopher in Weiss's *Minhath Yizhak*, no. 4.
68. Sometimes he is called: R. Eleazar, see E. Urbach, *Baale Ha-Tosaphoth*, p. 357.
69. Erroneously written in some works: Verdun.
70. *Vide supra* p. 216.

R. Eliezer[71] argued that since the Talmud states only 'such a woman must not re-marry' and not 'she must *never* re-marry' the Talmud had in mind that the prohibition of re-marrying is not meant to be permanent. It is left entirely to the Rabbis of each generation and God-fearing men to decide the cases which arise in their time. They should not decide a case merely by following the majority (in our case: the majority of ships which sink at sea sink with their passengers aboard). However, if there were other factors (*hazakoth*, presumptions) indicating that the husband must have died, then they could combine those *hazakoth* with the principle of 'following the majority'.

R. Eliezer gave his decision in the following case: in 1214 a ship sank on one Friday night during a great storm near Pesaro and Fano when according to one version sixty (according to another version, nine) ships sank. There was also another ship which was carrying Jews that was wrecked on the Sabbath. However, the passengers were saved and returned to their homes in Italy on the termination of the Sabbath.

In that ship which sank were R. Solomon b. Jacob of Verona and another Jew of Fano with his son whom he intended to bring to Verona to study there. At the sea shore two containers of oil were found which the wife[72] of R. Solomon's fellow passenger recognized as belonging to her husband. R. Solomon, the husband of the *agunah*, was about twenty-four years old (or less). His wife was about twenty years old. They had a son and a daughter. R. Jacob, R. Solomon's father, was still alive and had become rich through an inheritance, a fact which was commonly known. He had sent messengers to Spain (where his son had married and had children born to him) and brought them (i.e. the son and daughter mentioned above) to Verona. R. Solomon, who had remained in Spain, was then on his voyage from there to his family in Verona in accordance with his father's wish when his ship sank.

R. Eliezer of Verona then argued: there is a *hazakah* (presumption) that if R. Solomon and his fellow passengers were alive they would not have stayed away from their homes for seven years, since we can see that the passengers of another ship wrecked on the Sabbath returned home at the termination of the Sabbath. .... There is also a *hazakah* that a son does not transgress the commandment of honouring his father and mother (as his father had told him to return to Verona). There is a further *hazakah* that one does not transgress the law of one's marital duties (as his wife was in Verona). There is an additional

71. Parts of R. Eleazar's *Responsum* and the correspondence on it are found in the *Responsa* of R. Meir Rothenburg, Prague, no. 572; Mordechai on *Yebamot ad fin.*, no. 92; R. Judah b. Asher, *Zichron Yehudah*, no. 92, pp. 52f., Aptowitzer, *Mebo* to *Sepher RABIAH*, pp. 452f., see also pp. 193, 423, 429ff., 460. The full text of the *Responsum* is printed in Herzog's *Hechal Yizhak*, I, no. 23.
72. On the version see *Hechal Yizhak*, I, p. 114, note 36.

R

hazakah that a father has compassion on his little children (who were in Verona). Furthermore, R. Solomon had taken upon himself a legal commitment to teach the son of his landlord.

In view of all these *hazakoth* supported by the principle of following the majority (the majority of those sunk in endless waters are dead) R. Eliezer was of the opinion that the *agunah*, the wife of R. Solomon, may re-marry *ab initio*.

R. Eliezer's *Responsum* was sent to the Rabbis of the Rhine provinces; however, they did not accept R. Eliezer's *umdana* (supposition) and his interpretation of the Talmudic phrase.

R. Eliezer's decision was subject to controversy in the sixteenth century[73] and it was R. Joseph Caro who decided that ' "he who gives decisions in arrogance" (*Aboth* IV 7) to permit a woman to re-marry on the basis of that *Responsum* will have to account for it. Therefore "he that keepeth his soul holdeth himself far from it" (Prov. XXII 5).'[74]

It was later R. Moses Sopher (d. 1839)[75] who took R. Eliezer's view into consideration, namely, if the husband were alive he would have returned home eventually. Hence, if a certain time has elapsed and nothing has been heard of the man he could be regarded as dead and there would be no Biblical prohibition for his wife but only a Rabbinical injunction. The reason for R. Moses Sopher's view was the change of conditions at this time.

> Particularly in our country where there are post offices and traffic is frequent; even if a man were at the other end of the world he would be able to communicate with his family through the post. . . . If a certain time elapses required for his name to be forgotten and all memory of him being lost[76] and no communication from him has been received it is most probable that he is no longer alive. . . . Although far be it from me to permit re-marriage in the first instance on account of this view[77] . . . but every missing husband is in the category of a scholar (*vide supra* p. 216) so that prohibition of re-marriage would then be only of Rabbinical nature. . . .

R. Eliezer's assumptions (*umdanoth*) and R. Moses Sopher's distinction between former and current days 'to which even R. Joseph Caro would agree'[78] gained momentum in the period after the Nazi holocaust

---

73. See R. M.Meiri (Feuerwerger), *Ezrath Nashim*, II, pp. 111f., 147, 193.
74. *Beth Yoseph* on *Tur Eben Ha-Ezer*, Cap. XVII, *s.v. niseth.*
75. *Hatham Sopher E.H.*, Pressburg, 1965, no. 65, p. 43b; no. 58, p. 38b ('Nowadays times have changed, post offices are in every town and country. Even from Turkey we can receive letters after a short time and also newspapers can give information to one's family'); no. 48, p. 28b.
76. On the definition of the terms *abad zichro* and *nishtakah shemo*, see Herzog, *Hechal Yizhak*, I, no. 24, p. 127.
77-78. Cf. e.g. Kahana, in Breisch's, *Helkath Yaakob*, II, no. 30. Cf. also Herzog, *Hechal Yizhak* II nos. 1, 10; Meiri. *Ezrath Nashim*. II. p. 121.

when Rabbis had to deal not with a single case but with thousands of cases. These factors were taken into consideration particularly in view of the fact that changes have occurred even since R. Moses Sopher's time, which would strengthen R. Eliezer's view (i.e. had the husband been alive he would have informed his family). 'Currently when newspaper, telegraph, radio, special search bureaux and the Red Cross (Tracing Department) exist and people must hold identity cards no one who is alive could escape attention.'[79]

The phrase 'how much more should *umdana* apply nowadays' can be found again and again in the *Responsa* which deal with *agunoth* of the Nazi holocaust. 'The *umdana* of R. Eliezer has nowadays become seven times (a hundred times, a thousand times) stronger than it was in his days.'[80]

'Today three *umdanoth* can be considered: were the husband alive (1) he would have returned, (2) or he would have communicated with his family, (3) or his family would have discovered his whereabouts from the various search bureaux. Hence, even those who disagree with R. Eliezer of Verona would agree that these three *umdanoth* combined rank at least as strong as one "majority".'[81]

However, the acceptance of R. Eliezer's *umdana* is not in itself sufficient to permit re-marriage in the first instance. The effect of R. Eliezer's *umdana* is that re-marriage would not constitute an infringement of Biblical law, though it would still be prohibited by Rabbinic law. Nevertheless in certain cases[82] of *agunoth* there are additional grounds for permitting their re-marriage even in the first instance with the approval of Rabbinic law.[83] Among these grounds is the mitigating factor that the *agunah* might succumb to immorality[84] coupled with the fact that the vast number of women affected constitutes a *shaath ha-dehak* (time of emergency) which according to some authorities amounts at least to a *di-abad* case.[85]

---

79. Often stressed by the Rabbis. cf. e.g. Meiri. *Ezrath Nashim*; Herzog, *Hechal Yizhak*, I, no. 24, II, no. 10; Kahana in *Helkath Yaakob*, II, no. 30.
80. Cf. e.g. Herzog, *Hechal Yizhak*, I, nos. 24, 25, 31; II, nos. 1, 9, 11, 12.
81. Meiri, *Ezrath Nashim*, II, p. 122.
82. It should be pointed out that the the the entire problem of the *agunoth* of the Nazi holocaust is very complicated and requires special study. For a full understanding one must consult the classical works of Chief Rabbi Herzog's *Responsa* in *Hechal Yizhak* dealing with *agunoth*; Meiri, *Ezrath Nashim*; the *Kuntrasim* by R. Z.H.Meisels and R. E.Waldenberg; the *Responsa* of R. M.Breisch, R. I.J.Weiss, etc.
83. Cf. e.g. Meisels, *Kuntras Takkanoth Agunoth*, nos. 36, 49, pp. 13f., 16; Meiri, *Ezrath Nashim*, II, p. 146.
84–85. Cf. Breisch, *Helkath Yaakob*, I, no. 18; II, no. 29; Meisels, *Kuntras Takkanoth Agunoth*, nos. 54, 56ff., pp. 17ff.; Meiri, *Ezrath Nashim*, II, pp. 208ff.; Weiss, *Minhath Yizhak*, nos. 92, 99; Herzog, *Hechal Yizhak*, I, nos. 24, 29 (pp. 125, 160); II, nos. 10, 11 (pp. 51, 54); R. Jonathan (MhRI) Steif, *Responsa*, no. 21. On immorality after the liberation, *vide supra* Part I, pp. 143f.; *shaath ha-dehak* is more favourable than *di-abad*, cf. Meiri, *Ezrath Nashim* II, p. 208, and R. J. Zirelsohn in Meisels's *Mekaddshe*

So as to make no distinction some Rabbis suggest that the above grounds should apply also to a religious woman where the fear of immorality may not apply.[86] A phrase often used by the Rabbis is 'there is no greater "time of emergency" than that of our days. . . . Those who opposed R. Eliezer did not live at a time of such emergency.'[87]

Chief Rabbi Herzog is hesitant in applying the *umdana* of R. Eliezer of Verona in cases where the husband may have fled to Russia, as it was difficult to receive information about those in Siberia. In such cases the matter required further consideration.[88]

R. Eliezer's principle is not to be employed where the husband did not live in harmony with his wife or had left her because of a quarrel and later 'fell into waters the shores of which cannot be seen'. It is possible he may have been saved and changed his identity to conceal his whereabouts from his wife, or he had fled to evade repaying his creditors, or had left to live with another woman elsewhere. R. Eliezer had in mind an upright man whom he knew and who he was certain had lived peacefully with his wife and did not wish to escape from her.[89]

THE TIME FOR *Abad Zichro*

How much time must have elapsed before one can apply the principle of *abad zichro*? R. Toledano[90] suggests three years in accordance with a view expressed by one Rabbi who puts this time on the same footing as *hazakah* (the legal period of undisturbed possession entitling a man to claim land) which is three years.

Chief Rabbi Uzziel[91] suggests in a particular case twelve months of thorough investigation (after the cessation of war and occupation by the Allied forces) of records where the names of survivors are to be found and the name of the husband in question does not appear (then *abad zichro* applies).

However, Chief Rabbi Herzog[92] is of the opinion that the time of twelve months was not sufficient in that case since communications had

Ha-Shem, I, no. 28, quoting Isserles on *Eben Ha-Ezer*, cap. CXXVI, no. 4, and *Shebuth Yaakob*; Steif, *Responsa*, no. 21.

86. Cf. Breisch, *Helkath Yaakob*, II, no. 29, and Meisels, *Kuntras Takkanoth Agunah*, p. 17, where additional reasons are given.

87. Cf. Herzog, *Hechal Yizhak*, I, no. 24, p. 125; Kahana in Breisch's *Helkath Yaakob*, II, no. 30.

88. Herzog, *Hechal Yizhak*, II, no. 12 p. 57. Cf. ibid. no. 15, pp. 64ff. concerning communication between Russia and Latvia and the attitude of the Russians.

89. Ibid., pp. 18ff.

90. *Bath Ami*, p. 43.

91. *Mishpete Uzziel Eben Ha-Ezer*, no. 36, p. 145, and no. 44, p. 192.

92. Ibid. no. 45. Cf. his view in *Hechal Yizhak*, I, no. 24, pp. 127f.; Meisels, *Kuntras Takkanoth Agunoth*, nos. 28, 76; Meiri, *Ezrath Nashim*, II, pp. 143f. and the views quoted there.

not been restored by that time. The *agunoth* should be told to come again after twelve months and each case should be considered individually.

EVIDENCE

In some respects certain leniency in the attitude of the Rabbis can be observed in cases concerning admissibility of evidence where some other mitigating factors existed. As is well known, he who transgresses a Biblical commandment is disqualified from giving evidence. In one case the Rabbi questions the evidence given by people in a certain Polish town where there was no Rabbi or religious teacher acquainted with the laws of evidence. Hence he considers whether the witnesses were fit to give evidence as they might have been disqualified from the religious point of view. However, another Rabbi (R. Shlomoh David Kahana, formerly Ab Beth Din of Warsaw later in Jerusalem) tried to show that such a fear was far-fetched. 'There was some apprehension expressed in the literature of the Rabbis of the last generation whether soldiers are fit to give evidence as they might profane the Sabbath not in cases of saving life or eat *terephoth* (forbidden food) willingly (*le-razon*). But in our time, a time of general extermination, a time when many of the martyrs gave their lives for *kiddush ha-Shem* by saying *viddui* (reciting the confession of sin) and with the *shema* on the lips, one should not be afraid of such things. . . .'[93]

In another case where the evidence of witnesses who belonged to an irreligious *kibbuz* was discussed Chief Rabbi Herzog remarks: 'We are bound to give our life as a pledge to permit the re-marriage of an *agunah* whenever the words of truth are easily recognized and intellect obliges us to assume that the husband is dead. Concerning the objection to the evidence given by "a rasha de-hamas" (a wicked man of violence who is disqualified from giving evidence) behold the people of the *kibbuzim* even the free ones (irreligious ones, *hopheshim*) are known as very upright men in matters between one man and his fellow man and are not suspected of telling lies at all . . . and there is not even the possibility of their being a "rasha de-hamas" . . .'[94]

While all Rabbis showed great leniency in questions concerning *agunoth* (and often expressed their deep sympathy and tried to help them in every respect as far as halachically possible), the attitude of the Chief Rabbi of Israel, R. Yizhak Herzog, was outstanding. He was a father not only of the orphans whose parents had been killed by the Germans and tried successfully to save them from non-Jewish homes (*vide supra*, p. 163) where they would have been lost to Judaism, but he

---

93. Breisch, *Helkath Yaakob*, I, nos. 17, 21.
94. Herzog, *Hechal Yizhak*, II, no. 7, p. 42. See also the view of Weiss, *Minhath Yizhak*, I, no. 87.

cared also for the unfortunate *agunoth* who had lost everything dear to them and were wandering like forlorn sheep across Europe and other parts of the world. By this action his contribution to the rebuilding of our people was indeed magnificent. How great a spokesman he was in cases of *agunoth* can be seen from the expressions found in his *Responsa*,[95] and his pleas. 'My humble opinion is that when paying attention to the awful misfortune which had befallen our people when a third of our people has been exterminated through our sins one has to endeavour with all strength to permit *agunoth* to re-marry. . . . What I have still to explain at length with *pilpul* (casuistry), interpretations, etc., I leave for another time in order not to delay my decision in favour of the unfortunate woman. . . .' In another case of *agunah*, he concludes his *Responsum* with the words: 'May God have mercy upon this our sister and bring her forth from darkness to light, Amen, and Amen. . . . If I tried to go into particulars I am afraid I would commit a sin through extending the *iggun* of this unfortunate woman, "a brand plucked out of the fire" of the Gehenna of the Nazis. . . .'

To sum up: the case of *agunah* was regarded by the Rabbis as one of the most important problems of the post-war period; the reasons being: to help to rebuild our people of which a third had been lost; the unprecedented number of victims involved; the fear that young women particularly might succumb to immorality or not marry in accordance with the Law.

From rulings laid down in the *Shulhan Aruch* they sought to prove that:

1. falling into the hands of the Nazis was worse than falling into a lions' den;

2. falling into the hands of the Nazis was even worse than falling into a pit of snakes and scorpions;

3. the fear that a court's death sentence had not been carried out as a bribe had been paid did not apply by analogy to persons sent to the crematorium;

4. disappearing in the Nazi camps is halachically similar to (or, according to one view, halachically better than) falling into 'endless waters' and combined with other factors and principles the spouse (*agunah*) can be given permission to re-marry;

5. several Rabbis classified the cases of *agunoth* whose husbands disappeared in various circumstances under the Nazis and the Rabbis show within which category each *agunah* falls and which principles of the Talmud and Codes apply.

95. See *Hechal Yizhak*, I, no. 25, p. 151; II, no. 13, p. 59; no. 66, p. 240; no. 72, p. 258.

AGUNIM

Cases of *agunim*, i.e. husbands whose wives disappeared and cannot be traced and who wish to re-marry, are less frequently found in the *Responsa*. In general, cases of *agunim* could be treated more leniently as no Biblical prohibition was involved, but only the Ordinance of R. Gershom, the Light of the Exile, (d. 1040) would be infringed should it turn out after re-marriage that the first wife was alive. Apart from that the husband could stay with one of his two wives after divorcing the other and the children born from the second marriage were legitimate.

There is still another point to be mentioned. According to one Sephardi Rabbi of the sixteenth century[96] it was a greater merit to help a man[97] and free him from *iggun* than to help an *agunah*. The latter case was, as we have seen, highly praised by the Rabbis of all generations and particularly by those in the period of the Nazi holocaust. The question was discussed what should happen if the first wife reappears. (Such a case did indeed happen in our country recently and a great tragedy occurred.)[98] There are several Rabbis who deal with this particular problem. Mention should be made of the following three Rabbis who wrote on this subject: R. Hayyim Mordecai Roller of Neamt, author of the *Responsa Beer Hayyim Mordechai* (his *Responsum* appears to have been written during the war), Chief Rabbi Herzog of Israel and Chief Rabbi Jacob Mosheh Toledano of Tel Aviv-Jaffa.

R. Roller (Rabbi of Neamt who later emigrated to Israel where he died)[99] tries to prove that permission to re-marry could be given to a husband whose wife disappeared through the Nazis as the Ordinance of R. Gershom prohibiting bigamy does not apply where a *mizvah* is involved or where preventing many people from doing wrong is concerned. Even those authorities who hold that R. Gershom's Ordinance applied even to the former (a case where a *mizvah* is involved) would agree that it does not apply to the latter.[100] Furthermore, as nowadays thousands and perhaps even myriads of cases of *agunim* are affected everyone would agree that R. Gershom would not have intended his Ordinance to be applicable in such circumstances (*mizvah de-rabbim*).

This of course presupposes that the wives might be alive but for some reason do not return home. However, in our days when men, women

96. R. Shemuel di Medina, *Responsa, Yoreh Deah*, no. 140.
97. On the reason see Rashi on *Kethuboth* 64b.
98. Mentioned by Herzog, *Hechal Yizhak*, I, no. 26.
99. His *Responsum* is printed in Meisel's *Binyan Zebi*, II, no. 43, p. 61, and in R. Nathan Zebi Friedmann's *Nezer Mattai*, Tel Aviv, 1957, no. 39. Other Rabbis who dealt with this subject were: Meisels, *op. cit.*, nos. 38ff., 70; Weiss, *Minhath Yizhak*, no. 1.
100. On the references see note 99.

and children were led into captivity like sheep to the slaughter—to be killed, with unprecedented cruelty—they have lost their presumption of certainly being alive, it can be regarded only as doubtful. We are therefore in doubt whether the Ordinance of R. Gershom is at all applicable and so we may adopt a lenient view.

Those victims who had been taken to Auschwitz and placed on the left-hand side can certainly be presumed dead. So, if there is sufficient evidence that the woman had been led to the left side at Auschwitz her husband is free to re-marry.

However, we must consider that some women who had been saved by a miracle would return home. After all the suffering they had endured they would be happy to see their home-towns once again. However, on returning their joy would be turned to mourning on seeing their rivals in their husbands' homes. It is forbidden to perform *kiddushin* for the husband until he and his prospective second wife take upon themselves under the pain of a stringent ban, by vow and oath, orally as well as in writing that should the first wife return he would not live together with either of them until he comes to an agreement with one of them that she accept a bill of divorce according to the law of the Torah. All possessions would be divided into three parts one of which would be given to the woman who accepts the bill of divorce.

As far as *agunoth* are concerned permission to re-marry could only be given to a woman on the basis of clear evidence. (The same applies to an *agun* who wishes to marry his sister-in-law—wife's sister.) This cannot be done at present as long as the war continues.

In a *Responsum* to Dayan Abramski, Rosh Beth Din of London, Chief Rabbi Herzog of Israel deals with the problem of *agunim*, i.e. husbands whose wives disappeared during the Nazi holocaust.[101] 'Although I myself', R. Herzog says, 'am very stringent also in the case where the Ordinance of R. Gershom is involved this is only because in our Holy Land bigamy is not prohibited yet by law of the government and many breaches of morality have occurred. But in your country (England) where such fear does not exist one need not be so stringent.' Hence in the case submitted to the Chief Rabbi where husband and wife were living peacefully together and five years had elapsed during which there was no trace of the woman and on account of some other *halachic* factors (e.g. according to one view, R. Gershom's Ordinance was not applicable in cases where a *mizvah* was involved and where *iggun* would affect thousands of men—*mizvah be-rabbim*—etc.) permission could be granted to the husband to re-marry. This permission is not to be regarded as a general permit but each case must be treated and decided on its own merit.

101. Herzog, *Hechal Yizhak*, I, no. 26.

A special temporary Beth Din should be appointed under the auspices of the Beth Din in London to deal with such cases.

In spite of this, one must take into consideration the slightest possibility that the first woman might one day return (such miracles have happened with tragic results). Therefore the procedure should be as, I have heard, is customary in Hungary,[102] *Kiddushin* are not performed until both the husband and his prospective wife take upon themselves on oath and in writing by pain of excommunication that, should the first wife return, the husband would not live with either of them (*shtehen*) until he arranges that one wife receive a bill of divorce according to the law. A legal contract is drawn up binding him according to the law of the country to give substantial part of his property for the maintenance of his former wife, as the amount of money mentioned in the *ketubah* is in their country (Hungary) negligible. Such a procedure should, in my opinion, be adopted in Britain. . . .

In *Bath Ami* R. Toledano adds two sections (chapters five and six) on *agunim* to his treatise on *agunoth* (*supra* p. 223). They are:

(a) Cases of men whose wives disappeared in circumstances mentioned in chapters two and three (see above p. 224); whether they may re-marry and whether it is necessary to deposit a bill of divorce and *kethubah* at the Beth Din and to obtain permission of one hundred Rabbis (if Ashkenazim are involved among whom this practice is current). Also the question whether the husband may marry the sister of his wife who disappeared is considered.

(Rabbi Toledano tells us that in his Beth Din the practice has been adopted[103] that the husband should give an undertaking, that if by chance he learns that his first wife was alive, he would follow the directives given by the Beth Din concerning all claims and debts towards that wife with regard to alimentation, *kethubah*, as well as divorce if she wishes to be divorced. Only after such an undertaking shall the Beth Din give him permission to re-marry.)

(b) If a wife who had been missing returns after her husband had married another woman, which has he to divorce? Is there any reason to assume that since the first wife had been 'hidden' from her husband she would be forbidden to live with him? This question applies particularly to a *kohen* as he may not marry a 'captive'.

Since permission to re-marry was granted to the husband by the Beth Din, he may, if he wishes, and is able to maintain both wives, keep

102. See the *Responsum* quoted before.
103. *Op. cit.*, p. 61.

them both[104] or he could divorce whomever he wishes. The Rabbi is of the opinion (see further) that he should divorce the first wife. It depends also on the judgement of the Beth Din.

With regard to the question whether the first wife should become prohibited to him as she had been hidden and might have succumbed to immorality, the Rabbi shows that she is permitted to her husband as all Germans had been given strict warnings from their superiors and government not to associate with Jewish men and women.[105] The husband must not adopt a strict view and refuse to live with his wife as this might be a mere pretext to marry another woman. However, if he had married another woman in the meantime, with the permission of the Beth Din and is to divorce one of them, he should divorce his first wife. However, as is well known, a number of women had been taken to the 'houses of shame' and the well-known tattoo was marked on their flesh. Such women are prohibited to their husbands even if the latter are not *kohanim*.[106] If the husband is a *kohen* and his wife returns or if a bachelor who is a *kohen* wishes to marry a woman (spinster) who had been a captive of the Nazis the matter must be further considered.[107]

Of practical cases mention should be made of the following:

A man had lost every trace of his wife. He had received from her a letter informing him she would have to leave her home. Other people had told him she had been sent with many other victims to a well-known place where almost all those taken had been killed. Many years had elapsed since then, during which he heard nothing from her or from her children who had been with her. May he re-marry?

The reply was in the affirmative.[108]

LEVIRATE MARRIAGE AND HALIZAH

A different type of *agunah* was that where the fate of the husband was known and the woman could be regarded as a widow from the *halachic* point of view and yet re-marriage was not possible as *halizah* was still required. The latter could not always be performed as the fate of the brother-in-law was not known. The situation was similar where the order of death of father and child could not be ascertained. In such latter case *halizah* is required only if the child died first. The following is one of the problems of *halizah* which R. I.J.Weiss[109] describes as one

104. The Ordinance of R. Gershom prohibiting bigamy does not apply to Sephardim.
105. *Vide supra* pp. 195f.
106. See, however, *supra* pp. 199f.
107. See *supra* pp. 196ff.
108. R. Jonathan (MhRI) Steif, *Responsa*, Brooklyn, 1968, no. 20, where some suggestions are made. On other cases, see *infra* pp. 281f., 333ff. (*Helkath Yaakob*, I, no. 5; Herzog, *Hechal Yizhak*, I, no. 27).
109. *Minhath Yizhak*, I, nos. 32–34. The question was submitted to him by R. M.Meiri (author of *Ezrath Nashim*).

of the most difficult today. It concerns a husband and his son (or sons) who had been taken to the extermination camp. There were three possibilities to be taken into consideration:

1. where the time of death of neither was known;
2. where the time of the death of the father was known but not that of his son (or sons);
3. where the time of the death(s) of the son(s) was known but not that of the father.

In addition, the levir was living behind the Iron Curtain so that *halizah* was impossible and the woman would have to remain an *agunah* all her life.

There were other problems which are mentioned in the *Responsa* and were dealt with by the leading contemporary Rabbinic authorities.[110]

MARRYING THE SISTER OF ONE'S WIFE

In cases where the wife disappeared and her husband wishes to marry her sister, much care is required since the Biblical prohibition of Lev. XVIII 18 may be involved.

Whereas evidence of having seen a husband being sent to the left-hand side suffices to permit his wife to re-marry (even if given by only one witness) granting permission to a husband to marry his sister-in-law can only be done if there are two witnesses who testify that his wife had been sent to the left-hand side.[111]

As women had been separated from men and no evidence can be given by men about the fate of women the evidence of women is admissible.[112]

The Beth Din in Budapest gave the following decisions based on various Rabbinic sources:

(a) If two fit witnesses testify that they had seen the woman in the ghetto and there exists additional evidence by one woman that she had seen her on the left-hand side or she knew that the above woman was not among those who were sent to work, her sister may marry her brother-in-law (the husband of the missing woman) provided the sister-in-law asks the Beth Din for permission to marry him as she cannot find another such suitable partner.

(b) An *agunah* who can provide evidence that her husband was seen being placed in the extermination camp (e.g. Auschwitz) at the side leading to death is permitted to re-marry.[113]

---

110. See e.g. Part I, pp. 71f.; *Minhath Yizhak,* I, no. 101, Part III, pp. 315ff.
111. See R. Y.Z.Sopher in Weiss's *Minhath Yizhak,* I, no. 4 *ad fin.*
112. Steif, *Responsa,* no. 21.
113. Ibid.

7

How far can the Nazi Holocaust be termed 'shaath ha-shemad' (religious persecution)?

It has been mentioned at the beginning of this work[1] that the Nazi holocaust differed in several respects from all persecutions that befell our people. The only parallel to it mentioned by two Rabbis independently is the intended extermination of the Jews by Haman.[2]

One of the differences between the Nazi persecution and all other persecutions is seen by some Rabbis in the lack of any religious motive. The Nazis did not want the Jews to give up their religion.[3] Punishment was even meted out to those newly converted to Christianity. Hence the Nazi laws against the Jews in Germany (and Austria) did not bear any specific anti-religious character. Indeed when one studies the work of Blau[4] on the Nazi legislation one cannot find a single law which was directly anti-religious.[5] It is worth repeating that the prohibition of *shehitah* without prior stunning was not expressed to be part of a public anti-religious campaign but was issued, so they claimed, for humanitarian reasons to avoid cruelty to animals.

The burning of synagogues in Germany and Austria on 10 November 1938 and later in Poland during the war never bore a religious character. The synagogues were not turned into churches, but were destroyed or left bare for the time being. The burning of Hebrew books was by no means similar in nature to the burning of the Talmud in Paris in 1242 and in Rome in 1556. They were burned solely to offend the Jews. In fact the burning of Hebrew books was usually the work of the mob or soldiery as in some places the high value of the books was appreciated and they were confiscated and sent to Rosenberg's institute in Frankfurt am Main.

This policy of the Nazis was recognized immediately by the contemporary Rabbis and had some far-reaching *halachic* (legal) con-

1. *Vide supra* p. xv.
2. R. I.Z.Sopher in R. I.J.Weiss's *Minhath Yizhak*, I, no. 4; R. H.Y.Jeruchem, *Birkath Hayyim*, no. 51. See also ibid., no. 116.
3. *Vide infra* notes 5–7 and *supra* p. 59. At the end of October 1935, the Evangelical Lutheran Mission 'Under Israel' had to be dissolved as it was devoted particularly to the spreading of the Evangelical faith among Jews. See *The Yellow Spot: the Extermination of the Jews in Germany*, with an introduction by the Bishop of Durham, London 1936, p. 192.
4. Bruno Blau, *Das Ausnahmerecht der Juden in Deutschland 1933–1945*, Düsseldorf, 1954.
5. There is perhaps one exception: on 23 September 1939, the Jews were ordered to hand over their wireless sets personally to the local police. This day happened to be the Day of Atonement which fell on the Sabbath. See Blau, *Das Ausnahmerecht*, no. 253, p. 79.

sequences. In a letter addressed to R. Jonah Zebi Horowitz in Frankfurt am Main (dated 4 May 1933) from R. Yizhak Unna of Mannheim the latter refutes the former's view that the current persecution of prohibiting *shehitah* was to be regarded as a religious persecution (*le-haabir al dath, shaath ha-shemad*) in which case, 'we must not deviate from the old practice by trying to introduce the method of slaughtering poultry in the way required by the government (although this new method would not be entirely contrary to Jewish law)'.[6]

> I am greatly surprised to hear this. Had the Nazis decreed that we should eat meat of not-ritually slaughtered animals one could make the above statement. In fact they only wish to deprive us of food in order to annoy us, for the same reason as they remove the teachers from their positions and decree a ban against buying from Jews. All of it is done only to annoy them and to deprive them of their livelihood. Similarly, the prohibition of *shehitah* is aimed at annoying us. One of their bandits, Professor Müller of Munich, stated publicly that they do not wish to make us give up our religion (*le-haabir al dath*) . . .[7]

We learn from another source that Professor Max Müller who was abattoir director at Munich had perfected and introduced electric stunning machines throughout Germany (naturally he was interested in prohibiting *shehitah* without prior stunning) and was accused by Dr Klein of Lennep (a strong opponent of *shehitah*) who, however, was against introduction of electrical stunning. The latter had maintained that it had been promoted by Professor Müller for business reasons. In view of this a special committee of the *Reichsverband Deutscher Gemeindeärzte* was called to deal with this matter (17 March 1933).[8]

On another occasion[9] the Rabbi strongly rejects the view of those who would prohibit stunning because of the 'fact' alone that it was a time of religious persecution during which one has to sacrifice oneself even for the sake of 'changing the shoestrap',[10] although no fear of *terephah* might be involved in the process of stunning:

> At first let us see whether the reason 'because of religious persecution' applies. In fact this reason does not apply as this is only the case when the enemy intends to make Jews give up their religion (*le-haabir al*

6. On this method, *vide supra* p. 186.
7. The letter has been printed in R. Weinberg's *Seride Esh*,I, pp. 237f.
8. See *Religious Freedom: the Right to Practice Shehitah* ed. by R. Isaac Levin, R. Michael L.Munk, R. J.Berman, New York, 1946.
9. In *Seride Esh*, I, p. 387.
10. In the time of a religious persecution one must not change the shoestrap to one which has the colour used by non-Jews to try to conceal one's Jewish identity and in order to save one's life. *Sanhedrin* 74b.

dath). In our case the Government has only issued a decree forbidding killing an animal without prior stunning. The law of *shehitah* according to the Torah is not mentioned at all. Although we know their intention, which can be deduced from their action, nevertheless this *gezerah* (persecution) is not in the same category as the persecutions in olden times when they explicitly declared their aim was to cause us to give up our religion. Nowadays on the contrary they openly announce they do not mind us practising our religion. In fact their intention is not to cause us to give up our religion but only to annoy the Jews and to deprive them of their livelihood as we can see this in some other matters.

Apart from that the law of giving up one's life for one's religion applies only if this was directed against the Jews alone. But if the law involves the people of the whole country, although Jews were included this cannot be called 'shaath ha-shemad'. Hence when issuing the law of stunning the Germans did not mention the Jews at all. They decreed it for all inhabitants . . .

The same approach was taken by other Rabbis.[11] A similar view on the nature of the Nazi persecution in Germany was expressed by Chief Rabbi Unterman[12] of Jerusalem. 'All the evil decrees by the Nazis', he says, 'affecting also religious matters do not bear the character of *gezerath ha-shemad*, i.e. religious persecution, but are the outcome of their violent rule. The reason for this assumption is the fact that they imposed their harsh decrees also on apostates born as Jews. This proves that their intention was only to fulfil their murderous desire with all the venom of asps which was in them and their unclean soul which continues to long, unsatiated, for blood.'

'It can be assumed', says Chief Rabbi Herzog,[13] 'that in the case where armed robbers intended to exterminate the defenceless seed of our father Abraham they accomplished the task given to them by their government, a task which emanated from their wild, unclean hatred, not for the sake of material gain, not for any desirable thing (*hemdah*) but for the mere purpose of destruction . . .'

From all these quotations it can be seen that no religious motif is ever mentioned. The implications involved in this attitude were of great *halachic* consequence. These were dealt with in connection with questions concerning *shehitah*, acquisition of certificates of baptism or 'Aryan' papers to disguise one's identity, and the problem of *agunah*, etc.[14]

11. R. J.J.Weinberg, *op. cit.*, pp. 245f., 386.
12. *Shebet Mi-Yehudah*, I, Jerusalem, 1955, p. 47.
13. *Hechal Yizhak*, I, no. 24, p. 123.
14. On these problems, *vide infra* (*supra*).

There exists other direct evidence from which can be seen that the Nazis did not interfere directly in the religious matters of the Jews in Germany and Austria during the war. Holding religious services in the city synagogue in Vienna was possible until the end of the Nazi regime.[15] A *mikveh* too could be used there (1942–44).[16] *Mikvaoth* existed during those years in Berlin and Hamburg. Even in 1943 a new *mikveh* was built in Hamburg after the existing one had been bombed.[17] Public services were held in the house belonging to the community (1943).[18] With regard to Theresienstadt we are told that 'it is true that they did not explicitly permit services, but on the other hand they did not explicitly forbid them either. They simply looked on, as the Jews under the guidance of the Council of Elders set up prayer houses and established regular services. . . .'[19]

All this was in flagrant contradiction to the conditions in the conquered countries—Poland, Lithuania, etc. The decrees issued by the local police officers and governors and the various acts of desecration to which the Jews were forced to submit gave the persecution in those countries a religious character.

The Nazis compelled Jews to tear up scrolls of the Law[20] and forbade prayer. In Warsaw[21] an order was given by the Germans on 20 January 1940 to close all synagogues, houses of study (*Bathe Ha-Midrash*) and *mikvaoth*[22] as a preventive measure to avoid the spread of disease. Transgressors would be imprisoned. Nevertheless six hundred services were held secretly. On the intervention of the Council of the Elders permission was given by the Germans to open three synagogues (among them the great synagogue) at the end of April 1941 which, however, had to close again in March 1942.[23]

More severe were the decrees in Kaunas (Kovno). There the holding of public services was prohibited under pain of death. All *yeshiboth* and even *hadarim* (Hebrew schools for children) had to close and the study

---

15. See Herbert Rosenkranz, 'The Anschluss and the Tragedy of Austrian Jewry 1938–1945' in *The Jews of Austria*, ed. by Josef Fraenkel, p. 521.
16. See Hugo Gold, *Geschichte der Juden in Wien*, p. 111.
17. See *Beth Jacob*, Adar 721, no. 22, p. 23, quoted also by Mordecai Eliab, *Ani Maamin*, pp. 92f.
18. Ibid. *Beth Jacob*. Also a *sukkah* was erected in the courtyard of the house in September 1942.
19. Dr Richard Feder, 'Religious Life in Terezin', in *Terezin*, Prague, 1965, p. 53.
20. Cf. R. E.Oshry, *Mi-Maamakkim*, I, no. 1 (*vide infra* p. 320).
21. Cf. Joseph Kermish, Introduction to Adam Czerniakow, *Warsaw Ghetto Diary*, Jerusalem, 1968, pp. 14f.; see also entries pp. 38 (20 December 1939), 274 (3 March 1942); Chaim A. Kaplan, *Scroll of Agony*, ed. by Abraham I. Katsh, London, 1966, pp. 89 (24 January 1940), 122 (24 April 1940), 160 (12 August 1940), 183 (2 October 1940).
22. On the use of *mikvaoth* at first outside Warsaw and later even inside in spite of the threat of imprisonment and death, see R. S.Huberband, *Kiddush Ha-Shem*, pp. 88ff.
23. Joseph Kermish in Czerniakow's, *Warsaw Ghetto Diary*.

of the Law was forbidden (26 August 1942).[24] Similarly, all *mikvaoth* had to close and their use was prohibited under severe punishment. The result was that in the ghetto of Kovno with a population of thirty thousand no *mikveh*[25] was available and the river[26] had to be used instead.

In connection with the prohibition of holding public services and studying the Law the following question was addressed to Rabbi Oshry:[27]

Is it permitted to expose oneself to danger by studying Torah and attending public service?

On the 13th of Ellul, 702 (26 August 1942), the Nazi enemy issued a decree prohibiting the inmates of the ghetto (of Kovno) from holding public services and lectures in Synagogues and Houses of Study. The prisoners (of the ghetto) after a day's hard labour, broken in body and spirit, would forget their troubles by gathering in the Holy Places, and fixing special times for the study of the Torah, and forming groups for the study of the Talmud and Mishnah, to listen to words of instruction and encouragement from Rabbis and preachers. . . . I myself had the privilege to be one of those who led many to righteousness and continued to spread Torah among the people of God in the darkest period. I continued to deliver my discourses in my House of Study which was famous and known by the name of 'Abba Yehezkiel's Klaus'. After the cursed wicked men turned it into a prison I moved to the 'Halvayyath Ha-Meth Klaus' and into the Synagogue which was in Gapinowicz House in Vitna Street and into the Synagogue of Hayyim Schapir in Varena Street near 'Moazath Ha-Zekenim' (*Ältestenrat*). I devoted myself particularly to the daily *shiurim* (lectures, discourses) which I delivered to the group 'Tiphereth Bahurim' ('The Glory of Young Men'). In all these places I strengthened with the help of God those young Jews as well as the masses, who were weak in spirit, and I endeavoured to teach them understanding and knowledge that they should know that just as one must praise God for the good so one must praise Him for the evil and that we must hope in silence for His help. . . .

That source of strength and inspiration did not go unnoticed in the eyes of the wicked men. Since all their endeavour was to bring despair to the hearts of the prisoners they had issued a decree pro-

24. On this prohibition, see Oshry, *Mi-Maamakkim*, II, no. 11; L. Garfunkel, *The Destruction of Kovno's Jewry*, pp. 131ff. According to Garfunkel this decree was issued by the *Staatskommissar*.
25. See Oshry, *Mi-Maamakkim*, I, no. 4 (*supra* Part I, p. 48).
26. On the question of immersion in a river, see ibid., p. 31.
27. *Mi-Maamakkim*, II, no. 11.

hibiting the Jews from attending public services in the Synagogues and in the Houses of Study. Anyone who did not comply with that decree would be put to death.

At that time R. Naphtali Weintraub (who later died a martyr), *gabbai* (Head) of the synagogue of Gapinowicz, came and asked me (R. Oshry) whether he was bound according to the law to expose himself to danger by going to pray in the 'Klaus' where he had attended services mornings and evenings. Had he to sacrifice his life for the study of Torah and for attending service or not?

The Rabbi deals with that question from two angles: must one place oneself at risk (*a*) for the study of Torah, (*b*) for prayer?

He shows from Talmudic and Rabbinic sources that at a time of persecution for studying the Law one must indeed sacrifice one's life as the intention of the enemy was to 'silence the voice of the Torah' as could be seen from the fact that their anger was directed primarily and particularly against the Rabbis and scholars. They prohibited even the teaching of children and took away scrolls and holy books by force.

With regard to the question whether one must suffer martyrdom if the non-Jews decree that the Jews were not to attend public services in synagogues and houses of study (*Bathe Midrash*) it appears it is similar to the case of Daniel who, although threatened with death, did not submit to the king's decree and was ready to suffer death for the sake of prayer (see Daniel vi 7ff.). How much more has such a course to be taken when the Germans sought to abolish prayer entirely.

It was a time of persecution not only of the body of the ghetto prisoner but also of his faith and religion. If the main intention of the enemy was merely the destruction of the body there was no reason to close the houses of learning and prayer with the threat of the death penalty. It had also been seen that the wicked men would impose forced labour on the Jews with particular severity on the Sabbath and festivals to cause them to desecrate the holiness of those days and to extinguish belief in their hearts. The latter amounted to idolatry to which the law of suffering martyrdom applied.

However, one could not oblige others to suffer martyrdom for Torah and prayer. The case of Daniel and his associates (Hananyah, Mishael and Azaryah) could not serve as a precedent as they may have acted beyond the letter of the law.

Furthermore, the reason for the attitude of Daniel and his colleagues was mainly due to the fact that a great, pious and God-fearing man may suffer martyrdom, even if the case involves a minor *mizvah*, in order to teach people the way of loving and fearing God.

Although the Rabbi finds it difficult to give a decision on the question whether he should expose himself to danger for the sake of the

s

study of Torah and attending public services for 'who knows whether his thought is pure to the extent of being in the rank of Daniel and his colleagues' he is of the opinion that one may do so.

Indeed the holy people continued to study and attend prayers in public. . . .

On *Rosh Ha-Shanah*, 703 (12 and 13 September 1942), the Jews were not afraid the Germans would hear the sound of the *shophar* they blew during their prayers. . . . Not only did they gather to pray with a quorum at places of worship but services were held even in the Ghetto hospital[28] and those responsible for arranging them were the doctors who had belonged to the assimilated class who did not fear the decree and were prepared to suffer martyrdom for the sake of prayer.

I too continued my public *shiurim* daily. Furthermore, the members of 'Tiphereth Bahurim' renovated Mr Singer's building and installed electric lighting. They provided it with a bunker to be safe from the Germans. They were not satisfied until the house had been consecrated, all preparations completed, and we began our *shiurim* which had been fixed and the *derashoth* which I delivered to give them further encouragement. . . .

Reviewing the attitude of the Nazis towards the Jews in religious respects one can say briefly: there existed a difference in the treatment of the Jews of the *Altreich* and of those of the conquered countries. In the former no special law existed which bore a distinctive anti-religious character, unlike the laws issued by the governors in occupied territories where the decrees sometimes pertained to *shaath ha-shemad* i.e., religious persecution. However, while in olden times the religious persecution was aimed at forcing the Jew to renounce his religion in favour of a dominant religion, in the Nazi holocaust all anti-religious laws were aimed at annoying the Jew in any way possible, and emanated from hatred without special significance for religion itself.

28. See also Garfunkel, *Destruction of Kovno's Jewry*, p. 133, who mentions an incident which happened in the hospital on *Yom Ha-Kippurim*.

Part 3
Anthology of *Responsa*

1

Immigration, Refugees*

SPAIN

It has been mentioned already (*supra* p. 16) that in 1933 when emigration from Germany began the question was discussed whether it was permitted from the *halachic* point of view to settle in Spain as it was alleged that a *herem* had been imposed by the exiles from Spain in 1492 against Jewish resettlement without authority.

The problem of the existence of a *herem* in connection with emigration from Germany had been dealt with for the first time in a *Responsum* by R. Menahem Mendel Hayyim Landa of Zawiercie written in Otwock on the 14th of Iyyar 693 (10 May 1933). It is addressed to R. Weinberg in Berlin who had approached him concerning the slaughtering of fowls and at the same time put this question to him. The Rabbi, whom R. Weinberg regards as a great scholar well versed in all branches of Jewish knowledge, admits that he too had heard in his youth about a *herem* on Spain:

> but it appears to be only a rumour since it is not recorded in any book of the exiles from Spain.
>
> Even if they had issued such a decree, one province alone cannot impose a ban affecting the whole world. Furthermore, who could tell us that this *herem* had even been generally accepted? Whom do we regard greater than R. Gershom who was the Light of the Exile (b. *c.* 960, lived in Mayence in 1013, d. 1040) and his ordinance (concerning the prohibition of bigamy) nevertheless did not spread to countries where they refused to accept it. It was effective only where the people accepted it freely. The reason for Jews not taking up residence in Spain after the expulsion was that the country was closed to them for many centuries following the expulsion. . . .
>
> Furthermore, granted that such a decree existed, nevertheless it is not logical to say that it was intended to include a person who had been driven from his home because of oppression and seeks shelter. The land of Egypt should serve as proof, for according to the Torah one must not return there (see Deut. XVII 16) and yet we find *tannaim* who fled to Egypt[1] . . . how much more is it permitted nowadays to

---

* The reader is reminded that the decisions in the *Responsa* are not to be taken as a guide for practical cases without studying the sources and examining carefully the *halachic* reasoning in the Rabbis' replies.

1. See *Yerushalmi Talmud Hagigah*, III, 2, 77d, quoted in *Tosaphoth* on *Hagigah* 16b, *s.v. Ab.* On the whole question, see Chief Rabbi Herzog, *Hechal Yizhak*, I, no. 12.

emigrate there (to Spain) when the gates of other countries are closed to Jews. In general, I do not believe the rumour of the *herem* . . . how often were the Jews in the Middle Ages expelled from France, England, etc. where all Jewish settlements were wiped out for hundreds of years and the Jews later returned? Why should the expulsion from Spain be different from that from England and France about which we have no report of such a decree having been issued?[2]

1933.   The same question (regarding the existence of a *herem* on Spain) was put to R. Hayyim Eleazar Spira of Munkatsch when the persecution of the Jews began and a report spread that Spain had given permission to them to immigrate. The Rabbi was then asked whether one has to take into consideration the continuous rumour that our brethren at the time of their expulsion, because of the persecution and troubles, had taken upon themselves under pain of a stringent ban that both they and their descendants would never return to that country.

His decision was that this rumour was quite 'doubtful'. It is supposed that there was no truth at all in it. It is not mentioned in any book of previous Rabbis unlike the *herem* of R. Gershom[3] or that of R. Tam.[4] Furthermore, R. Joseph Caro who died in 5335 (1575) at the age of eighty-seven and lived during the persecution did not mention the *herem*. Therefore, we need have no apprehension. Apart from that, even if we would regard this rumour as even 'doubtful' we are not of the descendants of the exiles from Spain to whom this *herem* should apply. If the government would grant us freedom to live according to our holy Torah in public and let the Jews have their own cemetery also in the capital, Jews may take up residence there. Until this freedom is given a Jew is forbidden to live there.[5]

1945.   In his *Responsum* concerning a suggestion made at a conference of Israeli Rabbis after World War II to proclaim a ban against entering Germany (*supra* p. 130), R. Meshullam Rath, who opposed such a decision, deals also with the question of the *herem* against returning to Spain. He points out:

2. In R. J.J.Weinberg's *Seride Esh*, I, no. 6, p. 233. See also R. Weinberg's *Eth Ahai Anochi Mebakkesh*, Bene Berak, p. 33.
3. He refers to R. Gershom's ordinance concerning the prohibition of polygamy (*vide supra* p. 239).
4. On R. Jacob Tam's ordinance concerning the return of the dowry and other matters, see Finkelstein, *Jewish Self-Government in the Middle Ages*, pp. 43, 58, 168ff.
5. *Sepher Darche Hayyim Ve-Shalom, Minhagim* of R. Hayyim Eleazar Spira, edited by his student Yehiel Michal Gold (in Munkatsch, 1940) 3rd Ed., New York, 1948, p. 353, 'Hilchoth Herem', cap. 972.

Concerning the assertion that the exiles from Spain had issued a *herem* not to return to Spain, I found in no book anything to confirm this. On the contrary, the opposite could be deduced from a passage in a *Responsum* of R. Mosheh Trani,[6] I, no. 307, where it is said: 'There are no Jews in Aragon for 70 years and we are sure that no Jew will pitch his tent there any more as the Merciful will gather those banished of His people Israel to Erez Yisrael in the very near future'. Even if the rumour were true it could not serve as proof for us as the Exiles from Spain could decree a *herem* for themselves and their own countrymen (among them were great men, lights of the exile, R. Jacob Berab,[7] R. Levi ibn Habib,[8] Abravanel[9] and the author of *Akedath Yizhak*).[10] But how can we decree affecting the whole of Israel? In fact, in our generation, many Jews have settled in Spain where new communities have been established, as I have heard from people who lived there . . .'[11]

January 1951.   Although the following *Responsum* does not deal with refugees from Nazi oppression, it deserves to be included here as it presents a quite different view on the alleged *herem* against the return to Spain.

R. Eliezer Yehudah Waldenberg, Ab Beth Din of Jerusalem, was asked by his pupil R. Abraham David Shalem, Chief Rabbi of the Sephardi congregation of Peru, whether one may go to Spain on business and live there, as there was a *herem* with an oath issued by the exiles from Spain that neither they nor their children would enter that country.

The Rabbi at first refutes the assumption that there was certainly a *herem*. 'The historians', he says, 'have never found anything to confirm it. Nor did Abravanel[12] who was one of the first among the exiles, and who reports at length in the introduction to his books the exodus from Spain. He does not even allude to such a *herem*. It is not mentioned in

6. He was born at Salonica 1500, was a pupil of R. Jacob Berab (see next note) in Safed, where he later became Rabbi. He died in 1580. (I do not see how this passage proves that there was no *herem*. Should this proof be derived from the fact that R. M.Trani does not mention it explicitly? Cf. however, *infra* where this quotation is used as support for the existence of a *herem*!)
7. B. at Moqueda near Toledo (Spain) in 1474, d. at Safed in 1546. He intended to re-introduce the *Semichah* (Ordination). The plan did not materialize owing to the opposition of R. Levi ibn Habib, Chief Rabbi of Jerusalem (see next note).
8. R. Levi b. Jacob ibn Habib, b. in Zamora (Spain) about 1484, went with his parents to Portugal where after 1498 he was forced to conceal his Jewish identity, but soon escaped from there. Lived in Salonica and later in Jerusalem where he officiated as Chief Rabbi.
9. Don Isaac Abravanel, b. Lisbon, 1437, statesman and Bible commentator, left Spain at the expulsion of the Jews in 1492, d. at Venice 1508.
10. Its author was R. Isaac b. Moses Arama, b. in Spain about 1420, d. in Naples 1494.
11. R. M.Rath, *Kol Mebasser*, I, no. 13.
12. *Vide supra* note (9). See his commentary on Kings.

the famous books, e.g. *Shebet Yehudah*,[13] *Seder Ha-Doroth*,[14] *Sepher Yuhasin*[15] and *Shalsheleth Ha-Kabbalah*[16] which usually do not omit any current *agadah* (legend). I too made enquiries from experts in history and they were unable to show me any source for it.'

In view of this, the Rabbi tells us, he began to consider the law in a case where it is not clearly known whether there was such a *haskamah* (agreement) or not, and if there was a *haskamah* whether it was in the form of a *haskamah* only or in the form of a *herem* and oath and, if the latter, whether it was made for all future generations.

But I soon changed my mind. 'The conduct of Israel is Torah'[17] and 'Vox populi—vox Dei'[18] as it is a wide-spread *agadah* that the exiles had made such a *haskamah* and Jews have been apprehensive of it in all generations. In that case the saying of the Talmud applies: 'Leave it to Israel, if they are not prophets, yet they are the children of prophets.'[19] One should not grant permission outright to a person who wishes to take up permanent residence in Spain to do so particularly if he is a Sephardi, a descendant of the Jews exiled from Spain . . .

R. Waldenberg then asked the Sephardi Chief Rabbi of Israel, R. Uzziel, about this rumour. His reply was that in fact there was no source for it, but he knew that it was a tradition handed down from one generation to the next. The Sephardim had always been very particular not to transgress this traditional *haskamah* and he added that he was fully aware of a small number of Sephardim currently living in Spain but whenever a request was sent from there to supply them with *meshorthe kodesh* (religious officials) one always tried to evade compliance with their request. 'When I heard this', writes R. Waldenberg, 'the opinion I expressed before was strengthened so that I cannot permit in practice a person to live in Spain.'[20]

13. Composed by Solomon ibn Verga, b. in Spain, emigrated to Portugal in 1492, escaped from there to Italy (according to others: to Turkey).
14. Written by R. Jehiel ben Solomon Heilprin, Lithuanian Rabbi and chronicler, b. about 1660, d. at Minsk about 1746.
15. Its author being R. Abraham ben Samuel Zacuto, b. at Salamanca about 1450, d. in Turkey after 1510.
16. Written by Gedaliah ibn Yahya, b. in Italy 1515, d. probably in Alexandria 1587.
17. Cf. *Tosaphoth* on *Menahoth* 20b, *s.v. niphsal*.
18. 'Kol hamon she-hu ke-kol Shaddai', on this saying see Gur, *Dictionary* where the references can be found.
19. Cf. *Pesahim* 66a.
20. R. Waldenberg then refers to *Ner Ha-Maarab* (p. 75, note 9) by R. Toledano, Chief Rabbi of Tel Aviv and Jaffa, who, when explaining the origin of his name, says that 'our fathers have told us that the members of that family called themselves "Toleda-no" meaning in Spanish "Toledo-not" since they imposed a *herem* upon themselves not to return to Spain'. 'Hence from this remark too', says R. Waldenberg, 'it is confirmed that the exiles from Spain imposed upon themselves some kind of *herem* not to return to Spain both collectively and individually. . . .'

R. Waldenberg then quotes a great part of a *Responsum* of R. Mosheh Trani (b. 1500, Rabbi in Safed, d. 1580)[21] to substantiate his view.

The *Responsum* deals with a community with various congregations (of Jews from Italy, Portugal, Castile, and other countries). The Jews of that community made an agreement that anyone who had come there and had been born in Italy and his father too had been born in that country had to join the Italian congregation even though his grandfather may have hailed from Portugal, Castile, Aragon or elsewhere.[22] If, however, his father had been born in one of the countries mentioned above the son was to join the congregation of his countrymen even though he had been born in Italy. The members of the Aragonese congregation opposed that *haskamah* on the ground that it was unfair to force one who was known to be a descendant of a family which hailed from Aragon or another country to join the Italian congregation merely because he and his father had been born in Italy. R. Mosheh Trani was asked whether the Aragonese congregation had to accept the *haskamah*. His decision was in the negative for the following reason: as the acceptance of the *haskamah* would bring profit only to the Italian congregation and cause loss to the Aragonese congregation, and the latter had opposed that *haskamah* from the very beginning they could not be forced to accept it. R. Mosheh Trani points out that 'one should not argue that the Italian congregation would also suffer loss by accepting this *haskamah* if a Jew from Italy would come hither who and whose father had been born in another country and consequently the son would join another congregation, and shows a difference between the two cases. 'It is well known', he continues, 'that no Jew from Italy would ever come who and whose father had been born in Aragon as there have been no Jews in Aragon for the preceding seventy years. We are sure that no Jew will ever pitch his tent there for God, blessed be He, will gather those banished of His people Israel to Erez Yisrael in the near future.'

R. Waldenberg says:

From this phrase ('No Jew, etc.') we see that there is an allusion to a general *haskamah* never to return to Aragon. How did he (R. Mosheh Trani) know this if there had been no prior agreement to that effect? Furthermore, how can we be so certain of R. Mosheh Trani's assurance that no Jew will ever pitch his tent there if there had been no *herem* beforehand? One should not say that R. Mosheh Trani's assurances are based on the reason he gives 'For God, blessed be He, will gather those banished of His people Israel to Erez

---

21. *Responsa* I, no. 307.
22. Membership of a congregation entailed the duty of contributing to the charity fund of that congregation.

Yisrael in the near future', for if this were the case he ought also to have given an assurance that no Jews from anywhere would ever immigrate to the town whose members approached him, for instead of coming to that town they would immigrate to Israel. Moreover, the inhabitants of that town too[23] would for the same reason leave home and go to Israel. . . .

Therefore, the main reason for R. Mosheh Trani's assurance 'that no Jew would pitch his tent in Aragon' was the haskamah and herem against a return to Spain. Indeed, from R. Mosheh Trani's concluding words 'God, blessed be He, will gather . . .' it appears that a herem existed until such an occasion would arise, when God would gather those of Israel who had been banished. Thereupon, the herem would lose its validity and there would be no need to return to Aragon, for the eyes of all Jews would be directed towards Israel to flock to the holy heritage. The reason for R. Mosheh Trani's not having mentioned the herem and haskamah clearly was, one can say, that 'it is the glory of God to conceal a thing (Prov. xxv 2)' and owing to political and social factors for the sake of preservation of peace for Israel in the countries of the Diaspora . . . Verb. sap.[24]

Refugees in Switzerland

1938–39.	The following case came before the Rabbi[25] in Switzerland. A seventeen-year-old girl of a refugee family living in Switzerland married a man who had been born there but later emigrated to Uruguay (South America). He had come to visit his family and on seeing the girl had fallen in love. They went through a civil marriage (Zivilehe) but had no religious marriage. Two days after the civil marriage they left for his home in Uruguay. When the girl's father who was born in Poland was asked by the Rabbi why he had given his daughter permission to leave without a religious marriage (huppah and kiddushin) he replied that the fiancé had promised that after arriving in South

23. As one can see, R. Waldenberg is of the opinion that the town where the argument about the decree arose was outside Palestine. Indeed we hear of several communities in the sixteenth century with various congregations (see Cecil Roth 'The Spanish Exiles of 1492 in Italy', in Homenaje A Millas-Vallicrosa, vol. II, pp. 293ff., concerning Rome and Ferrara, and S. Rosanes, Dibre Yeme Yisrael Be-Togarmah, II, pp. 17, 19, concerning Constantinople and Salonica). However, from the word 'hither' in the phrase 'one should not argue . . . if a Jew from Italy would come hither' it appears that the town was Safed, the seat of R. Mosheh Trani. See also Rosanes, Dibre Yeme, II, p. 141.
24. R. E.Y.Waldenberg, Ziz Eliezer, V, no. 17. The Responsum is dated: 5th of Shebat 711 (12 January 1951).
25. R. M.J.Breisch, Helkath Yaakob, I, no. 1. The only date mentioned in the Responsum is that of Rabbi Steif's letter (14 March 1945). As four years had elapsed since the decree was granted and the proceedings took two years (even if we do not take the eight months of her stay in Uruguay into consideration) the case happened at the end of 1938 or at the beginning of 1939.

America he would help the girl's parents emigrate and he would arrange a festive wedding in the synagogue as he was a wealthy man. He claimed that in Switzerland the time had not been opportune. The father, a refugee, relying on the fact that he would help him and his family emigrate agreed to the proposal. After eight months had passed the woman returned from Uruguay. She asserted she had felt already on the ship to Uruguay that her union would not be successful as her fiancé differed from her in his nature, character and temperament. When she reached Uruguay, her fiancé's mother added to the strife between the couple. Through intervention of the Swiss Consul in Uruguay who had come to her assistance she succeeded in returning to Switzerland after eight months. It took two years before she received a divorce from the (non-Jewish) court.

The girl was willing to say on oath that *huppah* and *kiddushin* had never taken place, as quarrels had broken out straight away. Her fiancé had changed his intention of helping her parents emigrate to Uruguay as he had earlier promised—this was at the beginning of the war. Four years had elapsed since she was granted a divorce and became engaged to a man who was partly observant (her former fiancé was completely irreligious). The woman too knew a little of Judaism. The question was: was the Beth Din permitted to perform *huppah* and *kiddushin*, as two problems were involved.

1. Did the civil marriage require a *get* to comply with the strict view (*le-humra*) as the couple had lived as husband and wife?

2. Was the woman to be believed that she did not marry according to the law of Moses and Israel during the eight months she was in South America?

The Rabbi deals with these questions. While with regard to the first question he adopts a lenient view he is more stringent concerning the second. He came to the conclusion that one had first to make further inquiries in Uruguay if there had been a religious marriage or not.

The Rabbi had shown his *Responsum* to R. Joel Teitelbaum of Satmar who agreed with him and he prints a *Responsum* of R. Jonathan Steif of Budapest (who was at that time in Battenberg, Switzerland), dated Erev Rosh Hodesh Nisan 705 (14 March 1945) in which the latter also agreed with him.

1939–45.   There was no facility in the religious camp in Switzerland for having any warm food or drink on the Sabbath. Was it permitted to go to a non-Jewish public house (*Marzeah, Wirtschaft*) in the village and drink there hot (black) tea or coffee, particularly in winter when the atmosphere in the camp was very cold?

In view of the various mitigating factors, under certain conditions laid down by the Rabbi[26] it was permitted to do so as it was a time of emergency.

1938–45.   As is well known, the Swiss government had arranged camps for the refugees and the latter were to work for the government both on weekdays and Sabbaths. They were maintained by the government and received army rations. It was an act of grace that the government had arranged a special camp for religious people where they did not need to work on the Sabbath nor eat food inconsistent with Jewish dietary laws. The refugees could live there in accordance with the Torah and Jewish tradition.

The administration too of that camp was more favourable. When the minimum number of refugees for one camp was one hundred and the religious refugees did not make up that number, they were joined by irreligious refugees, in order to complete the required number. The latter were willing to join for they preferred to be there for, as mentioned above, the administration was more favourable.

One day, for reasons unknown, the authorities asked for five men from the camp to be sent to another camp. As the officials themselves did not know who was religious and who was not—they thought all inmates were religious—they chose five without making any previous inquiries. It just happened that all five were religious. The question then arose whether it was permitted to intervene on their behalf so that non-religious men be sent in their place. However, would such action amount to causing others to desecrate the Sabbath and to eat prohibited food in the other camp? Albeit the irreligious desecrated the Sabbath even in the religious camp and ate prohibited food, however, they did so on their own accord and were not compelled by the administration. In the other camp they would be forced to desecrate the Sabbath, etc.

The Rabbi decided that intervention on behalf of the religious did not amount to causing others to transgress the law. One of the reasons was that the authorities in permitting the religious Jews to have a camp for themselves showed that they wished each person to be able to live according to his religion and tradition. Had the authorities known when they selected the five who was religious and who was not, they would not have asked for the religious. Hence, the selection was based upon an error and therefore intervention on behalf of the religious inmates was in general permitted. However, this should not bring any disadvantage to other religious people.[27]

26. R. M.J.Breisch, *Helkath Yaakob*, I, no. 36.
27. R. M.J.Breisch, *Helkath Yaakob*, I, no. 73.

Torah Scroll as a Gift to a Clergyman (Switzerland? 1933-34)

I was approached by a communal worker who has connections with great and distinguished non-Jews who are very active in saving Jews in the land of blood (cf. Ezek. xxii 2), Germany and its provinces. Among them is a clergyman who is greatly distinguished for saving Jewish lives. May the communal worker give him a Scroll of the Law (which is no longer fit for use) as a present? The former assumes this present would be highly appreciated and would serve as an encouragement to continue his help on a greater scale.

The decision was in the affirmative.[28]

Refugees in France (Before 1939)

Rabbi Breisch of Zurich was asked by a Rabbi in Paris about some refugees who emigrated to overseas countries and had their fares paid by various institutions of the Joint, etc. Very often the ships taking them abroad arrived at the French port on the Sabbath so that *shebithah*[29] could not be acquired on Friday. Were the Jews permitted to start their sea-voyage on the Sabbath without having acquired *shebithah* at such a time of emergency as they depended on others and very often they could hardly avoid leaving the port on the Sabbath. Were they thus desecrating the Sabbath?

The decision was that they could leave the port on the Sabbath without having acquired *shebithah*. The reason was that it was a time of (great) emergency. (Were that not the case it would have been prohibited.)[30]

On his visit to Paris Rabbi Breisch was asked by refugees staying at hotels where each guest had his own room which he used for baking, cooking and eating if they were required to make an *erub hazeroth*[31] before being permitted to carry in other parts of the hotel on the Sabbath. It would be difficult for them to arrange an *erub* for various reasons.

---

28. R. M.J.Breisch, *Helkath Yaakob*, I, no. 83.
29. Lit. resting, acquiring (appointing) a place to be regarded as the centre of Sabbath movements.
30. *Helkath Yaakob*, I, no. 206.
31. Lit. combination by inhabitants of dwellings, i.e. an institution ascribed to King Solomon by which Jews living in different buildings with a common courtyard (or with a common corridor) could be able to carry from their houses into the courtyard and *vice versa*. Each occupier has to contribute towards some food which is deposited in one of the houses. Through this action all dwellings are considered 'common' and carrying is then permitted. There are various rulings on *erub* depending on the occupiers. If the owner or one of the occupiers is a non-Jew an *erub* is effective only when permission is obtained from him by renting his property usually for a nominal rent.

The decision was that arranging an *erub* in those circumstances was not necessary.[32]

ILLEGAL EMIGRATION

1938

R. Jeruchem advises his two grandsons who had succeeded in escaping from the Nazis and in entering a free country[33] illegally to recite the blessing *Hagomel* when they should enter the synagogue. Although normally the benediction should be recited within three days or at the most five days after the miraculous event had occurred, neverthless three days should in their case be counted from after their stay had become 'legal' and they would be able to attend the *Beth Ha-Midrash*. This would count as completion of the miracle. (Unless they were able to arrange service at their home where the Torah could be read before obtaining permission. The benediction should then be recited on that occasion. Since they were not able to make such arrangements, the three days began after they had been given permission to stay in the country.)

The *Responsum* is dated Thursday, *Seder* Gen. xxiv 1, 699[34] (17 November 1938).[35]

---

32. *Helkath Yaakob*, I, no. 207.
33. Most probably it refers either to Switzerland or Belgium.
34. It was just a week after *Kristallnacht*.
35. R. H.Y.Jeruchem, *Birkath Hayyim*, no. 16.

2

Religious Articles and Books saved on *Kristallnacht* (November 1938)

Many years ago, a generous man donated a silver *kiddush* cup and some other silver vessels (jug, etc.) to a synagogue in Germany. They were used for religious purposes only. The donor did not belong to that community. When the enemy broke into the synagogue in Germany,[1] one of the members of that synagogue (he was the brother of the donor) succeeded in saving the silver vessels and in bringing them to Israel.

He handed them over to the donor who inquired whether he may use them for his private purposes and regard them as his own property without any holiness being attached to them.

The decision was that he should first have the articles assessed by three experts and give their value to charity. He may then use the articles. The *Responsum* is dated 26th of Nisan 701 (23 April 1941).[2]

Among the religious articles saved from the countries of the diaspora and brought to Israel were crown ornaments of Torah scrolls. They were placed on the tombstone of the grave ascribed to King David. A man, a certain Mr Zebi Landsmann of Haifa, recognized one crown as having belonged to him. R. Dr S. Z. Kahana of the *Misrad Ha-Datoth* asked R. M.Rath what should be done with that crown—whether it should be returned to its claimant and taken off the grave of King David on the Mount Zion and removed from Jerusalem?

In R. Rath's view the crown had to be removed from the grave and to be given to a synagogue for the use of a Torah scroll. 'To sum up: (*a*) it was not necessary to return the crown to Mr Landsmann. (*b*) That crown and all other crowns of Torah scrolls which are on the tombstone had to be immediately removed from there and to be given to synagogues to be used for their original purpose. (*c*) From then onwards, no crown of a *Sepher Torah* should be placed on the tombstone.'[3]

Someone had saved books belonging to the library of the Hildesheimer Seminary in Berlin and taken them to Israel. He asked R. Weinberg whether he could keep the books for himself. He compared his action to the case mentioned in *Baba Mezia* 21b ('things found among the deposits of the sea belong to the finder'). R. Weinberg is of the opinion he must not keep them for himself, and gives the reason for his view. He

---

1. No doubt, this refers to the Crystal Night (*Kristallnacht*) on 10 November 1938 when synagogues were pillaged and burned down.
2. R. Simhah Ha-Levi Bamberger, *Sheerith Simhah*, no. 32.
3. R. M.Rath, *Kol Mebasser* I, no. 57.

also points out that the comparison with the case of *Baba Mezia* 21b
was not correct since it was well known that the wicked people took
possession of all the libraries and kept them in safe places. 'Also our
Library remained intact and lies in Prague as is well known. The hope
never went from our heart that "all wickedness shall be wholly consumed like smoke and the dominion of arrogance will pass away from
earth" '. The hope therefore existed that sometime in the future the
books would be returned to their former owners. He suggests this
matter be put to his colleagues with the question whether some books
could be given to the man as a gift in reward for his saving the books
despite danger to life. (R. Weinberg remarks that also his own books
had been taken away when he left Germany 'in nakedness and in want
of all things' (cf. Deut. xxviii 48), as is known to you.'4)

4. R. J.J.Weinberg, *Seride Esh*, III, no. 71. (The quotation: 'all wickedness etc.' is taken
from the *amidah* of *Rosh Ha-Shanah* and *Yom Ha-Kippurim*.)

3

Questions of Conscience

Is it permitted according to the *halachah* to expose oneself to danger in order to save one's fellow-man from danger?

When the German troops entered Lithuania[1] on the 28th of Sivan 5701 (23 June 1941) they immediately began to show their cruelty towards the Jews. Every day they went hunting Jews, men and women were seized in the streets of Kovno and sent to the Seventh Fortress where their fate was decided. In their search for Jews the wicked ones were helped by their accomplices the Lithuanians who were glad to have the opportunity of giving vent to their hatred of the Jews. . . . Hundreds of Jews were seized by them in the streets among the arrested being many *yeshibah* students. During one of those days R. Oshry (who wrote this *Responsum*) was asked by the head of the Slobodka *yeshibah*, R. Abraham Grodzinski (who later died a martyr) to go to the secretary of the '*Agudath Ha-Rabbanim*', R. David Itzkowitz (he too later died a martyr) to ask him to go to the Lithuanians who were responsible for hunting the Jews and whom he knew from before the war, and to plead for the release of the *yeshibah* students who had been detained by them.

The question arose whether R. David Itzkowitz was permitted according to the *halachah* to endanger his life, as he himself might be seized.[2] After a lengthy discussion the Rabbi decided that according to the law R. David was not bound to endanger his life by going to plead for the students' release. Nevertheless, if he wished to do so he was not to be held back, for he would be doing an act of piety, particularly as it concerned *yeshibah* students who study the Law and the intention of the enemy was to destroy both the body and the soul of the Jewish people.

R. David went to the Lithuanians in charge and succeeded in obtaining the release of the *yeshibah* students. He himself later became a victim of the Nazis.[3]

Transgression of the dietary laws in the concentration camps. A very religious man (a Rabbi?) from Vienna had been in the concentration camps of Dachau and Buchenwald and had to eat non-*kosher* food

1. On the marching of German troops into Lithuania in general and into Kovno in particular see L. Garfunkel, *The Destruction of Kovno's Jewry*, pp. 28ff.
2. On the question whether a person must expose himself to an action which may be dangerous (*saphek sakkanah*) in order to save his fellow-man from real danger, see also Chief Rabbi Unterman, *Shebet Mi-Yehudah*, I, pp. 19ff.
3. R. E.Oshry, *Mi-Maamakkim*, II, no. 1.

265

T

several times.[4] He succeeded in being released and reached London. From there he wrote a letter (June 1939) to Rabbi Jeruchem[5] asking him to prescribe an atonement for his having eaten non-*kosher* food. The Rabbi prescribed various fasts he had to observe.[6]

4. The case happened most probably in Austria after *Kristallnacht*. Many Jews had been sent from Austria into concentration camps and were released when they had proved that they could emigrate from that country. On eating prohibited food, *vide* also *supra* p. 111.

5. He had left Vienna for Poland and arrived in Cracow on Friday 14 October 1938. There he wrote his reply.

6. R. H.Y.Jeruchem, *Birkath Hayyim*, no. 42. On other questions of conscience, *vide supra* Part I, pp. 50ff., 61f. 72f., 84f., 113f.

4

Deportations

GERMANY-POLAND (1938); BRESLAU-RUSSIA (1941?); POLAND-RUSSIA

A Mr Blatt who had come from Breslau to England before the war left his wife and four children at home in Breslau. He was in correspondence with his wife through the Red Cross until the beginning of 1941. At the end of that year, he received a letter from his wife's brother in which he informed him that his wife Mrs Berta Blatt and her children had been seized and sent away with a transport from Breslau. Mr Blatt had a niece (i.e. a daughter of his brother) who too was named Berta Blatt and who had been deported to Poland in 1938. After the war in 1946 Mr Blatt saw the name Berta Blatt in the register of the Polish Committee, which contained the names of those who had survived in Russia. He immediately wrote to the Russian Consulate in London for the exact address of 'Mrs. Berta Blatt née Spiller'. After three months, he received a reply from the Consulate that 'Berta Blatt née Spiller was living in Pergana (North Russia)' in a certain street. There was no mention of the children. He wrote several letters to the address given to him; however, they were all returned as no woman of that name could be found. Mr Blatt wished to re-marry as at that time he had been without a wife for fifteen years.

In his reply dated 31st of Counting the Omer 713 (1 May 1953), Rabbi I.J.Weiss of Manchester says that it was obvious that were it not for the register of the Polish Committee and the letter of the Russian Consulate, the husband would have been permitted to re-marry

like all those husbands whose wives disappeared during the Nazi Holocaust, as I have written in a lengthy treatise (*kuntras*) to which many great Rabbis of Rumania have agreed. However, the main factors against permitting remarriage are the above-mentioned documents (which showed that the wife was still alive). However, it is possible that they referred to the niece Berta Blatt deported in 1938 (to Poland) and not to the wife of Mr Blatt. This is more plausible in view of the fact that we know many people left Poland for Russia before the latter joined the war against Germany. (Furthermore, I know that when the Russians made a pact with the Nazis and conquered a great part of Poland, they deported very many men and women to Russia itself, particularly those who did not belong to that district.) This was not so at the time when the woman and her four children were deported in 1941 as then war between the Nazis and the Russians had begun and there was no chance of escaping from Germany to Russia. . . .'

The Rabbi, after giving his reasons, concluded that the husband was permitted to re-marry after certain formalities were fulfilled.[1]

TARNOW—AUSCHWITZ—PLASZOW—GROSS-ROSEN—BELSEN (1939-43)

Hella Weitz and her husband Jacob Weitz were born and lived in Tarnow. After all the terrible experiences they had from the outbreak of the war in 1939 until 1943 when of about forty thousand Jews (both natives and refugees) in Tarnow,[2] a great portion was massacred and others were deported to the extermination camps of Auschwitz, Maidanek, Treblinka, etc., they were among the mere 150 persons who remained in the ghetto (of Tarnow). In October 1943 they too were deported to a concentration camp in Plaszow—Cracow, where they worked as tailors until the end of summer 1944. In October 1944 the husband was deported from there and people said he had been taken to the camp in Gross-Rosen in Silesia, where there were crematoria. From then onwards nothing more was heard of him. His wife too was deported one month later to the camps in Auschwitz and to Belsen, and by a great miracle remained alive. At the time when the question was put before the Rabbi[3] (at the end of 1947) she was living in Switzerland. After the war she made inquiries about her husband whom she dearly loved. She received written information from her friends who had returned to Tarnow after the war and who had heard that her husband had died in Gross-Rosen.

After the war when the wife was in Prague she heard from a certain Daniel Verstaendig of Tarnow who knew her and her husband, as he had worked as a tailor under them when still in Tarnow. He had seen her husband in Gross-Rosen but did not know what had happened to him afterwards. After several months during which he spent some time in Tarnow and returned to Prague she asked him again whether the report she had received in a letter from her friends in Tarnow (that her husband had died) was true. He replied that people in Tarnow said that was so.

Her brother-in-law, i.e. her sister's husband, Israel Rath of Austria, wrote to his wife, i.e. to the sister of the woman, on 21 July 1946, as follows (this being a translation from the Polish): 'I for my part have asked both Rosenbaums about the above mentioned Jacob Weitz, the husband of the above-mentioned Hella, and they confirmed that he is no longer alive only the little Jacob Weitz is alive (in Tarnow there was another Jacob Weitz called "Little Weitz" and his wife's name was Leah,

1. R. I.J.Weiss, *Minhath Yizhak*, I, no. 43. See also R. A.L.Grossnass, *Leb Aryeh*, no. 28.
2. On the actions against the Jews in May-June, and October 1942, see Gerald Reitlinger, *The Final Solution*, pp. 271, 283.
3. R. M.J.Breisch, *Helkath Yaakob*, I, no. 17.

both were saved by assuming non-Jewish names and lived in Hungary).'
The woman presented two statements she had received in reply to her
inquiries. One from the Jewish Committee in Tarnow translated from
Polish and dated 25 June 1947. It stated on the basis of evidence of
witnesses, that the husband of Hella Weitz who was then living in
Switzerland, i.e. Jacob Weitz of Tarnow, was deported in 1943 from the
ghetto in Tarnow to the camp in Plaszow and then was killed in
Gross-Rosen. The document was signed by the president, Mr M. Kohn,
and secretary, Mr T. Braun, no. 176.

The second statement was from the Jewish community of Tarnow
(dated 11 September 1947). Rabbi Breisch who dealt with the *Responsum*
says he advised the woman to write to the Beth Din in Tarnow and ask
for confirmation; however, there appeared to be no Rabbi or Ab Beth
Din there as the second statement was signed by two witnesses only
confirmed by the Jewish community (*Jüdische Religionsgemeinschaft*) of
Tarnow that Jacob Weitz died in Gross-Rosen in 1944.

After a lengthy discussion Rabbi Breisch decided that the woman
might re-marry.

R. J.J.Weinberg of Montreux agrees with this decision and Rabbi
Shlomoh David Kahana of Jerusalem, and Chief Rabbi Herzog also
agree with him.

FRANKFURT—LODZ (OCTOBER 1941)

R. Yizhak Unna dealt with the following question:

He and his sisters had twice kept the eve of *Rosh Hodesh Kislev* as
Yahrzeit for their sister, Mrs Zirla, brother-in-law Judah Leo Ha-Kohen
Grunfeld, and their son Asher Alfred, after he had learned that they had
been deported from Frankfurt to Lodz on the 28th of Tishri 702
(19 October 1941). As the Rabbinate of Israel later proclaimed the 10th
of Tebeth[4] as a day of national mourning for the victims of Nazism,
should they give up keeping the *Yahrzeit* on the eve of *Rosh Hodesh
Kislev* which they had been observing the past two years?

He decided they should continue keeping the eve of *Rosh Hodesh
Kislev* as the *Yahrzeit* but observe also the day proclaimed by the
Chief Rabbinate as a day of mourning for other relatives and for all
other Jewish victims.[5]

VIENNA—POLAND

This case concerns an *agunah* from Vienna whose husband had been
sent to a labour camp in Kielce[6] in Poland in 701 (1941) and did not

4. *Vide supra* Part I, p. 157.
5. R. Dr Joseph Unna, in *Kol Torah*, Jerusalem, Tishri-Tebet 709, III, nos. 1–4, p. 53.
6. This name occurs again once more later, but on one occasion it is written: Kalusz.

return after the end of the war. His wife was in possession of official letters from the court and the (Jewish?) community of Vienna verifying those facts.

She had given evidence before the Beth Din that when she had still been together with her husband and only daughter they had received affidavits (for immigration) from her brother-in-law in Chicago. However, the consul had said the affidavit was valid only for her husband. So she had waited for another affidavit. In the meantime she had had an opportunity to emigrate with her daughter to London and she made use of it while her husband remained in Vienna with the hope of receiving permission to emigrate to America as the consul had assured him. Before the couple separated they gave each other a firm assurance that after the end of the war they would meet in Chicago and would write to her brother-in-law so that they would be kept informed of each other.

When the husband was sent to Kielce he wrote to her regularly to London. His last letter had been written by someone else and only signed by her husband. In it he informed her that he could no longer see with both eyes and would remain blind. He expressed his wish to meet his family once more. The Holy One who knows the future knew whether he would have the merit as his position was desperate—he had nothing to eat. He was, however, satisfied that his wife and daughter had been saved.

Since the end of the war the woman had tried by all possible means available by making investigations through the consulate and Red Cross to learn the fate of her husband. She had always received the same reply that her husband's fate was unknown. She also consulted lists and registers of survivors, however, her husband's name did not appear on them.

The woman was still young and wished to re-marry but unfortunately could not find anyone who could assist her.

Rabbi Meisels shows at first that her re-marriage would be forbidden only from the Rabbinical standpoint of the Law (i.e. if she did re-marry without permission she could still stay with her husband). After expressing various mitigating factors Rabbi Meisels goes on to show that the woman may re-marry even in the first instance. One of the reasons was that her husband had been suffering from eye trouble which according to Jewish Law would be considered a dangerous disease. Such patients were unfit for work and no attempts were made to cure them. At the best they were placed in the hospital and sent to the crematorium at the next selection. In our case where the husband had been an invalid as early as 1941 he was surely not alive at the end of the war. The majority of forced labourers died for various reasons, some of them because of hard work, beating and starvation until they became *Mussulmans.*[7] Myriads died of various diseases which raged in the camp like stomach disorders, typhoid; even after the liberation, there was no possibility of providing the camps with sufficient medicaments. Because of that thousands-even tens of thousands-died after they had been liberated. This is well known.

In addition more than ten years had elapsed since she had received the last letter, hence all memory of him has been lost and that is on the same footing as an *umdana* that he is no longer alive. In view of this and some other important factors in favour of the woman the Rabbi decided that she may re-marry provided that three famous Rabbis would agree. This happened, one of them being R. Shlomoh David Kahana of Jerusalem. He tells the Rabbi he would be brief in his reply as he had to date dealt at length with three thousand cases of *agunoth.* He asked Rabbi Meisels to let him have another copy of his *Kuntras Agunoth* as the first one had been burned together with all his books in the Old City by the Arabs. The *Responsum* is dated: 23rd of Tishri 712 (23 October 1951).[8]

ANTWERP—CALAIS—BIRKENAU (SUMMER 1942)

Rabbi David Kahana (formerly Ab Beth Din in Warsaw) of Jerusalem was approached to look into the case of an agunah, a Mrs Berta Ramaszkowski of Zurich, 250 Badener Street, and to assist her obtain permission to re-marry.

According to her statement, her husband had been deported by the Germans together with a large group of Jews from Antwerp, to an unknown destination in the year 1942. From then she heard nothing of him. According to reports all members of that group had been lost and no one returned. On the basis of that information she had received a certificate from the ministry in Brussels stating that her husband was no longer alive. On the strength of that evidence she sought to obtain permission to re-marry. R. Kahana asked R. Breisch of Zurich to summon her and obtain, if possible, more details and particulars and to forward them to him.[9]

In his reply R. Breisch stated that he had immediately summoned Mrs Ramaszkowski from whom he heard the following particulars about her husband:

Levi (Leon) Ramaszkowski, born in Swenigrodka (Russia), had been taken by the Germans in midsummer 1942 from his house in Antwerp to the nearby town of Calais, France, for hard labour and from there to Birkenau—Auschwitz. In midsummer 1943, his wife, who was by then

7. See 'Glossary'.
8. R. Z.H.Meisels, *Binyan Zebi,* II, nos. 60–65.
9. The letter is dated: 10th of Shebat 711 (17 January 1951).

in Switzerland, received a letter from her husband in Birkenau (the letter was written by him to his non-Jewish maid in Antwerp who forwarded it to his wife in Switzerland) in which he asked the maid to send him parcels of food and to inform him whether she knew anything about his wife. Some lines had been deleted by the censor. From then onwards nothing was heard of him. Husband and wife were extremely happily married and had an only son. The husband had many relatives. His wife had been living in Zurich since the year mentioned above. She was religious and brought up her son in the religious way of life. She requested permission for re-marriage.

A statement from the Belgian authorities confirmed that her husband Leon ben Baruch Ramaszkowski, born in Swenigrodka, who lived in Antwerp, died in Auschwitz, Poland, some time between 1 November 1942 and 1 June 1943. That was recorded in the register of deaths.

Rabbi Breisch refers to a decision he had given on another occasion that all men who had been in camps under the Nazis were presumably dead and the position of their wives was better than that of those women whose husbands had disappeared 'in waters the shores of which cannot be seen' (in the latter case if they had re-married they could remain with their husbands, *vide supra* p. 216). What had to be proved in our case was that the woman could re-marry in the first instance. R. Breisch then tries to prove that Mrs Berta Ramaszkowski may do so and quotes Isserles concerning[10] the persecution in Austria[11] when the women who had been imprisoned had been permitted after their release to return to their husbands. The Rabbis were lenient because (he thinks) they feared that otherwise the women might succumb to immorality. Similarly, we too have to adopt a lenient view in cases of *agunah* after World War II since it is a time of emergency affecting thousands of women (this mitigating factor enables the woman to re-marry in the first instance).

In addition to other lenient factors R. Breisch believes that her husband had perished at the camp of Birkenau, known as *Zigeunerlager* (gipsy camp) and notorious for its having been the first to massacre all its inmates. Eight years had passed since Mrs Ramaszkowski had last heard of her husband. Could one imagine that her husband was still alive and did not care to return to his beloved wife and only child? Even if he were ill that could easily be established as there were special institutions which traced and assisted such people. Even if we were to assume he was mutilated and did not return home as he was ashamed (cf. *Yebamoth* 115a) we could argue the opposite: if he had been

10. *Darche Mosheh on Tur Eben Ha-Ezer*, VII, 13.
11. On this persecution which took place in 1420 see Isserlein, *Terumath Ha-Deshen* no. 241; *Pesakim U-Kethabim*, no. 34, and S. Krauss, *Die Wiener Geserah*, Vienna, 1920, pp. 97f.

injured he would have required the assistance of the Red Cross and similar institutions and could easily have been traced. He must therefore be presumed dead. In view of all that R. Breisch decided that the woman may re-marry provided R. Kahana agreed.

R. Solomon David Kahana who was in charge of *agunoth* cases agreed to that decision and added some other points to support it.[12]

FRANCE—BIRKENAU—AUSCHWITZ (SUMMER 1942)

Mr Abraham Elefand, husband of Mrs Juta Elefand of Zurich (formerly of France, born in Kalusz, Poland), was deported from the camp (in France) to the extermination camp of Birkenau-Auschwitz in midsummer 1942. A witness testified in writing that he had seen Mr Elefand in Birkenau. The witness was later taken to Auschwitz for forced labour. When he returned to Birkenau four weeks later he searched for Mr Elefand and for other acquaintances. However, none of them was to be found. The witness stated they were certainly massacred in Birkenau, the extermination place of Auschwitz.

There was also a confirmation of the government of Paris that Mr Elefand had died in Auschwitz on 13 July 1942—'it is well known Auschwitz and Birkenau were two places near each other'. R. Weinberg of Montreux was willing, in principle, to give Mrs Elefand permission to re-marry and concluded that if R. Breisch agreed he would join him in permitting the woman to re-marry.

In his *Responsum*[13] R. Breisch mentioned that two years previously on the 24th of Shebat 711 (31 January 1951) he had given permission to a Mrs Berta Ramaszkowski of Zurich[14] to re-marry on the strength of various principles which could apply likewise to the case of Mrs Elefand who had even better grounds for being granted permission, i.e. the above written evidence.

R. Breisch put the matter before R. Solomon David Kahana as he did not want to be the first to give a decision in that case. R. Kahana agreed to give Mrs Elefand permission to re-marry provided no question of *yibbum* was involved.[15]

BELGIUM—FRANCE—GERMANY (SEPTEMBER 1942)

This is the text of the report of the witnesses.

We were approached by Mrs Dushein who married according to the Law of Israel her husband Dr Samuel Jacob in Antwerp in 1939. She told us that when the Germans invaded Belgium she fled with her

12. R. M.J.Breisch, *Helkath Yaakob*, II, nos. 29–30.
13. Dated: 9th of Shebat 713 (29 January 1953).
14. See the case mentioned before.
15. R. M.J.Breisch, *Helkath Yaakob*, II, nos. 33–34.

husband to France. She and her mother succeeded afterwards in reaching London, while her husband remained in France with some other members of their family. In 1942 she ceased to hear from him. According to reports she received he had been deported to Germany by the Nazis in September of that year from the Camp in Milles in the South of France where he had been detained by the French Police. We then approached various people and enquired the whereabouts (fate) of her husband.

We received the following reply from the Grand Rabbi of Marseilles which we translated from the French:

'In reply to your letter of November 30 1954, I am able to inform you that the story of the family is well known to me. They were taken in front of my eyes from the Camp in Milles in the vicinity of Marseilles. Mr Samuel Jacob, the husband of Mrs Dushein at present in London, was with a group of several hundred taken in a transport to the death camps. The "official" report issued then was "Has been taken to an unknown destination".

To give you a precise reply I regret to confirm that from that date, September 1942, according to available reports, he must be regarded as dead. The letter of July 31 1946, to Mr Naftali Birnbaum, a copy of which you sent me, was written by me.

Do believe me that my religious feelings are sincerely orthodox.

Israel Selzer'.

We received the following reply from her brother-in-law Mr Naftali, New York (brother of her husband), which was translated from the English:

'I am sorry to inform you that the latest report on my brother, Samuel Jacob, which I received was the letter of July 1946 from Rabbi Selzer. I have heard the same from my wife's parents who were at the place to where our family was deported in 1942. They succeeded in escaping from that fate. After the end of the war, immediately communication with Europe was resumed, I tried at every source known to trace my family, but without any success. Also some relatives in Switzerland and Poland who survived helped me to trace them. However, they told me immediately afterwards that I should give up hope of finding them alive.

My brother, and my father too, knew our address in the United States. No doubt, they would have contacted us had they survived.'

From the Beth Din in Antwerp, we received the following evidence:

'We were in a session of three judges (one has since died), when there appeared before us the witness Petahia, son of Pinhas Eliezer Birnbaum, and, after caution with reference to Lev. v I, gave the following evidence: The missing person in question was taken together with the witness from the Camp at Drancy to the East. In the town Kozel, the Nazis said that all sick people, women and children should remain in the railway wagon, the remainder should get off for work. The person in question remained in the train because he thought he would be transferred to a hospital. As is known, they were taken to the extermination camps.

The witness knew him (the missing husband) only under the name of Dr Birnbaum but identified him on the photograph we enclose. We have been clearly informed that the missing man had no children but has a brother in the United States.

9th of Tebeth 715 (January 3, 1955)
(signed) Hayyim Yaakob Rothenberg, Rabbi and Ab Beth Din, son of R. Mordecai, Gershon Hillel, son of R. Yizhak Yaakov Fachler.'

The unfortunate woman is still in her prime and has not experienced life as she was separated from her husband a short time after the wedding when they fled from the enemy to save their lives. It is a terrible case of *iggun*.

Reply—The Rabbi decided that after performing *halizah* she may marry, but not a *kohen*.[16]

YUGOSLAVIA (1942)

A husband had been taken by the Germans in 1942 from Yugoslavia to an extermination camp (*mahaneh ha-hashmadah*) and did not return.[17] His wife brought three witnesses, two of whom said that they knew the woman and her husband who had two children, a boy and a girl. They knew that the husband had been taken by the Germans and did not return. However, they were not sure if the husband had been killed. The third witness stated that he knew for certain that her husband had been taken to the extermination camp in (?)[18] together with all the other Jews of the town. Only eighty of them returned and he heard from them and from others too that they alone had been saved, the others had been exterminated. They mentioned the name of her husband among those who had been killed.

The only clear evidence about the death of her husband is that of the third witness. However, the question is whether his evidence is admissible for the witness has declared his intention to marry the 'widow'. If one

16. R. I.J.Weiss, *Minhath Yizhak*, II, no. 64.
17. On the deportation and fate of the Yugoslav Jews, see Gerald Reitlinger, *The Final Solution*, pp. 389f.
18. Unfortunately I was unable to identify this camp with any of the camps mentioned in *The Crimes of the Fascist Occupants and their Collaborators against Jews in Yugoslavia*, ed. by Dr Zdenko Löwenthal, Belgrade, 1957.

gives evidence affecting a woman in order to marry her she may not marry at all. Furthermore, even if the evidence would enable her to re-marry, she would not be allowed to marry the witness.

However, the Rabbi proves that in view of the evidence of the two witnesses who testify that the husband had been taken by the Germans to the extermination camp where, as is well known, the vast majority (*rubba de-rubba*) of the Jews taken were killed[19] and on the strength of other persuasive factors there is no reason to refuse permission for her to marry anyone she wishes; she may even marry the witness.[20]

WESTERBORK (HOLLAND)—SOBIBOR (POLAND) (MARCH–JULY 1943)

On the 3rd of Iyyar 707 (23 April 1947) Chief Rabbi Aharon Schuster, Ab Beth Din of Amsterdam, submitted to the Chief Rabbi of Israel, R. Yizhak Herzog, the following case:

An *agunah*, Mrs G. D. of Holland, appeared before the Beth Din in Amsterdam. Her husband had been taken to the death camp in Sobibor. She showed the document (death certificate) she had received from the Red Cross informing her of her husband's death and stating also the date of his death. The woman had a son by her husband, who too had been deported by the evildoers to the death camp together with his father.

Through a thorough investigation which included the hearing of witnesses conducted in Amsterdam by a famous advocate, a religious Jew (Dr De Haas, the Chairman of the 'Agudath Yisrael' of Holland) it became known that all Jews from Holland who had been deported from the camp at Westerbork (Holland) to Eastern Europe from March 1943 till July 1943 were brought to Sobibor.[21] They numbered about 35,000 of whom only two women survived who then lived in Holland. The victims were massacred either in gas chambers or were shot. However, the entire transport was not killed at the same time. At first the young men and young women who appeared strong were separated from the rest to work in the camp, e.g. to sort out the garments of the corpses, etc. They were later killed.

This is, in short, the result of the investigation made by Dr De Haas who submitted a more lengthy report. All the courts and institutions, such as the Red Cross, rely on it. It was owing to this report that a certificate was given to the woman testifying to her husband's death, as he had surely died. It is almost certain (*karob le-vaddai*) that he

19. This evidence, says the Rabbi, makes our case at least like that of an *agunah* whose husband had disappeared in waters the shores of which cannot be seen and re-marriage is only Rabbinically forbidden.
20. R. E.Waldenberg, *Ziz Eliezer*, V, no. 24.
21. On deportations to Auschwitz, see the letter of the Red Cross *supra*, Part I, pp. 154f.

died soon after his arrival at the camp as he was about 46 years old. However, with regard to their son the exact time of death cannot be ascertained as he was only 16 years old and it is very possible that he had worked at the camp for a certain time. This is all that Dr De Haas told me.

The husband had left a brother who was living in Israel. A journey from Israel abroad entailed currently (April 1947) many difficulties both from the financial and political points of view.

Taking some mitigating factors into consideration Rabbi Schuster asked whether permission could be found for the woman to re-marry without *halizah*. The general position in Holland was that if no permission for re-marriage was granted the couple might live together without religious marriage and through this demoralization would increase.

Chief Rabbi Herzog decided, after giving his reasons, that no *halizah* was required taking also into consideration that the woman was young and could succumb to depravity, and it was almost certain that she would not obtain permission to go to Israel.

Rabbi Shlomoh David Kahana (formerly Rosh Beth Din of Warsaw, then Rabbi in the Old City in Jerusalem) thinks that the levir (who was in Israel) should be asked whether he was willing to participate in *halizah* and whether there was the possibility of doing so. If this could be done within three months endeavours should be made to perform *halizah*. Otherwise she is exempted from *halizah*. The *Responsum* is dated: 19th of Iyyar, 707 (9 May 1947).[22]

CRACOW—BELZEC (FEBRUARY 1943)

A woman and two witnesses testified before the Beth Din (of Melbourne) that her husband had been taken with about ten thousand Jews from the ghetto of Cracow[23] to the death camp in Belzec and that seven years had already elapsed and nothing of him was heard during that time. His name did not appear on the official list of those who had been saved nor was anything known about him in any office.

The respondent agrees with the Rabbi in Melbourne that the woman is allowed to re-marry if another distinguished Rabbi would agree. Among the various proofs for this decision the Rabbi quoted the statement in the Talmud that if a person is led to be executed on instructions of a non-Jewish court his wife may, according to some codifiers, re-marry as he is assumed to have died. But also the other codifiers would agree that the wife of a person led to be executed by a

22. Chief Rabbi Herzog, *Hechal Yizhak*, II, nos. 79–80.
23. The liquidation of the ghetto of Cracow took place on the 13th of Adar 703 (18 February 1943). See R. B.Halpern, Introduction to *Mishneh La-Melech*, p. 12.

non-Jewish court may re-marry if we are sure that the court does not accept bribes. 'And the wagons sent by the Nazis to the death camps on the instructions of the Gestapo and the Nazi government have the same character as that of a person taken to be executed by a non-Jewish court which does not accept any bribe to spare the condemned person. It is well known that the Germans did not take bribes, particularly as they had robbed their victims of everything beforehand and did not need any bribe.'[24]

KATOWITZ—DACHAU (1943, 1945)

Evidence before a Beth Din of three by a woman who testified as follows:

She, her husband and only son, aged three, lived in Katowitz, Poland, in 1939. When the Germans invaded Poland they were forced to work in the coal mines. Their son was taken from them by the Nazis in 1943 and from then they heard nothing more of him. The couple remained in Katowitz until the end of the war. In 1944[25] the Russians expelled the Germans from Poland and approached Katowitz. About eight weeks before the end of the war the Nazis seized the husband and sent him together with other men in a truck to Germany. After some days she too was arrested and sent in a truck to Germany. The journey took two to three weeks. A number of those with her died *en route* from hunger and thirst. Finally they reached Dachau. About three weeks after the end of the war she met a Jew whom she knew from Katowitz (she did not recall his name) who said to her: 'I'm sorry to have to give you bad news. I saw your husband when he was being taken from the truck to the hospital at Dachau swollen from hunger. Next morning I heard that your husband died. Later I saw him being taken out dead on a board from hospital.' She stated that in that hospital they used to kill the patients by administering lethal injections and they killed almost all the patients taken there. She added that her husband had a brother who had lived in America for more than thirty years and if he were still alive he would be about seventy years old. However, it was not known exactly where he was and they had not heard from him the whole time.

With regard to this testimony two points must be considered:

1. If we can accept that she did indeed hear from another person that her husband died in the extermination camp.
2. If we decide to accept her account, is she still forbidden to re-marry in view of the fact that she may be bound to her levir—perhaps her

---

24. R. M.Rath, *Kol Mebasser*, I, no. 84.
25. In *Minhath Yizhak* by R. I.J.Weiss, I, no. 101, it is said, 1945. This date is correct as the Russian troops entered Silesia on 21 January 1945.

son had died before her husband and her brother-in-law may still be alive. '

As far as the first point is concerned the Rabbi decided that she is reliable and her evidence acceptable.

With regard to the second point, he is of the opinion she requires *halizah*. The Rabbi tells us of the correspondence he had with Dayan I. J. Weiss of Manchester on this subject.[26]

HUNGARY—AUSCHWITZ (APRIL—MAY 1944)

Arrival, Selection

Hearing of witnesses.

R. Yizhak Hoffmann, son of the martyr R. Akiba Hoffman, came before us when we were in session and gave evidence concerning his late brother R. Moshe Aryeh (who died a martyr).

The witness had met a man in Pest in summer 705 (1945). The latter, named Rosenberg, son of the late R. Hayyim Rosenberg, was a native of Mihallipalwe. He told him he had seen during the persecution in Oswiecim, the city of blood (cf. Ezek. xxii 2, Nahum iii 1), the late aforementioned R. Mosheh Aryeh led to the left side and he probably shared the fate of those who perished.

Yizhak Meir Rath, son of the late R. Samuel, came before us too and gave evidence that in Oswiecim he saw the aforementioned R. Mosheh Aryeh in the barracks to where all men who had been sent to the right side were taken. In the barracks all Jewish prisoners were ordered to strip and wash. R. Mosheh was among them. He was extremely weak, so much so that he lost all human appearance. When still at home he had been suffering from consumption as was well known. By then his condition had certainly deteriorated and he became very weak. He resembled a dead man. The witness added that from that time onwards there were many men there from the district of Mihallipalwe but R. Mosheh Aryeh had perished and was seen no more.

Mihallipalwe, evening of the 20th Heshvan 707 (1 November 1946) signed by (the Rabbis) Naphtali Jacob son of R. Mosheh Ha-Kohen, Dayan; Shlomoh Jacob, son of Asher Isaiah; Zebi son of Zeeb Weiss.

Dayan E. Naphtali remarks that he was incapable of dealing with such a great problem particularly in view of the fact that there appeared to be a contradiction in the evidence of the two witnesses (according to one R. Mosheh Aryeh had been led to the left side, while according

26. R. A.L.Grossnass, *Leb Aryeh*, no. 45; R. Weiss, *Minhath Yizhak*, I, no. 101.

to the other he had been on the right side). In addition the Rabbi had not been at Oswiecim but only in Transnistria and therefore he thought himself unable to judge.

A reply was given by the Rabbi of Temesvar. He permitted Mrs Golda Hoffmann to re-marry after *halizah*. He believed there was no contradiction: 'It is well known that the murderers on seeing a young man unable to do work later put him on the left side together with old people. Hence when R. Mosheh was selected they did not know at that time he was unable to do work so they sent him to the right side. Later in the barracks after he had stripped his weakness became visible to all. He 'disappeared' for he had been led to the left side unnoticed except by the son of R. Hayyim Rosenberg, for the Germans had done this secretly so that others should not see. The evidence of the two witnesses was therefore not contradictory.'

The Rabbi then proceeds to discuss the question whether being sent to the left side was to be regarded as similar to the case of a man who had fallen into waters the shores of which cannot be seen (in which case the wife must not re-marry in the first instance, but if she had re-married she may stay with her second husband) or if it should be regarded similar to the case of a man who falls into a pit with snakes and scorpions in which case death can be assumed as certain. He quotes the decision of the Ab Beth Din of Neamt who had permitted a woman to re-marry on the evidence that her husband had been sent to the left side. The Rabbi of Temesvar, R. Yizhak Zebi Sopher, the writer of the *Responsum*, quotes another *Responsum* he wrote in which he cites the decision of 'one of the martyrs, R. Moses Werzberger', Dayan of Arschiva, who had worked on the left side and declared that in his view the wives of all those who were sent to the left side could be given permission to re-marry. Besides the above (i.e. even if the status is similar only to that of the wife of a man who had fallen into waters the shores of which cannot be seen) there were other mitigating factors: R. Mosheh Aryeh was weak and sick and nothing more was heard of him so most probably he had perished.

The Rabbi of Temesvar was inclined to give Mrs Hoffmann permission to re-marry, provided the Rabbi of Grosswardein (R. I.J.Weiss) would agree.

Indeed, R. Weiss agreed (as R. Yizhak Hoffmann was the brother-in-law of the *agunah* she had first to perform the act of *halizah* and she was not permitted to marry a *kohen*). Date: 3rd *Hanukkah* 707 (20 December 1946).[27]

---

27. R. I.J.Weiss, *Minhath Yizhak*, I, nos. 93–96. The deportations of Hungarian Jews to Auschwitz began in April-May 1944. See Jenö Levai, *Hungarian Jewry and the Papacy*, p. 118; Gerald Reitlinger, *The Final Solution*, p. 664.

(a) Theresienstadt, (b) Oswiecim (Auschwitz) (August 1944)

The following question was put before Rabbi Breisch in Zurich:

In August 1944 a man, his wife and their daughter aged 12, of Warsz, Hungary, were arrested by the evildoers. While the husband was sent to Theresienstadt, the mother and daugher were, according to a report the husband received from a soldier, sent to Auschwitz (Oswiecim) the place of the gas chamber where, as is well known, thousands and myriads of Jews had perished. From then onwards the husband heard nothing about them until the end of April 1945, the end of the war ... when many men and women came from Germany to Theresienstadt among whom were two women who knew the husband and who had been deported at the same time from Hungary. They reported that they had travelled together with his wife to Oswiecim; however, she had died *en route* in the wagon as she had been very ill. Already in 1938 she was suffering from a lung disease and in 1942 she underwent an operation for the removal of part of the lung. Since then she had always had a raised temperature and at the time she was deported she ran a temperature of 39 degrees (Celsius). In short, she had been dangerously ill. Both women did not mention the exact name of the dead woman. However, when they arrived in Theresienstadt and heard that the name of the husband was 'Hausmann' they recalled that the wife too was named 'Hausmann'. She had a daughter named 'Eliza' who was 12 years old. The woman died in the wagon and we know that the weak and the old remained in the wagon to travel to Oswiecim; however, the two women (who gave evidence), being healthy, were selected to be sent to work in Germany, for each time the healthy were selected from the weak.

In March 1946, the husband received a letter dated March 1946 from a non-Jewess who knew the family well from their home-town before the war. She informed the husband that the daughter who had survived was living in Kaschau while his wife had died in the camp, (*Lager*) when she was travelling from her home. That letter came in reply to the husband's enquiry to her whether she knew anything about the fate of his family.

In April 1946 he received another letter, dated April, from a non-Jewess who was living near Kaschau being a reply to the husband's query whether she knew anything about his daughter Eliza. She replied that she had spoken to his daughter Eliza in Kaschau a week before, who during the conversation mentioned that her mother had died in the wagon on the way to the camp. When writing the non-Jewess did not know the address of the daughter, Eliza.

v

The husband asked the Rabbi whether he may re-marry as he was only thirty-six years old and had not fulfilled the commandment of Genesis 1 28. He showed the letters he had received from the non-Jewesses. All the above evidence was supplied by the husband.

The Rabbi was inclined to decide leniently. In his reply, the following passage occurs:

> Anyone acquainted with these terrible events, unprecedented in history, knows that of all who had been taken to Auschwitz, those unfit for work had been doomed to die in the gas chamber. In our case with regard to a person dangerously ill there are greater grounds to assume he has been killed. He can be given the status of a person led to his execution upon the verdict of a non-Jewish court and according to some authorities is regarded as dead....[28]

LARISSA—CORFU—BIRKENAU (20–29 JUNE 1941)

The following *Responsum* was written by R. Ben Zion Hai Uzziel to the Chief Rabbinate in Tel Aviv-Jaffa on 21st of Tammuz 711 (25 July 1951):

> In reply to your letter of Tammuz 20 concerning the *agunah* Olga Maza I summoned the woman Olga Maza who gave the following oral evidence:
> 'I, Olga Maza, wife of Nissim Maza, married my husband in Larissa (Thessaly, Greece) in 1932 and lived with him together for 12 years, i.e. till 1944 when we were taken to Corfu and from there together with the whole community direct to Birkenau.[29] There the men were separated from the women and from then I never saw my husband again. We had no children. I had seen my husband's brothers in labour camps in Birkenau. I had three brothers-in-law: Yizhak Hayyim Maza, Yaakob Hayyim Maza, and Abraham Hayyim Maza. All of them said they had not seen my husband at all from the time they arrived there. My husband was suffering from ulkus (ulcers), my brother-in-law Yaakob Hayyim died in hospital according to the report of my youngest brother-in-law Abraham. Yizhak had been led away on the evening (of his arrival) to be taken to the furnace. Abraham told me that evening that they would transfer him next morning from his prison to Germany. I have since heard nothing of them. They all realized that those who were separated on their arrival in the camp were to be brought to the furnace'.

---

28. R. M.J. Breisch, *Helkath Yaakob*, I, no. 5.
29. On the plight of the Jews of Corfu, cf. Michael Molho and Joseph Nehama, *The Destruction of Greek Jewry, 1941–1944*, pp. 186ff.

From the words of the woman the following points become clear:

(a) Her husband Nissim Maza and her two brothers-in-law, Yizhak Maza and Abraham Maza, had been deported together with their community in Greece to Germany as 'captives of death'.

(b) The above-mentioned brothers had been separated for an ill fate in special camps for those who were unfit to work. They were to die by fire.

(c) The third brother, Yaakob Maza, died in hospital according to the declaration of Abraham, her youngest brother-in-law.

Since it is well known that the cursed Nazis transferred the whole community of Corfu to the death camps and that in those death camps furnaces were burning and that there existed gas chambers in which myriads of Jews were killed, our case is like that of a person who had fallen into a pit with serpents when death can be assumed as certain (*Shulhan Aruch, Eben Ha-Ezer*, Cap. XVII, No. 29). . . . .As they have not been found alive till this day (the *Responsum* was written on the 21st of Tammuz 711, 25 July 1951) their wives may re-marry.

Chief Rabbi Uzziel is of the opinion that a notice should appear in the Israeli press that anyone who knows anything about the members of the family Maza (their names are given) should inform the Beth Din in Tel Aviv, or should send there a statement legalized by a local Rabbi or by local authority. If a certain time elapses and nothing is heard the woman may re-marry. R. Uzziel gives the reasons for his decision.

Chief Rabbi Herzog agrees to this decision.[30]

LODZ—AUSCHWITZ-BIRKENAU (29 SEPTEMBER 1944)
LIBAU (LATVIA)—STUTTHOF—STALF (DECEMBER 1944)

Hannah (Anka), daughter of Yehezkiel Wiener, the wife of Pinhas Singer, both from Lodz, lived in the ghetto of Lodz under Nazi rule from the day of the outbreak of the war until 29 September 1944. On that day both were deported to Auschwitz and from then onwards nothing was heard of her husband. When they parted from each other they said that should they have the merit to survive the war both would send their addresses to Lodz, their home-town. The couple loved each other dearly, and at the time she reported this to the Rabbi her eyes shed tears continuously. She said that were her husband alive he would certainly have appeared. After the war at the end of 1945 she had heard

30. Chief Rabbi Ben Zion Meir Hai Uzziel, *Mishpete Uzziel, Eben Ha-Ezer*, no. 40.

from a man named Rosenthal, also from Lodz, who knew the Singer family well, i.e. the husband and wife. He had been together with her husband for three weeks in Birkenau, near Auschwitz, the place of the burning fire, known as *Zigeunerlager* where most of the men had been put to death. He, the witness, had luckily escaped by a miracle as he had been sent to work. In summer 1947 when the woman was in the hospital she received a reply dated 18 May 1947 from 'The Jewish National Committee in Lodz' from the section which dealt with tracing missing families, with regard to her question concerning the whereabouts of her husband. The committee knew nothing about him. The woman had been in Davos, Switzerland, for more than one year receiving medical treatment.

On the 7th of Heshvan, 708 (21 October 1947) the Beth Din of Zurich heard evidence from the *shohet* R. Abraham Shlomoh Kowalski. He had been in Davos on the 5th of Heshvan 708 (19 October 1947) and, in a session of three (judges), received the following evidence from the witness Baruch Lazar from Libau, Lettland. The latter testified that on about 5 December 1944, he and another man were among those who arrived at the 'Stalof (Stalf) workplace' from the concentration camp 'Struthof' Pommern, which was nearby.

The witness had worked together with that man in the field on the railway lines. About eight days later he saw the man lying ill in bed, his face swollen and his body leprous. He asked him what his name was, and he replied: 'Pinhas Singer of Lodz, a fruiterer'. He was of middle height and had black hair. That description corresponded to the one given by the *agunah*. After one month, on about 12 January 1945, he heard one morning that someone had died. When he asked who it was he was told by all that Pinhas Singer had died. The witness did not see him but he asked several times who had died and was told by all that it was Pinhas Singer (the *Lager* comprised a very large room where hundreds of men slept and lay. Pinhas Singer was lying at the end of the room so the witness did not see him often, and if a person died he was, naturally, carried out at once). This was all submitted by R. Abraham Shlomoh who concluded that the words of the above witness made a great impression on the three men—himself included,—who heard the evidence.

The above-mentioned woman wished to re-marry. She had no relatives whatsoever, was lonely and very poor. She had met a man who wished to marry her. If permission for re-marriage were not given it was feared she might succumb to immorality.

Rabbi Breisch decided that she may re-marry provided two famous Rabbis would agree and that an inquiry would be made once more of the community of Lodz whether anything about her husband had since been heard. Indeed, R. Weinberg of Montreux and R. Shlomoh D. Kahana, formerly Ab Beth Din in Warsaw, later Rabbi in Jerusalem, and Chief Rabbi Herzog agreed with him.[31]

LODZ—TREBLINKA (END OF 1940)

An *agunah* whose husband had been deported about six years previously from Lodz was in possession of a certificate issued by the Beth Din of Lodz confirming the death of her husband. Evidence was later received that her husband's three brothers had been sent about the same time to Treblinka, a place where all those deported had been exterminated. R. Meisels was asked to clarify the position as regards *halizah*.

In the course of his reply in which he is inclined to permit the woman to re-marry without *halizah* R. Meisels states *inter alia*: 'Treblinka had a reputation of being one of the worst camps from which not even one in a thousand escaped, for Treblinka was no labour camp but an extermination camp. . . .'[32]

---

31. R. M.J. Breisch, *Helkath Yaakob*, I, nos. 18–21.
32. R. Z.H.Meisels, *Binyan Zebi*, II, no. 71. The *Responsum* is dated, Thursday *Vayishlah* 707 (5 December 1946).

5

Cases of Mass Murder

LITHUANIA

A young woman, Judith, daughter of Isaac Lazenski, born in Israel, appeared before me[1] in Zurich and showed me her *kethubah* according to which she had married in accordance with Jewish Law a young man named Eliyahu son of Jacob Abramowitz in *Kibbutz* Masada (Mapai) on the 15th of Sivan 5706 (14 June 1946). She also produced a certificate from the Israeli Government, which stated as follows: 'We inform you with deep regret that Eliyahu Abramowitz died in action whilst exercising his duties on the 2nd of Tebeth 5709 (January 3, 1949) in the battle of Rafah.'

There were no children, and to the question whether her husband had any brothers she replied that he had a brother in Kovno named Gershon Abramowitz who had been murdered by the Nazis. She had learned that from her husband's parents Jacob Abramowitz and his wife who were living in Paris and were mourning for their two sons of whom they had been bereft.

A witness from Arosa gave R. Breisch a report over the telephone which the former later put in writing. It ran as follows:

I, Raphael, son of R. Judah Ha-Levi Levin from Kovno, saw the young Gershon Abramowitz for the last time two or three days after the outbreak of World War II, i.e. on June 24th or 25th, 1941.[2] He was standing on the threshold of his house in Kovno when he left for Wilno. In September of that year his parents received a letter from him in which he informed them that on his way to Wilno he had been arrested by the Germans and imprisoned in the Camp of Proviniski which was about 20 kilometres from Kovno in Lithuania. About two months later his parents, R. Jacob and Zila Abramowitz, learned from reports from Lithuanians that their son Gershon had together with other Jews of that camp been killed by the Germans and Lithuanian partisans. The destruction of the camp of Proviniski occurred at the time when the Germans exterminated the Jews of Lithuania and a great part of the Kovno ghetto, i.e. in October 1941.[3]

(This was the evidence of Raphael b. R. Judah Ha-Levi Levin.)

1. R. M.J.Breisch.
2. Russia was attacked by Germany on 22 June 1941. On the persecution of the Jews, see Gerald Reitlinger, *The Final Solution*, pp. 225ff.
3. On this persecution which took place on 28 and 29 October 1941, see L. Garfunkel, *The Destruction of Kovno's Jewry*, pp. 73ff. (see also *supra* pp. 50f.).

The same evidence was given by Eliezer Walfa of Kovno who knew Gershon Abramowitz from that town.

Mrs Judith Abramowitz met a man in Switzerland whom she wished to marry. She sought permission to do so. Two points were involved: the question of *agunah* and that of *halizah*.

The Rabbi decided that she could re-marry provided the Beth Din of Jerusalem would agree. He advised that one make new inquiries of the Israeli Government about Eliyahu Abramowitz as perhaps he was only wounded and during the war was wrongly listed as dead. Also particulars about the names of his father and home should be mentioned.

With regard to the question of *halizah* R. Breisch refers to his *Responsa* I, nos. 15–16 that those who had been in the hands of the Nazis were presumably dead. Their position was, as regards their wives' being permitted to re-marry, much better than that of one who had fallen into waters the shores of which cannot be seen (whose wife may not re-marry in the first instance but if she had married may remain with her second husband) particularly in view of the fact that so many years had elapsed and Gershon Abramowitz had not informed his parents whom he loved dearly that he was alive. Hence, in view of all this and some other reasons the Rabbi mentions, the levir can be regarded as dead.

R. Breisch requested R. Shlomoh David Kahana of the Beth Din in Jerusalem to deal with the matter as it was very urgent. The woman was anxious to marry as soon as possible because she feared she might be expelled from Switzerland. The *Responsum* was written on the eve of the New Moon of Nisan 711 (6 April 1951).

R. Shlomoh David Kahana of Jerusalem agreed.[4]

LATVIA

Civil Marriage, Refugees in Russia

An *agunah*, whose husband was in Latvia at the time of the Nazi invasion, entered into a civil marriage with a Jew in Belgium after many years had passed and nothing was heard of her former husband. She emigrated to England and approached the Beth Din to free her from the status of *agunah*. She testified before the Beth Din that a non-Jewish acquaintance from Latvia had informed her that one day the Germans had taken all the factory workmen, among them also her husband, to the outskirts of that town and shot them. The problem was that her husband left a brother who lived in Israel. The woman appeared before the Beth Din in Petah Tikvah. The levir told the Beth Din that

4. R. M.J. Breisch, *Helkath Yaakob*, II, nos. 31, 32.

he, too, had received at that time (*bizmano*) letters from Jewish friends
in South Africa reporting that they had received a letter from Latvia
stating that his brother, i.e. the husband of the *agunah*, had died. Now
there are two questions: (1) whether or not she is an *agunah*, and
(2) whether she may live with her second husband after the performance
of *halizah*. Naturally, a Jewish marriage according to the law of Moses
and Israel would first be performed.

In his reply to the Beth Din in Petah Tikvah Chief Rabbi Herzog is
inclined to adopt a lenient view and concluded: 'I am inclined to say
that after the performance of *halizah* one can permit her to live with
her second husband.'

There are some interesting facts mentioned by the Chief Rabbi in
his *Responsum*.

Many Jews, we hear, fled from Latvia to Russia. The Russians did
not as a rule kill but imprisoned the refugees. Often a man was put in
prison and nothing more was heard of him.

Furthermore, the Rabbis told me that in the first years, the Germans
used to arrange immediate 'aktia', i.e. immediate extermination. A
long time afterwards they changed their method by arranging first
a ghetto in the town and sending the Jews from there to the places
for extermination.There they made 'selektioth' (selections) who should
go to the furnace and who should be left for hard labour. But also of
those who had been sent to the right side (hard labour) it is presumed
the great majority died in the course of a few years.[5]

'KINDERAKTION'

Kinderaktion was the term used after World War I when children both
Jewish and non-Jewish were sent from the starving countries which lost
the war (e.g. Austria) to Holland where they found hospitality with the
families among which they were distributed. (Who knows how many
of these non-Jewish children later became Nazis and maltreated their
former hosts!) Before World War II when Germany and Austria were
already under the grip of the Nazis, the term *Kinderaktion* (and also
Kindertransport) denoted saving Jewish children by sending them to
countries particularly England where they would be safe.

Unfortunately, during the extermination policy of the Nazis in
World War II, this term obtained the meaning of 'extermination of
children'.

It is rather significant that one Rabbi[6] mentions incidentally that in

5. Chief Rabbi Herzog, *Hechal Yizhak*, II, no. 15.
6. R. N.Z.Friedmann, *Nezer Mattai*, no. 39.

one place 1,200,000 children's shoes were found which had been taken from the children before their execution.[7]

A cruel *Kinderaktion* in the ghetto of Kovno[8] is reported in the following *Responsum*.[9] After the Germans put their plan into operation on the 3rd and 4th of Nisan 5704 (27 and 28 March 1944) to massacre all Jewish children, which they called *Kinderaktion* (the children's operation) and killed 1,200 babies torn away from their mothers' breasts, a Rabbi was asked by the unfortunate parents if they must say *kaddish* for their children and if there was no need to say *kaddish* for young babies until what age were they to be regarded as 'young'? He decided that they should recite *kaddish* if the victim was older than thirty days.

<h2 style="text-align:center">ABDUCTING JEWS</h2>

The Germans abducted on an appointed day a group (*kebuzah*) of Jews of whom not even one survived. One witness testified that he knew that among the abducted was N.S. The latter's wife testified that non-Jews had told her that her husband had been abducted. Since then a long time elapsed and N.S. was still missing. What is the position of his wife? May she re-marry?

The answer is in the affirmative.[10]

<h2 style="text-align:center">HUNGARY: RE-INTERMENT OF VICTIMS</h2>

On the eve of *Rosh Ha-Shanah* (the year is not mentioned)[11] the members of the Jewish community of Sármás (Transylvania), 126 persons, were taken by the Germans and Hungarians to the foot of the mountain about six kilometres outside the town.[12] There they were stripped completely and whole families were mercilessly massacred, men and

7. According to R. Herzog, *Hechal Yizhak*, I, no. 24, p. 117, there were 1,200,000 children among the 6,000,000 victims. According to Karen Gershon, *Postscript*, p. 99, more than 1,000,000 children were killed.

8. On this *aktion* see L. Garfunkel, *The Destruction of Kovno's Jewry*, pp. 177f., 181. It occurred in various labour camps of Kovno, from where children under the age of twelve years and old people were taken and killed by the Germans helped by the Ukrainians. On the first day, 27 March 1944, of the *aktion* about a thousand children and old people were deported to the gas chambers of Auschwitz, and on the second day of the *aktion* about three hundred victims were taken to the Ninth Fortress and murdered. A full description of this *Kinderaktion* was given by a witness, Dr Aharon Peretz, at the Eichmann trial in Jerusalem which he calls 'the climax of horror' (see G. Hausner, *Justice in Jerusalem*, p. 330).

9. R. E.Oshry, *Mi-Maamakkim*, I, no. 16.

10. Chief Rabbi Herzog, *Hechal Yizhak*, II, no. 11.

11-12. See Bela Vago, 'The Destruction of the Jews of Transylvania', in *Hungarian Jewish Studies*, ed. by Randolph L. Braham, New York, 1966, pp. 200f., where it is said that the massacre happened on 17 and 18 September (on the eve of *Rosh Ha-Shanah* and on the following day) 1944, after the town had been occupied by Hungarian troops.

women, suckling and old. Their mingled corpses were thrown into a great pit. Since then they had been lying in shame and had become visible to passers by. The relatives of the martyrs sought to remove the corpses from the common grave and bury each separately in a Jewish cemetery. Was it permitted to do so?

In view of the seriousness of the question, the Rabbi was very hesitant to give a decision. However, as he was urgently requested to deal with this matter he would express his view with the proviso that it was to be carried out only if great Rabbinical scholars, among them the Rabbi of Sármás, would agree to his decision.

He laid down the conditions how and when the exhumation and reburial were to be carried out. Several Rabbis agreed to his decision. As men and women had been buried together an objection was raised that it would not be appropriate for men to carry out the exhumation of women. However, a suggestion was made how to avoid this. The reburial took place and the remains were transferred to the Jewish cemetery of Sármás. The *Responsum* was written on Sunday *Seder Va-Yehi* 705 (24 December 1944). The Rabbi remarks that in the meantime the Rumanian government[13] demanded the removal of the corpses from the place where the common grave was.[14]

MASS SHOOTING

A woman gave evidence she had seen her husband being shot in the head when he was in a group of Jews led from the town to be executed by German soldiers. The *Hazon Ish* is inclined to adopt a lenient view and permit his wife to re-marry. 'We need not fear that he had been saved as the crushing of the brain through shooting brings about death within a short time, if medical attention is not given immediately to the person in question. According to the conditions at that time this was impossible as all were destined to die being watched by the murderous soldiers. Had someone brought back the wounded the matter would have become known. . . .'[15]

13. In November 1944, the Hungarians were driven out and Transylvania was liberated. Vago, *loc. cit.*
14. R. B.Stern, *Be-Zel Ha-Hochmah*, 1, nos. 14–18.
15. R. A.Y.Karelitz, *Hazon Ish* on *Eben Ha-Ezer Hilchoth Ishshuth*, no. 28, p. 90.

6

Concealment of Identity

There were some problems which arose both during the Nazi terror and after the liberation as can be seen from the following cases.

We are told by a Rabbi that in 1942 he was approached by his friend R. Mordecai Jaffa (he later died a martyr) who told him he had received a letter from his relative who succeeded in escaping to Belgium disguised as a Christian where he found refuge in a village. As a result of the troubles and travails on his wanderings he fell ill and feared he would not recover. If he died, he feared, the non-Jews would bury him as a Christian in their cemetery. He therefore approached R. Mordecai to inquire whether he might ask the Christians to cremate his body after his death and thus he would be saved from being buried among non-Jews.[1]

The Rabbi proves that burial is one of the most important commandments. Furthermore, cremation is the practice current among sinners who reject the belief in resurrection. In view of that and some other reasons, the Rabbi decided that the man must not ask to be cremated. He advised the questioner to ask the non-Jews (with a gift, if required) to bury the man some distance away from other graves and later to inform his relatives of that. When with the will of God they will be liberated, they should endeavour to remove him from that place and bury him in a Jewish cemetery.[2]

One of the many problems concerning re-marriage of women after the war was the following: with the destruction of the Jewish communities and the extermination of the Jewish population many documents were destroyed. Women who survived and wished to re-marry often had nothing to prove their status and came to the Beth Din seeking permission to re-marry. Rabbi Efrati relates a case which occurred after the war when he was still Rabbi in Warsaw. One day a woman of about forty appeared and claimed to be a *gerushah* (divorced woman) but had no certificate or document of the Beth Din (*maaseh Beth Din*) in her possession to prove that her husband had divorced her at a certain Beth Din. During the persecution she, disguised as a Polish woman, succeeded in becoming a servant in the house of one of the murderers. She then not only burned all documents disclosing her Jewish identity

---

1. R. E.Oshry, *Mi-Maamakkim*, III, no. 3.
2. On a similar question about cremation *vide supra* p. 30.

but she also cut her nose with a knife (she pointed to her nose) to remove any sign which could possibly betray her. She would like to marry but it is not possible to inquire at the Beth Din where she had been divorced as in that place there remains only a vast common grave where the inhabitants had been buried alive together with their Rabbi.

Rabbi Efrati discusses the matter and shows that she is permitted to re-marry.[3]

Among the bodies the liberated Jews found in the infamous Kovno *Kazet Lager* and tried to inter was the corpse of a man in whose pocket there was a small *mezuzah* with a little note on which was written 'Israel, the son of Paltiel from Berlin'. This clearly indicated that the body was that of a Jew. In addition to that the man was circumcised. However, what caused great surprise was that on his neck a cord with a cross was hanging, which raised the question: was he to be regarded as a Jew or as an apostate with different burial rites? The Rabbi[4] decided that it was the duty of the Jews to attend to his burial. Even if he had been an apostate he had most probably changed his religion in the hope of escaping the Nazis . . . but he was to be buried at a little distance from the other martyrs.

A Jew fled to non-Jews in order to escape the Nazis. He disguised his Jewish identity completely. He used to go to church and wear a cross on his neck so that the Christians regarded him as a member of their religion, not suspecting at all that he was a Jew.

He fell ill and did not recover. When he died he was buried in the non-Jewish cemetery and a tombstone with a cross was put over his grave.

After the liberation his brother, without first consulting a Rabbi, removed the corpse to a Jewish cemetery. He intended to erect a tombstone over his brother's grave, particularly as he intended to emigrate from Lithuania where his whole family had been exterminated, thus no opportunity might again occur of erecting a tombstone. However, as he was poor and could not afford to pay for a tombstone he asked whether he could use the tombstone which the non-Jews had erected over his brother's grave and remove the cross and engrave his name in its place.

The decision was in the affirmative.[5]

AUSTRIA: SWASTIKA, GAUTAG

A *Responsum* dated: Friday, *Debarim*, 695 (2 August 1935). It concerns the dismissal of a Talmud-Torah teacher who profaned the Sabbath

3. R. S.Efrati, *Me-Emek Ha-Bacha*, no. 8.
4. R. E.Oshry, *Mi-Maamakkim*, II, no. 21.
5. R. E. Oshry, *Mi-Maamakkim*, II, no. 26.

in public by taking a photograph and who had expressed heretical views. Rabbi Jeruchem agrees that the teacher be dismissed. In addition 'there is sufficient reason to warrant such action as he pinned a swastika to his breast, on the day of their assembly (*Gautag*) which fell on *Rosh Hashanah*, so that he would not be recognized as a Jew when walking in the streets, although it was not a time of persecution (*shaath Hagezerah*) when he would have to save himself, nor was it necessary for him to walk there. . . .'[6]

6. R. H.Y.Jeruchem, *Birkath Hayyim*, no. 44.

7

Russia

FLEEING TO RUSSIA (SEPTEMBER 1939)

When the Germans entered Warsaw and began to maltreat the Jews some young people came to the hasidic Rabbi, R. Hayyim Jerahmiel Taub, asking him whether they might flee to the Russian side where they would be forced to desecrate the Sabbath and to eat non-ritually prepared food. The Rabbi decided in the affirmative as it was a matter of danger to life. He himself, however, remained in Warsaw with his family and hasidim. At the end his whole family was sent to Treblinka first and later he too was deported thither.[1]

REFUGEES DETAINED IN SIBERIA

An *agunah* about whom there was a strong supposition (*umdana*) that her husband was no longer alive received a letter from her sister-in-law (her husband's sister) that her husband had died. Might she re-marry?

After discussing the various points involved (particularly the reliability of her sister-in-law in such a case) Chief Rabbi Herzog decides in the affirmative. 'However, if there is reason to fear that the husband merely fled to Russia . . . where it is difficult to find out about those detained in Siberia we have to consider the case further. If this fear does not exist and Chief Rabbi Unterman (to whom the letter is addressed) agrees together with another Rabbi of repute (*rab mubhak be-horaah*) I herewith free our sister from the fetters of *iggun*).'[2]

REFUGEE ARRESTED AND HIS FATE IS UNKNOWN

A man had been taken away by the Nazis and after a long time his wife and son of about two years of age were sent to Auschwitz on the second day of *Shabuoth* 5704 (29 May 1944). Nothing was known of the fate of the child, as mother and child had been separated. The husband of that woman had a brother who fled to Russia but was arrested by the police (*shomerim*, guards) and it is not known what happened to him. After the war three famous Rabbis gave the woman permission to re-marry after evidence had been heard that the husband had died from hard work during *Hanukkah* 5705 (December 1944). She received permission to re-marry without performing *halizah*, although the Rabbis knew of the brother-in-law. She re-married and gave birth to children. She then received a letter from her brother-in-

---

1. Reported by Menasheh Ungar, *ADMORIM Shenispu*, p. 94 (quoted from *Elleh Ezkerah*, III, pp. 249ff.)
2. Chief Rabbi Herzog, *Hechal Yizhak*, II, no. 12. The *Responsum* is dated Monday *Hayye Sarah*, 708 (2 November 1947).

law in Russia that he was alive and under Soviet rule, but neither could he come to her nor could she go to him. The questioner was inclined to permit the woman to remain with her second husband without *halizah* for several reasons. However, R. Feinstein refuted all his proofs; he decided nevertheless leniently but with a proviso.[3]

DEPORTATION TO RUSSIA, HARSH DECREES, ATHEISM

In a case where the levir could not be traced R. Mosheh Feinstein remarks: If it is known that he is in Russia where most of those deported there, as a result of the harsh decrees, become irreligious, profane the Sabbath, transgress the whole Law and also deny the principles of Judaism (unity of God and His Torah) there might be grounds to be lenient towards his sister-in-law. . . .' (The *Responsum* is dated: 16th Heshvan 708, 30 October 1947).[4]

LABOUR CAMP IN RUSSIA, RELIGIOUS LIFE (OCTOBER 1941)

Students from Telz (Telsicai) worked together with other Jews in the forests of Biczoba(?), two hundred miles from the river Witka. Before *Sukkoth* 702 (6 October 1941) they asked for permission to borrow some planks which they intended to use for building a *sukkah*. Permission was granted. However, as the boards were too long they had to be cut, and the borrowers had not asked permission to cut them. The question arose whether they had fulfilled the commandment of *sukkah* since this *sukkah* would be similar to a '*sukkah* acquired by robbery'[5] with which one does not fulfil one's duty.

The answer was they had fulfilled the *mizvah*, and the Rabbi distinguishes the two cases.[6]

'MYRIADS OF REFUGEES IN RUSSIA'

In one of his *Responsa* dated 24th Heshvan 706 (31 November 1945) in connection with an *agunah* case Chief Rabbi Herzog of Israel tells us that 'myriads of refugees are still in Soviet Russia where investigations about them are difficult. However, it is not impossible that by our applying directly to the Soviet Government or through the special Russian section specially arranged for that purpose in the *sochnuth* (agency) we could succeed in improving the situation. But this requires work and preparation . . .'

3. R. M.Feinstein, *Iggeroth Mosheh, Eben Ha-Ezer*, nos. 149, 150. On imprisonment by the Russians, *vide infra* p. 309.
4. R. M.Feinstein, *Iggeroth Mosheh, Eben Ha-Ezer*, no. 42.
5. In the *Responsum* (see next note) reference is made to *Shulhan Aruch Orah Hayyim*, cap. DCXXXVII, showing the difference between 'timber belonging to a Jew' and that belonging to the government.
6. *Shomere Ha-Gaheleth*, ed. by R. Z.H.Harkavy and R. A.Shauli, no. 19.

He also says that with regard to the disappearance of persons, not all places are in the same category. 'In France[7] a little more than fifty per cent of people survived; the same applies to some other places.'[8]

THE JEWS—FRIENDS

A *kohen* was about to become engaged to marry a woman who had been in concentration camps during the war. She had always been in the company of Jewesses. After the liberation by the Russians she had been taken into their hospital as she was ill.When she recovered she was set free. The *kohen* feared she may be in the category of a captive owing to her stay in hospital (with regard to the time she spent in the camps there were various factors which permitted her to marry a *kohen*).[9]

The Rabbi proves that the *kohen* was permitted to marry her. She could not be classified as a captive as the Russians did not take captive those Jews found in the concentration camps, but saved them from the enemy. They regarded the Jews as friends who had fallen into the hands of their enemy and the Russians liberated them. Although Russians may have behaved immorally such fear was no greater than as regards a woman living in a Russian town.

The Rabbi mentions some other reasons in favour of the lady. Her stay in hospital could not affect her status as she was in a woman's ward where no man normally entered.[10]

7. On the figures of the victims killed and of the survivors of the Jews in France, cf. Gerald Reitlinger, *The Final Solution*, p. 538; on those in other countries, see ibid., pp. 535ff.
8. Chief Rabbi Herzog, *Hechal Yizhak*, I, no. 27.
9. On these factors, see R. I.J.Weiss, *Minhath Yizhak*, I, no. 87 (*supra* Part II, p. 197).
10. R. I.J.Weiss, *Minhath Yizhak*, I, no. 88.

8
Hungary

SENDING MONEY FOR CHARITY (1941)

It is well known that money set aside or even promised for a special charity fund must not be used for another charity. When the sending of money for the charity fund of R. Meir Baal Ha-Nes in Palestine was made impossible in Austria under the Nazis in the year before the outbreak of World War II the Jews used to give the money to those who were about to emigrate to Palestine. The writer cannot recall if this was done on the ruling of a Rabbi.

The question of sending money to the R. Meir Baal Ha-Nes fund was dealt with in Hungary during World War I when it became impossible to carry out the intention of the donors to send the money to Palestine. Furthermore, the money became devalued daily. The question was then asked whether the money could be used for the redemption of prisoners.

One Rabbi advises that each town should acquire property for the community with the money of R. Meir Baal Ha-Nes. Thus the capital would remain intact until the first opportunity arose to send money to Palestine to be distributed among those who study the Law. Or the communities should buy houses for letting to tenants. (Or they could be sold to use the money for fares for those who emigrate to Israel.) The rent could be added to the capital or used for the redemption of prisoners.[1]

KEEPING SHOPS OPEN ON THE SABBATH

An order was given by the Hungarian government that the Jews must keep their shops open on the Sabbath, otherwise they would be fined— they would not be permitted to open them even on weekdays and this would impose great financial hardship. Must they make this sacrifice or not? Can permission be found for them to keep their shops open on the Sabbath as it is a time of emergency (*shaath ha-dehak*) and great loss is involved?

The Rabbi of Grosswardein, R. Pinhas Zimetbaum (who died a martyr) deals with the matter from various angles and is of the opinion that if the owner has no other means of income permission could be found to keep the shop open on the Sabbath by making an arrangement with a non-Jew in the prescribed way and the Jewish owner would derive no benefit from business transacted on the Sabbath. The shopkeeper should give an undertaking before a Rabbi or Beth Din that

1. *Yerushath Peletah*, no. 21. See also no. 22 where another decision is to be found.

W

he himself would sell nothing on the Sabbath and when the government order is abrogated he would again keep his shop closed on the Sabbath. 'Great caution should be taken whether a decision either way should be given. This should be done after consulting the leading Rabbis. It should bear a general character applicable to the whole land; otherwise it could turn out that some decide this way and some another. . . .'

Even if permission could be given to a shopkeeper under the conditions mentioned above would this apply only to those who owned shops before the decree was issued or also to those who wished to open a shop after the order since the latter before opening a shop are aware that they would be forced to trade on the Sabbath?

The Rabbi is inclined to prohibit it.[2]

HUNGARIAN JEWS IN MILITARY LABOUR CAMPS (1940)[3]

Call up

In the year 1940 many Jews were called up by the authorities for labour. A teacher of the Talmud Torah of the community of Mád demanded his full wages from the community while the latter refused to pay him. The Rabbi of Sárospatak decided in his *Responsum* dated Sunday, *Seder Tabo* 700 (15 September 1940) that half of the wages for the term (*zeman*) should be paid. He writes that similar cases had occurred in his own community and in Uhely where the full wages had been paid to the teacher.[4]

Hungarian Jews in military service prohibited from putting on Tephillin

A decree was issued against the Jews in military service in a certain place that they were not to put on *tephillin* but were to send them home. Non-compliance with that decree would result in the *tephillin*, if found after a search among the Jews' belongings, being burned, or being subject to other disrespectful treatment. Some Jews complied with that

2. In *Yerushath Peletah*, no. 5, and in *Dibre Pinhas*, ed. by his son R. Aharon Zimetbaum, New York, no. 13. The same subject was discussed by R. Jonathan Steif, *Responsa*, no. 256.
3. Of all anti-Jewish measures in Hungary since 1939 the law concerning military service was the most harshly felt by the Jews. According to the law, all those who were unsuitable for, or excluded from, serving with the armed forces were called up for auxiliary labour. Although they were under the jurisdiction of military authorities they were deprived of all rights as soldiers. Their superiors were mostly pro-German Hungarians and great anti-Semites who behaved in a most brutal way towards the Jews.
   In the time between July 1939 and November 1940 about fifty-two thousand Jews served with auxiliary labour battalions.
   'In 1942 the call up was intensified, and fifty thousand Jews were sent to the Ukraine. Here they were employed under most severe conditions in road repairing, fortifications, and mine clearing between the lines.' See Nathaniel Katzburg, 'Hungarian Jewry in Modern Times', in *Hungarian Jewish Studies*, ed. by Randolph L. Braham, pp. 160ff.
4. R. Z.H.Meisels, *Mekaddshe Ha-Shem*, I, no. 98, see also note.

decree and sent their *tephillin* home. Other religious Jews did not wish to be included among 'the wrong-doers in Israel who sin with their body', i.e. by not putting on *tephillin* (see *Rosh Ha-Shanah* 17a). Therefore, they kept their *tephillin* despite the evil decree. The question was: which course of action was correct and whether it was permitted to bring about such a great disgrace by causing the *tephillin* to be burned if discovered.

It appears that the Rabbi was inclined to permit the keeping of the *tephillin*.

The *Responsum* was written in Des and is dated: Outgoing of the Sabbath of *Seder Va-yehi*, 704 (8 January 1944).[5]

'Evidence' (January 1943)

A translation from Hungarian.

Mr Joseph Goldstein and Mr Hershkovits gave evidence that in January 1943 they had been together in the hospital in Daresti with Mr Vanesh Joseph. They were lying near each other. The hands and legs of Mr Vanesh were frozen by the frost and he was suffering from typhus. On one occasion people were saying that the whole hospital would be set on fire to prevent the disease from spreading.[6] When Mr Vanesh heard this he felt he would not be able to escape. He handed over a photograph of his wife and child which was kept in a small silver locket together with his own photograph to his friend Hershkovits whom he had known from home. He asked Hershkovits to hand it to his wife on his behalf, when he returned home. That ornament was very dear to him. The friend carried out his mission.

On the 12/13th of January early in the morning the whole hospital went up in flames. The above witnesses escaped but Mr Vanesh was unable to do so both his hands and legs being frozen. Those two witnesses saw that the hospital had been burnt to the ground and no one was left alive. Mr Vanesh had been forced to remain there as he could not escape owing to his incapacity.

'We were sitting as a Beth Din (of three members) when Mr Joseph Goldstein and Mr Mordecai Asriel Hershkovits came and gave oral evidence in accordance with the above. Written and signed on Friday, *Toledoth* 706 (6 November 1945), Grosswardein. Yizhak Yaakob Weiss, Hayyim Katina, Hayyim Yehoushua Heschel Schön.'

May Mrs Vanesh re-marry? Answer: the woman is permitted to re-marry.[7]

5. R. Z.H.Meisels, *Mekaddshe Ha-Shem*, II, no. 8.
6. This means of preventing the spread of disease by setting fire to the hospital was used by the Nazis in Lithuania, *vide infra* p. 319.
7. R. I.J.Weiss, *Minhath Yizhak*, I, no. 99, where the reasons for his decision are given.

Evidence (1943)

1. We three judges were in session when R. David ben R. Jacob Hecht
   of Szeged appeared and after caution declared: During the withdrawal at the beginning of February 1943 four or five sick people
   from the 68th company stayed in Russia in a village Sztepanowka
   near Sumy. They were running a high temperature and were thus
   unable to march on. Among them was Archi Pollack of Masief.
   Ten or fifteen days later, two men joined the company. One of
   them whose name was Weiss was one of the sick (who had remained
   in the village). The other was his friend Kupferstein, who had
   not been ill but remained to watch over the sick people. I asked
   them why the others did not come. They replied that after 2 or 3
   days they all began to follow and on the high-road came across a
   German machine (vehicle?) and were ordered to help push the
   machine. They (Weiss and Kupferstein) could do so, the others
   were weak and could not help and stayed there (on the road). The
   illness was, as was later established, typhus which was called there
   'Ukrainian Fever'. It occurred that those who had stayed behind
   did arrive at the terminus; however, nothing had been heard of the
   others. Usually if people stayed behind without documents we can
   assume they were shot by the Hungarian Gendarmes or by the
   Germans or by the Ukrainian militia, or they died from illness, not
   having received medical attention and through starvation. All this
   we have heard from the witness . . . on Monday, 15th Adar Sheni,
   706 (18 March 1946), Temesvar.

   Yizhak Zebi Sopher, Ab Beth Din of the congregation Temesvar-
   Fabrik; Yizhak Eisack Rath; Raphael Horowitz.

2. We were in a session of three when R. Shemuel ben R. Abraham
   Jacob Tessler of Mittelwische came and gave the following evidence:
   'I was in Russia in 1943 in the village of Sztepanowka near Sumy,
   billeted with Archi Pollack of Masief. We rested there for eight days.
   On the withdrawal, it was about February, it was terribly cold.
   During our rest he had run a high temperature and fell ill. He could
   go no further and so he remained in the village. It was stated later
   that this fever was "Ukrainian typhus", a disease which had smitten
   most people and the great majority died. He (Archi Pollack)
   remained there without a doctor and without any attention. I heard
   nothing more about him.' All this we heard from the witness,
   Monday 15th Adar Sheni 706 (18 March 1946), Temesvar, Yizhak
   Zebi Sopher, Ab Beth Din of Temesvar-Fabrik; Shemuel ben Zebi
   Yehudah Guttmann; Yaakob Isachar ben Yehudah Ha-Levi
   Glückmann.

3. We were in a session of three when Mrs Mattel, daughter of Zeeb (Struhl), wife of R. Aharon Leb Pollack of Masief, came and declared: 'I was in Masief in summer 706 (1946) where Mr Alter Herstick, a good friend of my husband, told me that he had known already last year of my husband's fate but did not want to reveal it then. He had been in Kiev and my husband Aharon Leib Pollack being ill remained in Sztepanawka. He heard and knew and everyone talked about this, that my husband Aharon Leib Pollack died during his journey on his way to hospital. In May 1943 I received information from the Red Cross that my husband disappeared between January and March 1943. (On hearing this) Alter Herstick told me that at that time he did not live any more.' All this we heard from the woman mentioned above. Temesvar, 15th Kislev 707 (8 December 1946). Yizhak Zebi Sopher; Abraham ben Hillel Zebi; Yisrael Hayyim ben David.

R. Yizhak Yaakob Zebi Sopher and R. Weiss decided that the woman (after performing *halizah*) may re-marry.

When speaking of the danger in which the husband had been left, R. Sopher remarks that the Hungarian army had in their wickedness outlawed sick Jews and left them without food and drink and documents.[8]

Mourning

R. Zebi Hirsch Meisels of Waitzen (Vác, Hungary) approached R. Joel Teitelbaum of Szatmar on 1st of Nisan 703 (6 April 1943) on the following matter.

Many Jews from Hungary had been sent about two years earlier for hard labour to a distant place where they had to serve on government orders under the supervision of military officers. In the last few weeks before R. Meisels approached R. Teitelbaum wives of those servicemen had received letters signed by the commandant's officials that their husbands had died and had been buried.

The women had no intention of re-marrying, as they knew that there was at that time no system among the officers and errors occurred very often. Every woman was prepared to wait until the end of the period of military service which it had been reported, was not to be long and when all Jews would return home. The situation would then be clarified by Jewish friends who had been together with their husbands. Every woman who had received a letter from the commandant hoped that there had been a mistake as to the death of her husband.

However, their main question concerned the observance of the laws

8. R. I.J.Weiss, *Minhath Yizhak*, I, nos. 97–98.

of mourning and the recital of *kaddish*, etc. In some towns the Rabbis had decided on the strength of the above mentioned information that *abeluth* be observed and *kaddish* recited, while in other towns the Rabbis had forbidden that. (The observance of *abeluth* might lead people to assume that the person in question had died and consequently through indirect evidence at a Beth Din the *agunah* might be permitted to re-marry.) In Budapest, the capital of Hungary, the views were divided. R. Meisels too had been asked for a ruling on that matter. In his view neither *abeluth* was to be observed nor *kaddish* recited. R. Meisels sought R. Teitelbaum's opinion.

R. Teitelbaum believed that, while *abeluth* was not to be observed, *kaddish* was to be recited. He showed the difference between the former and the latter. However, he decided, quoting an authority, *kaddish* should be said under special circumstances.[9]

Evidence (May 1943)

1. Evidence was given by R. Moses (KZ) ben David of Kleinwardein concerning Neuwirth, *shohet* of Ramatschahaz. He declared that he met the *shohet* in hospital in Daraschitz (Ukraine) and spoke to him. On the following morning, when he left the hospital, he saw him lying among the dead and recognized him. The corpses were lying at the end of the room where the sick were. (This was the general practice to put the dead at the end of the hospital.) When he noticed the *shohet* dead, he asked a friend of his named Kon Miki of Kleinwardein whether the *shohet* had died, and he replied in the affirmative. The same (that the *shohet* Neuwirth had died) was said by R. Aharon Weiss of Rozwadi who was there too.

   Monday, *Seder Shemoth*, 14th of Tebeth, 704 (10 January 1944) Kleinwardein, (Rabbi) Shmuel Shmelka SGL Litsch Rosenbaum, Ab Beth Din;[10] (Rabbi) Abraham Hayyim ben Asher Ha-Levi; Pinhas Gefen.

2. On Thursday, *Seder Shemoth* 704 (13 January 1944) R. Aharon Weiss of Rozwadi which is under the rabbinical jurisdiction of Chelmez appeared before us in Chelmez and testified that he was in the military labour camp (*zeba ha-abodah*) in Daraschitz. He was together with a man called Shmuel David Neuwirth who had been a *shohet* in Ramatschahaz and whom he knew from his youth from Rahad. He fell ill from typhoid (which often happened to people— as the Rabbi remarks later—who were suffering from hunger). He had spoken to him several times during his illness and

9. R. Z.H.Meisels, *Binyan Zebi*, II, nos. 72, 73.
10. R. Shmuel Shmelka SGL Rosenbaum, *Elleh Dibre Shemuel*, nos. 4ff.

also two days before his death. The witness had seen him being taken out after his death but was not present at his funeral. There is no doubt that the *shohet* had died and had been buried. (The witness signed this evidence.) The death occurred on May 24 (1943). Chelmetz date as above (i.e. 13 January 1944). (Rabbi) Joel Wolf Glatstein, Ab Beth Din; (Rabbi) Aharon Weiss.

The question was whether this evidence suffices to permit the son to recite *kaddish* (since, as long as no clear proof exists of the death of the husband, his wife must not mourn and his sons may not say *kaddish*; see Isserles on *Shulhan Aruch Eben Ha-Ezer*, cap. XVII, no. 5).

The answer was in the affirmative: *kaddish* may be recited. According to one Rabbi, a certain condition concerning the hearing of evidence should, if possible, be fulfilled.

NON-JEWISH FRIENDS (MARCH-APRIL 1944)

It was on the eve of the Nazi invasion of Hungary[11] when the Rabbi of Kleinwardein (who later died a martyr) was asked by a Jew between *Purim* and *Pesah* 704 (9 March—8 April 1944), the following question. He had put wheat of *mazzoth shemuroth* in a sack properly sealed and hid it during autumn and winter in the loft of a house of a non-Jew who was the judge of that village. May this wheat be used for the *mazzoth shemuroth*? The reply written on 17 March 1944 was in the negative as it might have come in contact with water or other damp. However, it may be used for ordinary *mazzoth*.[12]

Another Rabbi tells us of an *Oberleutnant* (First Lieutenant) of the Hussars in Grosswardein, 'who are well known for their wickedness,' and his wife who have endangered their lives in hiding and helping Jews.[13]

---

11. Hungary was occupied by German troops on 19 March 1944. See the chronological table in Jenö Levai, *Hungarian Jewry and the Papacy*, p. 117.
12. R. Shmuel Shmelka SGL Rosenbaum, *Elleh Dibre Shemuel*, Jerusalem, 1961, no. 1.
13. R. A.Zimetbaum, 'Maaseh Nissim', in *Dibre Pinhas*, by his father R. P.Zimetbaum, p. 171.

9

Jews from Transylvania and Rumania in Labour Camps

Many Jews of Hermannstadt (Sibiu) had to leave their homes during World War II and were recruited by the Rumanian government for work in various villages near the town.[1] They were not permitted to leave their working place without special permission. After a certain time, they were released and returned to their homes. The question was raised whether or not their position was like that of prisoners set free who have to recite the benediction *Ha-Gomel* or should the place of work not be regarded as a prison when no benediction would be required?

In his reply the Rabbi points out that those Jews who had to do work in the neighbouring villages could still be regarded as possibly having been in danger of life (*sephek sakkanath nephashoth*) and would be required to recite the benediction. However, when returning home they had still to work in their own town and did not recite the benediction not knowing what the next day would bring. But the Jews who had been brought to Transnistria were in real danger as many of them died and only a small number returned home. Those Jews should recite the benediction and do so on behalf of the former.[2]

1. On 30 August 1940, at a Conference in Vienna, the Northern Part of Transylvania was given to Hungary while the southern part remained with Rumania. See Bela Vago, 'The Destruction of the Jews of Transylvania', in *Hungarian Jewish Studies*, p. 178.
2. R. B.Stern, *Be-Zel Ha-Hochmah*, I, no. 19.

10

Italy

An authorization (warrant) was written in German at the Beth Din in Trieste (Italy) by a certain Mosheh Maurice, son of Alexander Pajes, on 13 January 1940, in which he gave the order to arrange for a *get* (bill of divorce) to be written and given to his wife Malkah Malvine, the daughter of Zebi Kraemer (text of the authorization is printed in Hebrew in full). Signature: Maurice Pajes. Witnesses: Mosheh ben Eliyahu Baruch; Shlomoh Akiba ben Nethanel Mazliah.

The husband emigrated to America in 1941 and his address was unknown. His wife appeared before the Beth Din in Jerusalem in 1945 and presented the authorization which in accordance with the husband's wish had been handed over to her, to ask the Beth Din to write the *get*. However, some doubts arose about the validity of the authorization. The main question was whether the order given in the text referred to the special agent to whom the husband had handed over the authorization or was it meant to be of a general character not excluding others from acting on the husband's behalf. While Chief Rabbi Herzog was of the latter opinion one member of the Beth Din insisted on the interpretation that it referred to the special agent who unfortunately was no longer available. Consequently, the giving of the *get* had to be delayed.

While on a visit to Rome in Adar Sheni 706 (March 1946) on a mission for saving Jewish children Chief Rabbi Herzog succeeded in discovering the Rabbi who wrote the authorization and it turned out that the Chief Rabbi's assumption was correct. Evidence was given to that effect in Rome on the 19th of Adar Sheni 706 (22 March 1946) by Rabbi Zebi ben R. Raphael Friedenthal of Milano (formerly in Leghorn) who had arranged the authorization, before the Beth Din consisting of Chief Rabbi Herzog, R. David Prato and R. David Yizhak Panziri.

In a note the editor of the *Responsa Hechal Yizhak* (Mr Yaakob Goldman) remarks that when the representative of Mrs Pajes presented the case in her name before the Beth Din in Jerusalem for the first time he maintained that the authorization had been handed over to the agent in Trieste. The latter brought it to Mrs Pajes in Verona (where she was living). Mrs Pajes herself alleged she had travelled from Verona to Trieste where the Rabbi of Trieste handed over the authorization direct to her. The editor adds that the time when the authorization was written was a very confusing period, as Italy was on the brink of war.[1] Many Jews were afraid that their identity would become known to the

---

1. Italy declared war on Great Britain and France on 10 June 1940.

authorities. This was the reason for the authorization having been written in vague terms.

From the *Responsa* we can see that the performance of divorce by the Beth Din had been prohibited by the authorities in Italy. The great plight and fear of the Jews of being caught and killed is mentioned there. The Jews were anxious to leave Italy. They were afraid to keep writings as the police used to search every Jew passing through.[2]

AGUNIM (HUSBANDS WHOSE WIVES DISAPPEARED)

Rabbi David Prato, Chief Rabbi of Rome, asked Rabbi Herzog, Chief Rabbi of Israel, on the 18th Adar 707 (10 March 1947) the position of men whose wives disappeared during the Nazi holocaust and whether it was right to fix a memorial day (*yom zikkaron*) for saying *kaddish* for those who had disappeared.[3]

Reply. As infringing the *herem* of R. Gershom, the Light of the Exile, prohibiting bigamy is not as serious as the prohibition of marrying a married woman (*esheth ish*) there is a distinction between giving permission to men whose wives have disappeared and permitting women to re-marry whose husbands disappeared. Since the missing wives had been taken captive by the cursed evildoers and such a long time has elapsed and nothing has been heard of their whereabouts, permission can be granted to their husbands to re-marry. 'We have had many such cases and permitted many (husbands to re-marry). I have explained this case in a *Responsum* to London and Haifa.'

To add weight, the husband who seeks permission should deposit a bill of divorce at the Beth Din ready to be given should his first wife reappear. Similarly, he should deposit a bill of debt (document of obligation) to give her financial help. The exact amount should be fixed by the Beth Din of Rome with the Chief Rabbi as their head. If there is no time to arrange the writing of a *get* Chief Rabbi Herzog gives directives how to write a bill authorizing others to undertake the writing and handing over of the *get*.[4]

2. Chief Rabbi Herzog, *Hechal Yizhak*, II, nos. 71–74.
3. On the question of *Yom Zikkaron, vide supra* pp. 155ff. and *infra* pp. 347f.
4. Chief Rabbi Herzog, *Hechal Yizhak*, I, no. 28.

11

Fictitious, Civil, Illicit, Imperfectly-Performed and Mixed Marriages

FICTITIOUS MARRIAGE (1940)

We were together in session of three judges when the wife of Mr Shlomoh F. came and told us the following: 'When the Russians reached Wilno[1] I arranged for a Russian passport for myself. When I learned that the holder of a Russian passport would not be permitted to leave the country (*medinah*) but that the holder of a Polish passport could do so, I immediately married my husband who was a Pole and I obtained a Polish passport and permission to emigrate to Erez Yisrael. My husband did not receive permission for *aliyah*.

I went to Erez Yisrael and he remained in Wilno. When his friends came to Erez Yisrael, they informed me that he had been killed. I had not lived together with my husband. My only wish had been to receive a Polish passport through him. I later received a letter from Russia that my husband had been killed, and I hand the letter to you. He had no brother.'

The evidence of the first witness: 'We had been together in Wilno until the Germans were about to enter the town and the Russians were about to retreat.[2] Five or six friends decided to leave the town. When we reached the "green bridge" the Germans began to shoot. We saw Shlomoh F. fall. We thought he had been wounded and wished to take him with us. When we reached him, we saw that he was no longer alive.'

The evidence of the second witness: 'I had left the *kibbuz*. About half an hour later we reached the "green bridge" of Wilno where we saw the killed and wounded. We were interested to know what had happened as our friends had passed shortly before. We went nearer and recognized Shlomoh F. among the dead. When I reached the bridge the shooting had ceased. I knew him well. We also recognized other friends who had been killed. We had time to examine the bodies as the shooting had stopped. Many Jews had arrived to identify the dead . . . I know he (Shlomoh F.) had no brother.'

The evidence of the third witness: 'I am a member of the "Merkaz Ha-Noar Ha-Zioni". We have received letters from friends who wrote that our friend and other friends had been killed.'

Chief Rabbi Herzog after discussing the case and the problems involved

---

1. Most probably this refers to the marching in of Russian troops to Lithuania on 15 June 1940.
2. Germany attacked Russia on 22 June 1941.

comes to the conclusion that the woman may re-marry provided that a famous scholar would agree. Then a Beth Din of three judges should give her the required permission.[3]

CIVIL MARRIAGE

Mrs Hannah A. approached the Chief Rabbinate of Haifa and asked about arranging her marriage. She herself declared she had been both married and divorced by civil law in Czechoslovakia. Her mother confirmed this and added that the man whom she married gave her a ring at the time of registration in the presence of the officer, a non-Jew, but he did not say the Hebrew formula '*Hare ath* . . .'. There were also two witnesses: her uncle (the father's brother) and his wife. In her passport there is no mention that she had been married. The question was whether she should be believed. Furthermore, it was doubtful whether her husband was still alive as he might have been sent to an extermination camp and there are some other points to be clarified in favour of granting permission to re-marry.

The Chief Rabbinate of Haifa submitted the case to Chief Rabbi Herzog on the 12th of Tishri 707 (7 October 1946), who, in his letter dated 27th of Heshvan 707 (21 November 1946), decided that she might re-marry.[4]

1940. A woman from Warsaw, a member of an esteemed hasidic family of Ger (Gora Kalwarija), says that after the outbreak of the war in 1940 she fled to Bialystok. There she met a man whom she knew from Warsaw. In order to be 'protected by him' she registered a civil marriage in the register office and her brother-in-law signed as a witness. According to her statement, they did not think at that time that this ceremony would be regarded as a wedding. They arranged with each other, when they returned to Poland, to marry according to the Law of Moses and Israel.

After three months they were caught and sent to Siberia. She succeeded in getting set free and reached Israel with the Polish army but did not hear from the man any more. She approached all the institutions, e.g. the Red Cross, but all investigations proved fruitless. Since then, six years have elapsed and one can assume he died in prison. Now she wishes to be free from the fetters of *iggun* as she is sure that he is no longer alive.

This case was submitted to Chief Rabbi Herzog by R. David Kahana in a *kuntras* pointing out the mitigating factors and he asked the Chief Rabbi to let him know his opinion.

In his reply Chief Rabbi Herzog raised some points and dealt at

3. Chief Rabbi Herzog, *Hechal Yizhak*, II, no. 7.
4. Chief Rabbi Herzog, *Hechal Yizhak*, II, no. 31.

length with the validity of civil marriages. Although he is inclined to permit her to re-marry he would not like to give a definite decision before hearing again R. Kahana's view on the points he raised. Should R. Kahana believe without doubt that she may re-marry he would agree.

There are some interesting points as far as the refugees in Russia are concerned.

A person imprisoned by the Russians used to be sent to the concentration place of the prisoners in distant parts of Siberia known as TAMI. Although in Russian prisons there was no general extermination as there was in those of the Germans, it is known that in spite of the afflictions of lack of food and clothing and the terrible cold and heavy work the majority of the prisoners did not die; however, a great part of them fell ill and perished. R. Kahana says as six years had elapsed and nothing is known of the man's fate he is not presumed to be alive (*hezkath hai*). However, Chief Rabbi Herzog disagrees as the Russians sometimes do not give information on their prisoners. But it is known that some prisoners had died in prison. However, he thinks, they were only a minority. Many weak people remained alive in such conditions.

Being in prison in the hands of the Germans during the last war was surely more dangerous and fatal than even to have been in the hands of the soldiers of the wicked Titus. However, to be in the hands of the Russians was, as far as he knows, less dangerous than to have been in captivity at the time of the sages of the Talmud.[5]

A woman came before the Rabbi of Leeds asking for permission to marry a man to whom she had become engaged. She told the Rabbi the following story.

She had arrived in Leeds from Germany during the war. There she met a man who had come to Leeds after the war, having spent some time in a German concentration camp. She had married him in the registry office but not according to Jewish Law. He later died. She then wished to marry another man according to Jewish Law. After having been thoroughly questioned, the woman gave evidence that her husband had told her he had a brother who had been with him in the concentration camp but had died there. The woman had never met her brother-in-law (the levir). She had no information whether her husband had had other brothers. Furthermore, one later learned that her husband had been married before he had married his (second) wife (who came before the Rabbi in Leeds) in the registry office and that his first wife had given birth to a boy. Both mother and child had perished in the concentration camp, as her husband alleged.

5. Chief Rabbi Herzog, *Hechal Yizhak*, II, nos. 29–30.

It appeared that the man was unable to bring conclusive proof that his first wife had died. Perhaps he did not want to get involved with the Beth Din and therefore married his wife in the registry office.

It was therefore necessary to clarify whether the woman could marry the second man to whom she had become engaged as she may have been 'tied to the levir'. The decision was that she may re-marry.[6]

RELIGIOUS AND CIVIL MARRIAGES IN THE GHETTO (OCTOBER 1942)

On the 12th of Tishri, 702 (3 October 1941) a sad rumour spread among the inmates of the ghetto that the German murderers had decided to deport for killing those women whose husbands had already been massacred and would spare only those who still had husbands there. The reason for the plan was the fact that the number of women exceeded that of men since during the previous *aktionen* (actions) the heads of the families had been sent for extermination and their surviving wives had become widows. As a result of that continuous rumour many unmarried women tried to marry in order to be saved from death. Indeed they found men who were willing to marry them, and they approached the Rabbis to perform *kiddushin* for them according to the Law of Moses and Israel.

However, the Rabbis were at a great loss what to do since a problem confronted them. As in the ghetto there was no *mikveh* the problem presented itself whether a marriage may be performed for those women who were living under the shadow of death for through that action the Rabbis would be transgressing the prohibition of Lev. XIX 14, and they would be causing a serious infringement of the prohibition of Lev. XVIII 19; XX 18, by the woman and her husband punishable with *kareth*. Furthermore, the source of the rumour was not known. There was no one who could testify that it was true that the women who would marry would be saved. 'Even if one had heard this distinctly from the mouth of the cursed murderers, there was no guarantee it was true as we are handed over into their hands like sheep for slaughter, there is no one who could reproach them and every day they issue new decrees. Hence in our case too there is no certainty that the women who had married in the meantime would be spared. It is quite possible that in spite of their being married they would be deported for extermination together with their husbands.'

However, there was a possibility that those women in their great plight might approach the Jewish police of the ghetto and arrange civil marriages through them. The police would then enter in their passports which they issue that the couple were husband and wife. The Germans too would then regard such marriages as valid. A great calamity and

6. R. I.J.Weiss, *Minhath Yizhak*, III, no. 125.

confusion might arise since the police did not make proper inquiries about the couple's past and whenever a couple appeared and expressed their wish to marry they were immediately registered as husband and wife without investigation whether the first husband who had been deported was still alive, or whether he had fled. Furthermore, the woman would perhaps need to perform *halizah*. The couple might live as husband and wife and if the Rabbis would not perform the marriages they would be responsible for the consequences which would follow, i.e. great infringements of Jewish matrimonial laws and cases of illegitimacy. Therefore, it would be preferable for the Rabbi to perform the marriage because he would make the necessary inquiries before doing so.

In short, the question was: should the Rabbi refrain from performing *kiddushin* in order not to transgress the prohibition of Lev. xix 14, or should he perform the *kiddushin* to prevent serious consequences which might follow

Rabbi Ephraim Oshry was asked by R. Abraham Dob Kahana Schapira, the Ab Beth Din of Kovno, to deal with this matter.

R. Oshry came to the conclusion that marriages could be performed in view of the time of emergency involving danger to life particularly as the unfortunate women who came to the Rabbis did not say explicitly they would not observe the law of family purity. One had also to consider that there existed the possibility of having immersion in the river Njemen. The Rabbi should draw their attention to the stringency of that law. Only those women who declare with contempt they would not observe the laws of family purity should not have their marriages performed by the Rabbi. Rabbi Schapira agreed to this decision.

How successful those women were in being spared by the Germans is not mentioned. Nor is there any report about the new family life those women started. There is, however, one tragic case recorded which resulted from such a marriage. No doubt, this marriage was performed by officers of the Jewish police who were not so particular in ascertaining the permissibility of marriage.

ILLICIT MARRIAGES

There was a woman among the inmates of the ghetto whose husband had been taken away by the Germans. As he did not return to her she thought he had been killed. When the rumour of the killing of the widows, etc., spread she hastened to find a man who was willing to marry her. They married and she even gave birth to a son. They all succeeded in escaping from the ghetto and found a place of refuge. After the defeat of the Germans the family emigrated overseas. They managed to settle down and bring up their son who was educated in a *yeshibah* and he even obtained a Rabbinical diploma and soon married and took up a position as Rabbi in one of the communities. However, suddenly 'the world around him became dark' (see *San.* 22a). One day a man, the former husband of his mother, appeared and told him that he had been taken by the Germans who kept him for a long time; however, in spite of all that happened to him he remained alive. Immediately after the liberation he began to search for his wife, until he was told that she had re-married and even given birth to a son.

As he was very grieved because of the treacherous act of his wife, he decided to trace her and her son, the *mamzer*, and to put them publicly to shame particularly so that people should be able to refrain from marrying him in order not to increase *mamzerim* in Israel, and to separate her from her second husband. He was not successful as far as his wife was concerned as she had died in the meantime. However, he found his son had not only a family but was Rabbi and spiritual leader of a community. He therefore thought it his duty to make the matter public as a *mamzer* is not fit to be a Rabbi.

When the son heard this he collapsed and fell to the ground. He cried bitterly about his fate. He was particularly perturbed about the *hillul ha-shem*, the terrible disgrace which would result from this being disclosed. He begged the man not to reveal the matter and to wait until he, the young Rabbi, had consulted the Rabbis. Although the man was angry and wished to seek revenge, he acceded to the request.

The young Rabbi came before R. Oshry who was astounded when he saw the young man crushed and bent like an old man and also white hair had appeared on his head and beard. He told R. Oshry the whole case and asked him for his advice.

R. Oshry decided that the young Rabbi should leave his congregation and cease to be their spiritual leader. He also settled the matter affecting his wife and family. He then called the first husband and told him he must not make the affair public. His main object was that the young Rabbi should leave his community and this he had achieved. The son was a *shogeg*, he was blameless, and not responsible for what had been done.[7]

Illicit marriages occurred sometimes after the war when some survivors married women who thought their husbands had been killed by the Germans. In the first months after the liberation there was no religious leader in Munkatsch (Mukacevo), where some survivors settled, to draw the attention of the men to the grave implications involved in such a marriage should it transpire that the husbands of those women were still alive. Proper investigations had to be made beforehand to ascertain

7. R. E.Oshry, *Mi-Maamakkim*, I, no. 4 and III, no. 9.

whether the husbands were still alive or not. After six months or a year husbands began to return when some women were by then pregnant. Consequently the children born were *mamzerim*. In the above-mentioned town there were about ten young men born from such illicit marriages. They grew up and wished to marry; however, were unable to do so in view of their illegitimate status.

The Rabbis tried very hard to help those unfortunate people; a certain suggestion was made; however, no practical decision could be given as some difficulties were involved and the consent of great Rabbis was required.[8]

MARRIAGES WITHOUT 'KETHUBAH' PERFORMED BY LAYMEN

It has been mentioned already[9] that the president of the *Judenrat* of the ghetto of Lodz, Chaim Rumkowski, used to perform marriages without *huppah* and *kethubah* by letting the bridegroom give the bride a ring as *kiddushin* and recite the well-known formula *Hare ath.* . . .

It happened that a couple who had married in Lodz during the war emigrated afterwards to America. The woman had no *kethubah* as he who had arranged the *kiddushin* (*mesadder kiddushin*) was a layman who did not know that a *kethubah* was required. Ten people were present at the wedding, and a *tallith* was spread over the couple's heads like a *huppah*. The man[10] recited the benedictions from a prayerbook and the bridegroom placed a ring on the bride's finger and said '*Hare ath* . . .' and a cup was broken. No mention was made of a *kethubah*. After their arrival in America they attended a wedding of a member of their family and heard the reading of the *kethubah*. They then asked the Rabbi what should be done as they had no *kethubah*.

The Rabbi[11] decided that the text of an ordinary *kethubah* (and not that of a 'replacement *kethubah*') should be written and explained the necessary formalities.

MIXED MARRIAGE

A couple were divorced by the court in Germany. The husband married a non-Jewess and went to the part of France which was still unoccupied. His former wife emigrated to Palestine and approached the Beth Din in Haifa to help her obtain a bill of divorce. The Rabbinate in Haifa wrote to the husband to arrange an authorization by Rabbis for writing a *get*.

---

8. R. I.J.Weiss, *Minhath Yizhak*, V, nos. 47ff.; R. M.J.Breisch, *Helkath Yaakob*, III, nos. 91ff.
9. *Vide supra* Part I, pp. 145f.
10. He does not appear to be Chaim Rumkowski as the latter did not usually recite the 'Seven Benedictions' nor was a *huppah* arranged. For references, *vide supra* pp. 145f. and note 84.
11. R. J.Thumim, *Nehamath Yoseph*, New York, 1950, no. 27.

X

He replied by cable in German that in his place there was no Rabbi to assist the writing of an authorization but 'he has no objection (Ich habe nichts dagegen . . .) to giving a *get*'. The question was: can one rely and arrange a *get* on the basis of the telegram alone? As it was war-time it was impossible to get in touch with the husband again and the case was very urgent.

In his reply Chief Rabbi Herzog says, as far as he knew from reading the newspapers one could still travel from unoccupied France to the United States. Hence one must find out first whether one could get in touch with the husband. If this is the case one should ask him to send a more explicit telegram stating: 'I order . . . to write . . . to sign . . . to give a *get* to my wife according to the law of Moses and Israel.' Should this be impossible, one could rely on the telegram already received and a *get* should be written. There were some objections one could raise to writing a *get* on account of that cable which, however, the Chief Rabbi rejected. He had discussed this matter with two eminent Rabbis who agreed to this decision.[12]

No date is given but it was written before the unoccupied zone of France was seized by the Germans (11 November 1942).

---

12. Chief Rabbi Herzog, *Hechal Yizhak*, II, no. 66.

12
Yibbum and Halizah

R. Israel Welz, formerly Ab Beth Din of Pest, later in Jerusalem, approached Chief Rabbi Uzziel on the following matter.

Two days previously a Rabbinical student had told him of a man (a scholar in Rabbinics) who had come from Waitzen (Vác, Hungary) to Israel together with his sister-in-law (both had returned from Auschwitz) and went through the levirate marriage on permission given by Sephardi Rabbis who performed the marriage ceremony although they knew the couple were Ashkenazim. The Sephardi Rabbis had seen permission given to each by the Beth Din in Budapest absolving them from *iggun*. The couple had children and when the woman arrived in Israel she was pregnant. They had approached Rabbi Welz three years beforehand to perform the ceremony; however, the Rabbi refused as the couple were Ashkenazim who do not practise the law of *yibbum* (but that of *halizah* through which the brother-in-law is excluded from marrying his sister-in-law).

Chief Rabbi Uzziel shows how wrong this action was for the man who was learned and knew the law and for the Rabbi who performed the marriage. (Chief Rabbi Uzziel does not think that any Sephardi Beth Din would do this. Most probably it was done by a self-styled Sephardi Rabbi.) He concluded that nevertheless the couple could continue to live together. (The *Responsum* was written on the 21st of Ab 711 (23 August 1951)[1].

A deaf-mute woman appeared before the Rabbinate in Israel wishing to register for marriage with a deaf-mute man. The woman had previously been married to a deaf-mute man and had a son. The father and the son who was then eight years old were sent by the Nazis to Auschwitz. There is evidence that they had been exterminated but it is not known who died first. The father had a brother living in Israel. According to the law a deaf-mute woman cannot perform *halizah*[2] but according to some authorities, may marry the levir even nowadays. In our case, however, the possibility is not ruled out that the father might have died first so *yibbum* (levirate marriage) may not be performed. There is therefore no remedy for the woman. What is now the position of the woman?

After some discussion the Chief Rabbi gave the following ruling. As the woman (and her husband) had been brought up in an institute for the deaf and dumb and she is able to speak though inarticulately,

1. Chief Rabbi Ben Zion Meir Hai Uzziel, *Mishpete Uzziel, Eben Ha-Ezer*, no. 119.
2. *Tur Shulhan Aruch, Eben Ha-Ezer*, cap. CLXXII, no. 11.

halizah could be performed according to one view. Hence if the levir agrees to participate in *halizah*, *halizah* should be done. If he refuses she should not be prevented from marrying 'to save her from being lost . . .'. 'Thank God, she met a deaf-mute who is willing to marry her, may the Maker of both bless both.' The *Responsum* is dated: 4th Nisan, 711 (10 April 1951).[3]

The husband of a pregnant woman was taken in February 1943 to a camp near Auschwitz. There is evidence that the husband died in the beginning of 1943. No one remembers the month of his death. The woman gave birth to a child in July 1943. The baby died a few hours after birth. According to a statement of the woman the child had been carried for the complete time, the hair of its head and its nails were fully developed. Another woman who had been with her when the child was born said that the child was normal as other babies. She remembers that it had hair, but cannot recollect at present whether it had nails. The widow had become engaged to a *kohen* and had received presents from him. The question was asked whether she could marry without *halizah* as otherwise she may lose the chance of re-marrying—she would not find such an excellent match again.

The Rabbi is very indignant about the question. In his view *halizah* is required. It was not a real case of *iggun*. It involved only financial hardship. The woman had not married nor had she been betrothed to the *kohen* that we would have to make him divorce her. She had merely become engaged and that is of no significance. Hence as only financial loss is concerned, as the fiancé was rich, it is obvious she could not be released without *halizah*. (The *Responsum* is addressed to the Rabbis of Antwerp.)[4]

After the war a man in Warsaw whose entire family perished in the furnaces wished to re-marry and raise a family again. He married a widow whose husband was presumed to have no brothers. She re-married on account of evidence of witnesses (to this effect) and through the Beth Din and she gave birth to two children. It was later learnt that her first husband had a brother living overseas. He came and gave *halizah*. The husband came to the Rabbi with the request to permit him to continue living with his wife. Two questions had to be considered: (1) whether the *halizah* performed after the marriage was valid as her brother-in-law would not have been permitted to marry her himself as a levir at that time according to a ruling of the Talmud 'Whosoever may not go up to enter into levirate marriage may not go

3. Chief Rabbi Herzog, *Hechal Yizhak*, II, no. 82.
4. R. M.Rath, *Kol Mebasser*, I, no. 4.

up to perform *halizah* either' (*Yebamoth* 20a, 44a); (2) there are some authorities who forbid a woman in such a case to stay with her husband.

However, the Rabbi tries to show that on account of the lenient view expressed by some other Rabbis the husband who had experienced so many sufferings in his life could stay with his wife.

Rabbi Efrati submitted his decision to Chief Rabbi Herzog who was at that time in Warsaw. The Chief Rabbi agreed, regarding this case 'as a case of great emergency, almost as important as saving the life of our ill-fated sister'. He quotes the view expressed by a great authority shared by other Rabbis that in such a case which happened inadvertently and children had been born from the second husband the woman may stay with him. One must also consider the *halachic* position of the children. His *Responsum* is dated 18th Ellul 708 (22 September 1948).[5]

One man of our community who had come here (England) from Galicia, married a woman here. There were no children. When he fell ill the members of his family were anxious whether to ask him to give his wife a bill of divorce so that she should not require *halizah*, as he had had brothers in his native town. However, since the time of the Nazi holocaust which befell our brethren he had heard nothing from them. After some investigation and after I visited him, I learned that he had had a wife and two children and a younger brother and once during the war he had received a letter from his family. He had heard nothing since. All of them are presumed to be no longer alive. However, there is no certain evidence. The marriage to his wife in London was after permission by a hundred Rabbis. In that case I thought it unnecessary to give him grounds for anxiety and to talk about a bill of divorce as in all events his family in Cracow are presumed dead or alive and so in either case *halizah* was not required. The man has now died and the matter has become a practical question, and must be further discussed.

The decision was that the woman may re-marry. The *Responsum* is dated 6th Tebeth 723 (2 January 1963).[6]

5. R. S.Efrati, *Mi-Ge Ha-Haregah*, no. 12.
6. R. Hanoch Dob Padwa, *Hesheb Ha-Ephod*, no. 115.

13

Inside the Ghettos

RELIGIOUS REVIVAL

Assimilation and persecution

Most unfortunate was the fate of those who were assimilated and had severed their ties with Judaism. They had hoped to be accepted into the gentile aristocracy. With the advent of Hitler they experienced the fate of ordinary Jews who dressed in black cap and kaftan. They were bewildered to find themselves outcasts from their environment and in their despair they joined their brethren completely even taking upon themselves the ways of traditional Judaism without hesitating over the price they would have to pay for being accepted into the fold of the covenant of Abraham. (See the moving story told *supra* Part I, pp. 62f.)

Sterilization and Religious Service

When a service was to be held in the hospital of the ghetto in Kovno[1] on the high festivals despite the prohibition issued by the Germans under the penalty of death about two weeks before *Rosh Ha-Shanah*, 703,[2] the only person available to act as *hazzan* was a man who had been sterilized by the Nazis. The question arose whether he may act as a *hazzan*.

The decision was in the affirmative. 'I too attended that service which took place in the hospital[3] and preached after *Kol Nidre*. . . . My ears can still hear the weeping of the people in their prayer to God. Among the worshippers were all doctors and workers of the hospital who took no notice of the prohibition of evildoers. They were all seized by the fear of God and prayed with fervour and in tears for all were then captives and the *hazzan* prayed like a captive[4] imploring his captor that our petitions and requests be granted and we not return empty-handed. . . .[5]'

Taking Tephillin into the hospital, destruction of the hospital with its doctors, sisters and patients (October 1941)

The Germans gave the appearance of trying to help the sick and

1. There were several other places in the ghetto where services were held in spite of the prohibition. They were attended even by those who had lost any connection with Judaism and never used to pray.
2. *Rosh Ha-Shanah* 703 fell on 12 September 1942; The prohibition was issued on 26 August 1942, see Garfunkel, *Destruction of Kovno's Jewry*, pp. 131ff.
3. On the service in the hospital, see also Garfunkel, *Destruction of Kovno's Jewry*, p. 133.
4. Text taken from the *Selihah* of Rab Amram Gaon.
5. R. E.Oshry, *Mi-Maamakkim*, III, no. 10, where the reasons for his decision are given.

318

restoring them to health. They did so at a time when their hope and will to live was strengthened on seeing the medical aid given to them and the special hospitals built for that purpose. In fact the Germans intended from the very beginning to destroy the hospitals together with their patients.

When the Germans issued an order that a hospital be erected in the small ghetto of Kovno (apart from the Small Ghetto there was another ghetto known as the Big Ghetto; both were connected by a wooden bridge)[6] Rabbi E.Oshry was asked the following question.

In the hospital there lay a young man whose right leg had been amputated by the Germans before they had taken him there. The young man, a *baal teshubah*, wished to pray every day and put on *tephillin*. He had therefore asked for a pair of *tephillin* to be sent to him so that he could pray according to the Law. However, a rumour had spread that when one left the hospital, the Germans would burn everything one possessed. Was it permitted to send *tephillin* to the man in hospital, as the *tephillin* might be burned together with his personal belongings and by sending the *tephillin* one would cause them to be burned?

The Rabbi discusses the question from various angles as there was ground both for and against sending the *tephillin*. He eventually decided that the young man ought to be supplied with *tephillin* as it would make him happy that he was included among the faithful of Israel and not among those 'upon whose heads *tephillin* were not placed' (see *Rosh Ha-Shanah* 17a).

The Rabbi reports:

Dr Davidovitz who was physician to the hospital testified that he was present when the *tephillin* were given to the young man. When the latter put them on for the first time his happiness was boundless as if he had come out from the darkness to the great light, from slavery to freedom. . . .

Behold on the 3rd of Tishri 5702 (24 September 1941)[7] when the cursed Germans carried out their evil plan to destroy the small ghetto they burned down the hospital with all the sick patients, sisters and doctors.[8] About 60 Jewish lives were destroyed, among them also Dr Davidowitz and the young man to whom the *tephillin* had been sent. . . .

But what a miracle! A Jew who was at the hospital managed to

6. *Vide supra.*
7. According to L. Garfunkel, *The Destruction of Kovno's Jewry*, pp. 70, 109, the hospital in the Small Ghetto was burned down on the Sabbath, 4 October 1941 which corresponds to the 13th of Tishri, 702.
8. On a similar case, *vide supra*, p. 299.

escape by the grace of God and to save the *tephillin* which the young man had guarded with danger to his life. When the latter had learnt of the Germans' plan to liquidate the hospital and all its occupants he gave the *tephillin* to the man with the request that he should endeavour to hide them so that they would not fall into the hands of the wicked, unclean men who would make sport of them and burn them. . . .[9]

DESECRATION OF TORAH SCROLLS AND HOLY PLACES (AUGUST 1941)

Defilement

One of the sadistic attempts of the German soldiers to annoy the Jews was the following:

On the 4th of Ellul, 5701 (27 August 1941) the Germans went out to round up all the stray animals (cats and dogs) and placed them all in the New Beth Ha-Midrash (*die neue Klaus*) in Slobodka. The animals were killed by shooting.[10] But the wicked men were not satisfied with defiling the holy place in such a way by turning it into a dump of stinking carcasses for they later gathered many Jews who were taken to see the defilement of their holy place. Afterwards Jews were forced to tear up the Holy scrolls and cover the carcasses with them. The Jews who had witnessed the defiling of the scrolls later approached the Ab Beth Din of Kovno[11] and asked him to prescribe atonement for them and particularly for those who had taken an active part in tearing up the scrolls as well as for all the inhabitants of the ghetto who heard what had happened for they regarded it as an evil omen sent from heaven. As the Ab Beth Din of Kovno was very ill, R. Oshry was asked to deal with the matter.

After a lengthy discussion the Rabbi decided that those who witnessed the tearing up of the scrolls should, if possible, fast. However, if they were unable to do so as they were weak as a result of hunger and the sorrows which occurred daily in the ghetto, they need not fast. Only those who had taken an active part in tearing up the scrolls must fast, although they did it under duress. All the other inhabitants of the ghetto need not fast but should make gifts to charity. On the following Sabbath the Rabbi preached on making atonement.[12]

Jew forced to burn Sepher Torah but the Torah mantle was saved

A Jew who succeeded in escaping from the massacres of the Nazis came

9. R. E.Oshry, *Mi-Maamakkim*, III, no. 1.
10. According to L. Garfunkel, *The Destruction of Kovno's Jewry*, p. 126, the defilement of 'the Beth Ha-Midrash Ha-Gadol' of Slobodka occurred on 14 January 1942.
11. He was R. Abraham Dob Schapira who died on 22nd Adar I, 703 (27 February 1943).
12. Oshry, *Mi-Maamakkim*, I, no. 1, where also the question of performing *keriah* is discussed.

immediately after the liberation to the Rabbi asking for a decision in the following case.

His family had been in possession of a *Sepher Torah* for more than 300 years. It passed on as an heritage for generations from father to son. This *Sepher Torah* was distinguished by its beautiful script and unusual size. The mantle was made accordingly and it too was outstanding because of its material, colour and fascinating embroidery, which captivated the eye.

During the Nazi rule, the cursed murderers in the course of their decree against the *Siphre Torah* in particular and Hebrew books in general forced the man's father under torture to burn the Torah scroll.[13] However, the questioner succeeded, with great danger to life, in hiding the mantle to have it as a keepsake for generations.

After the liberation the man wished to use the mantle for a *Sepher Torah* which had been saved in Kovno. Unfortunately, the mantle was too large because of its extraordinary size. The questioner therefore asked the Rabbi whether the surplus material left after a mantle would be made could be used as a *tephillin* bag for his son who was about to become a *bar-mizvah*.

The reply was in the negative. The mantle should be used for a *Sepher Torah*, and if the former is too long, it should be adjusted by folding any surplus material inside and sewing it up. The (entire) mantle would then fit correctly.[14]

MALTREATMENT

Loss of speech, etc., caused by beating

In 1942 an honourable member of R. E.Oshry's Beth Ha-Midrash in Kovno was beaten so mercilessly that he lost his power of speech and his sense of hearing and almost his eyesight. However, his mental capacity did not suffer. He could communicate with the outside world by writing. The reason for this maltreatment was the following. The Germans decreed that no one working in the forced labour camp was allowed to leave the place and search the dung hills for food. When famine oppressed him and other Jewish forced labourers, he exposed himself to danger by leaving his place of work and going to find some food. He had always been helpful to his fellow-men. When he saw his brethren were working hard and their skin was shrivelled upon their

13. On a case where a Rabbi was forced to burn a Torah scroll, see Oshry, *Mi-Maamakkim*, II, no. 19. One Rabbi was forced to throw a Torah scroll into the river, see R. A.Jeruchem, 'Alim Bochim', in *Birkath Hayyim* by his father R. H.Y.Jeruchem, p. 21. On one occasion when a Rabbi refused to tear up a scroll petrol was poured over him and he was set alight. While he was burning the scroll was thrown at him and both burned—Huberband, *Kiddush Ha-Shem*, p. 29.

14. Oshry, *Mi-Maamakkim*, II, no. 22.

bones, he went out into the field at the time of the potato-harvest in the hope of finding some potatoes and other vegetables with which to keep them alive. However, he was discovered by the cursed wicked people and was beaten severely. He suffered the consequences mentioned above. He had learned to live with his disabilities. However, he felt very unfortunate that he could not pray to God and be called up to the Torah as he was unable to pronounce the words. He wished to know whether he could be counted among the ten people making up the quorum. Would the Rabbi[15] advise him how he could help to make up a quorum and be called up?

All this was submitted to the Rabbi in writing by the man, and he was watching the Rabbi's face for the words of his reply.

The decision was that he could be included in the quorum. However, with regard to being called up the Rabbi was reluctant to give permission. He suggested the man be called up together with the reader and both should recite the benedictions. On learning of my decision, his eyes became bright and he wrote down on a piece of paper: 'Rabbi, you have comforted me and preserved my life. May God so comfort you and preserve your life.'

Sterilization caused by beating

In 1942 R. Oshry was asked by one of the members of the Beth Ha-Midrash in Slobodka, R. Jehiel ben R. Meir Ha-Kohen (who was later killed by the Germans) the following question.

The Nazis had issued a decree that none of the labourers of the forced labour camp group were allowed to bring into the ghetto any food left over from their meagre meal. Their aim was to prevent the Jews from helping their starving families. To add insult to injury the Germans issued an order that all labourers returning from work should undress so that their bodies and garments could be thoroughly searched for food.[16] Because his little children were starving the above-mentioned martyr could not resist the temptation to hide a piece of bread in his private parts in the hope that the Germans would not notice it. Unfortunately they discovered the bread and became enraged. They beat him mercilessly mutilating his genitals. When the wounds healed a little he came to R. Oshry and poured out his heart to him. He was aware, he said, that the prohibition of Deut. XXIII 2, applied to him. In any case, he would most probably be killed by the Germans. He would not, however, refrain from attending services, morning and evening,

15. Oshry, *Mi-Maamakkim*, III, no. 2.
16. On such searches, see Garfunkel, *The Destruction of Kovno's Jewry*, p. 94. See also G. Hausner, *Justice in Jerusalem*, pp. 162f. about the report of a former inmate of the labour camp of Plaszow (today a judge in Tel Aviv).

although it entailed great sacrifice (*mesirath nephesh*). But having had his genitals mutilated he feared he could no longer be called up as a *kohen*, a fact which greatly distressed him. Was he still permitted to be called up as a *kohen*?

After discussing the case the Rabbi decided that he could still be regarded as a *kohen* and be called up first. On hearing this the man called out: 'Rabbi, you have comforted me, you have given me new life. Happy are you that you have brought a new spirit and hope in me for this world and the world to come. . . .' (He was later killed by the Germans.)[17]

Cross tattooed on the arm

It was before daybreak when the Nazis led those Jews who had been picked out for forced labour into the labour camp so that they were prevented from putting on *tephillin* before going to work. After having spent the whole day at hard labour they were brought back late at night.

There were among those some who nevertheless put on *tephillin* secretly on their way to work. However, on one occasion the Germans caught a Jew who was putting on *tephillin* on his way and after torturing him severely they tattooed a cross on his arm where he wore the *tephillah*. Afterwards he approached Rabbi Oshry and asked whether he could cover the spot with a plaster and put the *tephillah* over it. Would the plaster constitute an interposition? Answer: as many people put on *tephillin* at home and wear them when coming to synagogue he should put *tephillin* on at home and take off the *tephillah* from his arm after his return from synagogue. If not possible, he may put on the *tephillah* over a thin shirt-sleeve because it was a case of true hardship.[18]

IMMORALITY (JANUARY 1942)

In the ghetto of Kovno one of the most distinguished members of the town came to the Rabbi[19] on the 25th of Tebeth 5702 (14 January 1942) telling him that his only daughter had had intercourse with a man and had given birth to a boy. The seducer had fled and had probably been killed by the Germans. His query was whether other people had a duty to observe the *mizvah* of redeeming the first born (*pidyan ha-ben*) or whether on the other hand only if a person so wished need he do so as, even if the father were present, he would not redeem his son because of

17. Oshry, *Mi-Maamakkim*, II, no. 7.
18. Oshry, *Mi-Maamakkim*, I, no.26. On the recital of the benedictions, see ibid. On the question whether one may put on *tephillin* at night in the time of emergency and danger, see Oshry, 'Kuntras Me-Emek Ha-Bacha', no. 2.
19. Oshry, *Mi-Maamakkim*, 1, no. 9.

shame though he would be pleased, no doubt, if his son were redeemed.
Similarly, a decision was required concerning the benediction *She-heheyanu*. May other people (not the father) say that benediction?

The Rabbi decided that the *pidyan ha-ben* should be performed. With
regard to the benediction *She-heheyanu* the Rabbi was of the opinion
that it should be omitted in the case where the father himself does not
redeem his son as 'in the ghetto no new fruit or new garment which
requires the recital of *She-heheyanu* was available which could at the
same time refer to the redemption of the first born . . .'.

EUTHANASIA

Apart from abnormal oppression by the Germans, the Jews had to
suffer daily from their taskmasters when they left each morning to
forced labour and when they returned home. In addition to oral insults
they were beaten and smitten at every step to hasten them, sometimes
they were made to run to their place of slave labour where they had to
do work which crushes the body and breaks the soul. Their daily ration
was cut down and they were deprived of food.

One day, when the forced labourers were driven to work[20] it was
very cold. Many of the wretched people were wrapped only in rags and
were forced by their cursed taskmasters armed with lashes, to proceed
quickly. The feet of many of them were swollen owing to hunger and
the marching. They often stopped and fell to the ground. Many fell
and did not rise again.

On one occasion, one of those unfortunate marchers seeing what
was happening became sick of life and in his despair turned to the man
behind him and begged him to give him a strong push so that he
would fall to the ground, and then repeat it again and again, that he
might be unable to get up and expire. He repeated his request several
times so that the man behind him wished to oblige as in any case his
companion would die sooner or later. He therefore pushed him
violently several times causing the man to fall to the ground every time
until they eventually reached their destination when the man fell to the
ground for the last time.

When after the liberation religious services for the high festivals were
about to be arranged at the end of the year 704 (September 1944), a
hazzan was required who was a worthy man and had a pleasant voice.
The above-mentioned man appeared to comply with all the require-

20. Most probably this refers to going to work outside the ghetto, i.e. to the aerodrome
(on the work there see Garfunkel, *The Destruction of Kovno's Jewry*, pp. 86, 92, 233).
People had to appear before the ghetto gates at 5 a.m. to walk five kilometres to the
aerodrome in military formation and work hard under terrible conditions. When
returning they had to endure new cruelties from their German tormentors; ibid.

ments. However, there were some people who objected to his officiating because of his past. (He had caused a man's death.)

As it was a time of emergency and no other *hazzan* was available, R. Oshry was asked whether this man may act as a *hazzan* and whether he required special repentance and whether that would help.

The Rabbi prescribed a special act of *teshubah*. After this was done, the man was permitted to act as *hazzan*. The Rabbi tells us that the *hazzan* prayed with great fervour and wept so that all worshippers were overcome by his prayers. Among the congregation were Jewish soldiers of the Red Army who had come to pray together with their brethren. They too were stirred by him.[21]

GARMENTS AND BELONGINGS OF THE VICTIMS

September 1941. The Jews of the ghetto of Kovno had been ordered to work at the airport outside the town and to send a thousand men there every day for that purpose without fail. It happened that on the eve of *Rosh Ha-Shanah* 5702 (21 September 1941) the number fell short. When the Germans noticed this they roamed the ghetto under Corporal Neumann to seize Jews for forced labour. On the way they murdered many Jews among them R. Isaac Baum, the owner of an ironmonger shop, who was holding a *mahzor* for *Rosh Ha-Shanah* in his hands, and also Berl Mendelewicz. Afterwards the evildoers ordered the Jews to dig a pit and bury those who had been slain and strip them of their upper clothes which they were to hand to the Jews who performed the burial. The garments had no stains of blood (had they been stained they too would have required burial according to the Law). The Rabbi was asked whether the garments may be used as they had come from dead people. The Rabbi decided that the garments may be used by the children of the deceased. 'In such hard and troublesome times when "outside the sword bereaves and in the chambers terror"(Deut. xxxii 25) surely the martyrs would have satisfaction if their children who survived would be able to use those garments either to warm themselves or to sell them and buy food to sustain themselves. . . .'. He then proves that the garments are not prohibited from being used and should be given to the children of the victims.[22]

October 1941. It was after the great massacre on the 8th of Heshvan, 5702 (29 October 1941)[23] when about ten thousand Jews were killed in the Ninth Fortress of Kovno that R. Elijah Zedikow (later killed) who

21. Oshry, *Mi-Maamakkim*, III, no. 7.
22. Oshry, *Mi-Maamakkim*, I, no. 3. On this event see also Garfunkel, *The Destruction of Kovno's Jewry*, p. 88.
23. On this massacre called 'The Great aktia' *vide supra* p. 51; R. M.Breisch, *Helkath Yaakob*, II, nos. 31, 32; L. Garfunkel, *The Destruction of Kovno's Jewry*, pp. 73ff.

belonged to the forced labour camp named 'Jordan Brigade' appeared and reported that at the place of the Ninth Fortress there was a store containing the garments of the victims who had been stripped before their execution. These garments contained personal letters and photographs of the members of the families of the victims so that there was no doubt that the clothes were those of the victims. No blood was to be found on the garments, which indicated that they had been removed before the victims had been executed. R. Elijah inquired whether according to the *halachah* those garments could be used.

The answer was in the affirmative.[24]

October 1941. It was on the 10th of Heshvan 5702 (31 October 1941) after the wicked Germans had taken about ten thousand people old and young, men and women and their babies from the ghetto and massacred them.[25] Everyone who remained feared lest he would share the same fate next day. At that troublesome time one of the most distinguished men of the town came to Rabbi Oshry and asked him the following question. As his whole family was starving and dying from hunger and no money was left for food may he take possession of the property left by a family formerly living in the same house and whose members had all been killed during the great massacre? He would be able to sell the articles and buy food for his starving little ones.

The answer was in the affirmative.[26]

PROHIBITION OF ERECTING TOMBSTONES (1941)

In some places the Germans did not permit the putting up of tombstones. In the ghetto of Kovno[27] they did not allow even the marking of the graves. Afterwards they permitted marking them by numbers and later they did not care any more and the Jews began to erect *mazeboth* of wood with inscriptions in Yiddish and Hebrew.

A Rabbi tells us that his mother had been struck by an SS captain and died in great pain in the ghetto of Luncic on the 9th of Tebet 701 (8 January 1941). She was buried there at the old cemetery. No tombstone could be erected because 'of the fury of the oppressor' (cf. Isa. LI 13). Instead a sealed bottle containing a note with her name was placed in her grave.[28]

GHETTO OF LODZ (AUGUST 1944)

A husband and wife had been interned in the ghetto of Lodz. On

24. Oshry, *Mi-Maamakkim*, II, no. 5.
25. On this action, *vide supra*, Part II, p. 286.
26. Oshry, *Mi-Maamakkim*, III, no. 4.
27. Garfunkel, *The Destruction of Kovno's Jewry*, p. 112.
28. R. J.M.Aronzon, *Yeshuath Mosheh*, p. 307, n. 52.

25 August 1944, the husband was deported to a concentration camp.[29] They had no children. The husband had a brother who was in the concentration camp too. Both brothers died in the camp. One witness testified afterwards before the Beth Din in Lodz that one of them died in December 1944 and the other in May 1945, but he did not know which brother died first.

In March 1945 the woman gave birth to a daughter, who was taken away by the Germans about three or four days after birth and nothing is known of what happened to the baby.[30]

After the war the woman returned to Lodz and re-married without *halizah*, having received permission from the Beth Din (in Lodz) who investigated and decided that both husband and his brother had died. Nothing was known of the existence of another brother. (The woman did not inform the Beth Din about the birth of a daughter at that time— before it had become known that there was still another brother (levir) —such information was then of no significance. She later gave an acceptable explanation for not divulging the daughter's birth.)

After the (second) marriage the couple emigrated to Australia. It was there that they learned to their great surprise that the first husband had left a brother who, thirty years before, when still young, had emigrated to Palestine. Since then no connection had existed between him and his family in Poland. He was almost forgotten. Until that moment the woman knew nothing of that brother-in-law. The husband immediately withdrew from contact with his wife and was ready to send her to Israel to perform the act of *halizah*. However, she was prevented by the situation in 1947 and 1948 caused by the war of liberation at the end of the mandate.

The woman then disclosed to her husband the birth of a daughter born to her in the camp and gave a reasonable explanation why she kept it from him until then. She also told him of a woman who had been with her in the camp and who had returned with her to Lodz after the war and knew about the birth of the daughter. The husband, without asking the Rabbis, returned to his wife who afterwards gave birth to a son.

The Rabbi in Australia requested the Beth Din in Lodz to question the woman about the daughter. Evidence was received from the Beth Din in Lodz that the woman confirmed that a daughter had indeed been born 'about March 1945' after nine months of pregnancy; the birth was normal.

---

29. On deportations from Lodz, cf. Reitlinger, *The Final Solution*, pp. 323ff.

30. R. Herzog in his *Responsum* (*vide infra* note 31) regards it as possible that the baby was not killed but given to a non-Jewish family where she grew up as a non-Jewess not knowing her family background.

'The man and the woman are religious and would not have resumed living together had they not thought in their ignorance that they were permitted to do so.

The question concerns the position of the couple and that of their son. They are ready to do whatever the law requires.'

The following main problems were involved:

1. Assuming that *halizah* is required and that she could leave Australia and come to Israel for *halizah* to be performed, what would be the subsequent position of the woman and that of the child? Would she be permitted to stay with her husband, would the child be legitimate?
2. Is it necessary to give her a bill of divorce first and then let her perform the act of *halizah* and afterwards re-marry her husband?
3. If she could not obtain permission to return to Australia after she had been in Israel for *halizah*, this would ruin her, and 'who knows what would then happen, seeing she has already a child from her husband. Perhaps a solution can be found to permit her to live with her husband without *halizah*.'

Chief Rabbi Herzog discussed the problem from every angle making some suggestions and adopting a lenient view.[31]

WARSAW GHETTO AND UPRISING (19 APRIL 1943)

The *Responsum* was written on 1 May 1945.[32]

The case concerns an *agunah* whose husband had gone to Poland on business before the war. He remained there after the outbreak of the war and stayed in Warsaw. His wife received letters from him through the Red Cross informing her that he was living in the Warsaw Ghetto. A Jew who had escaped from the ghetto ('through a miracle') gave evidence that he had seen her husband in the Warsaw Ghetto during the time of the uprising when the ghetto was already 'straitly shut up' (see Joshua VI 1) by the cursed Germans. He, the witness, escaped 'through a miracle' making use of a false document (certificate). Since then no further information about the husband was received. Can the woman who was still young be granted permission to re-marry after the end of the war when the whole of Germany would be occupied by the Allied armies?

In his reply, the Rabbi (in Tel Aviv) said that the question was currently not pressing, however, as 'it was Torah which had to be discussed' he dealt at length with the case. He then stated that permission for re-marriage could perhaps be given but only when Nazi Germany was liberated and all camps of forced labourers were opened. Twelve

31. R. Herzog, *Hechal Yizhak*, II, no. 84.
32. The *Responsum* is dated: 33rd of Counting the Omer, 705 (1 May 1945).

months would have to elapse since the liberation and no news have been received about her husband. 'However, I stress that I am submitting this case to the great Rabbis and if two great scholars of renown give their permission, I too will agree.'

In his *Responsum* there are several interesting historical facts which he mentions to prove that the death of the husband can be taken as certain.

He says: As regards the Jews of Warsaw, their misfortune had been twofold. First, they had been subdued by the 'troops besieging a town' (see on this *Gittin* III 4, p. 28b) after the revolt, as the Jews had fought and killed many German soldiers in a desperate battle. The latter fought back with tanks, bombs and cannons. Hence the majority of Jews were killed like inhabitants of any town under siege taken by troops.

Second, all Jews had been under a death sentence of Hitler's wicked government who had decreed that they be destroyed, be slain and perish (cf. Esther III 13; VII 4). Indeed, he destroyed about six million people, all who had been in his hands. 'How much more did he murder the Jews of Warsaw who had rebelled against him.'

One cannot assume that there was a possibility of escape as the city was besieged, closely shut up. One could not hide either as the buildings were destroyed by bombs from the air and by shells of mortars. As regards the witness who escaped by a miracle 'one cannot derive a rule from miraculous events'.

In addition, from the Talmud[33] one can deduce that if a building collapses burying people underneath it can be assumed that the majority of them have been killed (*rubban le-mithah*). 'It is well known that the Germans caused a flood of bombs to pour down over the Jewish Ghetto of Warsaw. All houses were turned into ruins as we all know. Even to-day, one can see the ruins of the former ghetto. This is similar to the 'collapse of a building' where the majority of the inhabitants can be regarded as dead. In view of all this, our case is similar to that of a man who disappeared in 'waters the shores of which cannot be seen' (where re-marriage is only Rabbinically forbidden) as all countries of Europe subdued by the Germans were turned into a 'valley of slaughter' (Jer. VII 32) for all Jews. The Germans decreed that all non-Jews who hide and save a Jew would be killed as well as the Jews. The Germans enforced their decree. They sent out 'secret spies', who were paid for every Jew handed over. When a Jewish boy was once seen outside the Ghetto of Warsaw escaping into a house a hunt was arranged and every method was

---

33. *Yeb.* 114b and *Rashi* ibid.; *Yer. Gittin* III 4.

employed (all streets were closed) in search of him. This did indeed take place. Hence, even if one Jew fled the ghetto he was still in great danger of being handed over to the Germans by wicked non-Jews or of being found by the Germans who would pounce on any Jew outside the ghetto. They made use of especially trained dogs to track down the Jews. . . . The case is in some respects even worse than that of a man falling into waters without end. . . .[34]

34. R. Tobiah Yehudah Tabyomi (Guttentag), *Erez Tobah*, I, no. 60.

14

Liberation of the Concentration Camd of Gunskirchen

FAMILY SENT TO VIENNA

R. Ezekiel Lefkowitsch approached Rabbi Meisels on the following matter.

He had been together with his brother-in-law in the concentration camp of Gunskirchen,[1] 'the worst of all camps'. On the day of its liberation 'all inmates were very weak because of the troubles of the past'. Desperate for food they went out into the villages and towns to find some victuals and on that day an epidemic, typhoid and other stomach diseases broke out and the American military authorities had at their disposal medicaments to save only a small number of inmates. Within a few days the great majority died. Of the original number of about thirty thousand only about[2] thirteen thousand survived. He had seen the American soldiers continuously carrying thousands for burial. He himself made investigations at the hospitals there about his brother-in-law and looked up all lists of survivors but did not find his name listed. Rabbi Lefkowitsch was almost certain that his brother-in-law had died in the pestilence as otherwise he would have informed his family as he had been living in harmony with his wife and they were attached to each other and their dear child. Moreover, he knew that his wife and child survived for they had not been sent to Auschwitz but to Vienna where they stayed for a long time.

While still in the concentration camp he had expressed his joy at being able to see his wife and son alive. Most probably he had died. There is no question that he had been taken to Russia (Siberia) as he had been liberated together with Rabbi Lefkowitsch in Austria by the American army.

R. Meisels decided that the *agunah* may re-marry provided that two other Rabbis would agree.[3]

---

1. Sub-camp of Mauthausen in Austria; cf. Evelyn Le Chêne, *Mauthausen*, pp. 247f.
2. On the figures, *vide supra* Part I, p. 130.
3. R. Z.H.Meisels, *Binyan Zebi*, II, no. 66.

15

Return to Judaism

After the liberation a Jewish soldier of the Red Army came to Rabbi Oshry and told him that among the German prisoners in the camp were two people who maintained they were Jewish but they had been baptized and assimilated with the Germans. They were therefore seeking an opportunity to leave the camp of the wicked Nazis and to return to their Jewish brethren to follow the Jewish way of life.

After a certain time they succeeded indeed in leaving the camp and in reaching Kovno and settled among the Jews after they had returned to Judaism. The man was attending morning and evening services regularly. As he was a *kohen* the Rabbi was asked whether he might recite the priestly blessing. He decided in the affirmative but prescribed immersion.[1]

Immediately after the liberation R. Oshry was called to the hospital where a Jewish woman had given birth to a son and wished to speak to the Rabbi to reveal to him a secret she could tell no one else. When he arrived he found her distressed and crying. She asked everyone to leave the room. When this was done she told the Rabbi that the father of the child was a non-Jew who had saved her from death and had kept her in hiding all the time. She wished that the child be circumcised and brought up as a Jew. The Rabbi was asked to see that the boy was circumcised according to the Law. The Rabbi comforted her and she promised to conduct herself according to the religious way of life and to bring up her son accordingly.[2]

1. R. E.Oshry, *Mi-Maamakkim*, III, no. 13.
2. R. E.Oshry, *Mi-Maamakkim*, II, no. 27. For further cases, *vide supra* Part I, pp. 69f, 160ff., 165.

16

Repatriation

Deportation of married couples from Greece to Germany. Return of one spouse after liberation who wishes to re-marry and the problems involved.

Mr Michael Molho[1] of 'bereaved' Salonica asked Chief Rabbi Uzziel for advice on the following questions:

(1) At present deportees from Greece return from Poland.[2] They are men whose wives and children had been taken by the Germans direct to Birkenau and had been brought to the gas chambers and fiery furnaces and there is no hope of seeing them alive again.[3] Some of the men became engaged to Jewish women, a number had children and they wish that weddings be arranged for them according to the Law of Moses and Israel. How can it be proved that their first wives had died? May one in practice rely on general evidence to assume that a particular man's wife has died?

(2) If the husband or the wife who had no children or whose children had disappeared was not heard of, and now he (or she) wishes to re-marry and to begin a new family life, how long has he (or she) to wait before re-marrying?

(3) If a man or woman who had been married and had children or had no children returned without his (or her) spouse is the evidence of people who claim to have seen the spouse taken to the wagons leading to the crematoria sufficient for them to be regarded as dead and to permit the surviving spouse to re-marry?

(4) How should we deal with cases of men and women returning from Poland who claim to be single and to have never been married and wish now to marry? We have no archives[4] at our disposal and are therefore unable to check their statements. Is the evidence of witnesses who testify that they are single sufficient to permit them to marry?

R. Uzziel tried to deal with these points, and after expressing his view he sent the questions and his answers to Chief Rabbi Herzog. In spite

---

1. In the Chief Rabbi's reply he is addressed as 'Mar Michael Molho'. Also Chief Rabbi Herzog is of the opinion that there was no Rabbi in Salonica at that time (*vide infra*). However, from the book published by Molho jointly with Joseph Nehama, *The Destruction of Greek Jewry 1941–1944*, we can see that he was Rabbi in Salonica before the war and after the war; see p. 155 and Preface, p. 7.
2. On the deportations, see ibid., 172ff.
3. Ibid., pp. 219, 221, and *infra* note 5.
4. On the spoil of the archives, see ibid., p. 113.

of his illness, the former writes, he attended to the matter in view of the urgency and tried to answer the questions which are of manifold importance and concern the whole of Israel (*kelal Yisrael*). He therefore asks Chief Rabbi Herzog to let him know his view as soon as possible.[5]

In Chief Rabbi Herzog's reply[6] a few points deserve particular mention. As far as men (*agunim*) were concerned he agreed with Chief Rabbi Uzziel without any hesitation. However, the cases of *agunoth* required more consideration. 'It is known there are still myriads of refugees in Soviet Russia. Investigation is very difficult, though it is not impossible to approach the Soviet authorities about the matter (fate of survivors) . . .' He therefore does not agree to the suggestion made by Chief Rabbi Uzziel that women should be given permission to re-marry after twelve months had elapsed since the end of the war and despite thorough investigation nothing was heard of the missing husband as it was well known communications were not open immediately after the war and the matter of investigation and research was not even then complete. The women should therefore not re-marry but apply again after twelve months from then when their cases would be reviewed. Chief Rabbi Herzog then mentions the kind of evidence required in each case to permit an *agunah* to re-marry. No general permission could be given. Not all places under the Nazis suffered equally. Not everywhere was the majority of Jews exterminated. In France a little more than fifty per cent remained. He expresses his deep regret for the community of Salonica which 'came down wonderfully' (cf. Lam. I 9) and is very perturbed that, as it appears, there are no religious leaders and authorized teachers (*more horaah*) at all there. He asks Chief Rabbi Uzziel to draw the attention of the Jews of Salonica to the fact that there is a great difference between husbands whose wives are missing and women whose husbands have disappeared, so that it should not appear strange that men are treated differently from women. Among Ashkenazim the Ordinance of R. Gershom, the Light of the Exile, prohibiting bigamy, and among the Sephardim an oath not to marry an additional wife is involved. Women, however, would transgress a biblical prohibition if they 'married' a second man and grave consequences ensue.

In the light of what had been discussed by Chief Rabbis Uzziel and Herzog the former wrote on the 29th of Heshvan 706 (5 November 1945) to Mr Molho the following replies to his questions.

(1) If there exists evidence as to the identification of the women who had been taken by the Germans direct to Birkenau and sent to the gas

5. Chief Rabbi Ben Zion Meir Hai Uzziel, *Mishpete Uzziel, Eben Ha-Ezer*, nos. 44–46
6. Chief Rabbi Herzog's reply is also printed in his *Hechal Yizhak*, I, no. 27.

chambers and furnaces, one can rely on this evidence to permit their husbands to re-marry or to arrange *Huppah and Kiddushin* for those who became engaged on the assumption that their wives had died. This can be done only after a thorough investigation of the lists of all those who had survived which have hitherto been published by Jewish or government institutions.

If, however, it turns out in the course of time that those (first) wives had escaped and are still alive, their husbands have to maintain them until their divorce which must be with the women's consent and free will, by a bill of divorce, according to Jewish law.

(2) Jewish marriages can be annulled only by a bill of divorce or by the death of the spouse proved by reliable evidence. A man or woman whose spouse has disappeared may only re-marry if permission is granted by an authoritative Beth Din. The length of the period elapsed since the spouse was last seen is of no significance in annulling the marriage.

(3) Men and women cannot be treated alike for the following reason. If a man marries another woman after evidence and a decision of the Beth Din and it later transpires that his first wife is still alive, she does not become prohibited for him, but is his wife in every respect. Her husband must maintain her until he divorces her with her knowledge and consent.

In contradistinction if a woman re-marries after a decision of an authoritative Beth Din and it later transpires that her first husband is still alive, she is prohibited to her first husband, she cannot claim maintenance or her *kethubah*, nor may she live with the second husband and the children born from the second marriage are never permitted to marry.

Any woman whose husband died is not permitted to re-marry unless she performs *halizah*, if he had no children or if they died during his lifetime and her husband left brothers. As long as this is not done she may not re-marry. If the husband and his children were murdered together and it cannot be established whether the children died after their father's death or during his lifetime (in the former case their mother could marry without *halizah*, in the latter case *halizah* would be required if she wished to re-marry) as long as the matter is not clarified in accordance with Jewish law, no permission can be given to a woman to re-marry until it is clear that the husband had left children, otherwise one has to be sure that he had no brothers or that they had died.

Therefore, granting an *agunah* permission to re-marry requires great care. We have seen with our own eyes new lists of survivors who have emerged from their hiding places or revealed their true Jewish names which they concealed during the persecution when they pretended to be non-Jews.

In view of this, the Chief Rabbi suggests great caution before granting permission to *agunoth* to re-marry. They should not re-marry before the lapse of twelve months from that day (the *Responsum* is dated: Heshvan 706) during which time a thorough investigation should be made of all the lists of names of survivors. Particulars would probably come to light which were unknown at first. After twelve months the matter would be reconsidered on the basis of any new information.

If there are women who have some evidence of the death of their husbands from witnesses (even from one witness or reliable official report) their case will be dealt with.

(4) Any man or woman who comes before us claiming to be single is not to be regarded (*muhzakim*) as married. Therefore, permission for marriage can perhaps be given after evidence of reliable witnesses who would have to testify that the person was single and not bound by a previous marriage.

This applies only to a time when all communal records are destroyed and no certificate of one's single status can be obtained from the place the person had left. However, if such a certificate can be obtained, it is customary in most Jewish communities for such a document to be written by the Beth Din of the place the person had left. The document must state that the person concerned was single. Only after such a certificate can permission to marry be granted.[7]

REPATRIATION FROM RUSSIA

Although it was difficult to obtain information about people who fled or were deported to Russia during the war[8] 'the Russians permitted them to return after the defeat of Germany. Almost all of them left Russia particularly those who were married and had children.'[9]

This statement was made by R. Mosheh Feinstein in connection with a case dealt with in a *Responsum* dated 17th of Heshvan 710 (9 November, 1949). Two groups of Jews from Russia had tried to cross a river, a border with Russia. While the first group succeeded in crossing the border, the second group was drowned. The question arose whether one could assume that the husband in question was among those drowned or whether he had changed his mind and did not join his party and consequently was still in Russia. From the *Responsum* it appears

---

7. In a note by the editor ibid. we are informed that through the endeavours of the Chief Rabbis in Israel, a distinguished Rabbi was sent by the 'Joint' to Greece for several years to deal with religious questions, among them *agunah* problems.
8. *Vide supra* p. 295.
9. R. M.Feinstein, *Iggeroth Mosheh, Eben Ha-Ezer*, III, no. 50. See also R. Z.H.Meisels, *Binyan Zebi*, II, no. 64, who writes (in a letter dated 8th day of *Hanukkah* 712, 31 December 1951): 'It is known that permission has been given in Russia to every refugee to return to his country of origin if he wishes. Most refugees have made use of this permission and returned to their homes....'

that crossing the border involved danger of being killed by the Russians. (In view of what has been mentioned above it seems that such attempts to cross the border were probably illegal.)[10]

The wife of a famous scholar and their children had been deported by the Russians when the latter began to leave the town. When the husband came to the town he found they were no longer there. He was unable to join a transport and leave the place. Soon afterwards the Nazis occupied the town and killed all Jews and also the Jews of neighbouring places. Many years had passed since then and nothing had been heard of that scholar. Three years had elapsed since the end of the war and most of the survivors who had been in Russia had returned. His wife and children went from there to the United States and the wife heard nothing of her husband although he was known to many people, scholars and students of *yeshiboth* who were scattered over Russia, Europe and various camps. He had not been seen anywhere. He had relatives, men learned in Torah, in America and Israel. Were he alive he would have written to them to hear about his wife and children in order to enable him to emigrate to America or Israel, as many people did. Could the woman be permitted to re-marry? The Rabbi decided in the affirmative provided great scholars would agree.[11]

10. R. M.Feinstein, *Iggeroth Mosheh, Eben Ha-Ezer* III, no. 50.
11. R. M.Feinstein, *Iggeroth Mosheh, Eben Ha-Ezer*, no. 41.

17

Fraternization

An American Jewish soldier from Minneapolis, Minnesota, serving after World War II in the American Army Intelligence Corps in Germany met a young girl who told him she was a Jewess and said that she was born in a small town to parents who did not observe the Jewish religion. She therefore knew nothing of Jewish law and custom. She also informed him that her parents had been murdered by 'the cursed German murderers' and that during the war she had been working in a factory with four hundred young girls from Hungary. The young man made investigations which confirmed the things she had said but could not find out whether she was really a Jewess. He wished to marry her according to Jewish Law and approached his Rabbi on this matter.

The Rabbi decided that as there was no proof of her identity she could not be relied on and the Jewish officer could not marry her without her undergoing the process of *geruth* (conversion to Judaism) as prescribed by the Law.[1]

1. R. S.I.Levin, Rabbi in Minneapolis, Minnesota, formerly in Indianapolis, Indiana, *Minhath Shlomoh*, Brooklyn, 1963, no. 58.

More lucky was a British officer who was soon able to marry the girl he met in Belsen. Under the heading 'Wedding Memories from the Shadow of Belsen' a daily London newspaper published a report about a silver wedding which took place in London on 14 October 1970. A girl was working with other prisoners as a nurse in the Belsen Hospital after five years as a concentration camp inmate. She escaped the gas chambers, once actually being released from one after an hour because the gas did not function.

With the forces that liberated Belsen was a young British intelligence officer who wished to marry her. After the Chaplain to the British forces had made inquiries and found out that from the religious point of view there was no objection, the wedding ceremony was performed. The couple is happily married and they have three children one of them already married. (*Evening Standard*, 14 October 1970.)

18

Gratitude

There was a small number of non-Jews who, out of pure altruism and without any motive other than helping Jews survive, gave assistance to some Jews, despite the great personal danger involved as the Germans killed every non-Jew who had given shelter to a Jew.

After the liberation R. Moses Segal approached R. Oshry (in 1945) with the following question: was it permitted for him to recite *kaddish* after a non-Jewess who had endangered her life during the Nazi occupation by hiding him and another ten Jews in her cellar and providing them with food all the time? When after the liberation they wished to express their gratitude to her they learned, to their great regret, that she had died. They decided that one of those saved by her should recite *kaddish* as tribute to her. The lot fell on R. Moses Segal who asked R. Oshry whether he was permitted to do so.

Could *kaddish* be recited as tribute to her?

The reply was in the affirmative.[1]

---

1. R. E.Oshry, *Mi-Maamakkim*, III, no. 8. See also the case mentioned *supra* p. 261.

19

Places of Execution, Mass Graves, Cemeteries, Reburial

One Rabbi[1] tells us that when he came to a town in eastern Galicia he met one of the distinguished people of Tarnopol, a worthy Jew and scholar, a pupil of his uncle, the *Gaon* and *Zaddik* R. Aryeh Leb Babad, Ab Beth Din of Podwoloczyska (who died a martyr). After informing him of the troubles which had befallen him and his nephews who miraculously survived, he took the Rabbi to the place of execution where tens of thousands of people had later been buried, among them his uncle the *Gaon* and *Zaddik* and the Rabbi of Mazbiez—Tarnopol.

They entered the holy place and walked into the heart of the "cemetery"; the entire scene resembled the overthrow of Sodom and Gomorrah (Deut. xxix 22). There was neither fence, nor huts, only sandheaps, wilderness and waste. They went up hills and down dales. The terrible massacre revealed itself to them. The sand poured out as if it refused to conceal the valley of slaughter. It emitted human skeletons and many skulls and detached limbs. Here and there there were garments which had become old rags, strips with a *Magen David*, documents of Jews. Beside the skull of a woman there lay a very small shoe.

The Rabbi says he was then asked whether it was a duty to remove the bones to a Jewish cemetery. Although the Jews were very soon to leave the town there was still a Jewish cemetery there. Did the law of a *meth mitzvah* (the corpse of a person whose relatives are unknown and whose burial is obligatory on all) apply, according to which (see *Baba Kama* 81b) 'a dead body, which must be buried by anyone finding it, acquires the right to be buried on the spot where it is found' and therefore those remains must not be removed from the place where they were lying?[2]

The Rabbi quoting R. Solomon Luria (b. 1510, Brest Litowsk, d. Lublin, 1573) shows that the law of *meth mizvah* applied only in *Erez Yisrael* but not in countries outside the Holy Land where the fields belong to non-Jews. It would not be an honour for the dead to be buried in such a place, apart from that the bodies might be exposed to disrespect. He therefore thinks that it is a duty to transfer the corpses to Israel. (He gives directives how the exhumation should take place particularly with regard to the earth around the corpses which had absorbed the blood.) He then appeals to all Jews to help in bringing to Israel the remains of the victims. In a postscript he informs the public

1. R. S. Efrati.
2. There was also another problem involved: if removal should take place, has also the earth around the body, which had absorbed serous secretion, to be taken out?

that a committee had been formed with the task of transferring the bones of the martyrs to Israel and anyone wishing to know more about that should contact the committee. 'For the time being we are interested in collecting material as to where the martyrs are resting. He who has information should contact us at the following address: Rabbi S. Efrati, in the name of the Vaad Le-maan Haalath Azmoth Ha-Kedoshim Le-Erez Yisrael, Jerusalem, Rehov Aza 16.'[3]

When the survivors returned from hiding in the old forests of Siberia they began to search for the holy places which their brothers and sisters had sanctified with their blood. The first question which arose was whether the victims should be exhumed and be transferred to Jewish graves. The places where they were lying were trampled underfoot or became pasture-land for cattle. This was disrespect to the dead.

The answer was that not only was it permitted to transfer the victims to the local cemetery which had been sanctified through generations, until their bones could eventually be taken to *Erez Yisrael* but it is a great *mizvah* to do so. (The Rabbi says he had dealt at length with the question of *meth mizvah* in his book *Me-Emek Ha Bacha*.) However, the question arose: what should happen to those places which had become sanctified with the blood of the martyrs?

Although the place may be holy, being sanctified by the holiness of the blood, once the corpses are removed it does not defile *kohanim* if they tread upon it and a building may be erected on that ground. However, the Rabbi is of the opinion that those places where the martyrs expired with their last word *Ehad* should remain waste. Emptiness is the best symbol of destruction, better than any building or monument. Destruction can be defined only by negating all colour, by void and waste.

The Rabbi relates that, when he was still Rabbi in Warsaw after the war, Chief Rabbi Herzog came there and they went to visit the ruins of the Warsaw Ghetto. The Chief Rabbi then asked Rabbi Efrati why he opposed the erection of a memorial in honour of the victims of the ghetto. R. Efrati gave his reason by saying that, in his view, the only memorial which would symbolize the destruction would be those desolate hills. The Chief Rabbi agreed.

After the removal of the corpses, the area should be fenced in and lie waste. However, from the *halachic* point of view it may be used if necessary, as a building-site and does not defile *kohanim*.[4]

After the liberation of Kovno from the Germans when we came out from the hiding places, a terrible sight met our eyes: everywhere

3. R. S.Efrati, *Me-Emek Ha-Bacha*, no. 5.
4. R. S.Efrati, *Mi-Ge Ha-Haregah*, no. 11.

human skeletons, skulls, bones and limbs were scattered over the area where previously the so-called 'Kovner K Z Lager' stood, and underneath the ruins of houses set on fire by the Germans to kill those hiding in the cellars singed human organs protruded which showed that that place was used for hiding (*Melunah*).[5] Also at the place known as 'The Ninth Fortress' where about 14,000 people brought from all parts of Europe had been killed, heaps of bodies soaked with fuel were lying on wood which the Germans had no time to burn. . . . The question arose:

(1) Is it a religious duty to remove the bones from there and to bury them in a Jewish cemetery in the ghetto or should the law concerning a 'meth mizvah' (*vide supra*, p. 340) be applied, according to which a body must be buried where it has been found? However, if the latter were done the remains would be exposed to disrespect and become food for birds and animals who dig and burrow underground. Perhaps it was therefore better to remove the remains and bury them in a Jewish cemetery.

(2) Is it obligatory to take *tebusah* (i.e. three inches of soil beneath the corpse as it contains secretion of the body) which requires burial (together with the corpse)?

The Rabbi decided that the bodies should be buried in the Jewish cemetery, and, although in case of murdered people the law of *tebusah* did not apply, he still ordered that the loose earth under the corpses should be buried too.[6]

Those bodies and bones found in the infamous Ninth Fortress and in other places scattered around were buried in a common grave. The bodies found beneath the ruins were buried separately with their garments and the loose earth under them.

As the Jews who survived were very weak and unable to carry out the task of burying thousand of bodies the government placed German prisoners at their disposal to help them. Thus in the course of six weeks (15th Ab-28th Ellul 5704 = 4 August 1944-16 September 1944) about three thousand bodies were buried.[7]

When after the liberation (R. Oshry tells us) he went out to find the graves of the victims he was shown by the Lithuanians (who had helped in wiping out the communities) mass graves (pits) where the martyrs had been buried. After torture, the victims-some still alive-had been thrown into the pits and covered with earth.

5. On this expression, see 'Glossary'.
6. Concerning the law of *meth mizvah* he refers to the authorities who maintain that it does not apply outside Israel.
7. R. E.Oshry, *Mi-Maamakkim*, I, no. 23.

Most of the graves of the martyrs were unprotected; they were in fields which belonged to non-Jews and were used partly as pasture-land for cattle. To avoid the graves being ploughed up or trodden down by grazing cattle so that their location would no longer be known R. Oshry wanted to erect a wooden fence around those graves. Unfortunately, as wooden boards for the fence were unobtainable owing to lack of money, he was asked whether the trees which were growing in the Jewish cemetery could be cut down and used for that purpose.

The Rabbi decided that only those trees which stood at the edge of the Jewish cemetery should be cut down. One could then be sure that those trees had never stood over graves. Even they should be cut in such a way that part of the trunk and the roots remain untouched as they might have spread to the soil of the graves (in order to exclude the possibility of deriving a benefit from the graves). The Rabbi remarks that the decision was carried out in many Lithuanian towns. However, it was of no avail as the 'cruel Lithuanians' who were the accomplices of the German butchers (*rabbe ha-tabbahim*) and murderers, broke down and destroyed the fences which had been erected with great toil and trouble around the graves of our martyrs, scattered over the fields. They did that to wipe out the memory of the evil and abominable deeds which they wrought to our people and to show that they were innocent.

The same fate befell the infamous vast open land near Slobodka, the Ninth Fortress, the place where were buried about forty thousand Jews of Lithuania (Lita), Germany, Austria and France who were taken there to be murdered. That place too was ploughed and cultivated for growing potatoes and corn. The produce of that land saturated with the blood of martyrs, our brothers and sisters, is being eaten by the cruel Lithuanian murderers who, together with the cursed Germans, massacred myriads of our martyrs and robbed them of their possessions.[8]

8. Oshry, *Mi-Maamakkim*, I, no. 29.

20

Desecration of Cemeteries

R. S.Efrati gives a description of the lives of the Jews after the war.

When in the days after the war the individual survivors, 'brands plucked from the fires' of Treblinka, Belzec, Oswiecim (Auschwitz) and Maidanek, returned to their home towns dressed in mourning and in despair, harried by nightmares and shocking memories, the people of Poland did not receive them warmly. They were received by the 'pious' Poles with the question: 'What? Are there so many Jews left?' Those who pray to the heavenly kingdom and who during the Nazi occupation were not ashamed to squeeze out the last *perutoth* (small coins) from the fugitives of the ghettos, to strip them of their last shirt and to return them to the Gestapo to be killed, when they saw that there was still a remnant, asked in astonishment: 'from where do they come?' The life of the Jews in the small towns was at the mercy of the most wicked. The Jews therefore settled in the big cities, e.g. Warsaw, Lodz and in Silesia. Thus many towns which were formerly the seats of piety and learning, Kock, Ger, Sandz and Ropczyce, Zamosc and Bilgoraj, towns the air of which was filled with songs of Torah were silenced forever . . . the chanting never to return.

The inhabitants of the towns showed great concern for the cemeteries where great scholars and leaders of the Jewish nation had been resting for generations. Eventually they will be exposed to disrespect as the wicked and hateful people not only dig up the graves of the death camps but do so at every place where Jews are buried looking for treasures and they disturb the rest of those who lie in dust.

When the Chief Rabbi of Israel, Rabbi Herzog, came to Poland on his way from Lodz to Warsaw, while passing Sochaczew he expressed the wish to visit the grave of the *Gaon* and *Zaddik*, R. Abrumali, the son-in-law of the Rabbi of Kock. When we were standing at the grave of this *Zaddik* and noticed that his holy bones had been exhumed our eyes began to shed tears . . .

But also the pious gentiles will surely not let the entire place lie waste; no doubt they will plough it or let their cattle graze there and consequently disrespect to the dead will occur as in those towns not even a single Jew can now be found . . .

In Hrubieszow where I served as deputy (*segen*) to the Ab Beth Din, my father-in-law, R. I.Wertheim, the following occurred:

During the occupation the Germans built a main road from Chelm to Zamosc via Hrubieszow. They used the eastern side of the cemetery and destroyed all the *oholim* (mausoleums) of the *Zaddikim* resting there, among them the *ohel* of the Rabbi, the *Zaddik* R. Jacob Aryeh, the son of the *Maggid* of Trysk, and the *ohel* of my grandfather, the Rabbi and *Zaddik* R. Eliezer, Ab Beth Din of Ostilla (Ustilug) and many others. The road was built over their graves over which the wicked German soldiers tramped.

After the liberation the few Jews who had returned succeeded in removing the bones of the saintly men from underneath the paving and burying them in the part of the cemetery still standing. However, it extends over more than one kilometre. No doubt this whole place will be turned to pasture-land for the cattle of the remaining decent non-Jews. My only advice is to collect the bones and the remains into a small area and to build a construction of stone and iron and fence it off. The bones will then be in peace.

The Rabbi shows that there are two problems involved.

1. The prohibition of removing a corpse (*Tur Shulhan Aruch Yoreh Deah*, cap. CCCLXIII) which disturbs the rest of the deceased.
2. The way reburial is to be done as the new resting place is too narrow. How was it to be arranged, in accordance with *Tur* and *S.A. Y.D.* cap. CDIII?

As far as the first point is concerned he proves that as the bones would certainly be exposed to disrespect, exhumation and removal are not only permitted but even obligatory.

With regard to the second question, the Rabbi gives directives. 'As the matter affects the honour of myriads of Jews, my reply is submitted to our great Rabbis to express their view.'[1]

The following question was asked from Hungary.

It often happens in many places where Jews no longer live that the non-Jews steal the tombstones from the Jewish cemeteries and also break down the wall surrounding the cemetery so that the graves remain without any protection.

(1) Is it in such circumstances permitted to remove the tombstones before they are stolen and to place them where Jews are still living, or should the tombstones be sold and the money received used for building a fence around the cemeteries?

(2) What should happen to the cemeteries which have no wall and protection? Is it permitted to remove the bones from the graves and bury them in a neighbouring town, where Jews are living before the cemetery is desecrated?

1. R. S.Efrati, *Me-Emek Ha-Bacha*, no. 4.

Answer. As far as the first question is concerned, the decision is that the tombstones must not be sold. With regard to the second question, the bones may be removed to avoid desecration by the non-Jews. The Rabbi advises that at the same time also the tombstones should be removed to the neighbouring town.[2]

After the liberation it could be seen that the enemy not only killed young and old but even disturbed the dead in their graves. The enemy had destroyed cemeteries of almost all Lithuanian towns, desecrating the graves of famous scholars and righteous men. Tombstones had been removed so that the places of burial became unknown.

A Jew who survived the Nazi holocaust asked Rabbi Oshry whether he could erect a tombstone in the cemetery of Ponevezh for his parents whose tombstones had been removed. The register (*pinkas*) of the *Hebrah Kaddisha* had been lost so that the exact resting places were no longer known.

The reply was in the affirmative. He should erect a tombstone with the following inscription:

'In this cemetery my father and mother have been laid to rest . . . the location of their burial places was lost in the time of the cursed insolent ones.'[3]

2. R. M.Rath, *Kol Mebasser*, II, no. 9.
3. R. E.Oshry, *Mi-Maamakkim*, I, no. 28.

21

Memorial Days

Rabbi Weiss reports that he had been asked many times concerning observance of the *yahrzeit* of parents who perished during the Nazi persecution when it was not known whether they were killed together or on the same day of the same month but in different years. Can the *yahrzeit* for both parents be kept on one day?

There are two questions involved: if the day of the death of one of them is known but not that of the other parent, and if the day of the death of neither is known when should the *yahrzeit* be kept?

The Rabbi is of the opinion that the *yahrzeit* of each should be observed on different days unless it was certain that both perished on the same day. If there are other mourners in the synagogue, he must give them preference.[1]

The same Rabbi[2] was asked by a young man for a decision in the following case. His father had been in France during the Nazi holocaust. He received a notification from the French police that his father had been sent to Upper Silesia, Germany. After that all trace of him had been lost. The young man fixed a day to study *Mishnah*. He does not say *Kaddish* since his mother who is alive must not re-marry (nor does she wish to re-marry). Furthermore, he had heard from a Rabbi that there was no reason to allow an *agunah* to re-marry if she did not wish to re-marry but merely that *yahrzeit* for her husband could be observed, even if from the *halachic* point of view there were grounds for allowing re-marriage.

In his reply the Rabbi shows the difference in giving an *agunah* permission to re-marry if she wishes to do so, and not granting the right of re-marriage if she does not explicitly state her wish to re-marry. With regard to the question asked the Rabbi says that the matter should be investigated as far as possible. One had to clarify what had happened to all those who had been sent to Upper Silesia in general, and the fate of his father in particular.

The following question has been asked often as it affects those many people who lost their dear ones in the Polish towns where often the entire Jewish population was exterminated. The survivors know only the date of the massacre but are not certain that their relatives died on that day. The survivors regret that not only have they no hope of seeing their dear ones again but they are even deprived of the right of mourning

1. R. I.J.Weiss, *Minhath Yizhak*, I, no. 83.
2. R. I.J.Weiss, *Minhath Yizhak*, II, no. 90.

for them and of reciting prayers in their memory, as according to Isserles (*Eben Ha-Ezer*, cap. XVII, no. 5) a woman must not mourn or dress in black before there is suitable evidence of the death of her husband. People might presume that her husband had died and she might re-marry solely on the strength of that presumption.

Rabbi Efrati came to the following conclusion.[3] If the fate of both parents is not known, the son knows only that on a specific day the Jewish population of that town was massacred, since husband and wife had been together, one can permit the son to mourn, although such information would not permit the wife to re-marry. That specific day should be regarded as the anniversary of the death of the parents. If, however, the wife was not together with her husband when the massacre occurred but with other surviving relatives, since she must not re-marry until there is clear evidence that her husband was among those killed, his relatives must not mourn for him.

Rabbi Efrati, when still in Warsaw, suggested that the great men in Israel (*gedole Yisrael*) should fix a special day of mourning for the whole Jewish nation. All Jews would observe that day as a day of mourning and recite *kaddish*. There would then be no need for apprehension. Rabbi Efrati is disappointed that until this day, his suggestion has not been adopted.[4]

Rabbi Efrati sent a copy of his *Responsum* to Rabbi Waldenberg, who discussed this matter and made some comments. He came to the following conclusions:

(*a*) If the missing man did not leave a wife, his son or relative may fix the *yahrzeit* for the day on which they assume the victim was killed, and *kaddish* may be recited. (*b*) Even if the victim left a wife, a *yahrzeit* can be fixed provided that some change is made from a normal *yahrzeit*, e.g. to say *kaddish* only if there are no other mourners in the synagogue or to recite *kaddish* at a service specially arranged at home. If there are other mourners in the synagogue (although the relative should not recite *kaddish*) he may act as reader, as this is permitted even for those who are not mourners. (*c*) If it is probable that the victim was killed, he is in the same category as a person who had fallen into waters the shores of which cannot be seen from all sides (*vide supra*, p. 216). Although, in such a case we do not give his wife permission to re-marry in the first instance, the relatives can nevertheless fix a day for the *yahrzeit* and recite *kaddish* as on a normal *yahrzeit*.[5]

---

3. *Me-Emek Ha-Bacha*, no. 3.
4. In fact, the 10th of Tebeth has since been fixed as *Yom Ha-Shoah* (*Kaddish Kelali*) by the Chief Rabbinate of Israel.
5. R. E.Y.Waldenberg, *Ziz Eliezer*, III, no. 3.

22

Disused or Destroyed Synagogues, Cemeteries

On the 5th of Nisan 696 (28 March 1936)[1] R. Weinberg inquired of R. Hayyim Ozer Grodzinski whether the synagogue of a community the inhabitants of which had emigrated may be sold to the 'Congregation of Baptists'. R. Weinberg was of the opinion it was not permitted to do so. It would amount to a *hillul ha-Shem* (profanation of the Name). If the sale were forced on the community the latter was not responsible for that. R. Hayyim agrees with him.[2]

During the holocaust, when all Jewish inhabitants had been expelled from the town, the non-Jews seized the synagogue of the community. When after the war some members of the community returned they found the non-Jews in possession of the synagogue. In spite of various efforts the Jews could not regain possession. However, the non-Jews were willing to pay the price of the synagogue but under no circumstances were they willing to return it. In fact it was at that time impossible to bring any court action or by other means to force the non-Jews to return the synagogue. The Rabbi was asked whether it was permitted to accept the money from the non-Jews and whether it would not be regarded as selling the synagogue (which was a 'synagogue of a large town', where also people from neighbouring places sometimes prayed, unlike a synagogue in a village which is attended only by the inhabitants of that village)[3] which normally may not be sold. However, it was not a case of sale as it was impossible to regain possession from the non-Jews. (The Jews had been forced to part with it.) If the Jews refused to accept the payment offered, the synagogue would remain in non-Jewish hands. Or did that make no difference, as whenever money is taken the synagogue was to be regarded as having been sold. Furthermore, if the Jews refused payment perhaps later they would be able to regain possession which would not be the case if they accepted the money now.

The Rabbi's decision was that it was permitted to accept the money offered by the non-Jews for the synagogue. (He quotes the decision of *Dobeb Mesharim*, II, no. 44 who gave the same decision in a similar case.)[4]

The question concerned the Jewish community at Mattersdorf (Austria).

---

1. The date appears to be incorrect as the 5th of Nisan 696 was not a Wednesday but a Sabbath. (The 5th of Nisan was on a Wednesday in the years 694, i.e. 21 March 1934; 697 i.e. 17 March 1937; and 698 i.e. 6 April 1938.)
2. R. H.O.Grodzinski, *Ahiezer, Kobez Iggeroth*, II, Bene Berak, 1970, pp. 376f.
3. On the difference, see *Shulhan Aruch Orah Hayyim*, cap. CLIII, no. 7.
   R. B.Stern, *Be-Zel Ha-Hochmah*, I, no. 29.

There existed a ghetto with a synagogue, house of study, the Rabbi's house, *mikveh* and communal house which were later destroyed by the Nazis. However, the cemetery remained intact surrounded by a wall, part of which had been heavily damaged. It was closed and looked after by a former member of the community who had returned. He collected all fragments of tombstones which he put in a corner of the cemetery.

The local government of Mattersdorf intended to erect a big town-hall in the former Jewish area. It included the whole site where the communal building was standing. They requested the members of the former Jewish community to hand over without a right to compensation all the former Jewish communal places (they would, however, pay compensation to individual house-owners for their property). In return, the authorities had agreed to repair the wall of the cemetery properly and to give a guarantee that they would not interfere with the cemetery for sixty years. (It was well known that plans existed to make it a public park.)

Was it allowed to hand over the sites where formerly the synagogue and house of study stood even if a guarantee were obtained that nothing would happen to the cemetery? If the Jews would not agree the possibility existed that the authorities would take possession of the sites without giving any guarantee whatsoever. The questioner points out that there had been an old cemetery on a hill near the house of study which had been flattened to give way to a road leading through it.

The Rabbi decided that the sites should be handed over to the authorities who should guarantee that no public park would be made on the site of the cemetery for sixty years (or for longer if the Jews could obtain such an agreement) and to repair the cemetery wall. However, he advised that the ground of the cemetery should be raised by one metre (by adding earth) and plane trees should be planted there. (Raising the ground with the trees planted there would serve two purposes: avoidance of disrespect to the dead by treading direct on their graves, and of deriving a benefit from a matter which is prohibited.) The wall of the cemetery should immediately be repaired. If the local government refuses to raise the ground by one metre, the Jews should agree to less than one metre. They should even agree if no raising took place at all, as it was a time of emergency.[5]

5. R. M.Rath, *Kol Mebasser*, I, no. 6. On Mattersdorf (or 'Mattersburg' as it has been called since 1924) see Fritz P. Hodik, 'Geschichte der Juden in Mattersdorf (Mattersburg)', in *Gedenkbuch der untergegangenen Judengemeinden des Burgenlands*, ed. by Hugo Gold, Tel Aviv, 1970, pp. 91ff., 115ff. When speaking of the time after World War II he says that only individual Jews were returning to this town from where they soon emigrated. 'Die zerstörten und verfallenen Judenhäuser blieben eine Zeit lang leer, wurden danach abgerissen und an ihre Stelle stehen heute moderne Hochbauten. Nur ein verfallener Friedhof mit seinen Grabsteinen zeugt heute noch von der einstigen Grösse dieser musterhaften Siedlung, die es nicht mehr gibt.'

In 1946 R. I.J.Weiss was asked a question concerning what was a daily occurrence for synagogues and *Bathe Midrash* in many places in Europe, deserted by Jews, and not used. If they were to remain in that condition, it was feared the government would take them over and use them for their own purposes. Was it permitted to use the deserted synagogues as orphanages where orphans who remained after the persecution would be looked after? This had been done in many places without prior consultation with a Rabbi with those sections of the synagogues which had been used by women worshippers.

The Rabbi gives a ruling, and points out that the place where the synagogue for men was standing which bears the main holy character should remain empty.[6]

6. R. I.J.Weiss, *Minhath Yizhak*, I, no. 118. On similar cases *vide supra* Part I, p. 14.

23

Unclaimed Property

What is to be done with the property left behind by persons killed by the Germans, whose heirs are unknown?

This question was raised in connection with the following case, sent by R. Zebi Hirsch Meisels[1] to R. Mordecai Breisch.[2] During World War II a man gave a thousand dollars to a Jew in Belgium for safe keeping. No trace could later be found of the former. Despite thorough investigations and announcements in the press no heir appeared to claim the money. The man to whom the money had been given wished to hand it over to the Rabbi who was publishing the works of Rabbis killed by the Nazis. The man requested the money be used for that purpose. The Rabbi, however, was hesitant to accept the money and asked R. Breisch whether he could accept it.

In his *Responsum*, dated 20th of Sivan 722 (28 June 1962), R. Breisch pointed out that this question was one of many such cases where the owners and their heirs could not be traced. 'The public was shaken by the large sums of money deposited in Swiss banks by Jews who had been killed, and Jewish institutions would like to claim that money.' The problem was very acute and involved vast sums. His decision was that the money should be used for charitable purposes such as dowries for poor orphan girls and for poor and sick people.[3]

1. On him, *vide supra* Part I, p. 111 note 312.
2. Ibid., p. 3.
3. R. M.Breisch, *Helkath Yaakob*, III, nos. 1–5.

24

Adoption

It was during the *Kinderaktion* on the 3rd and 4th of Tishri 5704 (2 and 3 October 1943)[1] when the Germans massacred about 1,200 children that a Jew succeeded in saving one child whom he brought up. Both were saved during the Nazi regime of terror. As the man who had adopted the boy had no children he wished that the boy be regarded as his own son in every respect. The man asked the Rabbi[2] whether the boy when being called up to the Law could be called up as his son as if he had begotten him, as it is customary to call up a man by mentioning his name and that of his father. He pointed out that the boy was a *kohen*.

The Rabbi's decision was in the negative, the reason being that one has to honour one's father regardless of whether he were alive or dead. Being called up as 'son of Mr . . .' counts as honouring him. Hence the boy had to be called up as a son of his real (own) father. Otherwise it would be regarded as disrespectful to his father. Furthermore, as the boy was a *kohen* confusion in religious respects might arise if the boy would be called up after the name of his foster-father.

The Rabbi tried to comfort the questioner and to show him the great merit he had earned by saving the boy and bringing him up.[3]

1. The *Kinderaktion* took place on 27 and 28 March 1944; see L. Garfunkel, *The Destruction of Kovno's Jewry*, pp. 176ff. R. Oshry himself says that the *Kinderaktion* took place on 3rd and 4th of Nisan 704 (27 and 28 March 1944); see *Mi-Maamakkim*, I, no. 16.
2–3. Oshry, *Mi-Maamakkim*, III, no. 11.

Epilogue of the Greatest Tragedy of Mankind

According to our Sages[1] the pious men of the non-Jewish nations have a portion in the world to come. When Rabbi Haninah ben Teradyon, one of the martyrs during the persecution by the Roman Emperor Hadrian, was led out to be executed because he had transgressed the emperor's prohibition against studying the Law he was wrapped in a scroll of the Law and bundles of twigs were placed around him and set on fire. In order that he should not die quickly tufts of wool soaked in water were placed over his heart. The executioner asked the Rabbi: 'Rabbi, if I raise the flame and take away the tufts of wool from over your heart (thus reducing the pain by accelerating death) will you cause me to enter into the world to come?' When the Rabbi promised him that on oath the executioner raised the flames and removed the tufts. The Rabbi's soul departed speedily. Thereupon the executioner himself jumped into the fire, and a heavenly voice (*bath kol*) exclaimed: 'Rabbi Haninah ben Teradyon and his executioner have been assigned to the world to come.'[2]

After having heard of the atrocities committed by Nazi Germany, we must pay tribute to many noble gentiles, i.e. 'the pious men of the non-Jewish nations', who endangered their lives and to some who even sacrificed their lives to help the unfortunate victims.

Among those noble gentiles figures foremost, as is well known, Anton Schmid of Vienna who served as *Feldwebel* (sergeant) in the German army at Vilnyus. Many survivors owe their lives to him. One day when he tried to smuggle out five Jews from the ghetto he was arrested and executed.[3]

We are told also of a clergyman who hid the wife and children of Rabbi Israel Shalom Joseph Hager of Ontania (between Stanislawow and Kolomyja). They were discovered and all, the priest included, were murdered.[4]

Mention has been made of the 'greatly distinguished' clergyman who through his connections with great and distinguished gentiles saved Jews in 'the land of blood',[5] of the woman who saved Jews who wished to recite *kaddish* for her as she was no longer alive when they came after the war to express their gratitude to her,[6] of the Ukrainian peasants

---

1. Cf. Maimonides on Mishnah *Sanhedrin*, X, 2, and *Mishneh Torah, Hilchoth Teshubah*, III, 5; R. Obadiah of Bertinoro on Mishnah *Sanhedrin*, X, 2.
2. *Abodah Zarah* 18a.
3. See Simon Wiesenthal, *The Murderers Among Us*, pp. 245ff.
4. See M. Ungar, *ADMORIM Shenispu*, p. 189.
5. *Vide supra*, Part III, p. 261.
6. Ibid., p. 339.

who hid the Rabbi and his family[7] and of the Hungarian *Oberleutnant* (First Lieutenant) of the Hussars and his wife who gave shelter to Jews.[8] A unique epic of our times was the heroic attitude of the Danish and Swedish nationals in their attempts to save Jews.[9] Reports continue to appear in the Jewish press of such noble and dangerous acts of the pious of various nations. When one walks on the Mount of Memory on the outskirts of Jerusalem one can see the 'Avenue of the Righteous Gentiles' where trees were planted by *Yad Va-Shem*, each tree bearing the name of one gentile who risked his life to save Jewish life. Through these deeds they have secured for themselves a portion in the world to come, and of those who are no longer alive we say: 'The memory of the pious men of the non-Jewish nations shall be for a blessing.'

---

7. See R. M. Steinberg Introduction to *Mahazeh Abraham* 2nd Part, p. 5.
8. See R. Aron Zimetbaum, 'Maaseh Nissim', in his father's *Dibre Pinhas*, p. 171.
9. Cf. Leni Yahil, *The Rescue of Danish Jewry*, pp. 41ff.; Raul Hilberg, *The Destruction of European Jews*, pp. 356, 361ff. See also Gideon Hausner, *Justice in Jerusalem*, pp. 254ff. where cases of rescuing Jews by members of other nations are recorded.

Glossary

The Nazi holocaust has enriched the vocabulary by producing idioms, phrases and puns. In the following lines a list of such expressions is given without, however, claiming to be complete.

A. PHRASES

1. The term קיבוץ גלויות (Reunion of the Exiles) taken from the Talmud (*Pesahim* 88a: 'The reunion of the Exiles is as important as the day when heaven and earth were created') was used with bitter irony of the Jews from various countries deported to the extermination camps in Poland.

    R. S.Efrati, *Me-Emek Ha-Bacha*, no. 1; *Mi-Ge Ha-Haregah*, no. 4 (adding the words: 'in his [the enemy's] version').See also Chaim A. Kaplan, *Scroll of Agony*, p. 289: 'Jewish exiles from all the conquered countries are brought to this exile camp. . . . An ingathering of Jews on foreign soil!"

2. לא תחיה כל נשמה (Thou shalt save alive nothing that breatheth) (Deut. xx 16). Interpreting a Talmudic ruling concerning a town conquered by the enemy one Rabbi thinks it right to assume that all inhabitants had been killed. Ironically another Rabbi asks: 'Are they (the enemies) commanded "Thou shalt save alive nothing that breatheth"?' (see R. Nethanel Weil, *Korban Nethanel* on R. Asher on *Gittin* III, 4, no. 50). Unfortunately, when speaking of the mass murder of the Nazis in connection with certain *agunah* cases (women whose husbands disappeared) some Rabbis take the biblical phrase as applying to the Germans concerning the fate of the Jews: 'They were commanded to fulfil the order "Thou shalt save alive nothing that breatheth", so that death could be taken as certain.'

    R. M.J.Breisch, *Helkath Yaakob*, I, nos. 15, 17; R. I.J.Weiss, *Minhath Yizhak*, II, no. 62.

3. זבחי אדם עגלים ישקון (They that sacrifice men kiss calves. Hos. XIII 2). This phrase was used by a Rabbi to denote the Nazis who on one hand murdered human beings and on the other 'protected' animals from alleged sufferings caused by *shehitah* without prior stunning.

    R. Michael Dob Weissmandel, *Min Ha-Mezar*, New York, 1960, p. 32. See also Dob Rosen, *Shema Yisrael*, Jerusalem, 729, p. 353.

4. כל הגולה כמדורת אש (The whole exile was like a sea of fire). This expression found in Mishnah *Rosh Ha-Shanah* II, 4, described the lights kindled to announce that the New Moon had been fixed. It was used in the Rabbinic literature during the Nazi holocaust in connection with the large number of countries whose Jews had been murdered by the Nazis.

    See R. H.O.Grodzinski, Introduction to *Ahiezer* III; R. Shmuel Shmelka SGL Rosenbaum, *Elleh Dibre Shemuel*, Introduction by his son, p. vi.

5. להתראות בעולם האמת (To meet in the world of truth). People used these words when they parted from each other as they did not know whether they would meet again in this world.

    R. E.Oshry, *Mi-Maamakkim*, I, no. 13.

6. נחשבנו כצאן טבחה (We are accounted as sheep for the slaughter) (Ps. XLIV 23) is applied by the Talmud (*Gittin* 57b) to the four hundred children who committed suicide at the time of the destruction of the Temple in order to avoid being taken to Rome for immoral purposes. The

phrase is found subsequently in connection with persecutions, e.g. in the *tehinnah* recited on Mondays and Thursdays, in various *selihoth* and *kinoth* composed in the Middle Ages (particularly during the Crusades, cf. e.g. S.Bernfeld, *Sepher Ha-Demaoth*, II, pp. 207, 283) and in Maimonides', *Mishneh Torah, Hilchoth Yesode Ha-Torah*, V, 4, concerning martyrs 'like Daniel and his colleagues and R. Akibah and his colleagues'. It appears again and again in the *Responsa* of the Nazi holocaust.

Cf. e.g. R. H.M.Roller in *Nezer Mattai* of R. N.Z.Friedmann, no. 39; R. Y.Abramski in *Tebunah*, Jerusalem, Nisan 709, 5–(96) p. 44; Chief Rabbi Uzziel in his approbation to R. S.Efrati's *Mi-Ge Ha-Haregah*; Efrati, ibid. no. 3; R. E.Oshry, *Mi-Maamakkim*, Parts I–III several times.

7. The Jews of Poland used to say: 'He who enters "their wagons" may immediately say *kaddish* after himself.'

R. I.J.Weiss, 'Pirsume Nissa' in *Minhath Yizhak*, I, p. 267.

8. חגים וזמנים לאסון The well-known phrase recited on the three festivals in *kiddush* and in the *amidah* 'And Thou hast given us festivals and seasons *le-sason* (for joy)' was paraphrased by people in their conversations 'And . . . *le-ason* (for misfortune)', the reason being that the Germans had chosen festivals on which to impose harder work on the inmates and to make selections for the crematoria or to murder Jews by the *Einsatzgruppen*.

For the phrase, see Levinski, *Sepher Ha-Moadim*, p. 124. For harder work and selections, etc., see *supra* Part I, p. 48; evidence by Kleinmann at the Eichmann trial in Jerusalem, in Evidence Document Session 68–G1— NSK, 7.6.61 and Indictment against Eichmann Count One p. 3 (both in possession of the Wiener Library).

9. עלה על המוקד: עקדה (The binding or sacrifice of Isaac, to go up on the altar-hearth as sacrifice). Suffering martyrdom for the sake of the Jewish religion which is regarded as the highest degree of piety and devotion to God is described in the Talmud as *akedah* equal to that of Isaac (see *Gittin* 57b) and is found very often in the *selihoth* of the Middle Ages (cf. e.g. Bernfeld, *Sepher Ha-Demaoth*, I, pp. 200, 218, 225, etc.). In the time of the Nazi holocaust it was commonly used to denote the death of the martyrs in the crematoria.

Cf. e.g. R. S.Efrati, Introduction to *Mi-Ge Ha-Haregah*, and ibid. no. 3 *Me-Emek Ha-Bacha*, no. 2; R. E.Oshry, *Mi-Maamakkim*, Introduction to I; II, no. 16; R. Z.H.Meisels, *Mekaddshe Ha-Shem*, I, p. 7a; Rosenbaum, *Elleh Dibre Shemuel*, Title-page (he died a martyr).

10. ואני בתוך הגולה (And I was among the captives) (Ezek. ı 1). This phrase was used by some Rabbis immediately after the liberation.

E.g. R. J.Avigdor, *Helek Yaakob*, p. 67; R. Z.H.Meisels, *Kuntras Takkanoth Agunoth*, p. 5.

11. אוד מצל מאש (A brand plucked out of the fire). This phrase taken from Zech. ııı 2, was used for the first time with reference to a Rabbi who had escaped death by burning during the persecution of the Marranos in Ancona by Pope Paul IV (1555, 1556, see R. Joshua Soncin, *Nahalah Le-Yehoshua*, no. 40; Zimmels, *Die Marannen in der rabbinischen Literatur*, pp. 118ff.). In the time following the Nazi holocaust it is often found

denoting a victim who had survived the extermination camp, or books which had been saved from burning.

Cf. e.g. R. Z.H.Meisels, *Kuntras Takkanath Agunoth*, p. 5; *Binyan Zebi*, II, no. 38, 64, p. 58; Avigdor, *Helek Yaakob*, p. 67; R. E.Oshry, Introduction to *Mi-Maamakkim* I, nos. 7, 30 (the Rabbis apply the phrase to themselves); R. S.Efrati, *Me-Emek Ha-Bacha*, no. 4; *Mi-Ge Ha-Haregah* Introduction and Approbation; Chief Rabbi Herzog, *Hechal Yizhak*, II, no. 72, p. 258 (*ud muzzal me-esh ha-Gehinom shel ha-Nazim*); when speaking at a Mizrachi conference in London he said: 'A brand plucked from the Hitlerite fire' (*Jewish Chronicle*, 28 June 1946, p. 7); R. M.J. Breisch, *Helkath Yaakob*, I, Introduction and no. 21.

12. שארית הפליטה (The remnants that escaped). This phrase from Chr. I, IV, 43, became a familiar expression denoting the survivors of the Nazi holocaust. It was used for the first time in 1935 in connection with the Jews in Nazi Germany.[1] Following the war it became a common description of the survivors as well as of communal organizations caring for survivors, etc.[2]

B. EXPRESSIONS

Abortion   הפלה מלאכותית · אבארט
(R. E.Oshry, *Mi-Maamakkim*, I, no. 20.)

Aktion (denoting deportation and mass murder)

אקציאן, (אקציעס), פעולה (פעולות), קינדר אקציאן
אקציע, אקציה,

(Ibid. nos. 4, 7, 16, 19; III, nos. 4, 9, 11; Chief Rabbi Herzog, *Hechal Yizhak*, II, no. 15.)

Ältesten Rat see **Council of Elders**

Appel Roll call   אפעל
R. Z.H.Meisels, *Mekaddshe Ha-Shem*, I, p. 10.

Aussiedlungen (transfer of Jews to undisclosed destination) אויסזידדלונגן
(R. J.M.Aronzon, *Yeshuoth Mosheh*, p. 306.)

Barrack   באראקא (בארראקען)
(R. I.J.Weiss, *Minhath Yizhak*, I, no. 93.)

---

1. R. A.Munk in R. Weinberg's *Seride Esh*, I, p. 386 (when dealing with stunning animals before *shehitah*).
2. Cf. e.g. R. Z.H.Meisels, *Binyan Zebi*, II, nos. 35, 49; R. J.M.Aronzon, Introduction to his *Yeshuath Mosheh*, p. 6; R. E.Oshry, Introduction to his *Dibre Ephraim; Mi-Maamakkim*, II, no. 5; *Yerushath Peletah*, Collection of *Responsa* of Hungarian Rabbis, Introduction ibid. R. S.Efrati is described on the title-pages of his *Responsa* collections *Me-Emek Ha-Bacha* (see also ibid. no. 4.) and *Mi-Ge Ha-Haregah* as 'after the war Rabbi of *Sheerith Ha-Peletah*' in Warsaw'. Chief Rabbi Herzog went to Rome (1946) concerning the rescue of Jewish children of *sheerith ha-peletah* (*Hechal Yizhak* II, no. 71); see also Dr Philip Friedman, *Bibliography of Books in Hebrew on the Jewish Catastrophe and Heroism in Europe*, Index p. 414, p. 147 and pp. 153ff. See also Karen Gershon, *Postscript*, London, 1969, p. 40. ('The federation—Sheerith Hapletah—had as its principal purpose the protection of the survivors in the American zone of occupation and representation of the people *vis-à-vis* the military and civilian authorities, including Jewish relief and political agencies in Palestine and the United States . . .')

Block   בלוק, בלאק(בלאקען, בלאקים)
(R. Z.H.Meisels, *Mekaddshe Ha-Shem*, I, pp. 7, 10; *Binyan Zebi*, II.
no. 40)

Boycott   באיקעט, באיאקאט, החרמה, חרם
(R. Hayyim Eliezer Spira, in *Sepher Darche Hayyim Ve-Shalom*, p. 353;
and in *Seride Esh* of R. J.J.Weinberg, I, p. 223; Weinberg, ibid., p. 371;
R. B.Z.Jacobson, *Essa Dei Le-Merahok*, p. 123.)

Bunker   בונקר, בונקער, (בונקערס), מחבוא, מחבואה,
                     (מחבואים, מחבואות), מלינה, בור תחתיות
(R. S.Efrati, *Mi-Ge Ha-Haregah*, nos. 1, 11; Oshry, *Mi-Maamakkim*,
I, no. 23; II, nos. 11, 18, 21; Weiss, *Minhath Yizhak*, no. 92, pp. 265, 267;
R. M.Steinberg in his Introduction to *Mahaze Abraham* where also *bor
tappuhe adamah* (pit of potatoes) served as a bunker. On the expression
melunah (or *melinah*) see Garfunkel, *The Destruction of Kovno's Jewry*,
p. 163 note where he says that its derivation is not clear. He quotes the
view that *melinah* originated in the underworld and was used to denote
a place where articles acquired illegally had been hidden. Similarly, it was
used in the ghetto for a place where provisions could be easily obtained.
It appears, however, that the word is of Hebrew origin and a corrupted
form of *melunah* (shelter, hut), cf. Isa. I, 8.)

Camp

(a) Concentration Camp -קאנצענטראציאנס לאגער, קאנצענטראטראציע
                     לאגער, קאצע''ט לאגער, מחנה,מחנה(מחנות)רכוז
                     (הריכוז), מחנה הסגר(ההסגר)(רכוזים)
(Cf. e.g. Breisch, *Helkath Yaakob*, I, nos. 16ff., 21; Weiss, *Minhath Yizhak*,
I, nos. 87, 88; III, no. 125; R. Z.H.Meisels, *Kuntras Takkanoth Agunoth*,
pp. 9, 21, 27; *Binyan Zebi*, II, nos. 34, 60, 66. As a verb, to be sent to a
concentration camp, *pual* of the root *RKZ* is used, cf. e.g. Herzog, *Hechal
Yizhak*, II, no. 84).

(b) Extermination Camps מחנות הריגה, מחנה השמד,מחנה השמדה,
                     מחנה(מחנות) המות, מחנת האבדון, מקום(מקומות) ההשמדה,
                     בית התופת, בית הסקילה
(Cf. e.g. R. S.Efrati, *Me-Emek Ha-Bacha*, nos. 4, 6; Chief Rabbi Uzziel,
Mishpete Uzziel, E.H. nos. 40, 44; Breisch, *Helkath Yaakob*, II, nos. 33,
34; Meisels, *Kuntras Takkanoth*, p. 23; *Mekaddshe Ha-Shem*, I, p. 14;
R. Jonathan Steif, *Responsa*, no. 21; Herzog, *Hechal Yizhak*, I, nos. 24, 31;
II, no. 79).

(c) Forced Labour Camps ארבייטסלאגער, מחנה(מחנות) עבודה,
                     מחנות עבודת כפיה, מחנות של עבודת כפיה, מחנות פועלי כפיה
Forced Labour
                     עבודת פרך, עבודת הכפיה, אנגריא,
Forced Labourer   עובדי הכפיה
(Steif, *Responsa*, no. 21; Meisels, *Kuntras Takkanoth*, p. 21, no. 78;
Binyan Zebi, II, no. 60; Uzziel, *Mishpete Uzziel*, no. 45; Herzog, *Hechal*

Yizhak, I, no. 24; R. T.J.Tabyomi, *Erez Tobah*, no. 60; R. J.Avigdor, *Helek Yaakob*, p. 78; Breisch, *Helkath Yaakob* I, no. 15; Oshry, *Mi-Maamakkim*, I, nos. 2, 3, 5, 12; II, nos. 5, 7; R. Y.Abramski, in *Tebunah*, Nisan 706, p. 42. On *angaria*, see *Aruch*, I, p. 139.)

(d) Gipsy Camp　　　　　　　　　　　　　צִיגַיְינֶער לַאגֶער
(Breisch, *Helkath Yaakob*, I, nos. 18, 21; II, no. 29.)

Canada(s), Kanada(s)　　　　　　　　　　　　קַאנַאדֶעס
(Meisels, *Kuntras Takkanoth*, pp. 35, 36; *Binyan Zebi*, II, no. 56.) This word denoted at first the store of belongings of the victims who had arrived at Auschwitz but was applied later to the special squad of Jewish prisoners who dealt with the sorting out of the garments and articles of the victims. The *Canadas* were present at the arrival of the transports and accompanied those destined to die to the gas chambers.

On *Canadas*, see Reitlinger, *The Final Solution*, pp. 126, 464; Roger Manvel and Heinrich Fraenkel, *The Incomparable Crime*, pp. 156, 158, 173. The origin of the word is disputed; various suggestions were put forward (see R. Michael Dob Weissmandel, *Min Ha-Mezar*, pp. 30ff.; O. Kraus and E. Kulka, *The Death Factory*, p. 37.)

Certificates of Aryan Race, Baptism　　תְּעוּדָה אָרִית, טוֹיפְשַׁיְין, תְּעוּדַת
הִתְנַצְּרוּת, תְּעוּדַת עכו״ם, שְׁטַר הַהַמְרָה
(Herzog, *Hechal Yizhak*, II, no. 88; *Yerushath Peletah* no. 27; Oshry, *Mi-Maamakkim*, I, no. 15).

Council of Elders Council of Jews set up by the Germans.

עֶלְטֶסְטֶען־רָאט, עֶלְטְסְטֶען־רָאט
(Oshry, 'Kuntras Me-Emek Ha-Bacha' in *Dibre Ephraim*, no. 1; *Mi-Maamakkim*, I, no. 22.)

Crematorium　　　　קְרֶעמַא(ר)טָארְיוּם, קְרֶעמַאטָארְיעֶן, כִּבְשׁוֹן
(כִּבְשׁוֹנוֹת), כִּבְשׁוֹן (כִּבְשׁוֹנוֹת, כִּבְשׁוֹנִי) הָאֵשׁ, בֵּית מוֹקֵד אֵשׁ,
בֵּית הַמּוֹקֵד, תַּנּוּרֵי אֵשׁ, תַּנּוּרֵי גָאז, מַחֲנַת הַשְּׂרֵפָה, מִשְׂרְפוֹת
אֵשׁ, בָּתֵּי הַמִּשְׂרֵפוֹת, בֵּית הַתּוֹפֶת, אוֹר כַּשְׂדִּים
(Avigdor, *Helek Yaakob*, pp. 78, 86, 95, 98, 101, 103; Meisels, *Binyan Zebi*, II, nos. 33, 38; *Kuntras Takkanoth*, pp. 5, 21, 35, 38; *Mekaddshe Ha-Shem*, I, pp. 7, 14; Efrati, *Mi-Ge Ha-Haregah*, no. 12; Uzziel, *Mishpete Uzziel*, nos. 36, 40, 44; Breisch, *Helkath Yaakob*, I, nos. 18, 21; R. N.Z Freidmann, *Nezer Mattai*, Introduction.)

Crystal Night (Kristallnacht, Night of Broken Glass).
The name was derived from the fact that glass fragments of the windows of Jewish homes and stores were lying in the streets of German towns in consequence of the riots on 9 and 10 November 1938. I could not find this term mentioned in the *Responsa*. Reference is only made to 'when the enemy broke into the Synagogues in Germany'. *Vide* Part III, p. 263.

Deathmarch　　　　　　　　　　　　טוֹיטֶען־מַארְשׁ
(Breisch, *Helkath Yaakob*, II, no. 143.)

Deportation　　　　　　　　　　　　דֶעפָּארטַצִיאָן
(Breisch, *Helkath Yaakob*, I, no. 5; otherwise the *hiphil* or *hophal* of the

root *YBL* or the *kal* and *nıphal* of the root *ShLH* for deporting or being deported are used.)

Einsatzgruppe   ‎... גייס שעבר מעיר לעיר
(*Hazon Ish* on *Hilchoth Ishshuth*, XXXI, 7.) A mobile killing unit (action group) followed the advancing army and murdered the Jews by shooting on the spot and dumped them into a common grave.

Evionim (*EBIONIM*, lit. the needy)   ‎אביונים
(R. Y.H.Jeruchem, *Birkath Hayyim*, p. 21). Nickname given by one Rabbi to the participants in the conference at Evian.

Execution Place   ‎גיא ההריגה, שדה קטל, עמק הבכא, סף מזבח
‎הדמים העמקי
(Tabyomi, *Erez Tobah* no. 60; Oshry, *Mi-Maamakkim*, II, nos. 6, 16; Uzziel, *Mishpete Uzziel*, no. 36; Efrati, *Mi-Ge Ha-Haregah*, no. 4; *Me-Emek Ha-Bacha*, no. 5.)

Extermination Camp see **Camps**

Forced Labour (Camp) see **Camps**

Gas Chambers   ‎מקום הגאזקאממער, גאזקאממער, חדר (חדרי)
‎הגעז, חדר הגאז, תאי הגאז (הגז), תאי הגעזים, תנורי גאז
(Breisch, *Helkath Yaakob*, I, nos. 5, 17, 20; Herzog, *Hechal Yizhak* I, no. 24; II, no. 79; Efrati, *Mi-Ge Ha-Haregah*, no. 10; Avigdor, *Helek Yaakob*, p. xiii; Feinstein, *Iggeroth Mosheh*, III, nos. 43, 44; Uzziel, *Mishpete Uzziel*, nos. 36, 44, 45; Meisels, *Kuntras Takkanoth*, p. 5.)

Gautag–meeting of the Nazis of the *Gau* which was one of the territorial units into which Germany was divided.

Gestapo–abbreviation of: *Geheime Staats Polizei* (Secret Police)—
‎ה,גיסטאפו, הרשעה, פריצי הגיסטפו, גיסטפו, גיסטאפו
(Cf. e.g. Weinberg, *Seride Esh*, Introduction, p. 1, Oshry, *Mi-Maamakkim*, I, no. 19; Rath, *Kol Mebasser*, I, no. 84; Efrati, *Me-Emek Ha-Bacha*, no. 4.)

Ghetto (ם)(ה)יהודי)‏ ‎גיטא, (גיטאות), געטא, (געטאס), גיטו, רבע
(Avigdor, *Helek Yaakob*, pp. x, xii, xiii, 67, 81, 89, 95, 96; Meisels, *Kuntras Takkanoth*, pp. 12, 23, Oshry, *Mi-Maamakkim*, I, nos. 2, 13; II, nos. 23, 25; 'Kuntras Me-Emek Ha-Bacha' in *Dibre Ephraim*; Breisch, *Helkath Yaakob*, I, no. 18; Weinberg, *Seride Esh*; Rath, *Kol Mebasser*, nos. 6, 84; Herzog, *Hechal Yizhak*, I, no. 31; Tabyomi, *Erez Tobah*; Weiss, *Minhath Yizhak*, I, no. 92; Uzziel, *Mishpete Uzziel*, no. 36; Chief Rabbi J.M.Toledano, *Bath Ami*, p. 2.)

Gipsy Camp see **Camp**

Hitler   ‎הרשע הגרמני, בעל עגלה, השטן המשחית הנאצי, הצורר
‎הרשע מגרמניה היטלר, הצורר הטמא והמזוהם, הרשע המטורף
‎והמנוול, הרוצח האשמודאי
(R. H.I.Jeruchem, *Birkath Hayyim*, nos. 37, 116; Oshry, *Mi-Maamakkim*, I, no. 30; Friedman, *Nezer Mattai*, no. 39; Weinberg, *Seride Esh*, I, Introduction, p. 6; II, no. 12; Efrati, *Mi-Ge Ha-Haregah*, no. 4. On a different version, see *Me-Emek*, no. 1.)

B 1

Indemnification שלומים, פיצויים, דמי פרעון פצוי, דמי פצוי,
תשלומים, דמי שלומים בעד הפסקת פרנסה, שלומים (על
אבדתנו הגשמית), דמי פרעון ממה שלקחו וגזלו•

(Weiss, *Minhath Yizhak*, IV, no. 76; Chief Rabbi Unterman in *Mazkereth Le-Zecher Maran Ha-Rab Yizhak Herzog*, Jerusalem, 722, p. 68; Feinstein, *Iggeroth Morsheh E.H.* no. 103; Weinberg, *Seride Esh*, II, no. 161; R. S.I.Levin, *Minhath Shlomoh*, I, no. 29. R. E.Waldenberg, *Ziz Eliezer*, VI, no. 27.)

Kapo, Kapos–abbreviation of: *Kamp Polizei*, name given to inmate(s) of the camps who was (were) in charge of a section of fellow-prisoners.

קאפו, (קאפוס), שומרים, נוגש, (נוגשים), שוטרים

(Meisels, *Mekaddshe Ha-Shem*, I, pp. 7, 8, 11, 16; Oshry, *Mi-Maamakkim*, III, nos. 12, 14.)

Konzentrationslager see **Camp**

K.Z. Ibid.

Liquidation ליקווידאציע, חיסול

(Avigdor, *Helek Yaakob*, p. 79; Oshry, *Mi-Maamakkim*, II, no. 2.)

Mass Grave קבר אחים (הגדול), קברי אחים הגדולים,
קבר משותף

(Oshry, *Mi-Maamakkim*, I, nos. 23, 29; Efrati, *Mi-Ge Ha-Haregah*, nos. 4, 7; R. Z.Sorotzkin, *Mozenayim La-Mishpat*, II, no. 15; Stern, *Be-Zel Ha-Hochmah*, I, no. 14.)

Malina(s) or **Melunah** see **Bunker**

Monument מונומנט, אסטול של אבן, מצבת (מצבות) זכרון, גלעד

(Herzog in *Kol Torah*, Jerusalem, Iyyar, 707; Uzziel, *Mishpete Uzziel*, 2nd ed. *Y.D.*, 1st Part, no. 22; Weiss, *Minhath Yizhak*, I, no. 29; Efrati, *Mi-Ge Ha-Haregah*, no. 9.)

Mussulmänner מוסולמענער, מאזיל|מענער, term used to denote inmates of the camp (Auschwitz) who because of starvation became weak and were unable to sit or walk straight but rocked like praying Moslems. At selections for the gas chamber they were the first candidates.

(Meisels, *Kuntras Takkanoth*, pp. 21, 22; *Binyan Zebi*, II, no. 60; cf. Reitlinger, *Final Solution*, pp. 129; 498; Kraus and Kulka, *Death Factory*, p. 38.)

Judenrat see **Council of Elders**

Night of Broken Glass see **Crystal Night**

Nazi Germany (and the satellite states) אשכנז, גרמניה, (גרמניא),
ארץ הדמים, ארץ הטומאה, ארץ הדמים בסלאוואקיי, ארץ
הדמים מדינת ליטא, ארצות הדמים, ארצות השמד, האדמה
הטמאה, בית הסקילה ליהודים, גרמניא הארורה,
(The German capital is called— עיר הרשעות החבלנית והרצחנית,
בירת הרשעות העולמית

(Weinberg, *Seride Esh*, Introduction, pp. 1, 3; Breisch, *Helkath Yaakob*, in nos. 32, 136; Weiss, *Minhath Yizhak*, IV, no. 100; Efrati, *Mi-Ge Ha-Haregah*, no. 10; Oshry, *Mi-Maamakkim*, II, no. 26, Steinberg, Introduction to his grandfather's *Mahazeh Abraham*; Uzziel, *Mishpete Uzziel*, and *E.H.* nos. 36, 40; Rath, *Kol Mebasser*, no. 13.)

Nazi Government הממשלה הגרמנית, ממשלת הרשע, ממשלת
הרשע והזדון של הנאצים הצוררים, מלכות הרשעה אשכנז,
מלכות הרשעה של היטלר, שלטון הרשע והזדון.
(Wasserman, *Sheilath Mosheh*, no. 85; Avigdor, *Helek Yaakob*, p. 80; Uzziel, *Mishpete Uzziel*, *E.H.* no. 44; Breisch, *Helkath Yaakob*, I, no. 146; Tabyomi, *Erez Tobah*, no. 60; Weinberg, *Seride Esh*, p. 1.)

Nazis הנאצים הארורים, הנאצים, הנאצים האכזרים, הגרמנים
הנאציים, האשכנזים הארורים, הגרמנים (הארורים, עם שטן,
האכזרים, המנואצים), הרוצחים האכזרים, הטמאים הארורים,
הרוצחים הגרמנים, הארורים, הצר הצורר (הנאצי), צוררי
ישראל, הצוררים (הארורים, האכזרים), הרשעים (הארורים,
האכזרים, אנשי הדמים), הזדים הארורים, פריצי חיות,* כהני
אליל וטן הטיטוני חית-האדם הגרמנית
(Herzog, *Hechal Yizhak*, I, nos. 24, 27, 28; II, nos. 10, 11; Uzziel, *Mishpete Uzziel*, 2nd ed. *Y.D.* Part III, vol. II, no. 116; *E.H.* nos. 36, 40; Breisch, *Helkath Yaakob*, I, nos. 5, 6, 7, 18; II, nos. 143, 145; Rath, *Kol Mebasser*, I, no. 84; R. J.M. Aronzon, *Yeshuath Mosheh*, no. 61; Oshry, *Mi-Maamakkim*, I–III; Meisels, *Binyan Zebi*, II, nos. 33, 45, 49; Levin, *Minhath Shlomoh*, I, nos. 53, 58; Weinberg, *Seride Esh*, Introduction; Weiss, *Minhath Yizhak*, I, Introduction, no. 1. Efrati, *Mi-Ge Ha-Haregah*, Introduction, nos. 1, 3; *Me-Emek Ha-Bacha*, Introduction, p. 12, no. 1.)

The Nazi Period השואה, השואה הנוראה, השואה האיומה, שנות
השואה האיומה, ימי השואה והזעם, חורבן השואה האיום
והנורא, החורבן הנורא, שעת הזעם, שנות הזעם של שלטון
הנאצים, ימי הזעם והחורבן, ימי הרע והזעם, ימי שלטון הרשע
והזדון, ימי הזועה, השמד האיום והנורא, גזרת השמד והכליון,
שנות ההשמדה, גזרות השמד והמלחמה, שעת הגזרה, ימי
הגזרות דהנאצים
The biblical expression שואה denoting devastation and ruin is most frequently found in the *Responsa*. (Cf. Herzog, *Hechal Yizhak*, I, nos. 24, 25, 28; Uzziel, *Mishpete Uzziel*, 2nd ed. Part II, *Y.D.* vol. I, no. 22; *E.H.*, no. 36; Efrati, *Mi-Ge Ha-Haregah*, Introduction, p. 15, no. 12; Steinberg, *Mahaze Abraham*; Stern, *Be-Zel Ha-Hochmah*, I, no. 29; Friedman, *Nezer Mattai*, no. 39; Oshry, *Mi-Maamakkim*, I, Introduction, nos. 25, 28; II, nos. 24, 26; III, no. 8; Meisels, *Binyan Zebi*, II, Title-page; Weiss, *Minhath Yizhak*, I, nos. 23, 69, 83, 92; II, no. 90; IV, no. 100; Weinberg, *Seride Esh*, I, pp. 179; II, p. 122; Toledano, *Bath Ami*, p. 3; Breisch, *Helkath Yaakob* II no. 143; Feinstein, *Iggeroth Mosheh*, III, no. 41; *Yerushath Peletah*, no. 27.)

Neu Kosher נייא-כשר , expression coined in Germany after the issue of

---

*For the expression see Isa. xxxv 9.

364   *The Nazi Holocaust*

the prohibition of *shehitah* without prior stunning. Non-observant Jews bought meat from non-Jewish butchers and salted it (as if it were *kosher* meat) calling it *Neu kosher*.

(Weinberg, *Seride Esh*, I, p. 238; R. J.Unna, *Shoalin Ve-Dorshin*, no. 21.)

Nyilaases. *Vide supra*, Part I, p. 71, note 136.

Rasse Gesetz (Rassengesetz) הראססע געזעטץ Racial law. Cf. Weiss, *Minhath Yizhak*, I, no. 87, referring to the racial law proclaimed in Nuremberg on 15 September 1935. *Vide supra*, Part I, p. xviii, note 9.

Red Cross   רעד קראס, הצלב האדום, רויטען קרייץ

(Herzog, *Hechal Yizhak*, II, nos. 79, 80; Tabyomi, *Erez Tobah*, no. 60; Grossnass, *Leb Aryeh*, no. 28; Meisels, no. 60.)

Refugees   פליטים, גולים, נדחי ישראל,

(Breisch, *Helkath Yaakob*, I, nos. 1, 36, 73, 146, 206, 207; II, no. 4; Tabyomi, *Erez Tobah*, Jeruchem, *Birkath Hayyim*, 'Alim Bochim', p. 21, no. 42; Weiss, *Minhath Yizhak*, I, no. 23.)

Restitution see **Indemnification**

Survivors (Displaced Persons)   שרידים, שרידי חרב פליטי הגולה,

השרידים ניצולי הגיטו, שרידי פליטי להט החרב המתהפכת, פליטים, פליטי חרב, פליטי הגיטאות, נמלטים, ניצולים, ניצולי השואה, אודים המוצלים (הניצולים) מאשי...

(Efrati, *Mi-Ge Ha-Haregah*, nos. 11, 13; *Me-Emek Ha-Bacha*, p. 9 and no. 4; Stern, *Be-zel Ha-Hochmah*, Introduction, Oshry, *Mi-Maamakkim*, I nos. 23, 28, 30; II, no. 5; III, no. 8; Meisels, *Binyan Zebi*, II, no. 64; *Kuntras Takkanoth*, pp. 23, 24; Levin, *Minhath Shlomah*, no. 29; Uzziel, *Mishpete Uzziel*, E.H. nos. 36, 44.)

Selectia, Selection   סלקציה, סעלעקציע, סילעקציא, סילעקציע,

choosing inmates, (סילעקציעס), סעלעקציאן, בחירה, ביקורת of the ghetto for deportation or death and those in the death-camps for the furnace. This term was also used for sorting out the corpses to remove gold teeth and hair.

(Efrati, *Mi-Ge Ha-Haregah*, no. 10; Meisels, *Kuntras Takkanoth*, pp. 6, 13, 21, 22; *Binyan Zebi* II, nos. 38, 45, 60; *Mekaddshe Ha-Shem* I, p. 7; Waldenberg, *Ziz Eliezer*, III, no. 25, p. 117a; Oshry, *Mi-Maamakkim*, II, no. 4.)

Sonderkommando
(1) Jewish inmates of the extermination camp dealing with the corpses.
(2) Special detachment of the Security Police used mainly for liquidation. See **Einsatzgruppe**.

SS (abbreviation of *Schutzstaffel*)

ס·ס·, הס·ס·, העס עס, מלאכי חבלה צבאי ס·ס·

Originally a bodyguard for Hitler the SS were later in charge of the ghettos and camps and responsible for the massacre of millions of Jews.

(Breisch, *Helkath Yaakob*, Introduction to vol. I; Meisels, *Mekaddshe Ha-Shem*, I, pp. 7, 8, 11, 14; Weiss, *Minhath Yizhak*, I, p. 265.)

Star of David   ''מגן דוד'' הכתום, אות, הטלאי הצהוב

Badge Jews had to wear so as to be easily identifiable as members of the Jewish race.

(Oshry, *Mi-Maamakkim*, II, no. 12; Avigdor, *Helek Yaakob*, p. x; Weiss, *Minhath Yizhak*.)

Taufschein see **Certificates of Aryan Race/Baptism**

Totenmarsch see **Death-march**

Transport   טראנספורט (טראנספארטים, טראנספארטן)

(Meisels, *Kuntras Takkanoth*, p. 5; *Mekaddshe Ha-Shem*, I, p. 10.)

Umschlagplatz Collecting place for Deportation.

Zigeunerlager see **Gipsy Camp**

Index